THE CRISIS OF
ISRAELITE RELIGION

Transformation of Religious Tradition
in Exilic and Post-Exilic Times

EDITED BY

BOB BECKING

AND

MARJO C.A. KORPEL

BRILL
LEIDEN · BOSTON · KÖLN
1999

This book is printed on acid-free paper.

BM
176
.C75
1999

Library of Congress Cataloging in Publication Data is also available.

Die Deutsche Bibliothek – CIP-Einheitsaufnahme

The crisis of Israelite religion : transformation of religious tradition
in exilic and post exilic times / ed. by Bob Becking and Marjo C.A.
Korpel. – Leiden ; Boston ; Köln : Brill, 1999
   (Oudtestamentische Studiën ; Deel 42)
   ISBN 90–04–11496–3

ISSN   0169-7226
ISBN   90 04 11496 3

PRINTED IN THE NETHERLANDS

THE CRISIS OF ISRAELITE RELIGION

OUDTESTAMENTISCHE STUDIËN

NAMENS HET OUDTESTAMENTISCH
WERKGEZELSCHAP IN NEDERLAND EN BELGIË

UITGEGEVEN DOOR

JOHANNES C. DE MOOR

KAMPEN

DEEL XLII

Contents

Acknowledgments

When the Faculty of Theology of Utrecht University received the honor to become the administrative centre for the Netherlands' School for Advanced Studies in Theology and Religion (NOSTER), the board of Utrecht University rewarded this step with a major financial grant. The board of the Research Institute for Theology and Religious Studies (INTEGON), a common enterprise of the Faculty of Theology and the Catholic Theological University, both at Utrecht, decided to invite the various research groups in the institute to organize scholarly symposia on an important topic in their field. On that incentive Old Testament scholars from Utrecht designed a conference 'Israelite Religion under Stress: Continuity and Discontinuity in the sixth and fifth Centuries BCE'. 25 scholars accepted the invitation to participate in the symposium. Three PhD-students following the training-programme of NOSTER joined the conference. In the framework of the collaboration between the University of Münster in Westfalen and NOSTER two colleagues from Münster were invited. The symposium was held at the conference centre 'Kontakt der Kontinenten' in Soesterberg, 5-8 April 1998. This volume contains the proceedings of our meeting.

Our gratitude goes to the boards of Utrecht University and of INTEGON who made our symposium possible. We would like to thank all the participants to the conference, not only those who read a paper, but also those who took part in the stimulating exchange of ideas. Prof. Johannes C. de Moor, Kampen, kindly accepted the manuscript for publication in the series Oudtestamentische Studiën. Dr. Harm W.M. van Grol, who took the lead in the organization of the conference, is thanked for his efforts and his assistance in the preliminary work to this volume. Mirjam Muis, Utrecht, was very helpful both in converting the various contributions into a camera-ready manuscript and in the preparation of the indices.

The Editors

Bob Becking   *Utrecht – The Netherlands*

Continuity and Discontinuity after the Exile
Some Introductory Remarks

1   Introduction

These remarks intend to introduce the articles in this volume[1] to the
readers. It is not my aim to summarize the various contributions to
the theme both of the conference and of this book. I will, however,
sketch its contours by referring to the problems involved. This will
be done in a somewhat expressionistic way. Not by arguing, but by
putting some dots and lines on the canvas, I will introduce the reader
in the scholarly landscape related to period under consideration. In
doing so, I hope to make clear the various connections between the
papers in this volume.

2   Exile and Return

From a broader historical perspective the period between, roughly
speaking, 600 and 400 BCE in Israelite history is characterized by
changes. These changes can simply be indicated with the ideas 'exile'
and 'return'. In the beginning of the sixth century Judah lost the last
remains of its independence in the sack of Jerusalem by the Babylonians. Judahites – among them the royal family – were deported to
Babylonia. City and temple were destroyed. In 539 BCE Cyrus, King
of Persia, defeated the Babylonians and conquered their capital city.
Since that date, Judaeans (re)settled in Jerusalem and vicinity. They
rebuilt their temple and worshipped Yahweh as sole deity.[2]

   The outline given in the previous textual unit is wilfully vague.
I have my reasons for that. When it comes to a detailed reconstruction of the events in the sixth and fifth century BCE many problems arise. The main problem is yielded by the scarcity of evidence.
Moreover, much of the existing written evidence is imbued with Persian or Judaean ideology. This scarcity on the other hand has opened
the lane for a vivid scholarly discussion on what did and what did
not happen in the periods of exile and return. I would like to point
at three features here:

---

[1] The order of the articles follows the sequence of the respective lectures and
workshops during the congress.

[2] See most recently: B. Becking, "Babylonisches Exil", in: H.D. Betz *et al.*
(ed.), *Religion in Geschichte und Gegenwart: Handwörterbuch für Theologie und
Religionswissenschaft*, Bd. 1/A-B, Tübingen ⁴1998, 1044-1045.

1. *The myth of the empty land.* Traditionally, the view has been
   defended that Judah laid waste during the 'exilic' period. Hans
   Barstad, elaborating on ideas by Robert Carroll,[3] has convincingly made clear that the area was not uninhabited and that
   life went on as normal to some degree.[4]

2. *The pace of the return.* The Old Testament, especially Ezra 1–2,
   suggests an early return from the exile. Taking the Aramaic sections in the Book of Ezra for authentic documents, Baruch Halpern has presented the view that the return from exile, ordered
   by Cyrus in 538 BCE eventually took place in 521 BCE.[5] No direct evidence from Persian sources affirms the claim of an early
   return.[6] Others have claimed that archaeological evidence would
   support that 'the return' consisted in a process of waves of smaller groups that moved to Yehud and that lasted for more than
   a century.[7]

3. *Imperial authorization.* Did Judaism emerge as a reformulation
   of local Yahwistic traditions or was it the final product of the
   interference of the Persian empire in local matters as described
   in the Books of Ezra and Nehemiah? This is a longstanding debate in Old Testament scholarship.[8] The discussion now seems
   to concentrate on the question of the historicity of the imper-

---

[3]R.P. Carroll, "The Myth of the Empty Land", in: D. Jobling, T.Pippin (eds.), *Ideological Criticism of Biblical Texts* (Semeia, 59), Atlanta 1992, 79-93.

[4]H.M. Barstad, *The Myth of the Empty Land: A Study in the History and Archaeology of Judah during the 'Exilic' Period* (SO.S, 28), Oslo 1996.

[5]B. Halpern, "A Historiographic Commentary on Ezra 1-6: Achronological Narrative and Dual Chronology in Israelite Historiography", in: W.H. Propp *et al.* (eds.), *The Hebrew Bible and its Interpreters* (BibJS, 1), Winona Lake 1990, 81-142.

[6]On the historicity of the so-called Cyrus-cylinder see: A. Kuhrt, "The Cyrus Cylinder and Achaemenid Imperial Policy", *JSOT* 25 (1983), 83-97; J. Wiesehöfer, *Das antike Persien von 550 v. Chr. bis 650 n. Chr.*, München & Zürich 1994, 71-88. The famous Behistun inscription of Darius relates in its various versions his rebellion and rise to power but does not contain historical data on the return to Jerusalem or the rebuilding of the temple, see e.g. Wiesehöfer, *Antike Persien*, 33-43.

[7]See e.g. J.P. Weinberg, *The Citizen-Temple Community* (JSOT.S, 151), Sheffield 1992, 41; L.L. Grabbe, *Judaism from Cyrus to Hadrian*, London 1994, 126-40; P.R. Davies, *In Search of 'Ancient Israel'* (JSOT.S, 148), Sheffield ²1994, 80-2.

[8]See, e.g., the controversy between Wellhausen and Meyer as outlined by R.G. Kratz, "Die Entstehung des Judentums", *ZThK* 95 (1998), 167-84; and the studies by K.G. Hoglund, *Achaemenid Imperial Administration in Syria-Palestine and the Missions of Ezra and Nehemiah*, Atlanta 1992; J. Berquist, *Judaism in Persia's Shadow: A Social and Historical Approach*, Minneapolis 1995, esp. 131-59.

ial support of Ezra's mission. Frei compared Ezra 7:12-26 with other instances of imperial authorization known from Persian period written sources and concluded that the textual unit in Ezra reflects imperial customs.[9] The question, however, is still debated.[10]

A consensus is far away and can, in my view, only be reached when new evidence shows up or when the existing evidence is studied with new methods. Despite this lack of consensus the period under consideration is generally construed as a time of shifts and changes. The shift from the monarchic period to the Persian period provoked a change in selfunderstanding. 'Being Israelite' had changed from 'belonging to the Judaean nation' to 'being part of a Jewish family' or 'being member of a guild, be it in Yehud or in the Diaspora'.[11] The changed societal, political and mental circumstances provoked forms of a religion under stress.

3 Religion under Stress

Religion can be viewed and defined from different perspectives: doctrinal, theological, historical, sociological and a few more. The anthropologist Clifford Geertz has defined religion as "a system of symbols which acts to establish powerful, pervasive, and long lasting moods and motivations in men by formulating conceptions of a general order and clothing these conceptions with such an aura of factuality that the moods and motivations seem uniquely realistic".[12] In doing so, Geertz construes religion as in relation with a specific entity. In most religions this entity is personified and is seen – in an emic approach – as divine or supernatural. To this identity a network of concepts, rituals, conventions and codes is related. Since the factual existence of this divine entity is difficult to discuss, scholarly discussion about religion has to account for the human expressions in texts and artifacts of a specific system of symbols. It should be noted that a system

---

[9]P. Frei, "Zentralgewalt und Lokalautonomie im Achämenidenreich", in: P. Frei, K. Koch, *Reichsidee und Reichsorganisation im Perserreich* (OBO, 55), Freiburg & Göttingen [2]1996, 5-131.

[10]See the articles by P. Frei, J. Wiesehöfer and U. Rüterswörden in *ZAR* 1 (1995).

[11]See, e.g., A. Causse, *Du groupe ethnique à la communauté religieuse: la problème sociologique de la religion d'Israel*, Paris 1937, esp. 187; Weinberg, *Citizen-Temple Community, passim.*

[12]C. Geertz, "Religion as a Cultural System", in: M. Banton (ed.), *The Relevance of Models in Social Anthropology*, London, 1965, 2 (= C. Geertz, *The Interpretation of Cultures*, New York 1973, 90).

of symbols, especially in non-western civilizations, is not the idea of an individual, but should be seen as related to a society or a (powerful) group in a given society. In a way, the religious symbol-system reflects the patterns in a given society. Changes in the basic patterns of a society inflict the mechanisms of the symbol system.

'Exile' and 'restoration' provoked a crisis in the Israelite, Yahwistic religion. The ruination of the temple in Jerusalem, that functioned as the central sanctuary for the Yahwistic religion, and the collapse of the Davidic dynasty, that functioned as a symbol of divine presence and protection,[13] should be seen as a fundamental breach in the Yahwistic symbol system. The return from exile, no matter its size and pace, and the rebuilding of the temple as a place of worship for a religious minority group in the immense empire, were events that had a great impact on the symbol system of the Yahwistic group(s) in and around Jerusalem.

Obviously people react differently to fundamental changes. At least four ways to cope with the new reality are plausible:

1. Abandoning of the traditional religion and embracing of the world view of the conquering Babylonian power;

2. Reinforcement of indigenous, Canaanite elements in the Yahwistic religion;

3. A concentration on Yahwism in an orthodox, exclusive monotheistic form and

4. An attempt to reformulate Yahwism in the religious, political and social context.

Texts in the Old Testament reflect the variety of responses to the changes in ancient Israel. I will not discuss these texts here in full, but only use them as an indication. Zeph. 1:1-8 might be interpreted as the adoption of a Mesopotamian rite.[14] The opponents in the debate Jeremiah is said to have had in Egypt put their religious trust in the veneration of the 'Queen of Heaven' that – most probably – had been abandoned in the 'orthodox' reform of Josiah. 'Queen of Heaven' is to be seen as an epithet for Asherah who had been worshipped as

---

[13] On this, see most recently: W. Brueggemann, *Theology of the Old Testament: Testimony, Dispute, Advocacy*, Minneapolis 1997, 650-79.

[14] See H. Donner, "Die Schwellenhüpfer: Beobachtungen zu Zephanja 1,8f", *JSSt* 15 (1970), 42-55; K. Seybold, *Satirische Prophetie: Studien zum Buch Zefanja* (SBS, 120), Stuttgart 1985, 25-8; *pace* A. Berlin, *Zephaniah: A New Translation with Introduction and Commentary* (AncB, 25/A), New York 1994, 79-80.

the consort of YHWH in pre-exilic times[15] The Books of Ezra and Nehemiah reflect a form of religion that can be labeled as fundamentalistic.[16] Second Isaiah,[17] the final redactions of the Pentateuchal traditions and the deuteronomistic history writing as well as the rewriting
of the Story of Ancient Israel in the Books of Chronicles form good
examples of the creative process of reformulation of the tradition.

4 From Yahwism(s) to Judaism(s)

In the final decades before the fall of Jerusalem to the Babylonians,
the religion in Judah can be characterized as Yahwistic. In view of
the recent debate on religion in Ancient Israel,[18] this characterization
needs to be specified. The dominant form of Yahwism before the exile
should be characterized as monotheistic, aniconic and oriented on
one central sanctuary. With Diana Edelman this form of religion can

---

[15] Jer. 44; see, e.g., K. Koch, "Aschera als Himmelskönigin in Jerusalem", *UF*
20 (1988), 97-120; W. McKane, "Worship of the Queen of Heaven (Jer 44)", in:
I. Kottsieper *et al.* (eds.), *"Wer ist wie du, Herr, unter den Göttern?" Studien
zur Theologie und Religionsgeschichte Israels für Otto Kaiser zum 70. Geburtstag*,
Göttingen 1994, 318-24; C. Houtman, "Queen of Heaven", *DDD*, 1278-84, [2]*DDD*,
678-80.

[16] Although the articles by B. Becking and H.G.M. Williamson in this volume
give nuances to this view.

[17] Besides the contribution of M.C.A. Korpel to this volume see A. Laato, *"About
Zion I Will Not Be Silent": The Book of Isaiah as an Ideological Unity* (CB.OT,
44), Stockholm 1998, esp. 126-69.

[18] On this discussion see, e.g., J.C. de Moor, *The Rise of Yahwism: The Roots
of Israelite Monotheism* (BEThL, 91) Leuven 1990, [2]1997; M.S. Smith, *The Early
History of God: Yahweh and the Other Deities in Ancient Israel*, San Francisco
1990; H. Niehr, *Der höchste Gott: Alttestamentlicher* JHWH-*Glaube in Kontext
syrisch-kanaanäischer Religion des 1. Jahrtausend v. Chr.* (BZAW, 190), Berlin
& New York 1990; O. Keel, C. Uehlinger, *Göttinnen, Götter und Gottessymbole:
Neue Erkenntnisse zur Religionsgeschichte Kanaans und Israel aufgrund bislang
unerschlossener ikonographischer Quellen* (QD, 134), Freiburg, etc. 1992, [3]1995
(ET: *Gods, Goddesses, and Images of God in Ancient Israel*, Minneapolis & Edinburgh 1998); R. Albertz, *Religionsgeschichte Israels in alttestamentlicher Zeit
2* (GAT, 8/1-2), Göttingen 1992; T.N.D. Mettinger, *No Graven Image? Israel-
ite Aniconism in Its Near Eastern Context* (CB.OT, 42), Stockholm 1995; O.
Loretz, *Des Gottes Einzigkeit: Ein altorientalisches Argumentationsmodell zum
'Schma Jisrael'*, Darmstadt 1997; and the essays in W. Dietrich, M.A. Klopfen-
stein (eds.), *Ein Gott Allein?* JHWH-*Verehrung und biblischer Monotheismus im
Kontext der israelitischen und altorientalischen Religionsgeschichte* (OBO, 139),
Freiburg & Göttingen 1994; D.V. Edelman (ed.), *The Triumph of Elohim: From
Yahwisms to Judaisms* (CBET, 13), Kampen 1995; K. van der Toorn (ed.), *The
Image and the Book: Iconic Cults, Aniconism and the Rise of Book Religion in
Israel and the Ancient Near East* (CBET, 21), Leuven 1997.

be labeled as 'national Yahwism' or 'First Temple Yahwism'.[19] This
implies that other forms of Yahwism were marginalized by that time.

From the middle of the fourth century BCE onward, the Jewish religion is well documented. Two features should be noted. First, Judaism, especially in the period in which it developed, was not uniform
in its character.[20] Second, the scarcity of evidence makes it difficult
to qualify the religion of people living in Yehud who venerated YHWH
as either 'still Yahwism' or 'already Judaism'.

Although Yahwism and Judaism have much in common, they are
not identical and should be treated as two different forms of religion.
Traditionally, the exile is taken as the watershed between the two
forms.[21] Edelman has suggested a four-phase transition scheme: From
'national Yahwism' or 'First Temple Yahwism' via 'Intertemple Yahwisms'[22] and 'Second Temple Yahwism' to 'Early Judaism'.[23] Problematical for this view are:

1. Her assumption that already in 515 BCE the second temple was
   build and in use. This view is – to say the least – problematic
   in view of the enigmatic dates in Ezra 3-6.[24] The Persian king
   Darius mentioned in Ezra 6 in whose reign the second temple
   was inaugurated and consecrated most probably is to be identified with Darius II Ochus (424-405 BCE).

2. According to Edelman, 'early Judaism' emerged only in the Hasmonean state (143 BCE onward). It might be a matter of definition, but in my view this date is too late since it excludes e.g.
   the Maccabees, Jesus ben Sira and the early settlers at Qumran
   from Judaism.

---

[19]D.V. Edelman, "Introduction", in: Edelman (ed.), *Triumph of Elohim*, 23-4;
see also Albertz, *Religionsgeschichte*, Bd. 1, 304-73; K. van der Toorn, *Family
Religion in Babylonia, Syria and Israel: Continuity and Change in the Forms of
religious Life* (SHCANE, 7), Leiden 1996, 339-72.

[20]See, e.g., E. Ferguson, *Backgrounds of Early Christianity*, Grand Rapids
²1993, 373-546; Grabbe, *Judaism from Cyrus to Hadrian*, 204-20, 269-312.

[21]Connected with this idea is the – fortunately now obsolete – view that pre-
exilic Yahwism was a more pure form of religion, while Judaism was seen as a
detorioration or an inferior development; see e.g., J. Wellhausen, "Die Rückkehr der
Juden aus dem babylonischen Exil", *NGWG.PH*, Göttingen 1885, 166-86.

[22]Indicating the various forms of religion of those in exile and those who remained in the land from 587-515 BCE.

[23]Edelman, "Introduction", 23-4.

[24]See, e.g., L.L. Grabbe, *Ezra-Nehemiah* (OTR), London 1998, 123-38.

INTRODUCTORY REMARKS

3. The evidence for the period labeled by Edelman as 'Second Temple Judaism' hints at pluriformity.[25] The Book of Ezra can be seen as a good example of the struggle between various Yahwistic groups about the most appropriate form of veneration.

In my view the transition from one form to the other should be seen as a multidimensional process the pace of which has not been the same in different groups and places. This view opens the perspective for another question: How did this complex process of transition take place? Which forces were at work? Is the Persian period the lying-in room of Judaism?[26]

5 Scarcity and Variety of Evidence

As already stated above, the evidence for the period under consideration is scarce. When the research is not confined, however, to a historical reconstruction of exile and restoration, but also asks for ways in which people understood their time and integrated this understanding in their symbol-system, the evidence to be discussed increases. Next to 'historical' texts like Chronicles, Ezra, Nehemiah, Greek and Persian sources,[27] poetic and prophetic texts come within sight. It should be noted, however, that 'historical' texts do not by implication produce more historical evidence than poetic and prophetic texts, since both can be seen as steered by the belief-system of their respective authors.[28]

Moreover, it should be noted that texts are not the only source to build on our view of the past. The remains of the material culture of the period under consideration[29] could give insight in settlement

[25]See Ferguson, *Backgrounds*; Grabbe, *Judaism*; Ph.R. Davies, "Scenes from the Early History of Judaism", in: Edelman (ed.), *Triumph of Elohim*, 145-182; E. Nodet, *A Search for the Origins of Judaism* (JSOT.S, 248), Sheffield 1997, 337-66.

[26]This question stands in the background of some contributions in this volume.

[27]For a survey see Grabbe, *Judaism*, 27-67; Nodet, *Search for the Origins*.

[28]See, e.g., R.G. Collingwood, *The Idea of History: Revised Edition with Lectures 1926-1928*, Oxford 1994; H.M. Barstad, "History and the Hebrew Bible", in: L.L. Grabbe (ed.), *Can a 'History of Israel' be Written?* (ESHM, 1; JSOT.S, 245), Sheffield 1997, 37-64; B. Becking, "Ezra's Reenactment of the Exile", in: L.L. Grabbe (ed.), *Leading Captivity Captive* (ESHM, 2; JSOT.S, 278), Sheffield 1998, 40-61.

[29]For an outline of the available evidence see E. Stern, *Material Culture of the Land of the Bible in the Persian Period 538-332 B.C.*, Warminster 1982; H. Weippert, *Palästina in vorhellenistischer Zeit* (HdA, Vorderasien 2/1), München 1988, 682-728; Barstad, *Myth of the Empty Land*.

movements and in the way people lived. The iconography of Iron Age III[30] hints at the symbol system(s) that helped people to understand their age.

6   Pluriformity in Method

The contributions to this volume do not aim at a methodological uniformity. Recent years have seen a debate between 'diachronic' and 'synchronic' approaches[31] or between final-form-reading and traditional historical and literary criticism. It might seem trivial to say that both approaches are in need of each other, since they are supplementary in the process of interpreting texts. The final aim of this volume is to gain understanding of what was going on in the period under consideration. This aim should not be understood in a positivistic way as if a law steering history can be tested against the evidence of this period.[32] I do not exclude, however, that patterns can be detected. To reach this aim a variety of texts and artifacts are discussed and analysed using different methods. This has been done not with the illusion to present the final solution to all problems involved but in the hope that the presentations will stimulate the scholarly discussion on this sometimes dim but always intriguing period.

---

[30]Discussed in Keel, Uehlinger, *Göttinnen, Götter und Gottessymbole*, 430-52, and in Uehlinger's contribution to this volume.

[31]See, e.g., the essays in J.C. de Moor (ed.), *Synchrony or Diachrony? A Debate on Method in Old Testament Exegesis* (OTS, 34), Leiden 1995.

[32]*Pace* the so-called 'covering-law-model' in historical research as outlined by, e.g., K.R. Popper, *The Logic of Scientific Discovery*, London 1959; see the criticism by W.H. Dray, *Laws and Explanation in History*, Oxford 1970.

Lester L. Grabbe   *Hull – United Kingdom*

Israel's Historical Reality after the Exile

It has been stated that during the Bosnian war, the American news media omitted the Croats from their reportage. It was supposedly because the public could understand two opposing sides, the Bosnian Muslims and the Bosnian Serbs, but that having a three-sided situation was just too complicated for your average American to handle. Whether this is really true, I do not know, but as you are aware, there is nothing that we Europeans enjoy more than laughing at American foibles. If I might be so bold as to paraphrase Mr Bennett, "What are Americans for?"[1]

Before we laugh too hard, however, I cannot really say that reportage in the UK was necessarily much better. The fact is that the human mind often prefers stereotype to reality. Reality is infinitely detailed and extremely complex. Although we scholars may disdain the common herd, we are by no means immune to attachment to our own stereotypes and oversimplifications – to our own myths. And scholars have no greater myth than the belief in the rightness of their own individual theories or their past positions taken on various issues. We all know of scholars whose devotion to a particular theory has blinded them to what is plain to the rest of us. However, occasionally a favoured theory has become so broken-winded that we can no longer ride it, at which point we make a virtue of necessity by abandoning it – especially if someone else originated it in the first place – and pointing out that we are always ready to change our minds if the facts demand it.

The theme of this conference is continuity and discontinuity in religion. As the first paper in this conference, it is my duty to map out a broad overview which will touch on many areas of concern. It seems to have been my lot a number of times recently to try to survey large areas and digest them for others.[2] To attempt to give

---

[1] J. Austen, *Pride and Prejudice* (1913; ed. R.W. Chapman), Oxford 1926, 364; Mr Bennett says to Elizabeth, "For what do we live, but to make sport for our neighbours, and laugh at them in our turn?"

[2] See my *Judaism from Cyrus to Hadrian*, vol. 1: Persian and Greek Periods; vol. 2: Roman Period, Minneapolis 1992 (British edition in one-volume paperback, London 1994); *Leviticus* (OTGu), Sheffield 1993; *Priests, Prophets, Diviners, Sages: A Socio-historical Study of Religious Specialists in Ancient Israel*, Valley Forge, PA 1995; *An Introduction to First Century Judaism: Jewish Religion and History in the Second Temple Period*, Edinburgh 1996; *Wisdom of Solomon* (Guides to Apocrypha and Pseudepigrapha), Sheffield 1997; "The Book of Leviticus", *Currents in Research: Biblical Studies* 5 (1997), 91-110.

an overview is a formidable task because there is no area with which
I deal that someone else here does not know more about. But since
other papers in the conference will take up many of these issues in
more detail, and no doubt from a different perspective than mine, I
think an attempt at a broad synthesis may be helpful.

But in order to bring some order into such a large subject but
also to try to avoid the stereotyping and oversimplification just for-
sworn, I wish to conduct an exercise in agnosticism. In this paper I
want to focus on the most obvious data, especially those from extra-
biblical sources. It may seem strange to remain aloof from opinions
and positions which we all may currently accept, but in view of the
many scholarly consenses currently under attack – at least from some
quarters – I shall do my best to assume nothing in this particular
exercise. I shall go from the known to the unknown, using those periods for which we have a significant amount of information as fixed
points, much as a surveyor uses fixed points to measure an unknown
dimension by means of trigonometry.

The time period I shall be looking at is a lengthy one for a simple
reason: we have a long dark period following the fall of Jerusalem in
587/586 BCE which is not much relieved until the Seleucid period. My
comments fall into three main areas: (1) the use of 'Israel' as a self-
designation; (2) the particular communities in and outside Palestine
claiming a connection with the monarchic kingdoms before 587; and
(3) the development of Judahite religion.

1 'Israel' as a Self-Designation

Despite the frequent use of 'Israel' in the OT, the name seldom occurs in extra-biblical sources; however, it is not unknown. The most
famous example is the Merneptah stela (13th century BCE) which
states, "Israel is laid waste, his seed is not".[3] It is probably earlier
than any portion of the OT text. Although there is considerable debate as to whether it is a geographical or an ethnic designation, I
am not aware of any serious queries about the reading or that it is a

---

[3] *Ysr3r fkt bn prt.f.* For recent treatments of the inscription, see G.W. Ahlström,
D. Edelman, "Merneptah's Israel", *JNES* 44 (1985), 59-61; H. Engel, "Die Sie-
gesstele des Merenptah: Kritischer Überblick über die verschieden Versuche histor-
ischer Auswertung des Schlussabschnitts", *Bib.* 60 (1979), 373-99; D.B. Redford,
"The Ashkelon Relief at Karnak and the Israel Stela", *IEJ* 36 (1986), 188-200; I.
Singer, "Merneptah's Campaign to Canaan and the Egyptian Occupation of the
Southern Coastal Plain of Palestine in the Ramesside Period", *BASOR* 269 (Feb-
ruary 1988), 1-10; L.E. Stager, "Merenptah, Israel and Sea Peoples: New Light
on an Old Relief", *ErIs* 18 (1985), 56*-64*; F.J. Yurco, "Merenptah's Canaanite
Campaign", *JARCE* 23 (1986), 189-215; M.G. Hasel, "*Israel* in the Merneptah
Stela," *BASOR* 296 (1994), 45-61.

name of some sort. No clear evidence then occurs for several centuries until the time of Shalmaneser III (9th century) who refers to 'Ahab of Israel'.[4] This identification has been widely accepted, but it has recently been challenged.[5] The arguments against the identification with the biblical Ahab are well presented and understandable, but is it reasonable that in the mid-9th century there was an 'Ahab' in Syria from a country whose name was very similar to 'Israel', yet he had no connection with the Ahab of the Bible? It is always possible, but common sense says it is not likely.

Two other inscriptions with the name Israel also seem to be from the 9th century. The famous Tel Dan inscription seems now to be from approximately the late 9th century or possibly the early 8th. It refers to a 'king of Israel' (frag. 1, line 8, and what seems to be the last part of the name 'Israel' is preserved in line 4 and the first part in line 12).[6]

From approximately the same time comes the Mesha stela or the Moabite stone. It refers to 'Omri king of Israel' and has several other references to 'Israel' in the text.[7]

When we move to the Persian and Greek periods, there is little evidence for the name Israel in extra-biblical sources. The name does not occur among the Elephantine papyri. It *might* occur once among the Egyptian inscriptions in Greek (in a broken context in what seems to be a synagogue inscription from the Roman period), but some read *Isdraēl*.[8] Even if we read *Israēl*, there is no way of knowing whether it was being applied to contemporary Jews or perhaps only making a reference to something in the biblical tradition. The name also does not occur among the Greek papyri in Egypt. It occurs only once in

---

[4] *A-ḫa-ab-bu* ᵐᵃᵗ*Sir-'a-la-a-a.* For text and translation, see A.K. Grayson, *Assyrian Rulers of the Early First Millennium BC: II* (858-745 BC) (The Royal Inscriptions of Mesopotamia, Assyrian Period, 3), Toronto 1996, A.0.102.2 ii 91-92 (23).

[5] W. Gugler, *Jehu und seine Revolution*, Kampen 1996, 67-80. Gugler cites A.S. van der Woude, *Zacharia* (PredOT), Nijkerk 1984, 167, as the originator of the thesis, that the Achab from the monolith-inscription should be construed as a king from Northwestern Syria.

[6] מלך.ישראל. A. Biran, J. Naveh, "An Aramaic Stele Fragment from Tel Dan", *IEJ* 43 (1993), 81-98. In "The Tel Dan Inscription: A New Fragment ", *IEJ* 45 (1995), 1-18, it is now claimed that a new fragment of the inscription has been found though some questions of authenticity have been raised. In any case, since it does not have the name Israel on it, it is not relevant for our present concerns.

[7] KAI No. 181:3-4 = TSSI No. 16:3-4 (also lines 10-11, 14, 18, 26): עמרי מלך ישראל.

[8] W. Horbury, D. Noy, *Jewish Inscriptions of Graeco-Roman Egypt*, Cambridge 1992, No. 17 (p. 25).

Rome, but in a late inscription of the 3rd-4th century CE.[9] None of the Greek or Roman writers mention Israel until Pompeius Trogus at the turn of the Common Era (*apud* Justin, *Historiae Philippicae* 36, Epitome 2.3-4). He represents the origin of the Jews as from Damascus, one of whose kings is said to be *Israhel*. He had ten sons and divided his kingdom among them, naming them 'Jews' from Judas who died soon afterward.[10] Nevertheless, Trogus uses the common term 'Jews' for the people of his time, not Israel.

As far as I am aware the term 'Israelite' is used in pre-Christian Greco-Roman sources only to refer to members of a community on Delos associated with the cult on Mt Gerizim. Two inscriptions, one from about 200 BCE and one from about 100 BCE were written by "the Israelites in Delos who sent to sacred Argarizein" an offering.[11] Considering the fact that the Samaritan tradition claims that this community is descended from faithful Israelites of the Northern Kingdom (see next section), these inscriptions look very significant. Those who wrote the Delos inscriptions seem to have lived right next to a Jewish community (a nearby building has been identified by some as a synagogue) and evidently had friendly relations with it. Yet they appear to have kept their own identity. They were not 'Jews' but 'Israelites', while the Jews are nowhere called 'Israelites' at this time according to presently available sources.

When we look at the biblical literature, we face the problem of dating and the fact that any particular passage could have been put in by later editors with a particular point of view. Simply taking the literature at face value, however, we find the following general picture:[12] The term is used of 'all Israel' in the Pentateuch and Joshua

---

[9]D. Noy, *Jewish Inscriptions of Western Europe*, vol. 2, The City of Rome, Cambridge 1995, No. 489 (pp. 390-1), but the significance is puzzling. A woman is referred to as a 'proselyte' and a 'Jew, Israelite', but it is not clear why the double designation is given.

[10]Although somewhat garbled, Trogus' version looks like a summary of the story in the Pentateuch. Thus, his information most likely derives from a Jewish source.

[11]οι εν δηλω ισραελειται/ισραηλιται οι απαρξομενοι εις ιερον (αγιον) αργαριζειν. See P. Brunneau, "'Les Israélites de Délos' et la juiverie délienne", *BCH* 106 (1982), 465-504, especially 3-4, though he does not think the writers were Samaritans but Jews; however, his reasoning is somewhat circular. Cf. A.T. Kraabel, "New Evidence of the Samaritan Diaspora has been Found on Delos", *BA* (March 1984), 44-6; on the 'Samaritan diaspora' in general, see A.D. Crown, "III. The Samaritan Diaspora", in: Idem (ed.), *The Samaritans*, Tübingen 1989, 195-217. The mention of Mt Gerizim (Argarizein), although not decisive, is often an indication that this is a Samaritan community. Cf. R. Pummer, "Αργαριζειν: A Criterion for Samaritan Provenance?" *JSJ* 18 (1987), 18-25.

[12]See H.-J. Zobel, "יִשְׂרָאֵל", *ThWAT*, Bd. 4, 986-1011, especially 990-4 = TDOT

and Judges. Beginning in Samuel, we find Israel as the name of the Northern Kingdom (though it is still sometimes used of 'all Israel'). This usage characterizes the books of Samuel, Kings, and much of the prophetic literature. However, when we come to Chronicles, we see a greater tendency to have all Israel in mind, though it is still naturally used of the Northern Kingdom. In Ezra and Nehemiah, by contrast, 'Israel'/'descendents of Israel'/'people of Israel' is frequently used of the reconstituted community of returned Judahites, alongside the term 'Jews'.[13] Similarly, here and there in the supposed post-exilic prophets (e.g., Zech. 12:1) 'Israel' designates Judahites. Judahites are referred to as 'Israelites' in Daniel 1:3. Tobit normally refers to the exiled people in Assyria as 'Israel', but the fiction of the book is that Tobit is from the northern tribe of Naphtali; however, the writer slips at 11:18, stating it was a day of rejoicing for the 'Jews of Nineveh'. 1 Maccabees uses 'Israel' frequently to refer to the people, though normally in an ideological context as the people of God; 'Jews' is also used and is the only term in alleged treaties and communications with and from foreigners (e.g., 8:23-32; 10:18-20, 25-45; 11:30-37; 12:6-23; 13:36-40; 14:20-23; 15:2-9, 15-21). 2 Maccabees tends to use 'Jews', though 'Israel' occurs a few times.

To summarize, in the external references to peoples and kingdoms of Palestine, there is no evidence that 'Israel' ever refers to Judah or the Judahites; rather 'Judah', 'Jews', and similar designations are always used, at least until the Christian era. The only group referred to as 'Israelite' in Greco-Roman sources in the pre-Christian period is the Samaritan community associated with Mt Gerizim. On the other hand, in the biblical literature we find what seems to be an attempt by the Judahites to appropriate the name 'Israel' after the exile. Therefore, those who argue that 'Israel' was originally a term for the Northern Kingdom only and was only secondarily adopted by the inhabitants of Judah have a point.

Yet we need to apply a certain caution because gentilic usage is often complicated. White citizens of black African countries can quite

---

6, 397- 420, especially 401-4, for a convenient summary of the data.

[13] The usage is especially frequent in Ezra (e.g., 2:2, 70; 3:1; 6:16, 21; 7:7, 13; 8:25; 9:1; 10:5, 10) and also in Nehemiah in the parts outside the Nehemiah Memorial (e.g., 8:17; 9:1, 2; 10:34, 40; 11:3, 20; 12:47). The exception is Neh. 2:10, but whether it is authentic or secondary is debated, cf. U. Kellermann, *Nehemia: Quellen, Überlieferung, und Geschichte* (BZAW, 102), Berlin 1967, 12-3. The term 'Jews' is used in Ezra (4:12, 23; 5:5; 6:7, 8, 14), but these tend to be in the alleged Persian documents. In the Nehemiah Memorial the term 'Jews' is the normal term for the people of the community (e.g., 1:2; 2:5, 7, 16; 3:33, 34; 4:6; 5:1, 8, 17; 6:6).

appropriately call themselves 'Africans', yet in order to distinguish them from black citizens they are often referred to as 'Europeans', this despite the fact that they may be several generations removed from European settlers and may have no living member of the family who has ever been to Europe. Similarly, the United States is often referred to as 'America'. People from Canada, Mexico, and Central and South America might legitimately say they come from 'America' as well; they might even say with some justification that they are 'Americans'. Yet citizens of the USA have no gentilic based on the formal name of the country, such as 'USers' or 'Staters'; instead they are universally called 'Americans', both within and outside the country. In the same way, the name 'Israel' may have been used particularly of the inhabitants of the Northern Kingdom but still also have had a secondary usage of 'all Israel' which encompassed Judahites as well. Such usage is not clearly documented from non-biblical sources, but it cannot be excluded. I shall return to the question in my closing remarks.

2   Connections with Later Jewish Communities

The study of terminology indicates that when we ask about the continuity of 'Israel', we have to make clear what we are asking. If we are to believe the books of Kings and Chronicles, the Northern Kingdom of Israel was taken captive in 722 BCE, with their place taken by peoples deported from other parts of the Neo-Assyrian empire. For some, it is only this entity which should bear the name 'Israel'; that is, the name Israel was applied to Judahites and Jews only secondarily and inappropriately. Was there any continuation of this Israel?

There is a group which claims to be descended from the Northern Kingdom, the modern community of Samaritans. Unfortunately, many of their traditions are quite late, and determining which (if any) represent the state of things in the Persian or Greek periods – not to mention the Neo-Assyrian period – is difficult. Here we run into apologetic and polemic. The polemic is that the Samaritans come from foreign polytheists brought in to replace the deported population of Samaria; they developed a syncretistic form of Yahweh worship, but their religion and traditions are derivative from the Jews.[14] The apologetic is that the Samaritans are descendents of Israel who remained

---

[14]The base text for this picture is 2 Kings 17. Passages in Ezra 4, Nehemiah (2–3, 6, 13), and Josephus (especially Ant. 9.14.3 §§ 288-91; 11.7.2–8.7 §§ 302-47; 12.5.5 §§ 257-64) have expanded and built on this portrait. For a useful discussion of these sources, see R.J. Coggins, *The Samaritans and Jews* (Growing Points in Theology), London & Atlanta 1975.

true to their faith and God's temple on Gerizim and did not follow the false priesthood of Eli and his descendents in Jerusalem.[15] They have a scroll of the law copied by Abisha, the great grandson of Aaron, and follow that law to this day.[16] According to the Samaritan chronicles, Eli the priest usurped the post of high priest and led many in Israel astray, founding a cult site in Shiloh. The faithful Israelites continued to follow Ozzi (of the line of Eleazar) who remained on Mt Gerizim. Thus, the Jerusalem cult and its priesthood was apostate, but the true priesthood and religion was maintained at the 'place which God would choose', i.e., Shechem.

The relevant Samaritan Chronicles are Chronicle 2,[17] the Tolidah (Chronicle 3),[18] the Shalshalah (Chronicle 5),[19] Abu 'l-Fath (Chronicle 6),[20] and the Adler Chronicle (Chronicle 7).[21] The Chronicles are a minefield of problems. On the one hand, they claim to trace the Samaritan religion back to Moses and to give an account of their history independently (at least, in part) of the OT. On the other hand, all the Chronicles are late, some of them from the 19th or even 20th

---

[15] For a discussion of both the Jewish polemic and the Samaritan apologetic, especially as it relates to the Hellenistic and Maccabean periods, see L.L. Grabbe, "Betwixt and Between: The Samaritans in the Hasmonean Period," in: E.H. Lovering, Jr. (ed.), *Society of Biblical Literature 1993 Seminar Papers* (SBL.SPS, 32), Atlanta 1993, 334-47.

[13] This scenario is found in the various Samaritan chronicles. For a summary of primary and second sources on the Samaritan community, see Grabbe, *Judaism from Cyrus to Hadrian*, 501-5, and notes 17-22 below.

[17] J. Macdonald, *The Samaritan Chronicle No. II* (BZAW, 107), Berlin 1969, has published a portion of the manuscript. The section on the Persian period has not been published. For a summary of the entire contents, including the unpublished parts, see his article, "Samaritans", *EJ* 14, 728-32. From his description, the contents sound very similar to Abu 'l-Fath.

[18] A. Neubauer, "Chronique samaritaine, suivie d'un appendice contenant de courtes notices sur quelques autres ouvrages samaritains", *JA* 14 (1869), 385-470 (text and French translation); M. Heidenheim, "Die samaritan. Chronik des Hohenpriesters Elasar", *VDETF* 4 (1871), 347-89 (German translation only); J. Bowman, *Transcript of the Original Text of the Samaritan Chronicle Tolidah*, Leeds 1954 (text only, using a different manuscript from Neubauer).

[19] M. Gaster, "The Chain of Samaritan High Priests", *Studies and Texts*, London 1925-28, 1.483-502 (tr.), 3.131-8 (text).

[20] Transl.: P. Stenhouse, *The Kitāb al-Tarīkh of Abū 'l-Fath, Translated into English with Notes* (Mandelbaum Studies in Judaica, 1), Sydney 1985, though Stenhouse's own critical text of the Arabic original is still unpublished; partial translation in J. Bowman, *Samaritan Documents Relating to their History, Religion and Life* (Pittsburgh Original Texts and Translations, 2), Pittsburgh 1977, 114-213.

[21] E.N. Adler, M. Seligsohn, "Une nouvelle chronique samaritaine", *REJ* 44 (1902), 188-222; 45 (1902), 70-98, 223-54; 46 (1903), 123-46.

century in their present form. Study of them is not far advanced, and
Samaritan specialists have reached no consensus on their interrela-
tionships.[22]

Where the Chronicles relate Samaritan history to external events,
there is often confusion. In addition, some of the events which Jewish literature recounts with reference to the Jews is claimed for the
Samaritans by the Chronicles. For example, where Josephus and other
Jewish sources have Alexander the Great doing obeisance to the Jewish high priest, the Chronicles (Adler; Tolidah; Abu 'l-Fath; Chronicle
2, *apud* Macdonald) make him do it to the Samaritan high priest.[23]

The main early evidence we have are the two inscriptions from
Delos mentioned above from the 3rd to 1st centuries BCE. This is
about the only early (and non-literary) information we have. It is
of course possible that the Samaritan community is right about its
claims, but the lateness of most of the traditions means that they do
not meet the agnostic criteria I claimed to abide by in this paper.
For it is also possible that the Samaritans could have appropriated
Jewish traditions and turned them to their own ends. Even though
this is precisely the prejudicial polemic made against the Samaritans
and therefore very suspect, at this stage of study it does not seem
impossible. This means that we cannot yet demonstrate a continuity
of the Northern Kingdom even though that possibility remains.

So we now turn to the Judahites. Over a century after the fall of
Samaria Nebuchadnezzar similarly took the population of the Southern Kingdom of Judah captive; however, he did not replace it with
other peoples. We have a great deal of information, relatively speaking, about the last days of the kingdom of Judah. Thanks to the Babylonian Chronicles and other sources, we can reconstruct the events
almost year by year. The picture given by 2 Kings is confirmed to
a high degree by external sources, at least until 594 BCE.[24] At that

---

[22]It seems that each specialist prefers a different Chronicle as the most basic. Bowman thinks *Tolidah* is earliest. P. Stenhouse, "Samaritan Chronicles", in:
Crown (ed.), *The Samaritans*, 218-65, concentrates on Abu 'l-Fath. A.D. Crown,
"New Light on the Inter-relationships of Samaritan Chronicles from Some Manuscripts in the John Rylands Library", *BJRL* 54 (1971-72), 282-313; 55 (1972-73),
86-111, argues that the basis of all the Chronicles is the Samaritan Book of Joshua
(Chronicle 4) and a *Sefer ha-Yamim* (of which the Adler Chronicle and Chronicle
2 are late examples), with the former being incorporated into the latter at some
point.
[23]For a discussion of this event, its sources and historicity, see my article,
"Josephus and the Reconstruction of the Judean Restoration", *JBL* 106 (1987),
231-46, and *Judaism from Cyrus to Hadrian*, 181-3.
[24]For *Chronicles 1-5*, which are the main ones in question here, see A.K.
Grayson, *Assyrian and Babylonian Chronicles* (TCS, 5), Locust Valley, NY 1975,

point, the Chronicles break off, and our sources for Nebuchadnezzar's reign become fragmentary. Nevertheless, because the text of 2 Kings has been quite accurate in its general outline to that point, we can have considerable confidence in assuming that the next decade to the destruction of Jerusalem and the temple are also credible.

With the fall of Jerusalem, though, we suddenly find a huge hole in our information. For the time of the so-called 'exile' and the Persian period we have few sources, and the usability of their data is often questionable. Before looking at the sources for the Persian period, I want to leap ahead to another period of which we have some knowledge, the late Second Temple period. For the last century or two of the Second Temple period we have evidence of Jewish communities all over the ancient Near East and the Mediterranean world: Babylonia, Egypt and Cyrenaica, Syria, Asia Minor, Greece, Rome.[25] The origins and history of these communities is not always clear. The one in Babylonia is most naturally ascribed to the deportations under the Neo-Babylonian empire,[26] while those in Rome most likely postdate the Maccabean period and perhaps even the conquest of Jerusalem by Pompey.[27] We have little information on the ones in Asia Minor until the Roman period.

The Jews in Egypt are well documented from the mid-third century BCE, however, in a variety of sources. The papyri begin to men-

---

69-102. A survey of what we know of the events from external sources can be found in L.L. Grabbe, "'The Exile' under the Theodolite: Historiography as Triangulation", in: L.L. Grabbe (ed.), *Leading Captivity Captive: 'The Exile' as History and Propaganda* (ESHM, 2; JSOT.S, 278), Sheffield 1998, 80-100.

[25] A study of the most of these except Babylonia, see J.M.G. Barclay, *Jews in the Mediterranean Diaspora from Alexander to Trajan* (323 BCE-117 CE), Edinburgh 1996. Most of the information on the Jews in Egypt and Cyrenaica is collected in V.A. Tcherikover *et al.* (eds.), *Corpus Papyrorum Judaicarum* (3 vols.), Cambridge, Jerusalem 1957-64; W. Horbury, D. Noy (eds.), *Jewish Inscriptions of Graeco-Roman Egypt, with an Index of the Jewish Inscriptions of Egypt and Cyrenaica*, Cambridge 1992; and S. Applebaum, *Jews and Greeks in Ancient Cyrene* (SJLA, 28), Leiden 1979. On Asia Minor and Greece, see P. Trebilco, *Jewish Communities in Asia Minor* (MSSNTS, 69), Cambridge 1991. For Rome and other western areas, see D. Noy (ed.), *Jewish Inscriptions*: vol. 1: Italy (excluding the City of Rome), Spain and Gaul, Cambridge 1993; Idem, *Jewish Inscriptions of Western Europe*, vol. 2, The City of Rome, Cambridge 1995; L.V. Rutgers, *The Jews in Late Ancient Rome: Evidence of Cultural Interaction in the Roman Diaspora* (Religions in the Graeco-Roman World, 126), Leiden 1995; and H.J. Leon, *The Jews of Ancient Rome* (updated edition with new introduction by C.A. Osiek), Peabody, MA 1995.

[26] Unfortunately, most of our information on the Jews in Babylonia comes from the later rabbinic literature whose data must be used with great caution. For the Jews in Babylonia, see the study of J. Neusner, *A History of the Jews in Babylonia* (vols. 1-5), Leiden 1965-70.

[27] See Grabbe, *Judaism from Cyrus to Hadrian*, 397-8.

tion individuals identified as Jews as early as the mid-third-century.[28] They are mentioned not only as individuals but as an entity alongside 'the Greeks',[29] and an incidental reference to a synagogue (*proseuchè*) is found by 218 BCE.[30] Several synagogue inscriptions can be dated to the mid-third century.[31] The period of best documentation, the Roman period with writers such as Philo of Alexandria, simply affirms the picture from the earlier papyri and inscriptions. Inscriptions from Cyrenaica show a flourishing Jewish community there as well.[32]

Nevertheless, the earliest community attested in some detail is still that in Judah, with extra-biblical evidence going back to the early Greek period. Perhaps our most important early source is Hecataeus of Abdera, writing about 300 BCE:[33]

> "When in ancient times a pestilence arose in Egypt, the common people ascribed their troubles to the workings of a divine agency ... the natives of the land surmised that unless they removed the foreigners, their troubles would never be resolved. At once, therefore, the aliens were driven from the country, and the most outstanding and active among them banded together and, as some say, were cast ashore in Greece ... But the greater number were driven into what is now called Judaea, which is not far distant from Egypt and was at that time utterly uninhabited. The colony was headed by a man called Moses,

---

[28]These are collected in *CPJ*. Two Jews are mentioned among the Zenon papyri (*CPJ* 1 Nos. 8-9), but the earliest reference seems to be a deed of renunciation dated to 260 BCE (*CPJ* 1 No. 18). Tcherikover also used Jewish names as a means of determining or at least recording the presence of Jews. However, the names he used as criteria could also be those of Samaritans. In keeping with the agnostic stance of this article, I here refer only to papyri which actually use the term *Ioudaios* or something similar. In the third century BCE, Jews are mentioned in Nos. 33, 38, 125, and 129.

[29]*CPJ* 1 No. 33.

[30]*CPJ* 1 No. 129.

[31]Horbury, Noy, *Jewish Inscriptions of Graeco-Roman Egypt*, Nos. 22 and 117. For a general discussion, see J.G. Griffiths, "Egypt and the Rise of the Synagogue", *JThS n.s.*, 38 (1987), 1-15.

[32]See primarily Applebaum, *Jews and Greeks*.

[33]*Apud* Diodorus Siculus 40.3.1-8. For text, translation, and commentary, see M. Stern, *Jews and Judaism in Greek and Latin Literature* (3 vols.; Jerusalem 1974-84), 1.26-35. For a survey of the most recent scholarship on the work, see B. Bar-Kochva, *Pseudo-Hecataeus, "On the Jews": Legitimizing the Jewish Diaspora* (Hellenistic Culture and Society 21; Berkley & Los Angeles 1996), 7-43. Unfortunately, the quotations in Josephus are not likely to be authentic, as Bar-Kochva has now demonstrated.

outstanding both for his wisdom and for his courage. On taking possession of the land he founded, besides other cities, one that is now the most renowned of all, called Jerusalem. In addition he established the temple that they hold in chief veneration, instituted their forms of worship and ritual, drew up their laws and ordered their political institutions. He also divided them into twelve tribes, since this is regarded as the most perfect number and corresponds to the number of months that make up a year."

He describes a Jewish ethnic and national community centering on Jerusalem. They were founded by Moses who led a group out of Egypt, divided them into twelve tribes, and built Jerusalem and its temple. He goes on to say[34] that the Jews have never had a king but the priests provide leadership and act as judges, as well as running the cult and teaching the law. Chief authority is invested in the high priest who is chosen for his wisdom. It can be argued that the ultimate source of this picture is priestly teaching. For example, the period of the monarchy is completely unknown, and the priestly class is pictured as being in charge from the beginning. Our other Ptolemaic sources give us only a partial picture,[35] but the books of Maccabees confirm the picture of Hecataeus and other sources.[36]

When we ask whether we can bridge the gap between the mid-third century and the early 6th century by tracing the Jewish community back into the Persian period, we find an encouraging answer. Despite the skimpiness of the data, we do have some valuable pointers to the situation in Jerusalem. First of all, we have a number of coins for Persian Palestine.[37] The dating is not absolutely established for all of them, but there is agreement that a number with the inscription *YHD*

---

[34] See below under 'Religion' for a continuation of the quotation from Hecataeus.

[35] The best source is the Zenon papyri, especially on Tobias (*CPJ* 1 Nos. 1-6), but there is no real description of the community. The 'Tobiad Romance' found in Josephus (*Ant.* 12.4.1-11 §§ 157-236) is very interesting and important, despite its pathetic nature and many questionable details (cf. Grabbe, *Judaism from Cyrus to Hadrian*, 174-5, 192-8), but in keeping with the agnostic approach of my study, I shall not here use it as evidence.

[36] The situation in Jerusalem just before the Maccabean revolt (2 Macc. 3–5) fits well with the 'Tobiad Romance'.

[37] For a summary of most of the coins, see Y. Meshorer, *Ancient Jewish Coinage*, vol. 1: Persian Period through Hasmonaeans, New York 1982. For later finds and further discussion, see D. Barag, "Some Notes on a Silver Coin of Johanan the High Priest", *BA* 48 (1985), 166-8; Idem, "A Silver Coin of Yohanan the High Priest and the Coinage of Judea in the Fourth Century B.C.", *INJ* 9 (1986-87), 4-21; L. Mildenberg, "Yehud: A Preliminary Study of the Provincial Coinage of Judaea", in: O. Mørkholm, N.M. Waggoner (eds.), *Greek Numismatics and*

were products of the Persian province of Judah, known as *Yehud*.[38] Of particular interest are a number with the inscription 'Hezekiah the governor'.[39] Although these do not have the designation 'Yehud', the script, the name, the language, and the presumed location of the find all point to Judah as the place of minting. Again, the most natural interpretation is that these were produced by the governor of the province who was himself a native.

The most important source is the Elephantine papyri, in particular the letter from Jedaniah to Bagohi the governor of Judah, written in 410 BCE.[40] Within the letter is the following statement:

> "We sent a letter to our lord (Bagohi the governor) and to Yehohanan the high priest and his companions the priests who are in Jerusalem and to Ostan the brother of Anan and the nobles of the Jews. They did not send a single letter to us."[41]

These two brief lines give some very important data. There was not only the Persian province of Judah with its governor Bagohi; there was also a coterie of priests, with a high priest at their head and what is the point of a priest and high priests without a temple? In addition, there was community of some sort with Jewish 'nobles' as a part of its leadership, but a firm place in community leadership is also implied for the high priest and his fellow priests. Thus, the implication of this letter is that within the Persian province of Yehud (or perhaps co-extensive with it) is a Jewish community with a temple located at or centered on Jerusalem, having a leadership (in addition to the officially appointed governor) composed of the high priest and his fellow priests and the local nobility.

For an account of how the community in Judah was reconstituted after the deportation described in 2 Kings, we are heavily dependent on the books of Ezra and Nehemiah. It is Ezra which tells how the people returned from captivity in the late 6th century, at the decree of

---

Archaeology: Essays in Honor of Margaret Thompson, Wetteren 1979, 183-96; Idem, "*Yehūd* Münzen", in: H. Weippert (ed.), *Palästina in vorhellenistischer Zeit* (HdA, Vorderasien 2/1), München 1988, 721-8; A. Spaer, "Jaddua the High Priest?" *INJ* 9 (1986-87), 1-3.

[38] Meshorer. *Ancient Jewish Coinage*, Nos. 1-9.

[39] *Ibidem*, Nos. 10-13: יחזקיה הפחה.

[40] Cowley, Nos. 30 and 31 (= TAD A4.7 and A4.8) are two copies of the same document with only slight differences.

[41] My translation from the text in TAD A4.7:18-19: אגרה שלחן מראן ועל יהוחנן כהנא רבא וכנותה כהניא זי בירושלם ועל אוסתן אחויה זי ענני וחרי יהודיא אגרה חדה לא שלחו עלין:

Cyrus, and re-established the community which had been destroyed under Nebuchadnezzer and rebuilt the temple and restored the cult. Can we trust this picture? I must say that the more I read Ezra and the further I probe into its workings, the more problematic I find it.[42] Quite some time ago, Hugh Williamson pointed out that Ezra 1–6 was compiled from half a dozen sources and had no independent data beyond them.[43] The question is, then, how useful are the sources themselves? The Cyrus decree Ezra 1:1-4 is too problematic to accept. Although the alleged Persian documents have been widely accepted as authentic, they actually vary considerably: most of them have late grammatical features and other indications of reworking by Jewish scribes. They may be based on genuine Persian documents in some or even all cases, but a great deal of further study is needed before they can be accepted as trustworthy sources. As for Ezra 7–10, the harder one looks at Ezra, the more hazy he becomes as a historical figure. There may be history here, but it is very difficult to get at. On this, Bob Becking and I seem to agree.[44]

However, I am not so negative toward all our sources. I am impressed that Haggai and Zechariah give a picture of the rebuilding and restoration which differs in essential points from that in Ezra 1–6. It is difficult to be sure how to evaluate their information, but they have a certain independence. Ezra 2 ‖ Nehemiah 7 also contains not just a list of the alleged returnees but also indications of settlement patterns, which could argue for its genuineness in this area at least. However, the book of Nehemiah seems to be the best source, mainly because it appears to have an actual writing of Nehemiah at its core. There is a surprising consensus on this point.[45] The precise limits of the original 'Nehemiah Memorial/Memoir' are debated,[46] but there is

---

[42]See especially L.L. Grabbe, *Ezra-Nehemiah*, London 1998, ch. 6; also my earlier articles, 'Reconstructing History from the Book of Ezra', in: P.R. Davies (ed.), *Second Temple Studies* (JSOT.S, 117), vol. 1: The Persian Period, Sheffield 1991, 98-107; Idem, 'What Was Ezra's Mission?' in: T.C. Eskenazi, K.H. Richards (eds.), *Second Temple Studies* (JSOT.S, 175), vol. 2: Temple Community in the Persian Period, Sheffield 1994, 286-99.

[43]Cyrus edict (1:1-4), a list of temple vessels (1:9-11), a list of returnees (2:1-69), the prophetic books of Haggai and Zechariah, and several alleged Persian documents in Aramaic in 3–7, H.G.M. Williamson, "The Composition of Ezra i-vi", *JTS* 34 (1983), 1-30; cf. Idem, *Ezra, Nehemiah* (WBC, 16), Waco, TX 1985, xxiii-xxiv.

[44]See especially his article, "Ezra's Re-enactment of the Exile", in: Grabbe (ed.), *Leading Captivity Captive*, 40-61.

[45]Even A.H.J. Gunneweg, *Nehemiah* (KAT 19/2), Gütersloh 1987, 176-80, agrees with this, despite his skepticism about much of the material in Ezra.

[46]It is found mainly in Neh. 1–6 and 12:27-43. The main disagreement is over

sufficient agreement on the basic text to treat it almost as a contemporary source.[47] If it should be accepted as a genuinely contemporary source – however biased it may be – it goes a long way to show not only that a community existed in Judah and Jerusalem in the mid-Persian-period (even in the fifth century if Neh. 5:14 is accepted as a part of Nehemiah Memorial) but even to suggest some details of the shape of that community and the political maneuvering which affected it.

Especially important to the book of Ezra (and perhaps less explicitly in parts of Nehemiah) is the 'myth of the empty land'.[48] The book takes it for granted that only the golah community is legitimate and that all the others living in the land (the 'peoples of the land') are 'foreigners'. This is very unlikely. The bulk of the population was not deported but remained in the land. Despite the attempts to label them as outsiders and even to demonize them, these people seem to have become accepted as a part of the Jewish community so that by the time of the Maccabees there is no evidence that any of those living in Judah proper, whether 'peoples of the land' or otherwise, were viewed as 'foreigners'.[49] The significance of this point is that there is continuity with the kingdom of Judah in that many of the inhabitants of the former kingdom continued to live in the land and have children and grandchildren who also remained in the land. We could say that the kingdom of Judah continued on the DNA level, as well as in other ways.

As for the Jewish communities outside Palestine, our knowledge of their origin is uncertain in some cases and the continuation on the DNA level less provable. Nevertheless, they retained a strong ideological

---

Neh. 13. Perhaps the majority accept it as a part of the Nehemiah Memorial, but this view is rejected by P.R. Ackroyd, *The Age of the Chronicler* (Supplement to Colloquium – The Australian and New Zealand Theological Review), Auckland 1970, 28, 41, and G. Steins, *Die Chronik als kanonisches Abschlussphänomen: Studien zur Entstehung und Theologie von 1/2 Chronik* (BBB, 93), Weinheim 1995, 198-207.

[47]The fact that it has been edited and incorporated into a book with other material means that the present form of the book is probably rather later than the time of Nehemiah.

[48]R.P. Carroll, "The Myth of the Empty Land", in: D. Jobling, T. Pippin (eds.), *Ideological Criticism of Biblical Texts* (Semeia, 59), Atlanta 1992, 79-93; H.M. Barstad, *The Myth of the Empty Land: A Study in the History and Archaeology of Judah During the "Exilic" Period* (SO.S, 28), Oslo 1996.

[49]L.L. Grabbe, "Triumph of the Pious or Failure of the Xenophobes? The Ezra/Nehemiah Reforms and their *Nachgeschichte*", in: S. Jones, S. Pearce (eds.), *Studies in Jewish Local Patriotism and Self-Identification in the Graeco-Roman Period* (JSPE.S, 25), Sheffield 1998, 50-65.

attachment to the 'homeland', even when they were actually quite well integrated into their local community. Therefore, we can speak of a cultural and ideological continuity, especially on the level of self-identification.[50]

3   Judahite Religion in the Persian Period

There has been a great deal of interest in Israelite religion in recent years.[51] A lot of this has centred on the question of when monotheism developed, but this question is less important for our purposes than some others. When we compare the religion of Iron Age Palestine (as far as we can determine it) with that of Judaism toward the end of the Second Temple period, we see a remarkable amount of continuity but also a considerable amount of development. Again, we ask for actual evidence in datable sources.

To cover the religious question in detail would take much more than a few minutes in a single lecture. However, Judaic religion had two aspects which singled it out from other Northwest Semitic religions of which it was an integral part. These are worship of a god called YHWH; the other is the Jerusalem temple. It is on these that I shall focus for purposes of this exercise.

In broad outlines the present trend is to see the religion of monarchic Israel and Judah as polytheistic. Yet YHWH is especially associated with these two kingdoms. He seems to have been the national god or ethnic god in some sense, just as Chemosh was the Moabite

---

[50]For further discussion and documentation on the subject, consult W.C. van Unnik, *Das Selbstverständnis der jüdischen Diaspora in der hellenistisch-römischen Zeit* (aus dem Nachlaß herausgeben und bearbeitet von P.W. van der Horst), Leiden 1993; S.J.D. Cohen, E.S. Frerichs (eds.), *Diasporas in Antiquity* (BJSt, 288), Atlanta 1993; I.M. Gafni, *Land, Center and Diaspora: Jewish Constructs in Late Antiquity* (JSPE.S, 21), Sheffield 1997; and a number of the essays in: J.M. Scott (ed.), *Exile: Old Testament, Jewish, and Christian Conceptions* (JSJ.S, 56), Leiden 1997.

[51]A good survey to about 1990 or so is R. Albertz, *Religionsgeschichte Israels in alttestamentlicher Zeit* (GAT, 8), Göttingen 1992 (ET: *A History of Israelite Religion in the Old Testament Period*, vol. 1: From the Beginnings to the End of the Monarchy; vol. 2: From the Exile to the Maccabees, London 1994). More recent studies include J.C. de Moor, *The Rise of Yahwism: The Roots of Israelite Monotheism* (BEThL, 91A) Leuven ²1997; D.V. Edelman (ed.), *The Triumph of Elohim: From Yahwisms to Judaisms* (CBET, 13), Kampen & Grand Rapids, MI 1995; H. Niehr, *Der höchste Gott: Alttestamentlicher JHWH-Glaube im Context syrisch-kanaanäischer Religion des 1. Jahrtausends v. Chr.* (BZAW, 190), Berlin 1990; W. Dietrich, M.A. Klopfenstein, (eds.), *Ein Gott allein? JHWH-Verehrung und biblischer Monotheismus im Kontext der israelitischen und altorientalischen Religionsgeschichte* (OBO, 139), Freiburg & Göttingen 1994.

god and Qaus the Edomite god. He may well have had a consort, though whether his cult was aniconic is currently a moot point.[52] The name YHWH may be attested as early as the Late Bronze age in the Egyptian reference to the 'land of the Shasu of YHWH'.[53] YHWH is the most frequent divine element in personal names, whether in the inscriptions or in the biblical text, for whatever that is worth since not all see this as significant.[54] King Mesha of Moab refers to taking Nebo from Israel and dedicating the 'vessels of YHWH' to Chemosh, indicating that Omri and his son's god was YHWH.[55] The Kuntillet 'Ajrud inscriptions speak of both a YHWH of Samaria and a YHWH of Teman.[56]

Yet there is no evidence that YHWH was particularly confined to the Northern Kingdom; on the contrary, YHWH is equally the national/ethnic god of the Southern Kingdom. Among the Khirbet Beit Lei inscriptions is a reference to a YHWH god of Jerusalem.[57] A seal which has been dated paleographically to the early 8th century, allegedly found in Jerusalem, has the inscription, 'Miqneyahu servant of YHWH'.[58] The Lachish letters, probably dated to the last days of the Judean kingdom, mention YHWH as a matter of course in blessings,

---

[52] See T.N.D. Mettinger, *No Graven Image? Israelite Aniconism in Its Ancient Near Eastern Context* (CB.OT, 42), Stockholm 1995, and the various positions taken in K. van der Toorn (ed.), *The Image and the Book: Iconic Cults, Aniconism, and the Rise of Book Religion in Israel and the Ancient Near East* (CBET, 21), Leuven 1997.

[53] *t3 š3św yhw3*. R. Giveon, *Les bédouins Shosou des documents égyptiens* (DMOA, 22), Leiden 1971, Nos. 6 and 16. The name seems to be a geographical one; however, it is possible that the region got its name from the god associated with it. See V. Fritz, *Die Entstehung Israels im 12. und 11. Jahrhundert v. Chr.* (Biblische Enzyklopädie, 2), Stuttgart & Berlin, etc. 1996, 140-1.

[54] For a collection of much of the data, see M. Noth, *Die israelitischen Personennamen im Rahmen der gemeinsemitischen Namengebung* (BWANT, 3/10), Stuttgart 1928 (reprinted Hildesheim 1966); J.H. Tigay, *You Shall Have No Other Gods: Israelite Religion in the Light of Hebrew Inscriptions* (HSM, 31), Atlanta 1986; J.D. Fowler, *Theophoric Personal Names in Ancient Hebrew: A Comparative Study* (JSOT.S, 49), Sheffield 1988; and see Stern in this volume, p. 249, n.9.

[55] KAI No. 181:17-18; TSSI No. 16:17-18, [כלי יהוה]. This fits the OT picture as well since Omri's two sons (Ahaziah, Jehoram) both had YHWH names.

[56] G.I. Davies, *Ancient Hebrew Inscriptions: Corpus and Concordance*, Cambridge 1991, No. 8.017: ברכת . אתכם . ליהוה . שמרן . ולאשרתה; No. 8.021: . ברכתך ליהוה תמן ולאשרתה. The Khirbet el-Qom (No. 25.003) inscription also seems to mention YHWH, but the exact reading is difficult and disputed.

[57] Davies, *Ancient Hebrew Inscriptions*, No. 15.005. The precise reading has been disputed, but the name 'YHWH' and 'Jerusalem' are clear: /הו יהוה אלהי כל הארץ הרי / יהוה את ה[?יהד לו ?יהודה] אלהי. [?ולאאלהי.] ירשלם.

[58] N. Avigad, revised and completed by B. Sass, *Corpus of West Semitic Stamp Seals*, Jerusalem 1997. No. 27: מקניו עבד יהוה.

imprecations, and the like.[59] Much the same situation is found in the Arad ostraca (c. 600 BCE) where YHWH is mentioned a number of times in statements of blessing or imprecation.[60] In the fifth century the Elephantine colony which identified itself as 'Jews/Judeans'[61] and which may have originated before the fall of Jerusalem, worshipped mainly YHWH.[62]

But once again one of our main early sources about Judaic religion is Hecataeus of Abdera (see previous section). The description here is indicative of an aniconic and most likely a monotheistic temple-based religion (as quoted in Diodorus Siculus 40.3:3-6):

> "In addition he [Moses] established the temple that they hold in chief veneration, instituted their forms of worship and ritual, drew up their laws and ordered their political institutions ... But he had no images whatsoever of the gods made for them, being of the opinion that God is not in human form; rather the Heaven that surrounds the earth is alone divine, and rules the universe. The sacrifices that he established differ from those of other nations, as does their way of living, for as a result of their own expulsion from Egypt he introduced an unsocial and intolerant mode of life. He picked out the men of most refinement and with the greatest ability to head the entire nation, and appointed them priests; and he ordained that they should occupy themselves with the temple and the honours and sacrifices offered to their god. These same men he appointed to be judges in all major disputes, and entrusted to them the guardianship of the laws and customs. For this

---

[59] KAI Nos. 192:2, 5; 193:3; 194:3, 9; 195:1, 7-8; 196:1, 12; 197:1; TSSI Nos. 12:ii.2, 5; iii.3, 9; iv.1, v.7-8; vi.1, 12; ix.1.

[60] Y. Aharoni, *Arad Inscriptions* (in cooperation with J. Naveh) Jerusalem 1981, Nos. 16.3; 18.2; 21.2-3 (restored), 4; 40.3 (restored). In addition, No. 18.9 refers to a בית יהוה; Aharoni (p. 37) interprets this as a reference to the Jerusalem temple, but his argument is inferential, and he admits that other temples could serve as sanctuaries. It could be a reference to the Arad temple itself, cf. D. Ussishkin, "The Date of the Judaean Shrine at Arad", *IEJ* 38 (1988), 142-57, especially 155-6.

[61] E.g., TAD A4.1:2, 11 (Cowley, No. 21); A4.3:12 (Cowley, No. 38); A4.7:19, 22, 26 (Cowley, No. 30); A4.8:22, 26 (Cowley, No. 31); B2.9:2, 3 (Cowley, No. 20); C3.15:1 (Cowley, No. 22).

[62] Other divinities (or possibly hypostases of YHWH) also had a place in the form of Eshem-Bethel and Anat-Bethel (TAD C3.15:127-8 = Cowley, No. 22:127-8) and Anat-Yahu (TAD B7.3:3 = Cowley No. 44:3). For a further discussion, see K. van der Toorn, "Anat-Yahu, Some Other Deities, and the Jews of Elephantine", *Numen* 39 (1992), 80-101.

reason the Jews never have a king, and authority over the
people is regularly vested in whichever priest is regarded
as superior to his colleagues in wisdom and virtue. They
call this man the high priest [archiera], and believe that
he acts as a messenger to them of God's commandments.
It is he, we are told, who in their assemblies and other
gatherings announces what is ordained, and the Jews are
so docile in such matters that straightway they fall to the
ground and do reverence to the high priest when he ex-
pounds the commandments to them. And at the end of
their laws there is even appended the statement: 'These
are the words that Moses heard from God and declares
unto the Jews'."

The name of the God worshipped by the Jews is not given by Hecataeus, but a form of YHWH is mentioned by several classical writers.
Diodorus of Sicily says that Moses ascribed his laws to the god called
Iao (1.94.2). If Diodorus' source was Hecataeus of Abdera, that would
be very interesting, but this is probably not the case. Varro is also
quoted as saying that the Jewish God is called Iao in the Chaldean
mysteries.[63] Both Philo (*De Vita Mosis* 2.114-5; 2.132) and Josephus
(*War* 5.5.7 §235; *Ant.* 3.7.6 §178; 8.3.8 §93) make allusion to the
tetragrammaton as the name of the God of Israel.

It has been suggested that YHWH was not unique to Israel/Judah
but rather a deity common to a large part of Syria-Palestine.[64] This is
based on an apparent reference to individuals with YHWH names in a
cuneiform text relating to Hamath in Syria.[65] The reference seems to
be certain, but there is no supporting evidence that YHWH was part
of general worship over the region. Rather, it looks more likely that
YHWH worship had been transplanted from Palestine in some way
but remained isolated or confined to a minority.[66] Temple worship
was an important characteristic of Judahite religion, though precisely

---

[63] Apud Lydus, *De Mensibus* 4.53 (pp. 110-11). See M. Stern, *Jews and Judaism
in Greek and Latin Literature* (3 vols.), Jerusalem 1974-84, No. 75 (1.211-12).

[64] E.g., T.L. Thompson, "The Intellectual Matrix of Early Biblical Narrative:
Inclusive Monotheism in Persian Period Palestine", in: Edelman (ed.), *Triumph
of Elohim*, 107-24, especially 119, n. 13.

[65] S. Dalley, "Yahweh in Hamath in the 8th Century BC: Cuneiform Material
and Historical Deductions", *VT* 40 (1990), 21-32.

[66] E. Lipiński, "An Israelite King of Hamat", *VT* 21 (1971), 371-73; Z. Zevit,
"Yahweh Worship and Worshippers in 8th-Century Syria", *VT* 41 (1991), 363-6;
Van der Toorn, "Anat-Yahu", 88-90; Idem, "Yahweh", in: *DDD*, 1712-30, esp.
1713, [2]*DDD*, 910-9; cf. also M. Cogan, H. Tadmor, *II Kings* (AncB, 11), New
York 1988, 166.

when Jerusalem became the sole cult site is debated and may be a post-exilic development.[67] As noted above, the destruction of the Jerusalem temple by the Babylonians is virtually certain even though not confirmed by any external source. When we look ahead to later sources, we find that Hecataeus of Abdera mentions the temple (see the quote above). A century later in about 200 BCE a decree of Antiochus III lists the temple personnel and relieves some of their taxes temporarily so the temple can be repaired of war damage:[68]

> "In the first place we have decided, on account of their piety, to furnish them for their sacrifices an allowance of sacrificial animals, wine, oil and frankincense ... And it is my will that these things be made over to them as I have ordered, and that the work on the temple be completed, including the porticoes and any other part that it may be necessary to build ... And all the members of the nation shall have a form of government in accordance with the laws of their country, and the senate, the priests, the scribes of the temple and the temple-singers shall be relieved from the poll-tax and the crown-tax and the salt-tax which they pay."

Almost at the same time Ben Sira describes the high priest Simon in his duties in the temple (Ben Sira 50).[69] The temple is not mentioned explicitly in extra-biblical sources from the Persian period, but its existence by at least the 5th century can be inferred from the Elephantine letter quoted above. We also have a recently published coin

---

[67] It now seems likely that the Arad temple was active until near the end of the kingdom of Judah, cf. Ussishkin, "Date of the Judaean Shrine".

[68] Quoted in Josephus, *Ant.* 12.3.3-4 §§ 138-46, translation from H.St.J. Thackeray *et al.* (eds.), *Josephus* (LCL), London, Cambridge 1926-65, 7.71-5. This decree is widely accepted as authentic, even by some who are sceptical of other decrees quoted in Josephus. See E.J. Bickerman, "La charte séleucide de Jérusalem", *Studies in Jewish and Christian History* (AGJU, 9), Leiden 1980, 2.44-85, orig. *REJ* 100 (1935); Idem, "Une proclamation séleucide relative au temple de Jérusalem", *Studies in Jewish and Christian History* (AGJU, 9), Leiden 1980, 2.86-104, orig. *Syria* 25 (1946-48). J.-D. Gauger, *Beiträge zur jüdischen Apologetik: Untersuchungen zur Authentizität von Urkunden bei Flavius Josephus und im I. Makkabäerbuch* (BBB, 49), Köln & Bonn 1977, who is very skeptical of some of the alleged decrees in Josephus, nevertheless seems to accept the basic authenticity of this document, though he apparently allows that some reworking has taken place (cf. pp. 19, 23-4, 61-3, 136-8).

[69] It has often been argued that this is a description of ceremonies on the Day of Atonement, but this interpretation is opposed by F. O'Fearghail, "Sir 50,5-21: Yom Kippur or the Daily Whole-Offering?" *Bib.* 59 (1978), 301-16.

with the inscription 'Johanan the priest'.[70] Consequently, although the temple is not explicitly mentioned, it is implied; after all, a priest has little *raison d'être* without one, and this priest was important enough to have his own coins.

We have little in the way of a description of the temple and its cult. Most of the descriptions of the temple itself are likely to be stylized and their relationship to the actual physical temple uncertain: Ezekiel 40-48, *Letter of (Pseudo-)Aristeas*, the Qumran *Temple Scroll*, the Mishnah tractate *Middot*.[71] Josephus, as one who had seen the temple himself, is probably most reliable, but he is describing the edifice shortly before its destruction.

Precisely how the cult was carried out is also known only in broad outline.[72] It has often been proposed, quite plausibly, that the arrangements ascribed to David and Solomon in the books of Chronicles actually apply to the cult of the Second Temple. But we also have some indications of actual practice in other sources. It is often the incidental details without any ideological motivation mentioned in passing in the sources which are the best indicators of the reality of daily life. We have several such sporadic references which confirm the continuity of the temple observances over many centuries. I mention a few examples here:

1. Festival of the Wood Offering. Nothing is said about this in the Pentateuch. However, Nehemiah mentions bringing the wood for the altar at a particular time (10:35). The *Temple Scroll* (11QT 19–25) describes a Festival of the Wood Offering in which wood for the altar was brought. We cannot always be sure which details of the *Temple Scroll* are genuinely a reflection of real temple practice and which are ideological creations. Yet Josephus mentions in passing that the Edomites, despite a strict guard, managed to slip into Jerusalem during the ceremony of the bringing of the wood (*War* 2.17.6 § 425). Such a festival must have existed.

---

[70]יוחנן הכוהן, published in D. Barag, "Some Notes on a Silver Coin of Johanan the High Priest", *BA* 48 (1985), 166-8; Idem, "A Silver Coin of Yohanan the High Priest and the Coinage of Judea in the Fourth Century B.C.", *INJ* 9 (1986-87), 4-21.

[71]Much of the information on these later literary descriptions are discussed in detail in Th.A. Busink, *Der Tempel von Jerusalem von Salomo bis Herodes: Eine archäologisch-historische Studie unter Berücksichtigung des westsemitischen Tempelbaus, Bd.2, Von Ezechiel bis Middot*, Leiden 1980.

[72]The attempt by E.P. Sanders, *Judaism: Practice and Belief 63* BCE – *66* CE, Harrisburg, PA & London 1992, to describe the day-to-day functioning of the temple is an interesting – and even brave – exercise, but it has significant methodological flaws. See my review in *JTS* 44 (1993), 643-4.

2. Passover. The Passover celebration is described in two places in the Pentateuch (Exod. 12; Deut. 16:1-8). Whether either of these had much to do with the exact celebration is debatable. On the other hand, *Jubilees* 49 describes how the Passover was to be carried out. Potentially, some of the description could be taken from the biblical text, but some aspects do not conform to Exodus or Deuteronomy but to the later post-70 celebration. The precise time of the night after which the Passover could not be eaten is delineated (49:10-12, 19). It is to be eaten in the temple and nowhere else (49:16-17, 20-21), with certain portions burned on the altar (49:20). A feature also mentioned is the drinking of wine (49:6, 9) which is central to the post-70 Seder but does not feature in the biblical account. This suggests that its actual celebration in the second century BCE is being described in some way.

3. Sukkot (Festival of Booths). Plutarch (*Quaestiones Convivales* 4.6.1-2 671C-E) describes a table conversation in which the God worshipped by the Jews is discussed. This God is thought to be equivalent to Dionysus because at the time of the 'Fast' they set out tables of fruits and made huts of vegetation outside. This is called 'Tabernacles'. Then a few days later they march in a procession to the temple, carrying branches and the thyrsus while individuals called 'Levites' play on instruments. What is done after they enter the temple is unknown. Plutarch wrote about 100 CE, long after he destruction of the temple. Where exactly he got his information is uncertain, but it seems to have an eye-witness account at its base. On the other hand, it was a pagan eye-witness who described what he saw in Greek terms (with some slight confusions) and with a Greek interpretation. Yet this description fits well with the portrayal in Neh. 8:14-18 but also suggests a certain continued development of the celebration.

4. Temple Singers. Josephus relates how in the last days of the Second Temple, the temple singers from among the Levites appealed to Agrippa II to allow them to wear linen in their duties (*Ant.* 20.9.6 §§ 216-18). This is not just a reflex of the biblical description but appears to be a genuine event, illustrating the division of the priesthood into Levites and altar priests and showing that among the Levites were singers of hymns.

Putting together all our sources, we can made reasonable conjectures about the development of Judaic religion through the Second Temple period. However, if we stick to what we can demonstrate, we still find evidence for a continuity in religious belief and practice in certain areas. The most important of these is the worship of YHWH. YHWH was a markedly exclusivistic god. We find little evidence of his worship outside the Northern and Southern Kingdoms, but he is undeniably attested as the god of the people of central Palestine in extra-biblical texts. He continued to be worshipped in the Persian period, was found in a variety of Second Temple Jewish literature, and was plainly in evidence in late literature such as the Qumran scrolls, Philo, and Josephus. Although the name 'YHWH' is not usually found in Jewish literature in Greek or in Greco-Roman literature, the 'Jewish God' was well-known, and his connection with YHWH is plain.

4 Summary and Conclusions

We come back to our central question of the reality of Israel in the post-exilic period, in the context of continuity and discontinuity. The discontinuity is very clear: both the kingdom of Israel and the kingdom of Judah were conquered, the capital cities taken, and some of the population deported by a Mesopotamian empire. That would have caused enormous disruption and upheaval. Yet the extent of this disruption in some ways makes any continuity perhaps more remarkable.

It is true that no group connected with the Northern Kingdom – the 'Kingdom of Israel' proper – continued as such: the indications in most of our sources is that it became 'the lost ten tribes'. However, there may be an exception to this picture: the later Samaritan community associated with worship on Mt Gerizim claims to be direct descendents of the Northern Israelites. For this paper, that claim is left as a question mark. On the other hand, the Judahite community continued in some form, and it is a fact that appropriating the name Israel was important to some Judahites. This is clear from Ezra and Nehemiah and other biblical passages, as noted above. If the name had no special meaning to them, why try to adopt it? Is it likely that, out of the blue, they suddenly decided to appropriate a name with which they had had no past connection? The identity of 'Judah' and the name 'Jews' were the normal identification by outsiders and are widely attested in Mesopotamian and Greek writings. There was no reason for Jews/Judahites to take over the name Israel unless it had particular significance to them. Therefore, it seems perverse to me to ignore the fact that an entity called 'Israel' (at least as one of its names) continued to exist long after the Northern Kingdom had become only a memory from ancient history.

The continuity in the worship of YHWH is also significant. Why did the people of both the Northern and Southern Kingdoms – regardless of whether they had ever been one nation, as portrayed in the biblical text – worship YHWH? It is not as if there were not other gods available. Indeed, there is evidence that they did worship these other gods, but this does not explain the popularity of YHWH. We have evidence that the character of YHWH also changed somewhat over time, perhaps one of the most telling being his loss of a consort. It also seems likely that monotheism was a late development, first attested in Second Isaiah, whatever its earlier roots. Therefore, one of the discontinuities is the change from polytheism to monotheism, but the continuity is the dominance of YHWH worship as such. Eventually, the God of Israel is indicated by generic names or titles and is usually referred to without a special name; nevertheless, the idea that the tetagrammaton was somehow the special name of the Jewish God continued at least to the rabbinic period.

The temple was another example of both continuity and discontinuity. Temple worship was at the core of most ancient religions. The peculiarity we find in Palestine is the gradual decrease in the number of temples or cult places in the late Iron Age until finally only the Jerusalem temple remains in the region of Judah. The cultic activity at that temple seems to have remained quite conservative on the whole, but there are also indications of development and change over time.

As so often in scholarship, there is no simple answer to the question of Israel's continuity after the exile. There was certainly significant discontinuity. It also seems evident that the widespread theme of sin–deportation–return–restoration is a theological and ideological construct.[73] Yet I think that leaving the biblical text aside, we can still point to continuity of a certain sort and in certain areas. I don't doubt that much more could be said, and I don't necessarily assume that we should ignore the biblical text. Some of you will be saying more in your individual papers, and biblical material of various sorts will rightly be a part of this study. My purpose was to conduct a particular experimental exercise, to look for a critical minimum of what we might say from well-documented external data. In investigating this question, I have produced no new sources and no strikingly new data. Yet with what we currently have available, I believe that we can speak of the reality of Israel after the exile as long as we are clear what we are talking about.

---

[73] See especially the papers in Grabbe (ed.), *Leading Captivity Captive*.

As a sort of footnote, I want to mention that more and more
scholars are discussing the development of tradition in the Second
Temple period. Those of us who have specialized in this period are
often appalled at the lack of knowledge of recent scholarship on this
period. In many cases it does not seem to be any more recent than the
original Schürer,[74] and the work of such giants of the 20th century as
V. Tcherikover and E.J. Bickerman and many more recent studies of
quality are overlooked or ignored.[75] This does not mean scholarship
is any more cut and dried in this area than any other, but no one
who wants to work in the Second Temple period can avoid the duty
of becoming familiar with basic current scholarship in the area.

---

[74]E. Schürer, *Geschichte des jüdischen Volkes im Zeitalter Jesu Christi*, Leipzig
[4]1901-9. Unfortunately, the recent revision of Schürer left much of the text of vol.
1 intact, *The Jewish People in the Age of Jesus Christ* (revised G. Vermes *et al.*;
3 vols. in 4), Edinburgh 1973-87.

[75]This is one of the reasons that I wrote *Judaism from Cyrus to Hadrian*:
to summarize and make available to the non-specialist a lot of the more recent
scholarship on this period.

Sara Japhet *Jerusalem – Israel*

Exile and Restoration in the Book of Chronicles

1 The Chronological Master-Plan

The book of Chronicles does not fit well into the framework of the conference theme, as it is not a contemporary witness to the sixth or fifth centuries BCE. This, however, should not detract from its significance for the understanding of those centuries, and its relevance to the questions of identity and continuity posed by the conference. Written at the end of the Persian – or perhaps even better – at the beginning of the Hellenistic period, it observes the one that preceded it from without, and certainly relates to it.

As is generally accepted (although some differences of opinion exist on this as on any other matter), the book of Chronicles was composed in the last part of the fourth century, most probably after the Persian rule had come to an end. By its genre it is a historical work – although the debate about this definition continues. Whether, or to what degree, the Chronicler should be regarded as a historian, and whether – or to what degree – his work should be studied from a historical or a theological perspective, are questions that are still in the focus of attention.[1] Nevertheless, from a generic point of view Chronicles is a history. It is a description of the whereabouts of the people of Israel from its creation onwards, throughout the centuries.

Considering the two parameters that I have just mentioned – the point in time at which the book of Chronicles was written, and its topic – the question of its chronological master-plan immediately comes to mind: Why did the Chronicler deal with the distant past, from the beginning of humanity onwards, and did not recount the events of the immediate past, the last centuries of the Persian period? More specifically, why did he not bring the story up to his own time, stopping short two centuries earlier?

Before addressing the question, it should be presented in greater detail. The Chronicler's historical blueprint is well known and needs

---

[1] See the recent collection of essays dedicated to this topic: M.P. Graham *et al.* (eds.), *The Chronicler as Historian* (JSOT.S, 238), Sheffield 1997. In the most recent commentary on Chronicles, Johnstone denies the book any claim to history: "C [Chronicles] is a theological work" , or: "C's must be termed a work of Theology", W. Johnstone, *1 and 2 Chronicles* (JSOT.S, 253), Sheffield 1997, 10, 23.

no repeating.[2] Stated in the briefest terms, the story begins at the earliest possible point in time, that is, with Adam, the first human being, and continues with the history of Israel, omitting or epitomizing certain periods. It passes quickly to the history of the monarchical period, which is presented in great detail as the 'history of Israel'.[3] The story follows the kingdom to its end: the destruction of Jerusalem, the burning of the Temple, the termination of Davidic rule, and the exile (2 Chron. 36:20-21). The book concludes with a short fragment of the edict of Cyrus, cited from the book of Ezra (2 Chron. 36:22-23).

Thus, the general question of how the book ends may be approached from two directions:

(a) The relationship of Chronicles at this point to the book of Kings. Although the Chronicler's history draws very heavily on the book of Kings, and in particular on its historical and chronological framework,[4] the Chronicler chose a different ending for his story. Taking the historical outline of Kings as a point of departure, the Chronicler could have concluded the monarchical period at one of three points: destruction and exile (2 Kgs 25:21), the office of Gedaliahu the son of Ahikam, terminated by his assassination (25:22-26), or the rehabilitation of Jehoiachin by the Babylonian emperor in the thirty-seventh year of Jehoiachin's reign (25:27-30).

The Chronicler did not adopt any of these alternatives. He followed the story of Kings to the end of the reign of Zedekiah, described the fall of Jerusalem and the exile (2 Chron. 36:20),[5] skipped the story of Gedaliahu and the rehabilitation of Je-

---

[2]See the commentaries, e.g. H.G.M. Williamson, *1 and 2 Chronicles* (NCBC), London 1982, 33-6; S. Japhet, *I and II Chronicles – A Commentary* (OTL), London 1993, 8-13.

[3]The peculiarities of the Chronicler's historical sketch, such as the omission of the narrative portion of the Pentateuch (the Patriarchs, the servitude in Egypt, the Exodus, the wandering in the wilderness, etc.), and of the conquest of Canaan and the period of the Judges, and the refrainment from relating the history of the northern kingdom in its own right, have been discussed at some length in the scholarly literature. Although they all belong to the broad context of the present discussion, they will not be dealt with here.

[4]The general chronological structure of Chronicles follows faithfully that of Kings, in spite of differences in detail. On these differences see recently, W.B. Barnes, "Non-Synoptic Chronological References in the Books of Chronicles", in: Graham *et al.* (eds.), *The Chronicler as Historian*, 103-31.

[5]On the many differences in detail see S. Japhet, *The Ideology of the Book of Chronicles and its Place in Biblical Thought* (ET), Frankfurt & Bern, etc. 1989, 364-73; Idem, *I and II Chronicles*, 1061-77.

hoiachin, and moved directly to the conclusion of the exilic period. He bridged this gap in two ways: by rephrasing the wording of 2 Kgs 25:21 (in vv. 20-21) and adding the first sentences of the edict of Cyrus (in 36:22-23). Thus the final statement "So Judah went into exile out of its land" (2 Kgs 25:21) was replaced by: "He took into exile in Babylon those who had escaped from the sword, and they became servants to him and to his sons until the establishment of the kingdom of Persia. To fulfill the word of the Lord by the mouth of Jeremiah (until the land had made up for its sabbaths – all the days that it lay desolate it kept sabbath), to fulfill seventy years". This is then followed by: "In the first year of King Cyrus of Persia, in fulfillment of the word of the Lord spoken by Jeremiah, the Lord stirred up the spirit of King Cyrus of Persia so that he ... declared: '... whoever is among you of all his people, may the Lord his God be with him! Let him go up'."

(b) The second direction from which the book's ending should be analysed is by reviewing what is missing: Why did the Chronicler end his history with the edict of Cyrus and not go on to bring the story up to his own time? Would not such a procedure be almost 'natural' for a historian? Is he not expected to continue the historical narrative to the point at which he himself is writing? This question, too, should be presented in somewhat more detail.

In the history of scholarship this issue has received only passing attention, and to the extent that the question was raised, the solutions provided were either of a technical or a literary nature. A well-known answer, and for a long time the dominant one, was that this was not, indeed, the end of the book. Originally – so it had been claimed – the books of Chronicles and Ezra-Nehemiah were one long history, 'the Chronistic history', and its author, the Chronicler, indeed recorded the history of Israel up to his own time. Only at a later stage, and as a technical measure, was the book of Ezra-Nehemiah separated from Chronicles and placed earlier in the canon. Concluding the book with the edict of Cyrus was a technical means, an allusion to the original continuation of the work, and nothing more.[6]

---

[6] A recent advocate of this view is M. Haran. See, among others, his "Book-size and the Device of Catch-Lines in the Biblical Canon", *JJS* 36 (1985), 1-11. A direct reaction to his view may be found in H.G.M. Williamson, "Did the author of Chronicles also write the Books of Ezra-Nehemiah?", *BiRe* 3 (1987), 56-9.

I have dealt with the relationship between Chronicles and Ezra-Nehemiah on several occasions and do not intend to go into this question again.[7] I wonder, however, whether uneasiness with the conclusion of Chronicles did not play a perhaps unconscious role in the persistence of this view. The joining of Ezra-Nehemiah to the end of Chronicles certainly relieves this uneasiness.

I should add, however, that even among scholars who regard the books of Chronicles and Ezra-Nehemiah as separate works, the answer to the question I posed tends of being based on literary grounds. Such for example, is the claim made by Williamson and by some scholars following him, that the present conclusion of the book of Chronicles was not the original one. It ended – so they claim – in much greater similarity to the conclusion of Kings, that is, with the reference to the exile in 2 Chron. 36:20-21; the last two verses, taken from the edict of Cyrus, are a later addition, attached to the book for one reason or another.[8]

I will not dwell on the analysis of this view or its arguments, which seem to move in a circle and beg the question. To my mind, rather than providing an answer to the book's conclusion it manages to avoid the question, and as a result grossly misinterprets the Chronicler's message. The book's conclusion – no less than its beginning – is of great significance for understanding the Chronicler's view of history and his goals in writing this history.

The implications of the way in which Chronicles concludes are:

1. It ends on a positive note rather than with a catastrophe – be it the destruction, the exile, or the death of Gedaliahu. This ending looks to the future.

2. The book skips the actual period and experience of the exile. The details referring to this period found in the book of Kings are omitted and no others are supplied. In one sentence the book covers a period of seventy years.[9] In view of the detailed history of Israel up to this point, this omission cannot be accidental.

---

[7]For a summary of my views on this matter see: S. Japhet, "The Relationship between Chronicles and Ezra-Nehemiah", in: J.A. Emerton (ed.), *Congress Volume Leuven 1989* (VT.S, 43), Leiden 1991, 298-313.

[8]See H.G.M. Williamson, *Israel in the Books of Chronicles*, Cambridge 1977, 8-10. He is followed by Th. Willi, *Juda – Jehud – Israel: Studien zum Selbstverständniss des Judentums in persischer Zeit* (FAT, 12), Tübingen 1995, 21, n. 12, 53-5.

[9]The wording of these verses echoes the prophecies of Jeremiah in 27:7, "All the nations shall serve him and his son and his grandson, until the time of his own land comes", and 25:11-12 and 29:10 referring to the "seventy years".

One may claim, of course, that the Chronicler omitted the exilic period because he lacked sources, but this assertion cannot be sustained. He certainly had at his disposal the book of Ezekiel (whose influence on Chronicles is evident in several matters), the book of Lamentations (which he actually used) and probably other materials which are no longer extant. Lack of sources had never been an obstacle for his story.

3. The period of the Restoration too, is not described. Here, again, this is not due to a lack of sources. The Chronicler had at his disposal the book of Ezra-Nehemiah (which he actually used), contemporary prophetical sayings (such as Haggai, Zechariah and probably others), and most probably additional materials (some of which he actually employed for the description of earlier times). Yet, in contrast to his procedure regarding the books of Samuel and Kings, he did not rewrite these texts but omitted them altogether.

All these point to one conclusion: the Chronicler's plan is a conscious and powerful way of expressing his views. More specifically, his unique position on Exile and Restoration provides an important key to revealing his program.

2 Exile

What is the Chronicler's stand on the issue of 'Exile' – deportation of the people from their land – in the history of Israel? I have dealt elsewhere with this subject[10] but I believe that some repetition and further elaboration are in order.[11]

The place of 'Exile' in the Chronicler's history may be examined from three standpoints: the use of words and phrases from the semantic field of 'exile' (such as גל ה, נתש מעל האדמה), their frequency and distribution; the place of exile in the rhetoric of the book: in speeches, prophetical rebukes and historical overviews; and most importantly, the description of exile as a real historical event. I will skip the first two and move directly to the third: 'exile' in the Chronicler's historical narrative.

According to the book of Kings – and to the commonly held view of Israel's history – there were two major acts of exile in the Monarchical

---

[10] See Japhet, *Ideology*, 364-73.

[11] In particular after the criticism of my views by W. Johnstone, "The Use of Leviticus in Chronicles", in: J.F.A. Sawyer (ed.), *Reading Leviticus – A Conversation with Mary Douglas* (JSOT.S, 227), Sheffield 1996, 243-55.

period: the destruction of the northern kingdom of Israel and exile of its inhabitants by the Assyrians (in the eighth century BCE), and the destruction and exile of the kingdom of Judah by the Babylonians (in the sixth century BCE). In the book of Kings each of these events is described as a prolonged process, having occurred in two major stages. The Assyrians' first act was the conquest of the Galilee and the Gilead by Tiglath-pileser, in the days of Pekah of Israel and Ahaz of Judah (733-732 BCE). It is related in 2 Kgs 15:29 and confirmed by extra-biblical sources: "In the days of Pekah of Israel, King Tiglath-pileser of Assyria came and captured Ijon, Abel-beth-maacah, Janoah, Kedesh, Hazor, Gilead, and Galilee, all the land of Naphtali; and he carried the people captive[12] to Assyria".[13]

The second stage, about ten years later, was the final conquest of Samaria by Sargon II, in the reigns of Hosea of Israel and Hezekiah of Judah (722 BCE). This, too, is described rather briefly and confirmed by extra-biblical sources: "Then the king of Assyria invaded all the land and came to Samaria; for three years he besieged it. In the ninth year of Hosea the king of Assyria captured Samaria: he carried the Israelites away[14] to Assyria. He placed them in Halah on the Habor, the river of Gozan, and in the cities of the Medes" (2 Kgs 17:5-6; repeated in 18:11).[15]

The Babylonians' first act was the deportation of Jehoiachin, who had ruled for only three months (597 BCE). As described in great detail in 2 Kgs 24:10-16, the Babylonians took away "the king, his mother, his servants, his officers and his palace officials (24:12); the treasures of the house of the Lord, and the treasures of the king's house ... the vessels of gold (v. 13); he carried away (Hebrew: וְהִגְלָה) all Jerusalem, all the officials, all the warriors, ten thousand captives (Hebrew: גּוֹלֶה), all the artisans and the smiths (v. 14); He carried away (Hebrew: וַיֶּגֶל) Jehoiachin, the king's mother, the king's wives, his officials, and the elite of the land (v. 15)". In sum: the royal court, the ruling class, the artisans, the military force and the nobility of the land were all taken to Babylon.

The second stage, eleven years later, was the final destruction of Jerusalem and the deportation of the people of Judah in the time of Zedekiah, also described in great detail, in 2 Kgs 25:1-21: "Then they captured the king ... they slaughtered the sons of Zedekiah before his

---

[12]The NRSV translation of the Hebrew גל׳ה as "carry captive" or "carry away" seems to obscure the original emphasis on "exile".

[13]See M. Cogan, H. Tadmor, *II Kings* (AncB), Garden City, NY 1988, 173-80.

[14]See note 12.

[15]See Cogan, Tadmor, *II Kings*, 195-201.

eyes, they put out the eyes of Zedekiah, they bound him in fetters and took him to Babylon (vv. 6-7). He burned the house of the Lord, the king's house and all the houses of Jerusalem ... all the army broke down the walls around Jerusalem. Nebuzaradan ... carried into exile the rest of the people who were left in the city and the deserters ... all the rest of the population (vv. 9-11). The captain of the guard took ... So Judah went into exile out of its land" (vv. 18-21).[16]

In the book of Chronicles, the description of both the Assyrian conquest of Israel and the Babylonian conquest of Judah have undergone transformation. Since the history of northern Israel is described in Chronicles only from the perspective of the kingdom of Judah,[17] we would not have expected to find therein any reference to Israel's conquest and exile. Yet it is referred to four times: once at the appropriate historical point, during the reign of Hezekiah, and three times in the genealogical introduction.

In the genealogy of the tribe of Reuben a person by the name of Beera is identified as "whom King Tiglath-pilneser of Assyria carried away into exile" (1 Chron. 5:6). Then, in a summary referring to the two and a half tribes, it is said that "they lived in their territory until the exile" (1 Chron. 5:22). And finally, regarding these same tribes, we are told: "So the God of Israel stirred up the spirit of King Pul of Assyria, and he carried them away, namely the Reubenites, the Gadites, and the half-tribe of Manasseh, and brought them to Halah, Habor, Hara and the river Gozan, to this day" (1 Chron. 5:26).

These descriptions are certainly dependent on the narrative of Kings, but the differences are considerable and telling. According to 2 Kgs 15:29, the main objective of Tiglath-pileser was the Galilee, the northern part of Cisjordan. The only tribe mentioned by name was Naphtali, this in addition to the major cities such as Hazor, Kedesh, etc. Of all the territory of Transjordan, only the Gilead is mentioned. Moreover, the destination of the exiles is given in the most general terms: they were exiled "to Assyria".

In Chronicles, the area west of the Jordan is omitted altogether. As for Transjordan, rather than use the geographic designation of the Gilead, the Chronicler refers to all the Israelites dwelling there by their tribal names: Reuben, Gad and half of Manasseh were exiled to Assyria, never to return – they are there "to this day".[18] Moreover,

---

[16] For the interpretation of the historical details, see Cogan, Tadmor, *II Kings*, 310-24.

[17] See in detail, Japhet, *Ideology*, 311-8.

[18] It may be argued that the territory assumed by the two designations is the same, and therefore the difference between the two texts would have no historical

the destination of these deportees is specified in Chronicles as Halah, Habor, etc. – clearly dependent on 2 Kgs 17:5-6 and 18:11. But while in Kings these are the locations to which the deportees from Samaria were brought, in the case of Chronicles they are noted in reference to the Transjordanian tribes.

The last reference to the exile of northern Israel is in its generally appropriate historical context, during the reign of Hezekiah.[19] In his attempt to celebrate an "all Israel" Passover, Hezekiah turns to the northern tribes and invites them to come to Jerusalem for the celebration. According to Chronicles, these tribes reside in their original territory "from Beer-sheba to Dan" (2 Chron. 30:5), and explicit mention is made of Ephraim (vv. 1, 10), Manasseh (vv. 1, 10, 11), Zebulun (vv. 10, 11) and Asher (v. 11). In his call to these people Hezekiah mentions the assault of the kings of Assyria in the north. However, he does not speak of 'exile' or 'expulsion' but of 'captivity'[20]: "For as you return to the Lord, your kindred and your children will find compassion with their captors" (v. 9). Those remaining in the land are referred to earlier as "the remnant who have escaped from the hand of the kings of Assyria" (v. 6), but in fact they were found in the land, all throughout it. According to Chronicles there had been a setback in northern Israel during, or prior to, the time of Hezekiah, but it certainly had been no final exile or destruction of "Israel". On the contrary, Israel continued to live its life in the land, "from Beer-sheba to Dan".

I will return to this issue from another perspective, but it may be already said by way of summary, that the Chronicler had combined the two different stages of destruction and exile of northern Israel into one event. He defined it as the final expulsion "to this day", but limited it to the Transjordanian tribes. The conquests of Tiglath-pileser in the Galilee, and the final destruction of and deportation from Samaria have completely disappeared from his description.

As for the destruction and exile of Judah, this event, too, is mentioned in Chronicles in its appropriate historical sequence and twice in the genealogies, and it too has been transformed by the Chronicler's hand. Although the Chronicler adopts his description of the end of the

---

implication. Such a claim would only augment the theological significance of the Chronicler's phraseology.

[19] According to 2 Kgs 18:10 the conquest of Samaria occurred in the sixth year of Hezekiah, whereas according to the Chronicler's chronology, in the first year of Hezekiah (2 Chron. 29:37; 30:2) this event was already a matter of the past. One wonders whether this blurring of the historical sequence was not done on purpose.

[20] This difference is not reflected in the English version, either here or in the other passages, because of the inconsistent translation of גלה. See above, nn. 12, 14.

kingdom of Judah from the book of Kings, he introduces a series of
changes which put it in another light. Significant for our context are
the changes he introduced to the histories of Jehoiachin and Zedekiah.
As mentioned above, whereas the book of Kings elaborates on the deportation in the time of Jehoiachin, in Chronicles all this is reported
in one single verse: King Nebuchadnezzar brought to Babylon only
Jehoiachin himself and some[21] of the precious vessels of the house of
the Lord (2 Chron. 36:10). Nothing else was taken or transported.

The final destruction, during the reign of Zedekiah, is described
in Chronicles in greater detail than the fate of Judah in the time of
Jehoiachin, but if we read carefully it clearly emerges that the Chronicler limits the catastrophe to Jerusalem: "The king of the Chaldeans
who killed their youths in the house of their sanctuary, and had no
compassion on young man and young woman, the aged or the feeble
... All the vessels of the house of the Lord, large and small and
the treasures of the king and of his officials, all these he brought to
Babylon. They burned the house of God, broke down the wall of Jerusalem, burned all its palaces with fire and destroyed all its precious
vessels" (2 Chron. 36:17-19). And then finally: "he took into exile in
Babylon those who had escaped from the sword" (v. 20). Although
one may assume – as will soon become evident – that the Chronicler
knew of the blows that the land of Judah had suffered at the hand
of Nebuchadnezzar, in the relevant historical context he refrains from
relating them.[22] It is Jerusalem that was destroyed, and Jerusalem is
about to be rebuilt, by the authorization of Cyrus (vv. 22-23).

This portrayal changes somewhat when we turn to the other two
references in Chronicles to the exile of Judah. One is a cursory reference to the identity of Jehozadak, who "went into exile when the Lord
sent Judah and Jerusalem into exile by the hand of Nebuchadnezzar"
(1 Chron. 5:41).[23] The second reference, which is of great significance,
appears at the beginning of 1 Chron. 9. The Chronicler registered in
great detail the genealogies of all the tribes, in order to provide the
broadest possible sketch of "all Israel", the subject of the historical
narrative that follows. He summed up this section of his work with
the general statement: "So *all Israel* was enrolled by genealogies; and

---

[21] *NRSV*: "*the* precious vessels", is not a precise reflection of the original.

[22] He also avoids mention of the destruction of the land of Judah in the time of
Jehoiakim. Compare 2 Kgs 23:34–24:6 with 2 Chron. 36:4-6, and Japhet, *I and II
Chronicles*, 1064-7.

[23] This note might not have come from the hand of the Chronicler himself but
rather from the list that he was quoting, but this is of no consequence to our
discussion.

these are written in the book of *the Kings of Israel*. And *Judah* was taken into exile in Babylon because of their unfaithfulness" (1 Chron. 9:1).

It seems that what the Chronicler really meant by this short summary has totally escaped the attention of scholars, for understandable reasons. They have related it to the historical context that emerges from the book of Kings or as constructed by modern scholarship, but have not examined it in the context of the Chronicler's unique views. In the framework of the Chronicler's historical view it expresses an unusual, quite unexpected, concept of continuity. The contrast between "all Israel" on the one hand and "Judah" on the other [24] signifies that *"All Israel", in the true meaning of this term for the Chronicler, had never been exiled and never left the land!* The Chronicler admits that there were, indeed, partial acts of forced transfer in the history of Israel: the two and a half tribes were deported by the Assyrians and remained there "to this day" (1 Chron. 5:26); the king of Assyria had taken captive some of the children and kindred of the northern tribes – for whose return there was still hope (2 Chron. 30:9); and also, the tribe of Judah was taken into exile by the Babylonians. This exile, however, was a temporary measure, "for seventy years", enacted by the Lord as punishment for their transgressions and so that the land could enjoy its Sabbaths. In contrast to all these, "Israel" as an entity, in the broadest sense of the term, remained in the land despite all the tribulations that marked its history. It was "enrolled by genealogies" that "are written in the book of the Kings of Israel".

This view of the continuity of Israel in its land, despite all the dangers and upheavals, has no parallel in the Bible, and has been either ignored or played down by scholars. The conventional portrayal of the history of Israel, and the view of exile as a dominant factor in its history, prevented scholarship from understanding the full implications of the Chronicler's message.[25]

---

[24]The Chronicler systematically avoids this dichotomy when it is applied in his sources to the period of David and Solomon. See already E.L. Curtis, A.A. Madsen, *The Books of Chronicles* (ICC), Edinburgh 1910, 250.

[25]I find it difficult to understand how Willi could state dogmatically that "Israel war aufgrund seiner Schuld in die גולה gegangen", Willi, *Juda – Jehud – Israel*, 129. Or, how Johnstone, *1 and 2 Chronicles*, 119, could claim first that "beyond the debacle of Judean monarchy, the people of Israel remains", and then reach the general conclusion that: "Historically speaking C [Chronicles] is a post-exilic work; but theologically speaking it is 'exilic', written when Israel is still 'in exile', whether among the nations of the world or even in its own land" (p.10-1). I fail to see how these could be put together, even with the help of the metaphorization of 'exile' by means of the inverted commas.

3 Restoration

The last point of this paper is the Chronicler's attitude to the issue of 'Restoration'. As already mentioned, the Chronicler ends his story with the opening phrases of the edict of Cyrus and does not follow it up to his own time, although a detailed history of the Restoration, which he could rework to suit his taste, is found in the book of Ezra-Nehemiah. How should this omission be explained?

Once again, the explanation lies in terms of continuity and discontinuity. For the Chronicler, the restoration of Israel's destiny is not a matter of the past but a programme for the future – it has not yet occurred, but is to be expected and awaited. With this, the Chronicler's opposition to the facts and ideology of the book of Ezra-Nehemiah has reached its climax: it is not a matter of measure or degree but one of a total rejection. The Chronicler cannot accept the foundations of Ezra-Nehemiah's theology: the exclusive, narrow concept of Israel as a "holy seed", the supremacy of the "returned exiles" or simply "exiles", the attitude to the native inhabitants of the land and to intermarriage, and perhaps above all – the renunciation of the hope for political independence under the rule of the Davidic kings.[26] For the Chronicler, an era with these attributes was not one of 'Restoration' and should best be glossed over. The Chronicler places himself and his generation in the time of Cyrus. Restoration lies ahead and is about to begin.

This unique view of continuity may be more clearly understood when we compare it to the historical blue-print of I Esdras.[27] I Esdras' main design is to give expression to the continuity between the pre-exilic and the post-exilic periods. This he does by the combining of the end of Chronicles with the book of Ezra, and turning the destruction and exile into a passing episode in the historical continuity of Israel. For this author, the community of "returned exiles", with its history and ideology, is the true continuator of the kingdom of Judah. Only in a few matters, like the role of the Davidides in this history, does I Esdras deviate from the general lines of the book of Ezra.

This is precisely the opposite of what the Chronicler signified by his specific conclusion. In his view there was no continuation of the

---

[26] On the views of Ezra-Nehemiah on these matters see S. Japhet, "L'historiographie post-exilic: comment et pourquoi?", in: A. de Pury *et al.* (eds.), *Israël construit son histoire*, Genève 1996, 127-37.

[27] For more details on his views, see Japhet, "L'historiographie post-exilic", 145-50.

monarchical period; in the late fourth century BCE, 'Restoration' is still a matter for the future.

What should be the character of this 'Restoration'? Elaboration is unnecessary because the answer is abundantly clear from the peculiar lines of the Chronicler's history. It will be a continuation of the monarchical period as it was ideally realized in the time of David and Solomon. The contours of this period may be sketched briefly: It will encompass "all Israel", in the broadest ethnic, geographical and political terms; it will have a Davidic ruler, a descendant of David and Solomon; the people of Israel will live in full adherence to the Law given to them by Moses, and will be amply rewarded by God's providence; and it will be a time of peace.

Should we define the Chronicler's programme as 'eschatology'?[28] This is very much a matter of definition. If we waive the precision of terminology and conceptual distinctions and define any perspective toward the future as being eschatological, then the Chronicler may be included in this category. However, all we gain by this is generalization and metaphorization of basic religious concepts, which thus lose their precision and meaning. Not every future-oriented perspective should be defined as 'eschatology'. The Chronicler does not envisage a dramatic change in the structure and conduct of the world, nor does he expect a catastrophic transformation or a cosmic event. He does not await the appearance of God on earth. The Chronicler's aspirations are for a realistic transformation in the history of Israel, along the lines that characterized the kingdom of David and Solomon and in accordance with the laws and principles that govern the history of Israel. Historical Israel, delineated clearly throughout the entire book, is the bearer of the hopes, the realization of which is about to begin.

Going back, in conclusion, to the beginning of our paper, it should have become clear that the book of Chronicles does not fit into the framework of the conference theme neither chronologically nor theologically. The book of Chronicles does not represent 'religion under stress'. It is an expression of a religion that came to terms with the past, formed a solid theological basis for its existence, and was looking forward, to the future.

---

[28] This had been a common view in the scholarship about Chronicles, and has recently been strongly advocated by Johnstone, *1 and 2 Chronicles*, "The use of Leviticus in Chronicles", Willi, *Juda – Jehud – Israel*, and B.E. Kelly, *Retribution and Eschatology in Chronicles* (JSOT.S, 211), Sheffield 1996.

Walter Dietrich *Bern – Switzerland*

Niedergang und Neuanfang:

Die Haltung der Schlussredaktion des deuteronomistischen Geschichtswerkes zu den wichtigsten Fragen ihrer Zeit

Martin Noth hat Gestalt und Gehalt des deuteronomistischen (dtr) Geschichtswerkes, das die biblischen Bücher Deuteronomium bis 2 Könige umfasst habe, grundlegend beschrieben und es wegen seiner Abschlussperikope 2 Kön. 25:27-30 sowie aufgrund innerer Indizien auf die Mitte des 6. Jahrhunderts v.Chr. datiert.[1] Die epochemachende Untersuchung Noths hat inzwischen verschiedenartige Differenzierungen erfahren,[2] von denen die wichtigsten das sog. Blockmodell im Gefolge von Frank Moore Cross[3] und das sog. Schichtenmodell im Gefolge von Rudolf Smend[4] sind. Nimmt das Blockmodell eine oder mehrere Ausgaben des Geschichtswerkes noch in der Königszeit und seine Endredaktion in der Mitte des 6. Jahrhunderts an, so hält das Schichtenmodell gerade diese Redaktion für die Erstausgabe des Geschichtswerkes, das danach noch mehrfach erweitert worden sei. Um in die ausgehende Exilszeit und den Beginn der nachexilischen Zeit zu gelangen, müsste demnach auf das Schichtenmodell zurückgegriffen werden. Ich tue das gern und wende mich gezielt der letzten, der

---

[1] M. Noth, *Überlieferungsgeschichtliche Studien: Die sammelnden und bearbeitenden Geschichtswerke im Alten Testament*, Tübingen 1942, [2]1957. ET: *The Deuteronomistic History* (JSOT.S, 15), Sheffield 1981, [2]1991. Noth benannte bereits eine Reihe von Passagen, die dem Werk erst nachträglich zugefügt worden seien, ohne dass er sie auf ihre Zusammengehörigkeit untersuchte und einordnete; vgl. die Zusammenstellung bei W. Dietrich, "Martin Noth and the Future of the Deuteronomistic History", in: S.L. McKenzie, M.P. Graham (eds.), *The History of Israel's Traditions: The Heritage of Martin Noth* (JSOT.S, 182), Sheffield 1994, 128-52, n.2.

[2] Vgl. die zusammenfassenden Berichte von H. Weippert, "Das deuteronomistische Geschichtswerk: Sein Ziel und Ende in der neueren Forschung", *ThR* 50 (1985), 213-49, und von H.D. Preuss, "Zum deuteronomistischen Geschichtswerk", *ThR* 58 (1993), 229-64, 341-95.

[3] F.M. Cross, *Canaanite Myth and Hebrew Epic: Essays in the History of the Religion of Israel*, Cambridge, MA 1973, 274-89.

[4] R. Smend eröffnete diese Sichtweise in "Das Gesetz und die Völker: Ein Beitrag zur deuteronomistischen Redaktionsgeschichte", in: H.W. Wolff (ed.), *Probleme biblischer Theologie (Festschrift G. von Rad)*, München 1971, 494-509 = R. Smend, *Die Mitte des Alten Testaments: Gesammelte Studien* (BEvTh, 99), München 1986, 124-37. Zusammenfassend stellt er sie dar in: *Die Entstehung des Alten Testaments*, Stuttgart 1978, [4]1989, § 19.

sog. 'nomistischen' Textschicht 'DtrN' zu. Dabei kann offenbleiben, ob es sich um einen Autor oder um mehrere, und ob es sich um eine planvolle Gesamtredaktion oder um eine Vielzahl verschiedener Ergänzungen handelt. Nur darum geht es vorerst, Prinzipien und Intentionen der spät-dtr Texte in den Blick zu bekommen. Das sich dabei einstellende Bild könnte, je nach Kohärenz und Prägnanz, das Profil und die Eigenart von DtrN klären und damit die Evidenz des gesamten Erklärungsansatzes stützen helfen.

Als Textbasis dienen diejenigen Passagen zwischen Deuteronomium und 2 Könige, welche von Forschern, die nach dem Schichtenmodell gearbeitet haben,[5] mit hinreichender Plausibilität für DtrN in Anspruch genommen worden sind (oder hiermit in Anspruch genommen werden).[6] Es handelt sich um:

Dtn.[7] 1:36-38; 6:5, *6; 8:1, 11b, 18b-20; 9:7-21; 12:1-7, 29-31; 13:1-18; 17:2-5, 18-19, 20aβb; 18:15-22; 20:15-18; 25:17-19; 31:9-13, 24-29; 32:45-47;

---

[5] Ausser R. Smend sind das vornehmlich: L. Camp, *Hiskija und Hiskijabild: Analyse und Interpretation von 2. Kön 18–20* (MThA, 9), Altenberge 1990; W. Dietrich, *Prophetie und Geschichte: Eine redaktionsgeschichtliche Untersuchung zum deuteronomistischen Geschichtswerk* (FRLANT, 108), Göttingen 1972; Idem, "Histoire et Loi: Historiographie deutéronomiste et Loi deutéronomique à l'exemple du passage de l'époque des Juges à l'époque royale", in: A. de Pury *et al.* (eds.), *Israël construit son histoire*, Genève 1996, 297-323; F. Foresti, *The Rejection of Saul in the Perspective of the Deuteronomistic School: A Study of 1 Sm 15 and Related Texts*, Roma 1984; P.S.F. van Keulen, *Manasseh through the Eyes of the Deuteronomists: The Manasseh Account (2 Kings 21:1-18) and the Final Chapters of the Deuteronomistic History* (OTS, 38), Leiden 1996; W. Roth, "Deuteronomistisches Geschichtswerk/Deuteronomistische Schule", *TRE* 8, Berlin 1981, 543-52; T. Veijola, *Die ewige Dynastie: David und die Entstehung seiner Dynastie nach der deuteronomistischen Darstellung* (AASF Ser. B, 193), Helsinki 1975; Idem, *Das Königtum in der Beurteilung der deuteronomistischen Historiographie: Eine redaktionsgeschichtliche Untersuchung* (AASF Ser. B, 198), Helsinki 1977; S. Wälchli, *Der weise König Salomo: Eine Studie zu den Erzählungen von der Weisheit Salomos in ihrem alttestamentlichen und altorientalischen Kontext* (BWANT, 141), Stuttgart 1998; E. Würthwein, *Das erste Buch der Könige, Kap. 1-16*, (ATD, 11/1), Göttingen ²1985; Idem, *Die Bücher der Könige: 1. Kön 17 – 2. Kön 25* (ATD, 11/2), Göttingen 1984. Diese Liste ist weder den Namen noch den Titeln nach exklusiv oder auch vereinnahmend gemeint; auch sind nicht alle dort vertretenen Thesen zu DtrN hier übernommen.

[6] Die im folgenden gebotene Textliste erhebt keinen Anspruch auf Vollständigkeit oder Endgültigkeit; sie hat den Charakter einer Ausgangshypothese, welche offen ist für Ergänzung oder Modifizierung.

[7] Auf die diffizile neueste Deuteronomiumforschung kann hier nicht näher eingetreten werden. Guten Einblick bieten drei Sammelbände: N. Lohfink (ed.), *Das Deuteronomium: Entstehung, Gestalt und Botschaft* (BEThL, 68), Leuven 1985;

Jos.   1:7-9; 6:17-19; 7,1-26; 8:30-35; 13:1bβ-6; 23:1-16;

Ri.   2:1-5, 17, 20-23; 3:5-6; 6:7-10, 13, 14aα; 8:22-23, 27b, 33-35;
          9:16b-19a, *24b, 57; 10:10-16;

1 Sam. 7:*2, 3-4; 8:6-10, 18-20a; 10:18aβγb, 19a; 12:1-25; 13:13-14;
          15:10-11, 19; 28:17-19aα;

2 Sam. 5:12b; 7:1b, 5b-8aα, 10, 11a, 22-24; 22:1, 22-25;

1 Kön. 2:3, 4aβ; 3:3, 6b, 12, 14a; 6:11-13; 8:16, 22-26, 55-58, 61, *66;
          9:1-9; 10:9; 11:4-5, 9-13, 32-33, 34b, 35bβ-37aα, 38abα; 14:8b,
          9a, 15-16, 24; 15:3b-5, 30; 16:13; 21:25-26;

2 Kön. 10:30, 31a; 13:6, 23; 14:6, 26-27; 15:12; 16:3; 17:12-19; 18:5-
          7a, 9-12, 22; 19:15-19, 34; 20:*1-6; 21:4, 6, 7b-9, 15-16, 21-22;
          23:1-3, 10, 13b, 15, 21-27; 24:3-4, 20a; 25:21b.

1 JHWH und die anderen Götter

Die Feststellung, dass ein Deuteronomist Monotheist ist, kommt einer
Tautologie gleich. Doch während der ältere Deuteronomismus im Gefolge des Deuteronomiums einen *praktischen* Monotheismus propa-
giert – es gibt *für Israel* keinen anderen Gott als JHWH –, vertritt
DtrN einen *theoretischen* Monotheismus: Es gibt überhaupt keinen
Gott ausser JHWH. König David, soeben mit der Dynastieverheissung
beschenkt, betet: "Gross bist du, Herr JHWH, denn es ist keiner wie
du und es ist kein Gott neben dir" (זולתך, 2 Sam. 7:22). Und König
Hiskija, von den Assyrern bedrängt, betet: "Du allein (לבדך) bist
der Gott für alle Königreiche der Erde, du hast den Himmel und
die Erde gemacht" (2 Kön. 19:15). Diese Aussagen zeigen DtrN in
unmittelbarer geistiger – etwa auch in geographischer? – Nähe zu

---

T. Veijola (ed.), *Das Deuteronomium und seine Querbeziehungen* (SESJ, 62), Helsinki, Göttingen 1996; M. Vervenne, J. Lust (eds.), *Deuteronomy and Deuteronomic Literature: Festschrift C.H.W. Brekelmans* (BEThL, 133), Leuven 1997. Eine
Tendenz der Forschung scheint dahin zu gehen, dass grössere Partien namentlich
in der Einleitung des Deuteronomiums noch später datiert werden als die Schlussredaktion des dtr Geschichtswerkes – ein Umstand, der mit dem Verhältnis des
Deuteronomiums zum Tetrateuch bzw. des Pentateuchs zum dtr Geschichtswerk
in Zusammenhang stehen mag. Im Blick darauf ist die obige Textauswahl bewusst
klein gehalten. Umgekehrt sind dort manche Texte für DtrN reklamiert, die von
einigen Forschern mit Entschiedenheit älteren Stadien zugewiesen werden. Gerade
im Bereich des Deuteronomiums also sind die oben gemachten Angaben nur als
tastende Versuche zu sehen.

Deuterojesaja[8] und zur Priesterschrift[9].[10] Wenn JHWH allein Gott ist, hat dies eine logische Doppelkonsequenz: Wer sich an ihn hält, hat Gott für sich, wer sich nicht an ihn bzw. wer sich an andere (vermeintliche) Götter hält, hat Gott gegen sich. Daran aber, ob man Gott für oder gegen sich hat, entscheidet sich das eigene Geschick.

Warum durfte aus der ersten Generation der aus Ägypten Aufgebrochenen nur Kaleb das Gelobte Land sehen und seinen Anteil davon in Besitz nehmen? "Weil er vollkommen bei JHWH blieb" (Dtn. 1:36) – während bekanntlich alle anderen, abgesehen nur von Josua, anlässlich der Kundschafter-Episode an ihm gezweifelt hatten. Was wird Israel, wenn es denn doch ins Land gekommen ist, auf die Dauer zur grössten Bedrohung werden? Schon Mose wusste es: "Wenn du JHWH, deinen Gott, vergisst und hinter anderen Göttern herläufst und ihnen dienst und sie anbetest, bezeuge ich euch heute, dass ihr sicher zugrundegehen werdet" (Dtn. 8:19). Worin wurzelten die Erfolge der Landnahme und wie liessen sie sich für die Zukunft sichern? Josua weiss es: "JHWH, eurem Gott, müsst ihr anhangen, so wie ihr es bis jetzt getan habt" (Jos. 23:8). Warum werden die siebzig Söhne Gideons von Abimelech ermordet? Weil Gideon nach seinem glanzvollen Sieg über die Midianiter aus gespendetem Beuteschmuck einen goldenen Efod anfertigte und in seiner Heimatstadt Ofra aufstellte – ein Vorgang, den DtrN als eindeutigen Fall von Abgötterei einschätzt: "Ganz Israel hurte[11]dort hinter ihm (wohl: dem Efod) her, und das wurde Gideon und seinem Haus zum Fallstrick"[12] (Ri. 8:27). Warum

---

[8]Die Präposition זולה wird wie in 2 Sam. 7:22 sonst nur bei Deuterojesaja (Jes. 45:5, 21) und danach verwendet (vgl. Jes. 26:13; 64:3; Ps. 18:32 sowie 1 Chr. 17:20). Der Ursprung der Wendung dürfte in Hos. 13:4 zu suchen sein; dort freilich äussert sich noch ein praktischer, kein theoretischer Monotheismus, bezieht sich die Präposition זולה hier doch 'nur' auf das Helfersein, nicht das Gottsein JHWHs. Ähnliches gilt für den Begriff בד(ל) in dieser Verwendung, vgl. Jes. 44:24 sowie dann wieder Jes. 26:13 und die spät- bzw. nach-dtr Belege Ex. 22:19; Dtn. 4:35; 32:12; 1 Kön. 8:39; Neh. 9:6. Zur Polemik gegen Götter "aus Holz und Stein" vgl. Dtn. 4:28 und Ez. 20:32.

[9]Das Theologumenon vom Schöpfer "des Himmels und der Erde" begegnet prominent in Gen. 1:1 – allerdings mit dem Verb ברא, doch fehlt עשה in dem (nicht von ungefähr eminent monotheistischen) Kapitel Gen. 1 ja nicht.

[10]Dazu würde auch die Verwendung des Begriffs תהו in 1 Sam. 12:21 passen, von dessen 18 übrigen Vorkommen acht (in ganz ähnlicher Verwendung!) bei Deuterojesaja und natürlich eines in Gen. 1:2 zu finden sind.

[11]Die Wurzel זנה als drastischer Ausdruck für religiöse Untreue begegnet wohl erstmals in der Jehu-Überlieferung (2 Kön. 9:22) und dann vor allem bei Hosea (z.B. Hos. 1:2; 2:7 und mehrfach in Hos. 4) und Jeremia (2:20; 3:1, 6, 8, vgl. auch die 12 Belege in Ez. 16 und 23); DtrN verwendet sie noch in Ri. 2:17; 8:33.

[12]Der Ausdruck מוקש wird in ähnlicher Weise, bezogen freilich auf das ganze Volk Israel, schon in Ri. 2:3 gebraucht.

waren die Israeliten bald danach den Ammonitern lange Jahre hilflos ausgeliefert? Gott selber klärt sie, als sie sich endlich an ihn wenden, auf: Gegen alle früheren Feinde habe er ihnen doch zur Seite gestanden; nun aber, da sie sich anderen Göttern zugewendet hätten, wolle er ihnen nicht mehr helfen: "Geht doch und schreit zu den Göttern, die ihr erwählt habt – sollen die euch helfen in eurer Notzeit!" Der Sarkasmus ist hörbar: Diese Götter sind Nichtse und können nicht helfen; Israel spürt das, entfernt sie aus seiner Mitte (Ri. 10:10-16) – und schon naht Hilfe in der Gestalt Jiftachs. Unter welchen Umständen wird Israel, nachdem es einen König über sich meinte setzen zu sollen, überleben? Samuel sagt es: "Weicht nicht von JHWH ab" und lauft nicht[13] "hinter den Nichtsen (תהו) her, die nicht helfen und nicht retten, weil sie Nichtse sind" (1 Sam. 12:20-21). Wodurch wird die Heilsgabe des JHWH-Tempels in Jerusalem aufs Spiel gesetzt? JHWH selbst klärt Salomo auf: Indem man ihn verlässt und anderen Göttern dient und sie anbetet (1 Kön. 9:6, 9). Warum ist der Staat Nordisrael untergegangen? Der Prophet Ahia weiss es im voraus: "Weil sie sich Ascheren machen" (1 Kön. 14:15), und DtrN bestätigt es hernach: weil sie "den Götzen (גללים) dienten" (2 Kön. 17:12). Warum konnten die Assyrer all die anderen Völker unterwerfen, die doch allesamt auf ihre Götter trauten? Hiskija weiss es: "Weil diese keine Götter waren, sondern Werk von Menschenhänden, Holz und Stein" (2 Kön. 19:18).

Während also Israel den einzig wahren Gott für sich hat bzw. hätte, läuft es doch immer wieder den Nicht-Göttern anderer Völker nach. Die Gefahr kommt von aussen. Israel ist von lauter Völkern mit falschen Göttern umgeben; nicht so sehr auf militärischem Gebiet als vielmehr auf religiösem liegt die Bedrohung. Durch die Überlieferungsgeschichte des dtr Geschichtswerkes hindurch lässt sich hier eine fortlaufende Akzentverschiebung beobachten: In den relativ ältesten Traditionen – Landnahmesagen des Stammes Benjamin, Rettergeschichten, Ladeerzählung, Saul- und Davidgeschichten, Königsannalen – sind wenn, dann nicht die Religionen, sondern die Truppen der Nachbarvölker eine Gefahr für Israel.[14] In dem wohl ins 7. Jahrhundert zu datierenden "Prophetischen Erzählwerk von JHWHs Kampf gegen Baal", das im wesentlichen Prophetenerzählungen zwischen 1 Kön. 17 und 2 Kön. 10 umfasst,[15] kommt ein anderer Ton auf; jetzt geht

---

[13] Der Text ist hier etwas unklar; anscheinend ist ein Wortspiel mit dem Verb סור beabsichtigt, das einmal 'abweichen von JHWH' und einmal 'abweichen zu den Göttern' meint; das störende כי in V.21 fehlt in einigen Handschriften und den Versionen.

[14] In 1 Sam. 5 taucht Dagon auf – aber nicht als Gefahr für Israel.

[15] Zu dieser These vgl. W. Dietrich, "Prophetie im deuteronomistischen Ge-

es vorrangig um die Abwehr der von aussen[16] nach Israel eindringenden Baalreligion. Der Erstausgabe des dtr Geschichtswerkes (DtrH) zufolge wurden die fremden Völker und Religionen bei der Landnahme aus dem Land hinausgedrängt, von wo sie aber religiös wie militärisch-politisch immer wieder auf Israel einwirkten. DtrN sieht an den anderen Völkern nur mehr die religiöse Gefahr, zumal sie jetzt sogar einen Brückenkopf mitten in Israel haben: die nicht vertriebenen Reste der kanaanitischen Vorbevölkerung. Ist es zu gewagt, hinter dieser Akzentverschiebung eine veränderte politische Gesamtsituation für Israel und den gesamten Vorderen Orient zu vermuten? Die militärische Lage ist geklärt: so gründlich, wie dies erst nach der Errichtung des persischen Grossreiches der Fall war; das jüdische Volk ist nicht mehr durch feindliche Armeen bedroht, sondern durch fremdreligiöse Einflüsse, und diese dringen nicht mehr nur von aussen ein, sondern entfalten inmitten 'Israels' – sei es in der judäischen Heimat, sei es in der jüdischen Diaspora – ihre Anziehungskraft. Solchen Verlockungen setzt DtrN ein dezidiert monotheistisches Bekenntnis entgegen.

Die Kulte, gegen die sich das Judentum hier abgrenzt, sind nicht spezifisch persische, sondern die in Syrien-Palästina und Mesopotamien alteingesessenen, die – wie der Jhwh-Kult ja auch! – von der relativ liberalen Religionspolitik der Achämeniden profitierten. Die Liste der fremden (Nicht-) Götter bei DtrN ist lang und bunt: den von Jerobeam I. installierten Staatskult um goldene Stiere in Bet-El und Dan rechnet er hierher (2 Kön. 10:31; 17:16) und natürlich Aschera (1 Kön. 14:15; 2 Kön. 13:6; 17:16) bzw. Astarte (1 Sam. 7:3-4; 12:10; 1 Kön. 11:33) und Baal (meistens neben Aschera oder Astarte genannt), dazu die Götter der ostjordanischen Nachbarvölker (1 Kön. 11:33) und die mesopotamischen Gestirnsgötter, das "Himmelsheer" (2 Kön. 17:16; 21:4). Hinzu kommen animistisch-magische Praktiken verschiedenster Art (2 Kön. 17:17; 21:6; 23:24). Alles das fasst DtrN unter dem Begriff der אלהים אחרים zusammen, zuweilen auch unter גללים "Götzen" (1 Kön. 15:12; 21:26; 2 Kön. 17:12; 21:21; 23:24) – einem Begriff, der fast rein ezechielisch geprägt ist und insofern einen weiteren Hinweis auf Ort und Zeit der dtr Schlussredaktion geben könnte.[17] Anscheinend hatten sich die Juden zur Zeit von DtrN

---

schichtswerk" (demnächst in einem von T. Römer edierten BEThL-Band erscheinend) und "Samuel- und Königsbücher" (demnächst in TRE erscheinend).

[16]In erster Linie ist Baal der Feind; seine Heimat ist Phönizien (Isebel ist sidonische Königstochter) und Philistäa (der Baal von Ekron, 2 Kön. 1). Doch auch die Kämpfe mit Aram tragen Züge eines Religionskriegs, vgl. 1 Kön. 20, auch 2 Kön. 5.

[17]Von 48 Belegen stehen 39 im Ezechielbuch und mindestens fünf bei DtrN.

auf einem internationalen religiösen (und sicher auch ökonomischen!) Markt zu behaupten, und DtrN reagiert darauf mit der Proklamation eines streng exklusiven JHWH-Monotheismus.

Dieses Postulat nimmt mitunter ausgesprochen militante Züge an, jedenfalls bei der Rückprojektion in die Geschichte Israels. Gleich das erste Gebot, das DtrN Mose in der deuteronomischen Tora erteilen lässt, lautet: "Völlig zerstören sollt ihr all die Stätten, an denen die Völker, die ihr vertreiben werdet, ihren Göttern gedient haben . . . Ihre Altäre sollt ihr niederreissen und ihre Mazzeben zerbrechen und ihre Ascheren mit Feuer verbrennen und die Bilder ihrer Götter zerschlagen" (Dtn. 12:2-3).[18] Und in das Kriegsgesetz bringt DtrN einen Passus ein,[19] wonach die gesamte Bewohnerschaft von bei der Landnahme eroberten Städten der Vernichtungsweihe (dem "Bann") zu unterwerfen sei, "damit sie euch nicht nach all ihren Greueln zu tun lehren, die sie für ihre Götter getan haben, sodass ihr euch gegen JHWH, euern Gott, verfehlt" (Dtn. 20:18).[20]

Bemerkenswert ist das Vorkommen in 2 Kön. 21:11 – einer Stelle, die ich immer noch DtrP zurechnen würde (vgl. *Prophetie und Geschichte*, 14) und eben aus sprachlichen Gründen *nicht* DtrH (gegen Van Keulen, *Manasseh*, 204).

[18]Das Kapitel Dtn. 12 schliesst in einer Art Inclusio wiederum mit Warnungen zum Thema des Götzendienstes, woran Dtn. 13 thematisch eng anschliesst, indem hier die Liquidierung bzw. Bannung von Einzelpersonen (speziell Propheten) bzw. Städten gefordert wird, die zum Abfall von JHWH aufgerufen bzw. sich entschlossen haben. Das gleiche wird im Blick auf Einzelpersonen noch einmal in Dtn. 17:2-5 eingeschärft. Zwar möchte E. Otto, "Treueid und Gesetz: Die Ursprünge des Deuteronomiums im Horizont neuassyrischen Vertragsrechts", *ZAR* 2 (1996), 1-52, hinter Dtn. 13:2-10 (und 28:20-44) eine Polemik gegen assyrische Loyalitätseide (VTE §§ 10; 12; 18; 57) sehen, welche nur vor dem Untergang des neuassyrischen Reiches Sinn mache und darum geradezu als archimedischer Punkt zur Datierung des (Kern-) Deuteronomiums gelten könne. Ob aber Dtn. 13 zu diesem Kern gehört, erscheint angesichts der vielfältigen nomistischen Nomenklatur und auch der Stellung des Kapitels im Kontext als fraglich. Möglicherweise haben die spät-dtr Verfasser aber Nachklänge von (anti-) assyrischen Texten oder sogar diese selbst gekannt und vom Grosskönig-Vasallen- auf das JHWH-Israel-Verhältnis transponiert.

[19]Dtn. 20:15-18 ist von DtrN nachgetragen, vgl. W. Dietrich, "The 'Ban' in the Age of the Early Kings", in: V. Fritz, P.R. Davies (eds.), *The Origins of the Ancient Israelite States* (JSOT.S, 228), Sheffield 1996, 196-210. Eine Anweisung gleichen Inhalts findet sich schon in Dtn. 7:1-5.

[20]Es scheint, als werde später dann an den Amalekitern ein (virtuelles) Exempel statuiert: Laut Dtn. 25:17-19 sind sie als die allerersten Feinde Israels nach dem Auszug aus Ägypten per Bannung auszulöschen, sobald Israel dazu die Kraft hat. Über die Doppelthematik von JHWH-Feindschaft (falls man 25:18b so deuten kann, doch vgl. etwa 1 Sam. 12:14, DtrN) und Bann ist dieser Passus mit den einschlägigen DtrN-Passagen im Deuteronomium verbunden. König Saul wird bekanntlich über dieses Gebot stolpern (1 Sam. 15) – was aber über das Altersverhältnis beider Texte noch nicht viel sagt: DtrN kann Dtn. 25:17-19 gerade

Bekanntlich blieben bei der Landnahme Nichtisraeliten am Leben, und prompt verfiel Israel ein ums andere Mal der Fremdgötterei. DtrN hat darüber sehr viel Beklagenswertes zu vermelden. Schon in der Richterzeit "hurte Israel hinter den Baalen her" (Ri. 8:33). Seit der Zeit des Exodus aus Ägypten bis an die Schwelle zur Königszeit haben die Israeliten nach JHWHs Urteil den wahren Gott "verlassen und anderen Göttern gedient" (1 Sam. 8:8). Mit den Königen wurde alles noch schlimmer (vgl. z.B. 1 Kön. 11:10; 21:26; 2 Kön. 10:31; 13:6; 17:12; 21:6), und das traurige Ende ist bekannt.

Das einzige, was hülfe – und in der Geschichte mehrfach geholfen hat –, wäre die Abrenuntiation, die Lossagung von den fremden Göttern und die Beseitigung ihrer Symbole. In der Richterzeit fand eine solche Aktion statt (Ri. 10:16), eine vor Beginn der Königszeit (1 Sam. 7:3-4) und eine an deren Ende, durch Joschija (2 Kön. 23).[21] Bekanntlich konnte diese letzte grosse Selbstreinigung Judas den Schmutz der Manassezeit nicht mehr ganz beseitigen, und so kam das Exil. Der Appell an die Leserschaft ist kaum zu überhören: JHWHs Volk hat von allen fremden Göttern zu lassen – am besten von vornherein, notfalls aber auch im nachhinein; andernfalls setzt es seine Zukunft aufs Spiel.

2   Erwählung und Heilsgeschichte

DtrN lässt keinen Zweifel daran: Der Gott, der da von Israel ungeteilte Zuwendung verlangt, hat sich zuvor Israel in unbegreiflicher Grosszügigkeit zugewandt. Immer wieder werden wichtige Daten der Heilsgeschichte aufgerufen: die Herausführung aus Ägypten und die Hineinführung ins Land vornean, dann aber auch die militärischen Erfolge der Richter- und der frühen Königszeit.

Zuweilen werden Exodus (1 Sam. 8:8) und Landgabe (Jos. 23:14) als Grundpfeiler der Heilsgeschichte einzeln, zuweilen auch zusammen genannt (Ri. 2:1; 6:7-10). In längeren Geschichtsrückblicken bilden sie den Ausgangspunkt (Ri. 10:11;[22] 1 Sam. 12:8), an den sich die Siege über die Nachbarvölker anschliessen (nach Ri. 10:11f über die Ammoniter, Philister, Sidonier, Amalekiter und Midianiter, nach 1 Sam. 12:9

---

im Blick auf eine schon ältere Saul-Amalek- und eine noch ältere David-Amalek-Geschichte (1 Sam. 30) entworfen haben.

[21] In dem Kapitel sind nur relativ wenige Verse mit einiger Wahrscheinlichkeit DtrN zuzuweisen, doch genügt allein 2 Kön. 23:26, um seine spezifische Haltung deutlich zu machen.

[22] Hier in Gestalt der "Ägypter" und "Amoriter" in einer längeren Liste von Feinden.

über die Kanaaniter und Moabiter)[23]. So hat Gott sein Volk an einem Ort "eingepflanzt", an dem es ohne Angst leben konnte (2 Sam. 7:10), hat ihm Ruhe verschafft vor seinen Feinden (1 Sam. 12:11; 2 Sam. 7:1; 1 Kön. 8:56), ja hat es "gross" gemacht (2 Sam. 7:23-24).

Es liegt DtrN viel daran, die glänzende Frühzeit Israels als göttliches Geschenk und Einlösung göttlicher Verheissung hinzustellen. JHWHs Verlässlichkeit ist ein wichtiger Topos, die schöne Metapher von den Worten JHWHs, von denen keines "zu Boden gefallen ist", eine von DtrN geprägte Wendung (Jos. 23:14; 1 Kön. 8:56). Die volle Bedeutung solcher Aussagen entfaltet sich angesichts des weiteren Verlaufs der Geschichte Israels, die ja nach dem dtr Geschichtswerk im Untergang der beiden israelitischen Staaten und damit in einem doppelten Fiasko endet. War dies nicht gerade der Beweis von JHWHs Unzuverlässigkeit?

DtrN setzt sich mit dieser Frage besonders intensiv auseinander und argumentiert dabei auf zwei Linien.

Erstens hat die enge Beziehung, die JHWH mit Israel eingegangen ist, als grundsätzlich unauflösbar zu gelten. Sie kann beschädigt, sie kann aber durch keine noch so dramatische geschichtliche Entwicklung zerbrochen werden. Schon dass Israel bei der Landnahme nicht so rabiat vorging wie vorgesehen, barg den Keim künftigen Unheils in sich; doch seinen Bund (ברית) mit Israel wird JHWH niemals brechen (Ri. 2:1). Wohl werden durch die Einführung des Königtums mancherlei Schwierigkeiten heraufbeschworen; doch dass JHWH deshalb Israel verstossen würde, ist ausgeschlossen, hat es ihm doch nun einmal "gefallen" (הוֹאִיל), es "zu seinem Volk zu machen" (1 Sam. 12:22). Ganz in diesem Sinn kann Salomo beten:[24] "JHWH, du Gott Israels, es ist kein Gott wie du droben im Himmel noch drunten unter der Erde, der du den Bund und die Huld bewahrst deinen Dienern" (1 Kön. 8:23).

Zweitens gibt DtrN zu verstehen, dass die Epoche der Staatlichkeit Israels, auch wenn sie jetzt vorüber sei, doch über Erwarten lang gedauert habe, und dass dies nur aufgrund des erwählenden und helfenden Handelns JHWHs möglich gewesen sei. Freilich: Juda profi-

---

[23] Es ist, als ob die beiden Reihen sich ergänzten. Dabei ist die Erwähnung der Ammoniter vor Jiftach erstaunlich, rechtfertigt sich aber von der kurzen Notiz Ri. 3:13 her. Dort werden mit den Moabitern die Ammoniter und die Amalekiter zusammengefasst, letztere mit den Midianitern wiederholt in der Gideonüberlieferung (Ri. 6:3, 33; 7:12). Die phönizischen Sidonier tauchen in Jos. 13:4, 6 und Ri. 3:3 auf: eher als Übriggebliebene denn als Besiegte.

[24] Überhaupt ist nach DtrN das Gebet ein den Gläubigen jederzeit – auch in schwerer Schuld – offenstehender Weg zur Güte JHWHs, vgl. neben 1 Kön. 8 und 2 Sam. 7 (mit DtrN-Anteilen) noch 2 Sam. 22:1–23:5 (von DtrN eingebracht) sowie Jos. 7:6-9; Ri. 6:13; 10:10; 2 Kön. 13:4; 20:5 (alles DtrN).

tierte weit mehr von JHWHs Zuwendung als Nordisrael – und existierte darum bedeutend länger. Immerhin hat JHWH auch dem Nordreich eine Chance gegeben: Es hätte dort wie im Süden eine beständige, von Gott beschützte Dynastie entstehen können (1 Kön. *11:37-38); das war infolge des Versagens schon des ersten Königs, Jerobeams I., nicht der Fall. Die nun einsetzenden, relativ raschen Dynastiewechsel verschlimmerten die Lage noch.[25] Dann aber folgte, unter der Jehu-Dynastie, ein Jahrhundert leidlicher Stabilität – ein Faktum, das DtrN interessierte. Warum ging das Nordreich, nachdem es mit der Omri-Dynastie den Gipfel der Gottlosigkeit erreicht hatte, nicht sogleich unter? Die Antwort ist eine doppelte: Weil Jehu vergleichsweise got-tesfürchtig war, war ihm eine relativ langlebige Dynastie beschieden ("bis ins vierte Glied": 2 Kön. 10:30, 31a), und: Weil (Nord-)Israel zum erwählten Volk Gottes gehörte, blieb dem Nordstaat Israel noch eine Zeitlang die staatliche Selbständigkeit erhalten. Unter Joahas ben Jehu "gab JHWH Israel einen Helfer" gegen die Aramäer – wobei völlig rätselhaft bleibt, wer damit gemeint sein könnte (2 Kön. 13:5). Unter Joasch ben Joahas[26] erwies JHWH den Israeliten "Gnade und Erbarmen und wandte sich ihnen zu – um seines Bundes (ברית) willen, den er mit Abraham, Isaak und Jakob geschlossen hatte; er wollte sie bis dahin (!) nicht vernichten und sie nicht von seinem Antlitz verwerfen" (2 Kön. 13:23). Unter Jerobeam ben Joasch "hatte JHWH ein Einsehen mit dem Elend Israels …; da war kein Helfer[27] für Israel. Doch JHWH hatte nicht gesagt, dass er den Namen Israels auslöschen wolle unter dem Himmel, und so half er ihnen durch Jerobeam ben Joasch" (2 Kön. 14:26-27). Unter Sacharja ben Jerobeam aber vollendete sich das Schicksal auch dieser Dynastie (2 Kön. 15:12).

Noch viel intensiver als mit dem Ende Nordisraels hat sich DtrN mit demjenigen Judas auseinandergesetzt – kein Wunder, standen hier doch ganz spezifische göttliche Gnadengaben und Verheissungen auf dem Spiel. Immer wieder hebt DtrN die besondere Beziehung JHWHs

[25]Vgl. die DtrN-Kommentare in 1 Kön. 14:*8-9; 15:30; 16:13; 21:25-26 sowie unten Abschnitt 6.

[26]Irritierenderweise ist gerade vorher, in 2 Kön. 13:22, von Angriffen des Ara-mäers Hasaël zur Zeit des *Joahas* die Rede, dessen Tod aber schon in 13:9 vermeldet worden war. Es dürfte sich um eine mit 13:24-25 zusammengehö-rende Annalennotiz handeln, die bei ihrem Einbau (oder dem des "Prophetischen Erzählwerks", s.o. Anm. 15) ins dtr Geschichtswerk an einen nicht ganz sach-gemässen Platz geriet.

[27]Die hier schon das zweite Mal auftauchende Gestalt eines "Helfers" (vgl. 2 Kön. 13:5) bleibt rätselhaft: An einen Propheten denkt DtrN nicht, da ja in 14:25 Jona ben Amittai erwähnt wird. Auch ein König dürfte nicht gemeint sein, da Jerobeam II. ja erfolgreich agiert. Ist an einen himmlischen Helfer gedacht?

zu David sowie zu Jerusalem und seinem Tempel hervor – und die positiven Folgen, die dies für das Südreich hatte.

David ist betontermassen עבד יהוה, er ist ein kaum je erreichtes Vorbild an JHWH-Treue, ihm und seinen Nachfolgern gilt die grosse Verheissung Natans (1 Kön. 8:24, 66; 11:34 u.ö.). Als Salomo sich gegen das Gebot der Alleinverehrung JHWHs versündigt, verschiebt JHWH die fällige Strafe "um Davids willen" von Salomo auf dessen Sohn und Nachfolger; doch auch diesem will er nicht das ganze Reich abnehmen, sondern ihm einen Stamm – Juda – belassen "um meines Dieners David und um Jerusalems willen, das ich erwählt (בחר) habe" (1 Kön. 11:12-13).[28] Wiederholt spricht DtrN in sehr eigenständiger Redeweise davon, dass JHWH in der schlimmen Zeit bei und nach der Reichsteilung "für David" (1 Kön. 11:36) oder "um Davids willen" (1 Kön. 15:4) in Jerusalem eine "Leuchte" (ניר) belassen habe. All dies führt später, in Zeiten akuter innerer und äusserer Bedrohung Judas, zu einem analogen Gedankengang wie bei Nordisrael: "Doch JHWH wollte Juda nicht vernichten um seines Dieners David willen, wie er denn zugesagt hatte,[29] ihm 'und'[30] seinen Söhnen allezeit eine Leuchte geben zu wollen" (2 Kön. 8:19). Und in direkter Verheissungsrede: "Ich will diese Stadt beschirmen, ihr zu helfen[31] – um meinetwillen und um meines Dieners David willen" (2 Kön. 19:34).

Um zu erklären, warum Gottes Erwählungswille Juda, Jerusalem und die Daviddynastie am Ende doch nicht vor dem Untergang bewahrt hat, entwickelt DtrN einen regelrechten Mechanismus zur Ausserkraftsetzung der Verheissung. Den entscheidenden Umschlag führt Manasse, der Ketzerkönig des Südreichs, herbei.[32] Zwar hofft man, der fromme Joschija könne das Schlimmste noch verhüten, doch belehrt uns DtrN mehrfach, dass die Chance dafür gar nicht mehr bestanden habe. JHWH habe, heisst es am Ende der Joschija-Perikope, die Gottlosigkeit Manasses derart erbittert, dass er zu sich gesagt habe: "Auch Juda will ich von meinem Antlitz wegtun, wie ich Israel weggetan habe, und verwerfen will ich diese Stadt, die ich erwählt habe (בחר), und das Haus, von dem ich gesagt habe: Mein Name soll dort sein" (2 Kön. 23:26-27). Dass es die Sünde Manasses gewesen sei, welche die besondere Beziehung JHWHs zum Davidshaus

---

[28] Noch einmal ähnlich: 1 Kön. 11:32.

[29] Das לו ist wohl in Anlehnung an LXX wegzulassen, da nirgendwo eine entsprechende Anrede an David berichtet wird.

[30] Mit 2 Chr. 21:7 einzufügen.

[31] Die Wurzel ישע ist uns, in ganz ähnlicher Verwendung, aber auf das Nordreich angewandt, in 2 Kön. 13:5 und 14:26 begegnet.

[32] Seinem schon zuvor randvollen Sündenregister fügt DtrN noch einige Ungeheuerlichkeiten hinzu; dazu unten Abschnitt 3.

und zu Jerusalem endgültig zerstört habe, wird anlässlich der ersten
wie der zweiten Eroberung Jerusalems nochmals bekräftigt (2 Kön.
24:3-4, 20). Immerhin hatte diese Beziehung doch zur Folge, dass das
Königtum Juda rund einhalb Jahrhunderte länger Bestand hatte
als das Königtum Israel.

3   Toratreue und Frömmigkeit

Das "N" im Siglum DtrN steht für "Nomismus". Mit dem Begriff as-
soziiert sich christlichem Denken die Vorstellung einer Leistungs- und
Verdienstreligion: so als ob der Fromme Gesetzesgehorsam vorzuwei-
sen hätte, um Gottes Gunst zu erfahren. Dieses bis in die Gegenwart
gepflegte Bild jüdischer Religion müsste, wenn irgendwo im Kanons-
teil der Vorderen Propheten, dann in der Textschicht Anhalt finden,
die wir "DtrN" nennen. Doch auch hier erweist es sich als Zerrbild.
Gottes Erwählungshandeln an Israel, Juda, Jerusalem und dem Davidshaus erfolgte vollkommen ungeschuldet; da war kein Verdienst,
das die Begünstigten zuvor hätten erbringen müssen oder können.
Als unverdient Erwählte indes, und davon soll nun die Rede sein,
schulden sie Gott Dankbarkeit und Hingabe.

Die von DtrN in diesem Zusammenhang gebrauchte Terminologie
offenbart ein gar nicht 'gesetzliches' Denken. Auf die berühmte, wohl
in joschijanischer Zeit ausgegebene Parole שמע ישראל יהוה אלהינו יהוה
אחד lässt DtrN die Erläuterung folgen:[33] "Und du sollst JHWH, deinen
Gott, lieben mit deinem ganzen Herzen und deinem ganzen Trachten[34]
und deiner ganzen Kraft" (Dtn. 6:5). Liebe also wird von Israel er-
wartet,[35] nicht Unterwerfung und Anstrengung. Und auch wenn man
von dem Begriff 'Herz' (לבב) unangebrachte sentimentale Konnota-
tionen fernhält, wird hier doch die willige und freie Personhingabe
des Glaubenden und nicht die Erfüllung ihm auferlegter Leistungen
beschrieben. Im gleichen Atemzug freilich werden dem Glaubenden
"die Worte, die ich dir heute gebiete, aufs Herz" gebunden (Dtn. 6:6).
Hier nun geht es doch um Leistungen, nämlich um die Einhaltung

---

[33]So mit T. Veijola, "Das Bekenntnis Israels. Beobachtungen zur Geschichte
und Theologie von Dtn 6,4-9", *ThZ* 48 (1992), 369-381.

[34]Wenn die Urmeinung des Wortes נפש ("Kehle, Begehren") hier so zur Geltung
gebracht werden darf. Möglich wäre natürlich auch "mit deinem ganzen Leben"
oder das alte "von ganzer Seele".

[35]Von *Liebe* zu Gott redet DtrN noch in Dtn. 13:4; Jos. 23:11. Umgekehrt
von der Liebe JHWHs zu Israel ist in 1 Kön. 10:9 die Rede, einer Stelle, die P.
Särkiö, *Die Weisheit und Macht Salomos in der israelitischen Historiographie:
Eine traditions- und redaktionskritische Untersuchung über 1 Kön 3–5 und 9–11*
(SESJ, 60), Helsinki, Göttingen 1994, 183, im Gefolge Veijolas ebenfalls DtrN
zuweist, während Wälchli (*Salomo*) zu DtrH tendiert.

von Gottes Gebot. Dieses aber tritt dem Glaubenden nicht als ein ihm Fremdes entgegen, sondern ist seinem Personkern eingeprägt, so dass sein Gehorsam nichts als selbstverständlich, reine Tat der Liebe ist.[36]

Die von DtrN propagierte Haltung gegenüber JHWH und seiner Tora hat überhaupt nichts Berechnendes und Rechthaberisches an sich. Man soll an JHWH "kleben" (דבק, Dtn. 13:5; Jos. 23:8), ihm "trauen" (בטח, 2 Kön. 18:5), "hinter ihm her laufen" (... הלך אחר, 1 Kön. 14:8 u.o.), "auf seinen Wegen gehen" (הלך בדרכים, 1 Kön. 2:3), "vor ihm wandeln" (... הלך לפני, 1 Kön. 8:25), "in seiner Tora wandeln" (הלך בתורה, 2 Kön. 10:31), "voll zu ihm halten" (... מלא אחר, Dtn. 1:36), sein "Herz vollkommen auf ihn richten" (לבב שלם עם, 1 Kön. 8:61, vgl. 15:3). Viel ist vom "Herzen" die Rede, vom "Starksein" (חזק), von "Beständigkeit" (אמת, 1 Kön. 2:4), vom "Vollkommensein" (תמם). Kurzum: eine bestimmte Lebenshaltung und Lebensgestaltung ist im Blick.

Worin besteht diese näherhin? Eben in der Einhaltung der Tora, und zwar deutlich: der deuteronomischen Tora. Mit den "Worten, die ich dir heute gebiete" (Dtn. 6:6) ist die nachfolgende Gesetzesmitteilung gemeint. Nur und erst DtrN spricht im Geschichtswerk von "der Tora" oder den "Geboten", die "Mose befohlen" hat (1 Kön. 2:3; 2 Kön. 18:6, 12; 23:25) und die "(in einem Buch) aufgeschrieben" sind (1 Kön. 2:3; 2 Kön. 22:13; 23:24). Gottes Weisung liegt indes nicht nur in schriftlicher Form vor, sie wird immer wieder in "Worten" (דברים) oder als "Stimme" (קול) hörbar – und überhörbar.[37] "JHWH verwarnte Israel und Juda ...: Kehrt um von euren bösen Wegen und haltet meine Gebote und Anweisungen gemäss der ganzen Tora, die ich euren Vätern befohlen und die ich zu euch gesandt habe durch meine Diener, die Propheten! Doch sie hörten nicht" (2 Kön. 17:13, 14a).[38]

Solche Formulierungen machen klar, dass sich der Wille Gottes keineswegs nur auf bestimmte Segmente menschlicher Daseinsgestaltung richtet – auf das religiöse oder kultische Leben etwa –, sondern auf die ganze Breite des Lebens, wie sie im Deuteronomium und in der prophetischen Predigt angesprochen ist. Entsprechend ist oftmals

---

[36] Auch in 1 Kön. 8:55-58, 61 kommt die Einsicht von DtrN zum Vorschein, dass überhaupt erst durch Gottes Gnade das Gesetz gehalten werden kann.

[37] Beide Ausdrücke werden z.B. dazu gebraucht, den Ungehorsam Sauls zu kennzeichnen (1 Sam. 15:11, 19) – was dessen Fall paradigmatisch für jeden und jede in Israel macht.

[38] Das Nicht-Hören auf die Worte der Tora ist in der Sicht von DtrN geradezu ein Leitmotiv der Geschichte Israels: Ri. 2:2; 1 Sam. 15:19; 28:18; 2 Kön. 17:14; 18:12; 21:8; 22:13.

nicht einfach von der Tora als ganzer, sondern von der Vielzahl der in ihr enthaltenen משפטים, חקים, מצות die Rede. DtrN ist also mitnichten nur auf *ein* Thema fixiert: die Einhaltung oder Nichteinhaltung der Gebote zu Kultreinheit und Kulteinheit. Oberflächlicher Betrachtung könnte sich, etwa angesichts der Beurteilung der Könige, der Eindruck einstellen, Gut und Böse bemesse sich einzig an diesem Massstab; an Manasse etwa interessiere nur seine Vielgötterei, an Joschija nur die Beseitigung der Fremdkulte. Doch gerade DtrN betont mehrmals auch, dass Manasse "unschuldiges Blut vergossen" habe (2 Kön. 21:16; 24:4), und Joschija rühmt er nach, er habe sich an "die *ganze* Tora Moses" gehalten (2 Kön. 23:25).

Auf der anderen Seite ist natürlich nicht zu verkennen, dass für DtrN – wie für die gesamte dtr Bewegung – das Erste Gebot von zentraler Bedeutung ist. So sieht DtrN die Geschichte Israels als eine Beispielsammlung für Bewährung oder Versagen gerade in dieser Hinsicht. Es gibt positive Beispiele: Kaleb (Dtn. 1:36), David vor allem (2 Sam. 22:22-25; 1 Kön. 9:4; 11:34; 15:3, 5), Salomo (zu Beginn seiner Herrschaft: 1 Kön. 3:3), Hiskija (2 Kön. 18:5-6). Negative Beispiele sind Saul (1 Sam. 13:13; 15:11), Salomo (in seiner Spätzeit: 1 Kön. 11:33),[39] Jerobeam I. (1 Kön. 14:8)[40] – und, dies am erschreckendsten, ganz Israel und Juda (2 Kön. 17:15, 19).[41]

Die gewisse Einseitigkeit und Pauschalität, die in dieser Art der Geschichtsbeurteilung liegt, erklärt sich aus den Zeitumständen und der Zielsetzung dieser und überhaupt der dtr Redaktion. Sie beabsichtigte, unter *theologischen* Gesichtspunkten eine *politische* Geschichte zu schreiben. Sie ging ans Werk, als es keinen israelitischen Staat und also keine politischen Institutionen und Strukturen mehr gab, die der jüdischen Gemeinschaft Halt und Zusammenhalt hätten bieten können. Damit wurde die Frage nach der Religion – und zwar in einer möglichst einheitsstiftenden Ausformung – zur Schicksalsfrage. Diese Problemstellung spiegelt die dtr Geschichtsschreibung in die Geschichte Israels zurück. Das bedeutet einen gewissen Anachronismus, ermöglicht aber eine markante Lehre: An der Haltung zur Tora und insbesondere zum Ersten Gebot hat sich das Wohl und Wehe Israels schon immer entschieden – und wird es sich auch künftig entscheiden.

Darin, dass die Schlussredaktion DtrN diese dtr Grundüberzeugung voll teilt, dürfte sich abzeichnen, dass zu ihrer Zeit die Neu-

---

[39] Hier ist pluralisch formuliert: Nicht bei Salomo allein liegt die Verfehlung, sondern bei ganz Israel.

[40] Dass die 'Sünde Jerobeams' ganz Israel in ihren Bann gezogen hat, ist für die Deuteronomisten ebenfalls klar.

[41] Jehu (2 Kön. 10:30-31a) ist weiss *und* schwarz gezeichnet – wie in anderer Weise ja auch Salomo.

bildung fester politischer Strukturen und Institutionen in Juda noch nicht abzusehen, mithin die Ära Esras und Nehemias noch nicht angebrochen war. Andererseits ist, wie sich bereits angedeutet hat und noch deutlicher zeigen wird, die babylonische Ära mit ihren doch klaren Herrschaftsstrukturen zu Ende. In einer Zeit weltweiter Krisen und unsicherer Perspektiven stellt DtrN die jüdische Gemeinschaft vor eine klare Alternative: entweder treu zu JHWH halten und eine Zukunft haben – oder JHWH untreu werden und die Zukunft verspielen.

Kein Geringerer als Mose stellt Israel schon zu Beginn seiner Geschichte in einer sog. Alternativpredigt vor diese Wahl: "Gedenke JHWHs, deines Gottes, denn er gibt dir Kraft, um seinen Bund aufrechtzuerhalten, den er deinen Vätern zugeschworen hat, so wie es heute ist. Wenn du aber JHWHs, deines Gottes, unbedingt vergessen und anderen Göttern nachlaufen und ihnen dienen und sie anbeten willst, so bezeuge ich euch heute, dass ihr gewiss zugrundegehen werdet" (Dtn. 8:18-19).

Natürlich hofft und glaubt DtrN, das Volk, dem JHWH seinen "Bund zugeschworen hat", werde *nicht* "zugrundegehen". Doch kann es sich für die Zukunft nicht mehr auf die drei grossen Heilsgaben stützen, die ihm bisher Halt verliehen hatten: den Besitz des Landes, den Tempel in Jerusalem und das davidische Königtum. Den Verlust jeder einzelnen von ihnen reflektiert und kommentiert DtrN, wovon nun noch die Rede sein muss.

4   Landbesitz und Fremdherrschaft

In seiner Abschiedsrede vermahnt Josua die Israeliten: "So wie all das Gute, das JHWH euer Gott euch zugesagt hat, über euch gekommen ist, so wird JHWH über euch kommen lassen all das Schlimme, das er euch angesagt hat – bis er euch ausgerottet hat aus diesem guten Kulturland, das euch JHWH euer Gott gegeben hat: wenn ihr den Bund JHWHs eures Gottes übertretet, den er euch geboten hat, und anderen Göttern nachlauft und ihnen dient und sie anbetet, dann wird der Zorn JHWHs über euch entbrennen und er wird euch eilends beseitigen von dem guten Land, das er euch gegeben hat" (Jos. 23:15-16). So wenig also die Gabe des Landes an Bedingungen geknüpft war, so sehr ist es der dauerhafte Besitz des Landes. Von allem Anfang an ist deutlich: diese Gabe kann verloren gehen.

Eben in diese Richtung werden bei DtrN von vornherein die Weichen gestellt. In der Tora wurde Israel streng davor gewarnt, sich auf die Kulte der Vorbewohner des Landes einzulassen (Dtn. 12:29-31). Um diese Gefahr grundsätzlich auszuschliessen, sollten am besten überhaupt keine Nichtisraeliten im Land am Leben bleiben (Dtn. 20:15-18). Die Landnahme erfolgte nach dem Josuabuch zwar überaus rabiat, aber nicht so rabiat, wie sie nach DtrN hätte sein müssen. Die Verschonung der Hure Rahab und ihrer Familie in Jericho (Jos. 6:22-23) mochte noch angehen. Schlimmer war schon, dass es den Gibeonitern gelang, einen Vertrag mit Israel zu erschleichen (Jos. 9). DtrN selber fügt, in bewusster Störung des doch noch immer recht schnittigen Landnahmebildes von DtrH, umfangreiche Listen von uneroberten Landstrichen (Jos. 13:1bβ-6) und Städten (Ri. 1:27-35) bei.[42] Damit ist der Keim des Verderbens gelegt. Der "Engel JHWHs" persönlich hält den Israeliten vor, sie hätten "mit den Bewohnern des Landes keinen Bund schliessen" dürfen und "ihre Altäre niederreissen" müssen; "doch ihr habt nicht gehört" (Ri. 2:2). Zwar spricht Josua noch die Warnung aus, auf keinen Fall dürfe man zu den "übriggebliebenen Völkern hineingehen"[43] und sich von ihnen zum Dienst fremder Götter verführen lassen (Jos. 23:7). Doch es kommt, was kommen musste: "Die Israeliten wohnten inmitten der Kanaaniter ... und nahmen sich deren Töchter zu Frauen und gaben ihre Töchter deren Söhnen und dienten deren Göttern" (Ri. 3:5-6).

Nicht schon die Vermischung der Ethnien, sondern die dadurch bewirkte Verwischung der Religionsgrenzen ist der Sündenfall. DtrN wird das später an Salomo noch einmal exemplifizieren: Ihn brachten "im Alter seine (ausländischen) Frauen dazu, sein Herz anderen Göttern zuzuneigen" (1 Kön. 11:4).[44] Unschwer ist zu merken, dass es sich dabei weniger um historische Feststellungen als vielmehr um Stellungnahmen zu Gegenwartsfragen handelt. Nachdem Juda kein abgegrenzter Staat mehr war, sondern die Juden sowohl in der Gola wie in Judäa mit Menschen anderer Nationen und Religionen zusammenzuleben hatten, stellte sich die Frage nach der Fortexistenz einer eigenen jüdischen Gemeinschaft mit grosser Schärfe. Esra und Nehemia werden auf diese Frage eine harte (und letztlich sicher untaugliche) Antwort geben (Esra 10; Neh. 10).

Was bedeutet es angesichts dessen, dass sich für DtrN die Alternative von Landbesitz und Landverlust an ethnischer und religiöser Abgrenzung des Judentums entscheidet? Josua hatte sein Volk gewarnt: "Wenn ihr euch (von JHWH) abkehrt und an dem Rest dieser Völker klebt, die bei euch übriggeblieben sind, und euch mit ihnen

---

[42]Vgl. R. Smend, "Das Gesetz und die Völker".

[43]בוא hat hier, wie sonst oft, sexuelle Konnotation; gemeint ist das Konnubium.

[44]DtrN betont dies noch einmal ausdrücklich und fügt eine Liste der falschen Götter an (1 Kön. 11:4-5), nachdem DtrH nur eine schwache Andeutung in dieser Richtung gemacht hatte (1 Kön. 11:3b).

verschwägert und zu ihnen hineingeht und sie zu euch, dann wisset wohl, dass JHWH euer Gott diese Völker nicht mehr vor euch vertreiben wird, und sie werden euch zur Falle und zum Fangholz, zur Geissel an euren Seiten und zu Dornen in euren Augen, bis ihr vertrieben seid aus diesem guten Kulturland, welches euch JHWH euer Gott gegeben hat" (Jos. 23:12-13). Man kann solche Sätze historisch verstehen oder assertorisch. Sie besagen dann entweder, dass man das Land nicht mehr besitzt, weil man versagt hat, oder dass man es nicht besitzen wird, wenn man versagt.

Die historische Lesart liegt nahe. Die Landgabe war ein unverdientes Geschenk. Ein der Tora treues Israel hätte das Geschenk nehmen und behalten dürfen (Dtn. 6:17-19). Stattdessen kam die unvollständige Inbesitznahme und alsbald die Durchmischung der Ethnien und Religionen. In der Königszeit wurde es damit nicht besser, sondern schlimmer. Schon Salomo wird ins Stammbuch geschrieben: "Wenn ihr euch von mir abkehrt ... und hinter fremden Göttern herlauft und ihnen dient, werde ich Israel aus dem Kulturland aushauen, das ich ihnen gegeben habe" (1 Kön. 9:6-7). Und dem ersten König des Nordreichs, Jerobeam I., kündigt der Prophet Ahia an, JHWH werde "Israel ausreissen aus diesem schönen Kulturland, das er ihren Vätern gegeben hat, und sie aussäen jenseits des (Eufrat-) Stromes, weil sie sich Ascheren[45] gemacht und JHWH gereizt haben" (1 Kön. 14:15). So kam es denn auch: "Der König von Assur deportierte Israel nach Assur ..., weil sie nicht auf die Stimme JHWHs ihres Gottes gehört hatten" (2 Kön. 18:11-12). Juda war mittlerweile längst auf dem gleichen Weg, und spätestens seit Manasse gab es kein Zurück mehr: Er "verführte" seine Untertanen, "noch Schlimmeres zu tun als die Völker, die JHWH vor den Israeliten vertrieben hatte" (2 Kön. 21:9). Die Folge konnte nicht ausbleiben: Der König von Babel "deportierte Juda aus seinem Kulturland" (2 Kön. 25:21b).

Diese Deportationsnotizen, die beide auf DtrN zurückgehen dürften,[46] sind auffällig pauschal formuliert: so als ob ganz Israel und ganz

---

[45] Dieser Vorwurf kommt insofern überraschend, als an sich ja Jerobeams Missetat in der Aufstellung von Stieren in Bet-El und Dan bestand, hingegen von "Ascheren" bisher gar nicht, sondern nur von "Aschera" in Ri. 6:25ff die Rede war. Die "Aschera" war – ausweislich von 1 Kön. 15:13; 2 Kön. 18:4; 21:3; 23:4, 6 und den Inschriften von Kuntillet Adschrud – in der Königszeit mindestens ebensosehr im Süden wie im Norden zuhause. In der dtr Vorstellung bevölkern die "Ascheren" vorwiegend (doch vgl. 1 Kön. 14:23) den Norden (1 Kön. 14:15; 2 Kön. 13:6; 17:10, 16; 23:15 – bis auf 2 Kön. 17:10 alles DtrN-Belege!). Anscheinend ist die reale Göttin und ihre Präsenz in einem Kultgegenstand gar nicht mehr vor Augen, ist der – seltsam in einen maskulinen Plural gesetzte – Begriff zur blossen Chiffre für Abkehr von JHWH geworden; als solcher darf er eben beim Reichsgründer des Nordens nicht fehlen!

[46] 2 Kön. 25:21b kommt nach 25:21a, der Nachricht von der Hinrichtung Zidki-

Juda exiliert worden wären.[47] Diese Meinung ist historisch sicher un-
zutreffend, erklärt sich aber aus der Landtheologie von DtrN: Das
von JHWH einst verliehene Land musste infolge der Untreue Israels
verlorengehen, und das geschah, als die Staaten Israel und Juda unter-
gingen. Der theologischen Systematik geht es um das Gottesvolk als
ganzes – und nicht um soziologische Differenzierungen, wie sie DtrH
bzw. dessen Quelle in der Unterscheidung von politisch-militärischer
Elite und "niederem Landvolk" noch vorgenommen hatten (2 Kön.
25:11-12, 22). Die Chronik wird später die Theorie vertreten, die gesamte Bevölkerung Jerusalems und seines Umlandes sei in die Babylonische Gefangenschaft geraten, das Land Juda während des Exils
unbewohnt gewesen und erst von den Rückwanderern neu besiedelt
worden. DtrN hat dieser Theorie kaum schon angehangen, hat ihr aber
vorgearbeitet, indem er die babylonische Gola generös als "Juda" ti-
tulierte. Verrät sich darin womöglich eine hohe Wertschätzung des
Golajudentums?

Aus solcher Perspektive bekommt die Landtheologie von DtrN etwas Hintergründiges. Jene warnenden Sätze Josuas, Gott werde, wenn
Israel sich mit den anderen Völkern einlasse, diese nicht mehr vertreiben (Jos. 23:12-13), sind ja auffälligerweise *nach* der Landnahme
gesprochen und dennoch *futurisch* formuliert. Sollte an eine Fortsetzung der Landnahme bzw. eine neue Landnahme gedacht sein?
Setzte nicht nach dem persischen Sieg über Babylon tatsächlich eine
Rückwanderung von Golajuden nach Judäa ein? Haben die von DtrN
ins Josuabuch eingefügten Listen einst unerobert gebliebener Land-
striche und Städte einen appellativen Unterton? Gefährdete die von
DtrN befürchtete Assimilation der Juden die erhoffte Rückgewinnung
des Landes? War die geforderte scharfe Abgrenzung Teil des Pro-
gramms zu deren Realisierung?

5 Kult und Tempel

In der dtr Geschichtstheologie spielt der Tempel von Jerusalem eine
zentrale Rolle, insofern er gemäss dem Zentralisationsgebot (und nach
der Reform Joschijas zumindest eine Zeitlang auch faktisch) der einzige legitime Ort zur Ausübung des Opferkults für JHWH war. DtrN
teilt diese Auffassung durchaus. In einer eigenen, betont an die Spitze

---

jas, einigermassen überraschend, und bereitet auch 25:22-26, die Gedalja-Episode,
nicht recht vor. Der Ausdruck das "übriggebliebene Volk" von 25:22 erklärt sich
gut aus den detaillierten Deportationsnotizen 25:18-19, passt aber schlecht nach
der überaus pauschalen Formulierung von 25:21b.

[47] Ähnlich, aber ohne nachfolgende theologische Explikation, schon DtrH (aus
älterer Quelle?) in 2 Kön. 17:6.

des gesamten deuteronomischen Gesetzeskorpus gestellten Einfügung unterstreicht er das Verbot jeglichen Opferdienstes ausserhalb der "Stätte, die euer Gott JHWH erwählen wird aus allen euren Stämmen, um seinen Namen dort wohnen zu lassen" (Dtn. 12:5). Jahrhunderte später, nachdem Salomo den Jerusalemer Tempel gebaut und geweiht hat, bestätigt ihm JHWH in einer Erscheinung ausdrücklich: "Ich habe dieses Haus, das du gebaut hast, geheiligt, um meinen Namen dort wohnen zu lassen für ewig" (עד־עולם, 1 Kön. 9:3). Eine solche Versicherung hatte es in den älteren, auch den dtr Texten, noch nicht gegeben. Es ist, als wolle DtrN unterstreichen, dass das, was früher selbstverständlich erschien, was jetzt aber immer unwahrscheinlicher wirkte, tatsächlich zutreffend gewesen war: An diesem Ort wohnte der "Name"[48] JHWHs.

Es verdient Beachtung, dass hier von Gott persönlich dem Jerusalemer Tempel "ewiges" Bestehen prognostiziert wird. Dem Befund mit der Annahme vorexilischer Textentstehung beikommen zu wollen, ist, wenn irgendwo, dann hier vollkommen aussichtslos. Wir haben es mit der spätesten dtr Textschicht zu tun, und entsprechend weit liegt die Zerstörung des Tempels zurück. Dennoch nimmt DtrN den vorexilischen Tempelglauben voll auf, um ihn dann – ähnlich wie den Glauben an die Unverlierbarkeit des Gelobten Landes – durch die geschichtliche Entwicklung destruiert werden zu lassen. Dabei fällt ein schlechtes Licht nicht etwa auf Gottes, sondern auf Israels Verlässlichkeit. Wie der Besitz des Landes, so gilt auch das Vorhandensein des Tempels DtrN als reine Gnadengabe Gottes (und nicht etwa als Verdienst Salomos, wovon gleich noch zu reden ist). Doch wie jene, so zieht auch diese Gabe gewisse Verpflichtungen nach sich. Kommt Israel ihnen nicht nach, wird Gott sein Geschenk zurückziehen.

Wieder wird in einer Alternativpredigt von allem Anfang an klargemacht, was auf dem Spiel steht. Ginge es nach dem Willen Gottes, würde der Tempel auf dem Zion "ewig" stehen. Sollten aber die Könige die Tora missachten und anderen Göttern dienen, dann "werde ich", so droht Gott dem Salomo, "das Haus, das ich meinem Namen geheiligt habe, wegwerfen von meinem Angesicht" und es "wird zu einem 'Trümmerhaufen'[49] werden" (1 Kön. 9:7, 8).

Die Könige von Juda übertreten nach der dtr Darstellung die Tora,

---

[48] Dass dieser Ausdruck dtr ist und eine gewisse scheue Distanz zwischen das Gebäude auf dem Zionsberg und den heiligen Gott legen will, ist oft betont worden. Er wird nicht erst von DtrN gebraucht, vgl. z.B. 2 Sam. 7:13 (DtrH).

[49] Das עליון des MT dürfte dogmatisch bedingte Verschreibung aus לעיין sein, vgl. BHS.

namentlich das Zentralisationsgebot, ungezählte Male, doch erst in der Spätzeit wagen sie es, nichtjahwistische Symbole und Kulte direkt in den Jerusalemer Tempel hineinzutragen. Den neuen Altar des Ahas, in dtr Augen sicher ein Sakrileg, kommentiert DtrN nur indirekt durch die Bemerkung, dies sei ein König gewesen, der nicht einmal vor Kinderopfern zurückschreckte,[50] einem "Greuel der Völker, die JHWH vor den Israeliten vertrieben hatte" (2 Kön. 16:3). Manasse dann hält er den gleichen und noch eine Reihe anderer "Greuel" vor (2 Kön. 21:6) – und überdies den Bau gleich mehrerer Altäre in dem Tempel, "von dem der JHWH doch gesagt hatte: Zu Jerusalem will ich meinen Namen wohnen lassen" (2 Kön. 21:4). Das Schlimmste aber: "Er stellte das Gottesbild der Aschera, das er gemacht hatte,[51] in das Haus, von dem JHWH zu David und seinem Sohn Salomo gesagt hatte:[52] In diesem Haus und in Jerusalem ... will ich meinen Namen auf ewig wohnen lassen" (2 Kön. 21:7).

Wieder ist klar: Die anfangs aufgestellte Alternative ist zum Negativen entschieden. Ungeachtet der verzweifelten Bemühungen Joschijas kann JHWHs Entschluss nur lauten: "Ich verwerfe diese Stadt, die ich erwählt habe, Jerusalem und das Haus, von dem ich gesagt habe: Mein Name soll dort sein" (2 Kön. 23:27). Am Ende wird die Plünderung und Brandschatzung[53] des Tempels durch die Babylonier stehen.

---

[50]Die allermeisten Belege für den Ausdruck העביר באש im dtr Geschichtswerk – ausser 2 Kön. 16:3 noch 17:17; 21:6; 23:10, wohl auch Dtn. 18:10 – scheinen DtrN zuzuweisen zu sein. Interessanterweise finden sich sonst Belege nur bei Ezechiel: 20:31; 23:37. Nah verwandt, aber nicht identisch – und ebenfalls frühestens spätdtr – ist der Ausdruck mit dem Verb שרף in 2 Kön. 17:31; Jer. 7:31; 19:5. O. Kaiser , "Den Erstgeborenen deiner Söhne sollst du mir geben. Erwägungen zum Kinderopfer im Alten Testament", in: *Festschr. C.H. Ratschow*, Berlin 1976, 24-48, legt dar, dass vor allem im phönizischen Einflussbereich Kinderopfer tatsächlich dargebracht wurden, dass aber die Belege im dtr Geschichtswerk sich historischer Auswertung entziehen, weil sie bereits von der Polemik im Jer- und im Ez-Buch beeinflusst sind.

[51]Damit bezieht sich DtrN zurück auf die Aussage von DtrH in 21:3, Manasse habe "eine Aschera gemacht"; dort dürfte ein stilisierter Kultpfahl gemeint sein, der einen Baum und damit den Fruchtbarkeitsaspekt der Göttin – oder inzwischen wohl eher: JHWHs – symbolisierte. DtrN macht daraus eine regelrechte Götterstatue (פסל), die er ausdrücklich im JHWH-Tempel aufgestellt werden lässt. Hierbei verwendet er sicher mit Bedacht das Verb שׂים, das er auch für das "Wohnenlassen" des JHWH-Namens im Tempel verwendet.

[52]Eine entsprechende Verheissung ergeht nur an Salomo, nicht eigentlich an David; doch wird sein Name als der eines weiteren Verheissungsträgers hier bewusst eingeführt, zumal es natürlich in 2 Sam. 7:13 die (dtr hergestellte!) Verbindung zwischen dem 'Haus JHWHs' und 'Davids Haus' gibt.

[53]In 2 Kön. 25:9, 13-17 begegnen diese beiden Aktionen in verkehrter Reihenfolge: ein Hinweis darauf, dass wir es hier mit zwei verschiedenen Quellen zu tun haben dürften.

DtrN arbeitet auf das traurige Ende von vornherein hin – und er gibt seinen Zeitgenossen darüber hinaus zu verstehen, dass sie sich einen neuen Anfang nicht wünschen sollten. Zwar war Salomos Tempelbau ein achtbarer Versuch, Israel der Präsenz seines Gottes zu versichern: ein Versuch, auf den sich auch Gott mit Wohlwollen eingelassen hat. Doch sollte unvergessen bleiben, dass der Wunsch dazu nicht von Gott ausgegangen war, sondern vom König.[54] David hatte – wie alle altorientalischen Herrscher, die auf sich hielten – das Bedürfnis, die Gottheit mit einem Tempel zu beglücken. Durch den Einspruch Natans wurde die Herrscherlogik des 'Do ut des' durchkreuzt; Gott wollte ohne Gegenleistung schenken (die Dynastieverheissung nämlich), und erst später sollte Davids Nachfolger den Tempel bauen.

Diesen Gedankengang von DtrH (2 Sam. 7:1-5a, 11b-16) unterbrach DtrN, um eine grundsätzliche Reflexion über die Frage einzufügen, ob Tempelbau und Tempelkult für die JHWH-Religion eigentlich unverzichtbar seien (2 Sam. 7:5b-11a). Die Antwort fällt eher negativ aus. Seit den Tagen des Exodus, sagt JHWH, habe er in keinem Haus gewohnt, sondern sei umhergezogen "in einem Zelt und in einer Wohnstatt" (באהל ובמשכן, 7:6). Mit dem ersten Begriff ist auf das Zeltheiligtum angespielt, in dem die Lade untergebracht war, ehe sie ins Allerheiligste des salomonischen Tempels verbracht wurde.[55] Überraschend ist die Ergänzung durch einen zweiten Begriff, משכן, der sonst nirgendwo im dtr Geschichtswerk begegnet. Ursprünglich bezeichnete er in der Jerusalemer Kultsprache just den Tempel auf dem Zion.[56] DtrN verlegt Gottes Wohnsitz aus Jerusalem weg und in die vorstaatliche Zeit zurück. Damals war JHWH ganz gewiss bei seinem Volk – und nie hat ein Richter Israels[57] den Befehl vernommen, JHWH ein Zedernhaus zu bauen (2 Sam. 7:7). Wie könnte man daraus, nachdem der Tempel Salomos – mit Fug und Recht! – in Trümmer gesunken ist, nicht einen Schluss auf die Gegenwart und Zukunft des (nach-) exilischen Judentums ziehen?

Es will beachtet sein, dass sich DtrN, indem er die Begriffe אהל und משכן braucht, in grosser Nähe zum priesterschriftlichen Sprach- und

---

[54]Vgl. zum folgenden W. Dietrich, *David, Saul und die Propheten. Das Verhältnis von Religion und Politik nach den prophetischen Überlieferungen vom frühesten Königtum in Israel* (BWANT, 122), ²1992, 114-136.

[55]Vgl. 2 Sam. 6:17; 1 Kön. 8:4, auch 1 Kön. 1:39; 2:28, 29, 30. Die Priesterschrift (auch in Dtn. 31:14-15!) macht daraus – vielleicht unter Aufnahme von 1 Sam. 2:22 – den אהל מועד).

[56]Prominent in Ps. 46:5.

[57]In 2 Sam. 7:7 wird – auch ohne Anhalt an der Texttradition – שבטי in שפטי zu ändern sein. Ein "Stamm" kann ja schlecht Israel "weiden"; das war Aufgabe einzelner Führer.

Denkbereich bewegt. Dort sind das "Zelt der Begegnung" und Gottes "Wohnstatt" *termini technici* für das Wüstenheiligtum, welches der innerste Zielpunkt des Schöpfungsgeschehens und bereits Vorabbild des (Zweiten) Tempels in Jerusalem ist.[58] So weit geht DtrN nicht: vermutlich deshalb, weil in dtr Sicht der Tempel von Jerusalem unlösbar mit der Geschichte des davidischen Königtums verknüpft war. Die Möglichkeit, beide Grössen voneinander zu trennen, wie sie unter persischer Herrschaft und unter kräftiger Mitwirkung der Gola beim Bau eines neuen Tempels faktisch realisiert wurde, stand dtr Denken offenbar noch nicht offen. Dies führt zu dem letzten, hier zu betrachtenden Teilaspekt.

6 Königtum und (Nicht-) Staatlichkeit

DtrN vertritt im Geschichtswerk die am dezidiertesten königskritische Sicht. Entgegen dem inneren Duktus von DtrH, der die vorstaatliche Zeit als Zeit allmählichen und am Ende rapiden inneren und äusseren Niedergangs und folglich die Staatsgründung als unausweichlich und gar als hoffnungsvollen Neuaufbruch beschrieben hat,[59] wertet DtrN die Richterzeit auf und stellt die Einführung des Königtums als nachgerade überflüssig, ja schädlich hin.[60] Der letzte Richter, Samuel, darf sich bei seinem Rücktritt als untadeliger und erfolgreicher Regent präsentieren; er und seine Vorgänger hätten noch jeden Aggressor aus dem Land geschlagen (1 Sam. 12:3-4, 11-12). Und augenfällig demonstriert er abschliessend noch etwas, das keinem noch so tüchtigen König gegeben ist: Wundermacht (1 Sam. 12:16-18). Damit ist klar: Israel kann durch die Einführung des Königtums weder innen- noch aussenpolitisch noch geistlich irgendwie hinzugewinnen.

So hat denn auch der bewährte Richter Gideon, als man ihm die Königswürde antrug, dieses Ansinnen weit von sich gewiesen: "Ich will nicht über euch herrschen, und auch mein Sohn soll nicht über euch herrschen. JHWH soll über euch herrschen" (Ri. 8:33). Die Vorstellung vom Königtum eines Gottes ist im Orient verbreitet, doch tritt

---

[58]Vgl. B. Janowski, "Tempel und Schöpfung", in: Ders., *Gottesgegenwart in Israel*, Neukirchen 1993, 214-246.

[59]Simson (Ri. 13–16) ist kein vertrauenswürdiger 'Richter' mehr, nach ihm machen sich dann vollends chaotische und mörderische Zustände breit (Ri. 17–21), und wiederholt beklagt DtrH, dies sei eben die Zeit gewesen, zu der es noch keinen König gab in Israel (Ri. 17:6; 18:1; 19:1; 21:25). Schliesslich wird die Dominanz der Philister so erdrückend (1 Sam. 4), dass der Leser dringlichst einen Wechsel erhofft. Vgl. dazu Veijola, *Das Königtum*; Dietrich, "Histoire et Loi" (s.o. Anm.5).

[60]In der im vorigen Abschnitt behandelten Tempelbaufrage werden die Verhältnisse zur Richterzeit als vorbildlich hingestellt (2 Sam. 7:5-8); Gott braucht die Könige nicht, auch nicht für den Bau eines Tempels.

der im Himmel thronende Götterkönig kaum je in Konkurrenz zum irdischen Herrscher. In Israel aber erklärt Gott, als der Königswunsch laut wird, dem enttäuschten Samuel: "Nicht dich haben sie verworfen (מאס), sondern mich haben sie verworfen (מאס) vom Königsein über sie" (1 Sam. 8:7). Und als dann Saul in das Amt installiert werden soll, hält Samuel dem Volk noch einmal vor, es habe Jhwh "verworfen" (מאס), der doch ein zuverlässiger Helfer gegen alle Feinde gewesen sei (1 Sam. 10:19).

Jhwh ist also bis zur Staatsgründung König Israels gewesen, danach nicht mehr. Wie lange nicht? Sehr wohl könnte DtrN der Meinung sein, nach dem Untergang der israelitischen Staaten habe Gott seine alte Stelle wieder eingenommen. Aus anderen Quellen ist bekannt, dass in spät- und frühnachexilischer Zeit gewisse Kreise vor allem in der babylonischen Gola die Restauration des davidischen Königtums erhofft und auch betrieben haben.[61] In ihren Ohren dürfte eine Stimme wie die von DtrN nicht sonderlich wohl getönt haben. Immer wieder wird hier herausgestrichen, dass das eigentliche Gegenüber Jhwhs, Träger seiner Verheissungen und auch vorrangiges Objekt seiner Geschichtslenkung nicht das (davidische) Königtum, sondern das Gottesvolk Israel war und ist. Viel stärker als in den älteren Redaktionsschichten tritt bei DtrN ein kollektives, um nicht zu sagen: demokratisches Element in den Vordergrund. Zwar werden Davids Verdienste nicht geleugnet, doch war ihm Erfolg "um des Volkes Israel willen" beschieden (2 Sam. 5:12). Die an ihn ergangene Dynastieverheissung ist nur ein weiteres Glied in der Kette von Heilstaten Jhwhs an Israel (2 Sam. 7:22-24). Die in älteren Textschichten gerade David geltende Mitseins-Formel wird jetzt betont auf das Volk Israel übertragen (1 Kön. 8:57). Das davidische Königtum ist kein Zweck an sich, es hat bestenfalls dienende Funktion für das Volk Israel (2 Sam. 7:10, 11a) oder für Jerusalem und den dortigen Tempel (1 Kön. 11:36) – bzw. *könnte* sie haben, wenn die Könige nicht so oft und gründlich die ihnen gesetzten Ziele verfehlten (2 Kön. 21:7).

Wiederholt werden gerade die Könige als die bezeichnet, die "das Volk zum Sündigen brachten" (חטא hif.: 1 Kön. 15:30; 16:13; 2 Kön. 10:31). Andererseits kann es DtrN in seiner Hochschätzung des Gottesvolkes nicht zulassen, dass dieses lediglich Objekt und nicht viel-

---

[61] Vielleicht darf man bereits den Schluss des Werkes von DtrH, der von der Rehabilitierung des gefangenen Königs Jojachin im Jahr 562 berichtet (2 Kön. 25:27-30), hierher rechnen, jedenfalls aber die Serubbabel-Prophetien bei Haggai und Sacharja. Zwischen dem fünften Nachtgesicht Sach. 4 und der Weissagung Sach. 6:9-15 ist Serubbabel aber – vielleicht auf Anordnung der persischen Zentralmacht – abhanden gekommen.

mehr Subjekt des Sündigens gewesen wäre. Lassen die Königsbeurteilungen von DtrH zuweilen den Eindruck aufkommen, die Schuld am Niedergang und Untergang der Staaten läge allein bei den Königen, so betont DtrN immer wieder die Mitschuld, wenn nicht Hauptschuld des Volkes.

In 1 Kön. 11:33 erklärt der Prophet Ahia dem Jerobeam, warum dem Salomo (bzw. seinem Sohn) nur ein Stamm, Juda, bleiben und die zehn Nordstämme genommen werden sollen: "weil sie mich verlassen haben ... und sie nicht auf meinen Wegen gegangen sind". Die pluralen Verbformen sind im Kontext einigermassen befremdlich;[62] offenbar liegt DtrN daran, die Gründe für die Reichsteilung nicht einzig und allein bei Salomo zu suchen. In 1 Kön. 14 hat Ahia in göttlichem Auftrag das Haus Jerobeams wieder zu verwerfen. DtrN fügt in V.15-16 eine Drohung gegen ganz Israel an und verweist zur Begründung auf Ascheren, die sie, d.h. die Israeliten, angefertigt hätten – ohne dass davon zuvor etwas berichtet worden wäre; auch hier soll nicht der König allein schuld an dem Unheil sein, das über Israel kommt. Hiernach verwundert es nicht mehr, dass in der Schlussreflexion über die Geschichte und den Untergang des Nordreichs gerade DtrN[63] betont von der Schuld aller Israeliten, nicht nur und nicht einmal in erster Linie der Könige redet (2 Kön. 17:12-19). Und damit nichts missverständlich bleibt, heisst es im Abschnitt über Hiskija noch einmal zusammenfassend, der König von Assur habe Israel deportiert, "weil sie nicht auf die Stimme JHWHs, ihres Gottes, gehört und seinen Bund übertreten hatten ...; sie hatten's nicht gehört und nicht getan" (2 Kön. 18:12).

Dementsprechend richtet Samuel eine Alternativpredigt über das Thema Staat und Königtum betont an *Israel*: "Wenn *ihr* nur JHWH fürchtet ... und sowohl *ihr* als auch der König, der über euch herrscht, hinter JHWH bleibt! Wenn *ihr* aber nicht auf JHWHs Stimme hört ..., wird JHWHs Hand gegen *euch* 'und euern König'[64] sein" (1 Sam. 12:14-15). Nach dem vorhin Gesagten ist kaum anzunehmen, dass hier einem *künftigen* Königtum – in nachexilischer Zeit – eine bedingt-positive Perspektive eröffnet würde. Vielmehr hält DtrN die Leserschaft an, das strenge Licht der Selbstprüfung auf das Verhalten des

---

[62]Die Versionen haben sie denn auch in den Singular umgesetzt, doch ist das die lectio facilior. Verblüffenderweise ist am Ende des Verses wieder von "seinem (Salomos) Vater David" die Rede.

[63]Falls man die Unterscheidung beider Schichten in diesem Text aufrechterhalten will, allerdings auch schon DtrH: 2 Kön. 17:7-11.

[64]Die "Väter" des MT machen hier, zumal nach einer futurischen Verbform, keinen Sinn und sind nach LXX zu verbessern.

Volkes während der Epoche des Königtums zu richten: An der Tora-
Treue (bzw. -Untreue) Israels hat sich das Schicksal des Staates entschieden.

DtrN geht indes nicht so weit, dem Königtum alle Verantwortung
für das abzusprechen, was in der Vergangenheit geschehen war und
noch die Gegenwart bestimmte. Im deuteronomischen Königsgesetz
findet sich ein Passus, der dem König schon im vorhinein die Pflicht
auferlegt – nicht so sehr zu regieren, als vielmehr die Tora zu studie-
ren, "damit sich nicht sein Herz erhebe über seine Brüder und damit
er nicht nach rechts oder links abweiche vom Gebot, so dass er lange
auf 'dem Thron'[65] seines Königtums sitze, er und seine Söhne, inmitten Israels" (Dtn. 17:18-20). Es ist bezeichnend, dass die Gefahr des
Königtums in der Selbstüberhebung der Regenten über die "Brüder"
ihres Volkes gesehen wird und dass der Passus mit dem Wort "Israel"
endet!

Es sind demnach keineswegs nur religiöse Verfehlungen, die DtrN
bei den Königen ortet, sondern auch gesellschaftlich-soziale. Das wird
sogleich bei der Inaugurierung des Königtums deutlich. Das stark von
DtrN geprägte Kapitel 1 Sam. 8 enthält in seinem Kern ein offenbar
vor-dtr 'Königsrecht': ein vermutlich recht altes Pamphlet[66] gegen die
sozialen Erschütterungen, die durch die Umgestaltung eines tribalen
Gesellschaftssystems in eine Monarchie hervorgerufen wurden. DtrN
ist offenbar der Meinung, dass dagegen wie gegen religiöse Verirrun-
gen nur eines hilft: unbedingter Gehorsam gegenüber der Tora. Einige wenige Könige, und nur solche aus dem Davidshaus, sind dieser
Forderung annähernd gerecht geworden: David selbst, dazu Salomo
(in seiner Anfangszeit), Asa, Hiskija, Joschija (1 Kön. 3:12; 15:3b-5;
2 Kön. 18:5-7a; 23:24-27) – das ist achtbar, genügt aber bei weitem
nicht, die grundsätzliche Skepsis von DtrN gegen das Königtum aufzu-
wiegen. Gleich der erste König, Saul, wird des Ungehorsams gegen
Gottes Weisung bezichtigt (1 Sam. 13:13-14). Salomo, von Anfang an
und immer wieder über die Konditionen göttlichen Wohlwollens auf-
geklärt (1 Kön. 2:4; 3:14; 9:4), versagt dann doch kläglich (1 Kön.
11:33). Doch die zur Strafe eingesetzten Könige des Nordens genügen
dem Massstab der Tora noch viel weniger. An sich hätte auch Jerobeam I. der Begründer eines בית נאמן werden können – aber nur
bei Einhaltung klarer Bedingungen: "Wenn du auf alles hörst, was
ich dir befehle, und auf meinen Wegen wandelst und das Rechte in

---

[65] Der Samaritanus bietet כסא zusätzlich, was nach der Präposition על als sinn-
voll erscheint.

[66] Veijola, *Das Königtum*, 65-66, wagt es, 1 Sam. 8:11-17 auf die Salomozeit
zurückzuführen.

meinen Augen tust, nämlich meine Anordnungen und Befehle beach-
test, wie es mein Diener David getan hat" (1 Kön. 11:38). Man weiss,
was daraus bei Jerobeam geworden ist, und dass alle seine Nachfolger
die von ihm eingeleitete Fehlentwicklung nicht korrigiert haben. Doch
auch die judäischen Könige verspielten mehr und mehr den Kredit, der
mit der Erwählung Davids (und Jerusalems) eröffnet war. Spätestens
seit Manasse, der sowohl im religiösen wie im sozialen Bereich aufs
schwerste gegen die Tora verstiess (2 Kön. 21:9, 16), war der Untergang auch des Südreichs beschlossene Sache. So wird das Königtum
insgesamt als missglücktes Experiment in der Geschichte Israels hingestellt. Die Wiedererrichtung eines jüdischen Staates, und wäre es
unter davidischer Führung, erscheint nicht als erstrebenswertes Ziel.
Statt dessen liegt alles daran, dass Israel in konzentrierter Ausrich-
tung auf die Tora seine Identität als Gottes Volk neu findet. Darin
liegt seine Zukunft.

John van Seters *Chapel Hill – USA*

In the Babylonian Exile with J

Between Judgment in Ezekiel and Salvation in Second Isaiah

For over 25 years now I have been advocating the view that the non-Priestly corpus of the Tetrateuch, which I call the Yahwist for convenience and lack of a better term, is exilic in date. I have argued that it was a history written to expand the national tradition of the DtrH in order to give an account of Israel's origins and the beginnings of humanity itself. A similar view has been adopted by E. Blum with his conception of a D composition of the Pentateuch,[1] but there are two important differences in our understanding of this non-P material that I want to stress.

The first is that I regard this author as un-Deuteronomistic in certain fundamental ways and therefore it seems misleading to give this work the new label of D composition. This may be demonstrated by a few simple examples. Basic to the Dtr perspective is the view that Deuteronomy is the Torah, the law of Yahweh that is indispensible and the basis of Israel's covenantal relationship with Yahweh. Yet J speaks of a quite different law in Exod. 20:22–23:33 that is the basis of the covenant that follows and he even calls it by the term 'Book of the Covenant', which is language borrowed from Deuteronomy to mean something quite different from the Deuteronomic Code. He also has God inscribe this law of the Covenant Code, and not the Decalogue, on the tablets of stone (Exod. 24:12), the same law that Moses has already written in the scroll. Again Abraham is spoken of by God as the father of his people who will be able to "charge his children and his household after him to keep the way of Yahweh by doing what is right and just" (Gen. 18:19). The language is from Deuteronomy's admonition to fathers to teach their children the Deuteronomic law (Deut. 6:5-9), but Abraham cannot teach his children Deuteronomy. Yet so long as he can teach them what is right and just that is enough for them to receive the promised blessing. And Abraham's own obedience to God's command to sacrifice Isaac is later described by God as obedience to "my charge, my commandments, my statues and my laws" (Gen. 26:5). The language is Dtr, as so many have observed,

---

[1]E. Blum, *Die Komposition der Vätergeschichte* (WMANT, 57), Neukirchen-Vluyn 1984; Idem, *Studien zur Komposition des Pentateuch* (BZAW, 189), Berlin 1990.

but the intention is anything but Dtr. If Abraham's singular act of
obedience is the equivalent of the whole Deuteronomic Code, then
an entirely different perspective is present in this corpus and not the
work of some Dtr redactor who foolishly inserted some phrases in a
most inappropriate place.[2]

The second difference I have with Blum is the dating of this non-
P material to the Persian period and virtually contemporary with P.
The issue is not that two very different works could not arise in the
same period of time, but that this creates a gap between Deuteronomy in the late monarchy and P in the post-exilic reconstruction
with virtually nothing to reflect one of the most creative periods of
Hebrew literature, the time of the Babylonian exile.[3] The dating of
the D composition to the Persian period may be convenient for Blum's
theory about the creation of the Pentateuch as a compromise document, but it has nothing else to tie it to this period. On the contrary,
it is the special impact of the exilic environment so clearly reflected
in J that transforms the national tradition of the DtrH, giving it a
radically new perspective.

Perhaps the best window that we have on the Babylonian Golah
between the first exile in 598 BCE and the "liberation" of Babylon by
Cyrus that permitted the return, is that given by the two prophets
Ezekiel and Second Isaiah, the one at the beginning of this period
and the other at the end. It is my thesis that the Yahwist fits into
this period between these two prophets, responding to the theological
perspectives and issues dealt with by Ezekiel and his school, while
at the same time providing an extended tradition of sacred history
for Second Isaiah, his close contemporary. It is not possible in the
limited scope of this one paper to lay out all the intricacies of these
two prophecies and then compare them with J as this topic requires.
So I will have to be selective in my sketch, and rely on some previous
treatment of topics for greater detail. It will be enough merely to show
that the relationship of J to the exilic prophets is extensive and that
J addresses many of the same pressing issues that preoccupied these
prophets in the stress and ferment of the Babylonian Golah.

---

[2]Dtr clearly condemns child sacrifice (Deut. 18:10; 2 Kgs 16:3; 17:17; 21:6;
23:10; Jer. 32:35) so it is very unlikely that he would commend Abraham's willingness to sacrifice Isaac in such a strong way.

[3]This gap is not filled in my view by numerous editions of the DtrH (DtrG,
DtrP, DtrN, etc.). The whole Dtr corpus belongs within the early exilic period.

1   Ezekiel and J

Ezekiel's prophecy, coming as it does after the first military catastrophe of 598 BCE and focused on the second in 587, both as an
imminent threat and then as a reality, "is entirely concentrated upon
the reality of disaster" and "is concerned in this situation to justify
the ways of God to man".[4] In his effort to do so Ezekiel is both heavily
indebted to tradition and wildly creative.[5] On the one hand, Ezekiel
stands in the tradition of the Jerusalem priesthood and this has called
forth much discussion about his relationship to the Priestly corpus of
the Pentateuch. That is not a topic that I will deal with here. On the
other hand, Ezekiel is also in debt to the prior prophetic tradition,
especially Jeremiah, from which he borrows rather liberally and with
the freedom to reshape it for his own purposes. In addition, he is
also a strong adherent of the Deuteronomic reform and shares with
it a number of its concerns and language, without, however, being a
Deuteronomist. I emphasize this point at the outset because Ezekiel's
relationship to the large body of literary tradition that had accumu-
lated by the end of the monarchy is a useful model when we come
to consider the relationship of J to Deuteronomy and to the prior
prophetic tradition, especially Ezekiel.

The call of Ezekiel stands in the tradition of both Isaiah 6 and
Jeremiah 1. From Isaiah comes the context of the theophany in a
sacred place (?) and the emphasis on Yahweh's 'glory' (כָּבוֹד), as well
as the theme of 'obduracy' in the rejection of the message. From
Jeremiah comes the theme of placing words in the prophet's mouth
as well as warnings not to be a complaining prophet (like Jeremiah).
The call of Moses by J in Exod. 3–4 is a complex literary construction
that draws upon a number of different sources and traditions, all
of which cannot be discussed here.[6] Yet to pick just one example,
in the theme of Moses' objections, scholars have clearly identified
the similarity with Jeremiah, especially in the matter of their shared
inability to speak, and the motif of God's/Moses' placing words in
the mouth. However, the speech difficulty is different in Moses' case
(an impediment) from that of Jeremiah (his youth). God's response
to Moses is that he can give a person speech or make him dumb. In
Ezek. 3:26-27, Ezekiel too is unable to speak from the time of his call

---

[4] P.R. Ackroyd, *Exile and Restoration* (OTL), London 1968, 104.

[5] See W. Zimmerli, "The Message of the Prophet of Ezekiel", *Interpretation* 23
(1969), 136-8.

[6] See J. van Seters, *Life of Moses: The Yahwist as Historian in Exodus-
Numbers*, Louisville, KY & Kampen 1995, 35-63.

onwards unless God gives him the power to speak the divine word.[7]
It seems that J has taken over from the Ezekiel tradition this motif
of a speech impediment and combined it with the complaint motif of
Jeremiah.

Ezekiel is a prophet of judgment who justifies the divine activity
by the use of the so-called *Erweiswort* ('word of demonstration'): "and
you/they shall know that I am Yahweh",[8] with some variations. It is
through these acts of judgment as announced in the name of Yahweh
that he reveals himself to his people. This *Erweiswort* is likewise used
in the oracles against the nations, particularly in the collection against
Egypt in chs. 29-32 ("Then all who live in Egypt will know that I am
Yahweh"), as a response to the Pharaoh's hubris.

Now in J's story of Moses' (and Aaron's) confrontation of Pharaoh
requesting the people's release Pharaoh responds in arrogance: "Who
is Yahweh, that I should heed his voice, and let Israel go?" (Exod.
5:2) The plagues that follow are a series of divine judgments that are
meant to answer this question. Within the plagues we have a number
of examples of the *Erweiswort* or modifications on it (Exod. 7:17; 8:6
[10], 18 [22]; 9:14, 29) by which the Egyptians come to know that
Yahweh is the source of judgment, but also that there is none other
like him, that he is present in the land, and that the whole earth
belongs to him. This is certainly a creative expansion of Ezekiel's
Erweiswort. The plagues also function in a positive way as signs of
God's salvation to his people, and here too the *Erweiswort* is used:
"Thus you (the Israelites) will know that I am Yahweh" (10:2). This
form of prophetic speech in J is borrowed directly from Ezekiel.[9]

Ezekiel's treatment of the history of Israel in the exodus and the
wilderness in Ezek. 20 invites comparison with J.[10] It must be stated

---

[7]As Zimmerli has pointed out ("Message", 149-50), originally the motif of
Ezekiel's dumbness belonged to the narrative about the fall of the city of Jerusalem
in Ezek. 33:21-22. The account suggests that Yahweh made the prophet dumb the
evening before the messenger arrived and that it was only in the morning that
God restored his power of speech. Yet, someone of the Ezekiel school has read this
event back into the call narrative in Ezek. 3:26-27. J's version, therefore, depends
upon this development within the Ezekiel school.

[8]Zimmerli, "Message", 147-9; also Idem, "Erkenntnis Gottes nach dem Buche
Ezechiel", in: Idem, *Gottes Offenbarung* (TB, 19), München 1963, 41-119; Idem,
"Das Wortes des göttlichen Selbsterweises (Erweiswort), eine prophetische Gat-
tung", in: Zimmerli, *Gottes Offenbarung* , 120-32.

[9]Zimmerli ("Erkenntnis Gottes", 61-6) has some difficulty explaining how this
formula so distinctive of Ezekiel and later works can be present in the 'early'
sources of the Pentateuch. For a critique of Zimmerli on this point see H.H.
Schmid, *Der sogennante Jahwist*, Zürich 1976, 50.

[10]In the recent article by C. Patton, "'I Myself Gave them Laws that Were Not

at the outset that it is hard to see how Ezekiel could have had a copy
of J in front of him. There is an original revelation to the people in
Egypt, but not through Moses, and a promise for the first time to
give them a land that he had chosen for them, but no prior promise
to the patriarchs. There is a reference to the worship of foreign gods
by Israel in Egypt which threatened their existence, about which J
says nothing. The deliverance in Ezekiel is referred to only in the
"bringing Israel out of Egypt" with no reference to a sea event, or
plagues or the role of Moses. The wilderness is a record of continuous
disobedience against God's laws and the desecration of the sabbaths,
but no Sinai.

I think it is possible to account for J's development of the tradition, beyond that of Ezekiel. J clearly accepts the theme of continuous
disobedience as presented in the murmuring tradition, but in place of
the Israelite apostasy in Egypt before the exodus, J uses Deuteronomy's account of the apostasy after Horeb (Sinai) as an alternative
(Deut. 9:7–10:10; cf. Exod. 32).[11] At the same time J could make use
of the divine provisions in the wilderness enumerated in Deut. 8:2-4,
14-16, placing these before Sinai. For J the problem of the Israelites
in Egypt was not the worship of other gods but their lack of faith
in the revelation of their imminent deliverance from their oppressors.
Such talk of deliverance by the prophet Moses made life difficult for
them and they only wanted to be left alone (Exod. 5). The plagues
then become signs that Yahweh is who he says he is and can deliver
them. The divine threat of destruction is directed at the Egyptians,
not the Israelites as in Ezekiel.

Likewise, the treatment of the wilderness period by Ezekiel in comparison with J is noteworthy in a number of respects. First, Ezekiel
suggests that there was a continuous pattern of disobedience over
two generations in which the total destruction of the people was
threatened, but in which Yahweh relented on a number of success-
ive occasions "for the honor of my name that it might not be pro-
phaned among the nations ..." (20:9, 14, 22). This is a major theme
of Ezekiel, often in close association with the *Erweiswort*, and occurs
elsewhere as the reason for future hope and a new beginning (see also
36:16ff).[12] Once it is said that Yahweh relented out of pity and reluct-

---

Good': Ezekiel 20 and the Exodus Traditions", *JSOT* 69 (1996), 73-90, the author
assumes that all the Pentateuchal traditions are older than Ezekiel and that the
parallels all point to dependence of Ezekiel on various parts of the Pentateuch.
For the present discussion it is not helpful.

[11] Deut. 9:7 actually suggests continuous disobedience "from the day you left
Egypt until now (Moab)" and so may have Ezekiel in mind.

[12] Zimmerli, "Message", 154; also G. von Rad, *Old Testament Theology*, vol. 2,
Edinburgh & London 1965, 236-7.

ance to wipe them out and warned their children against continuing in their fathers' evil ways (20:17-20), a motif that fits well with the theme of ch. 18 where the children are not to be punished for their fathers' sins and God does not desire the death of anyone.

The pattern of threat and forgiveness is similar to that of punishment for apostasy, repentance and deliverance in Judges (DtrH), with similar concerns about the keeping of laws and the rejection of idolatry. But it stands even closer to the Yahwist's murmuring stories. The Yahwist has made this colorless series from Ezekiel into a number of quite specific murmuring stories from the golden calf episode onwards. Furthermore, he has incorporated the motif of not destroying the people because it might bring dishonor to Yahweh's name into Moses' prayer of intercession on two occasions (Exod. 32:11-13; Num. 14:13-16; cf. Deut. 9:28), along with other arguments not in Ezekiel,[13] suggesting that it was Moses' intercession that was responsible for Yahweh's decision to forgive his people. Ezekiel also states that it was already in the wilderness that Yahweh predicted that the people would one day experience the dispersion because of their disobedience to his laws (Ezek. 20:23-24). This too is included by J in God's concluding remark to Moses in the golden calf episode: "But a day of judgment will come when I shall punish them for their sin" (Exod. 32:34b).

The Yahwist also gives far greater prominence to the element of divine mercy and forgiveness. In Moses' prayer to Yahweh in Exod. 32:31-32, he suggests that if God is not willing to forgive the people, then God should also blot out Moses' name from the book that Yahweh has written, to which the deity responds that only the one who has sinned will be blotted out of God's book. To what could this book refer? Ezekiel, in his diatribe against false prophets, speaks about their names being excluded from a registry of the future citizens of Israel who will return to the land.[14] It is only such a notion that makes sense here in Moses' prayer and refers to those who will or will not reach the promised land. The motif is either borrowed directly from Ezekiel or was a current exilic concept.

Ezekiel also makes the rather remarkable statement about God giving the people laws in the wilderness that were not good and regulations by which they could not live, i.e., the command to sacrifice

---

[13] J adds the motivation of the promises to the patriarchs (Exod. 32:13) and the theme of God's forgiving nature (Num. 14:17-19; cf. Exod. 34:6-7) which is a considerable elaboration on Ezekiel's statement of divine pity (Ezek. 20:17).

[14] See Von Rad, *Theology* 2, 234.

their first-born sons. This must relate to a practice of child sacrifice
in the late monarchy which became associated with the wilderness
legislation.[15] It is not part of the firstlings law in Deuteronomy, but
it does have a parallel in the law specifically commanded by Moses in
Exod. 22:28b [29b]. In J's revision in Exod. 13:11-16 (see also 34:19-
20), however, the law has been modified to require the redemption of
the first-born sons by animal sacrifice. It hardly seems possible that
Ezekiel knew of the law in this modified version.[16]

A prominent feature of Ezekiel's wilderness portrait is the giving
of laws and sabbaths (pl.) in the wilderness. Likewise in Deuteronomy,
God gave Israel laws by which the people might live, but nothing is
said about the sabbaths, except the one law in the Decalogue. Exod.
16, however, contains an account of the institution of the sabbath
(sg.) in the wilderness by J, overlaid by P but discernable in 16:1a,
2-7, 13b-15, 21, 27-31, 35a.[17] The sabbath's origin is connected in a
creative way by J to the giving of manna, derived from Deut. 8:3,
such that according to God's instructions, his תּוֹרָה, the people would
receive manna six days but not on the seventh. To allow for this they
would be able to gather twice as much on the sixth day. All of this was
to be a test "to see whether they follow my תּוֹרָה or not." Moses (and
Aaron) further declare that by means of the event "you will know
that it was Yahweh who brought you out of Egypt", a variation of
the *Erweiswort* (Exod. 16:6-7).

Of course, the manna came and the people gathered it as instruc-
ted. But on the seventh day some went out to gather manna when
there was none. This brought the response from Yahweh: "How long
will the people refuse to obey my commands and laws?" (Exod. 16:28).
For J this event becomes the discovery of the seventh day sabbath
and the reason for its existence as a test of identity with the people of
Yahweh. This institution of a seventh-day sabbath is a major development of the exilic period. J's story is a very creative filling out of
a detail in Ezekiel in combination with Deuteronomy's manna motif.
The development could hardly be in the other direction.

---

[15] The issue of child-sacrifice is a hotly debated topic which cannot be reviewed
here. For the literature and a brief review see C. Houtman, *Das Bundesbuch:
Ein Kommentar*, Leiden 1997, 241-55. See especially J.D. Levenson, *The Death
and Resurrection of the Beloved Son*, New Haven & London 1993, 3-17. Levenson
argues, in my view correctly, against those who reject the possibility of child
sacrifice in the late monarchy period.

[16] The same applies to the statements in Jer. 19:5-6 and Mic. 6:7. So also Levenson, *The Death and Resurrection*, 11.

[17] See the discussion in my *Life of Moses*, 181-91.

A major problem that Ezekiel and his contemporaries in the Golah had to face was the lack of the divine presence associated with the
temple in Jerusalem and symbolized by the 'glory' (כָּבוֹד) of Yahweh.
In this respect Ezekiel was fully committed to the Deuteronomic reform. Yet with the imminent destruction of the temple and because of
its pollution, Ezekiel witnesses in a vision the departure of the glory
from the temple. With this Ezekiel also receives the assurance that
in the lands of the dispersion God would still be a small sanctuary
(מִקְדָּשׁ) to them (11:16).[18] We do not know what this sanctuary en-
tailed or what Ezekiel's role in its activity was in Babylonia. There
is no indication that it involved much cultic activity. Zimmerli specu-
lates that it was the locus for his vision of the כָּבוֹד.[19]

The Yahwist is also preoccupied with the issue of the divine presence, especially as a consequence of the people's apostasy in the worship of the golden calf (Exod. 32–34).[20] Yet, in the middle of an
extended theological discussion about God's presence there is a brief
description of a little sanctuary, the Tent of Meeting, which is without
a priesthood, and only one attendant, Joshua, besides Moses. Yet it
was the place where the pillar of cloud (J's form of the כָּבוֹד) appeared
and where the deity spoke with Moses. It was also the place where
one 'enquired of Yahweh' (Exod. 33:7-11).[21] J's Tent of Meeting, both
small and temporary, is Ezekiel's מִקְדָּשׁ in the diaspora.

It has been observed by Zimmerli, Von Rad and others how Ezekiel
stands apart from the earlier classical prophets by his emphasis on the
spirit as the motivation for his activity.[22] This is often understood as
an archaism in its similarity to such prophets as Elijah and Elisha.
But if so, Ezekiel's emphasis on the spirit is in an altogether different
direction, having to do with the delivery of the word of the deity, and
in this he also has many followers. In J's presentation of Moses as
prophet he says little about spirit possession, but in the story of the
appointment of the 70 elders in Num. 11:16-17, 24-30, a portion of
Moses' spirit is sufficient to cause them all to prophecy ecstatically.
The assumption by J is that great prophets like Moses are motivated
by the spirit of God. For the rest Moses does not resemble Ezekiel.

---

[18] Or perhaps a sanctuary "for a short time". The term מְעַט is ambiguous.

[19] Zimmerli, "Message", 138-9.

[20] See my *Life of Moses*, 319-60.

[21] I have likewise argued in another place that the burning bush of Exod. 3
represents a menorah, and the sound of the shofar on Mount Sinai, the voice of
God, so that when these are used in a simple sanctuary they symbolize the divine
presence, as they did later in the synagogue.

[22] Zimmerli, "Message", 134-6.

The case for Balaam, however, is altogether different. Here Ezekiel is very likely the prophetic model.[23] Ezekiel is often presented as standing in a certain place and facing in a certain direction to utter his oracles (Ezek. 6:1; 13:17; 21:2, 7; 25:2) and this is a feature of Balaam's oracles (Num. 22:41; 23:13; 24:2). Balaam also utters his oracles when inspired by the spirit (24:2), and, like Ezekiel, the words are placed in his mouth and he insists that he can only speak what Yahweh permits him to say. Balaam tells Balak: "See, I have come to you. Have I now any power to say anything? The word that Yahweh places in my mouth, that I can speak" (Num. 22:38). The motifs here are from Ezekiel. Balaam, like Ezekiel, is also visited by delegations who want him to give one kind of message, but instead he is compelled to give another. Balaam's oracles even use imagery that in style and in particular details are very similar to those of Ezekiel.[24]

Ezekiel and the Yahwist also share some traditions about the earliest pre-history of Israel as reflected in Genesis. Scholars have long noted the close association between the oracle against Tyre in Ezek. 28:12-19 and the Garden of Eden story in Gen. 2–3 and have debated the relationship between the two. But it is only recently that a newly discovered myth about the creation of the king has made clear the priority of the Ezekiel version over that of Genesis and J's dependence upon Ezekiel. I have dealt with this in another place and will not repeat myself here.[25]

Ezekiel also mentions Noah, although not specifically in connection with the flood (14:12-20). He is included with Job and Daniel as an example of a very righteous person. The argument is that even if these three righteous persons were in the land that was under divine judgment, they would not be able to save it or any other persons, including sons and daughters, but only themselves. This may work for the biblical story of Job but not for Noah because he does save his family! According to J, Noah's wife, his three sons and their wives are all included in the ark, even though the story speaks only of the righteousness of Noah.[26] The argument in Ezek. 14:12-20 goes together with that of ch. 18 in which it is argued that the righteousness of the father, as well as the sins of the father, are not passed on from

---

[23]Zimmerli ("Message", 136) observes some of these similarities but does not draw the same conclusions.

[24]See H. Rouillard, *La péricope de Balaam (Nombres 22–24): La prose et les 'oracles'* (EtB, 4), Paris 1985, 363-4; Van Seters, *Life of Moses*, 426-7.

[25]Van Seters, *Prologue to History*, 119-22; Idem, "The Creation of Man and the Creation of the King", *ZAW* 101 (1989), 333-42.

[26]It may be that Ezekiel knows a version of the story in which Noah and his wife alone go into the ark, as in the Greek version of the myth.

one generation to another. It is interesting that in J God says to Noah (Gen. 7:1): "Go into the ark, you and all your household; for you alone have I found to be righteous before me **in this generation**." The story of Sodom and Gomorrah addresses the same issue, especially in the dialogue between Abraham and God. Von Rad has already pointed out the close association between the discussion in Ezekiel and Gen. 18:16-33.[27] The issue is not about just one righteous person within a nation, or generation, as in the flood story, but about whether any number of righteous persons can avert disaster. In the story of the destruction in ch. 19 there is only **one** righteous person, Lot, and he is made a prophet of doom who is allowed to persuade and rescue his entire extended family if they will heed him. In the end he succeeds in saving only his two daughters. The basic unit of the faith community for J is not the nation as a whole, as in the Deuteronomic threat of judgment, nor is it just the individual, as in Ezekiel, but the "patriarchal" family unit. This also comes out in the post-Dtr text of Josh. 24:15, in which Joshua challenges the people:

> "If you do not want to serve Yahweh, choose for yourselves today whom you will serve, whether the gods of your forefathers in Mesopotamia or the gods of the Amorites in whose land you dwell, but I and my household will serve Yahweh."[28]

This patriarchal family unit not only makes Abraham the model of the righteous parent who instructs his offspring and household in the way of Yahweh and how to do what is right and just (Gen. 18:19), but as ancestor and head of household his righteousness and obedience is able to bring about the promised destiny to his descendents (Gen. 22:15-18; 26:3-5). It is not just any righteous person that can save the nation from disaster, not even a king like David, as in DtrH (1 Kgs 11:34-39), but only the first ancestor and father of the people.

This raises the question of Ezekiel's attitude to the patriarch Abraham as reflected in 33:24. The inhabitants of Judah who were left in the land after the second exile of 586 BCE laid claim to it as the rightful heirs of the patriarch Abraham. Their statement attests to the existence of a pre-exilic tradition about the ancestor Abraham 'inheriting' the land, but Ezekiel clearly understands this tradition as distinct from, and at variance with, the conditional appropriation of

---

[27]G. von Rad, *Old Testament Theology*, vol. 1, New York 1962, 394-5.

[28]See also the story of Rahab in Josh. 2. I am inclined to attribute both texts to J.

the land as set forth in the Deuteronomistic tradition, and it is only those who survive in the exile who will inherit the land (33:25-29; 36). The whole discussion would surely have been entirely different if the Abraham tradition used by the Judeans and known to Ezekiel had contained the call of Abraham from Mesopotamia and the bringing up of the patriarch from Ur of the Chaldeans, i.e., the land of the exiles.

With Second Isaiah, however, the matter is altogether different. It is precisely because Abraham was "taken from the ends of the earth and called from its farthest corners" (i.e., Mesopotamia), that the patriarchs can serve as models of hope for the exiles in particular (Isa. 41:8-9). This theme of Abraham's call and blessing is picked up again in Isa. 51:1-2, where it seem to refer quite specifically to the Yahwist's presentation in Gen. 12:1-3. The change in the role of the patriarchal traditions between Ezekiel and Second Isaiah can only be explained by J's history, which comes between the two.[29]

2 Second Isaiah and J

This brings us to the further comparison of Second Isaiah with J, and here I wish to argue the thesis that it is the 'publication' of J's work that accounts for much of the difference between Ezekiel and Second Isaiah. This is already evident in the treatment of the patriarchal promises, as we have seen. But it is equally evident in the greatly extented stage of world history beyond that of the DtrH, reaching back to creation and inclusive of all the nations as the arena of Yahweh's activity. The parallels to the details of J's historical account are now quite precise and numerous, and the role of Moses in J gives legitimation to the prophecy of salvation in Second Isaiah that was so problematic in Jeremiah and Ezekiel.

To take up this last point, it is well recognized that the burden of Second Isaiah's message is no longer concerned with obedience to God's laws and the threat of punishment, but faith in Yahweh's ability and willingness to deliver his people from their present situation and belief that Second Isaiah has received such a revelation from God.[30] Second Isaiah must counter the former emphasis on divine judgment and the complete discouragement of the people to convince them of his true calling as a prophet with this revelation of hope from Yahweh. Likewise in J, Moses is commissioned as a prophet of judgment

---

[29]See Van Seters, "Confessional Reformulation in the Exilic Period", *VT* 22 (1972), 448-59; Idem, *Prologue to History*, 227-45.

[30]See Von Rad, *Theology*, 2, 249; P.R. Ackroyd, *Exile and Restoration*, 123-4; R.N. Whybray, *Isaiah 40-66* (NCeB), London 1975, 32-4.

only for Pharaoh and the Egyptians, but for the Israelites he is a
prophet of salvation. Moses' objections, while similar in form to those
of Jeremiah, do not have to do with an unpopular message of judgment, but how he will be able to get the people to believe that he
has received a message of deliverance from God and to have faith
in Yahweh's imminent deliverance (Exod. 3:13–4:17). This theme of
believing in Yahweh and in Moses as his prophet becomes a *leitmotif*
of the Yahwist's presentation (4:29-31; 5:20–6:1; 14:10-14, 30-31).

Second Isaiah is the first prophet to make use of the theme of
creation as a way of introducing into prophecy an entirely new understanding of the nature of Yahweh.[31] A reason for the appeal to creation may have been due to the shift from the parochial situation of
the Judean homeland to the new environment of Babylonian religion
and culture and the temptation for the exiles to assimilation within
it.[32] Ezekiel makes use of a creation myth in his diatribe against Tyre
(Ezek. 28:12-19), but this was quite in isolation from his treatment of
Israel's origins and relationship to Yahweh. Ezekiel also makes use of
ברא in a reference to Ammon, "in the place where you were created
(ברא niph.), the land of your origin (מכרה)" (21:35 [30]), and this is
parallel to his treatment of the primeval 'origin' (מכרה) of Jerusalem
as a birth to primordial ancestors (16:3). So it is likely that ברא could
have had the sense of ancestral origin as well as creation.[33] But the
concepts play no positive role in Ezekiel.

With Second Isaiah, however, the matter is altogether different.
Yahweh as creator has now become a basic way of speaking about
Israel's origins, the object of Yahweh's attention and concern. It expresses the reason for both his willingness and ability to 'redeem'
Israel from its enforced exile in Babylonia. Second Isaiah's terms relating to Yahweh's creation, election and redemption come together
in Isa. 43:1:

"And now, thus says Yahweh, the one who created (ברא)
you, Jacob, the one who formed (יצר) you, Israel: 'fear not,
for I have redeemed (גאל) you; I have called (קרא) you by
my name, you are mine'."[34]

---

[31]See Von Rad, *Theology*, 2, 241-2; H.E. von Waldow, "The Message of Deutero-
Isaiah", *Interpretation* 22 (1968), 259-87, esp. 277-8; Whybray, *Isaiah 40-66*, 36-7;
P.B. Harner, "Creation Faith in Deutero-Isaiah", *VT* 17 (1967), 298-306.

[32]Von Rad, *Theology*, 2, 241.

[33]The rendering of בְּמְקוֹם אֲשֶׁר־נִבְרֵאת in REB as "in the place where you were
born" has much to commend it.

[34]Following the reading of BHS.

There was a tendency in the past, beginning with Von Rad,[35] to identify all of these references to the creation or forming of Israel as merely ways of speaking about the election of Israel through the exodus event and so to regard the theme of creation in Second Isaiah as ancilliary to that of the redemptive event of deliverance from Egypt. There can be no dispute regarding the importance of the exodus theme in this prophet, but such a way of characterizing the creation theme in Second Isaiah has obscured its character and understanding.[36] First of all, while the designation of God as 'redeemer' (גאל) and his act of redemption is frequently mentioned throughout Second Isaiah, it is only rather rarely brought into conjunction with the theme of God as creator, as above and in 54:5, and when they are used together it is to suggest that God as creator is able to redeem his people. Redemption has reference primarily to the present situation of release from exile and only occasionally by analogy with the past event of the exodus.

When one compares the language used of the creation theme with J, there is a striking similarity in the use of יצר 'to form' as descriptive of the act of creation of humankind by J and Israel by Second Isaiah. While the verb can be used to refer to the act of creation as a whole, using the image of the potter shaping clay, it can also refer specifically to God's forming one in the womb. And since ברא can also have this double sense of referring to ancestral origins by genealogical descent, it is very likely that the prophet is thinking primarily of God's creation and election through the ancestors. This is supported by the exhortation in 51:1-2:

> "Consider the rock from which you were hewn and the quarry from which you were cut; consider Abraham your father and Sarah who gave you birth! When he was only one I called him and blessed him and made him many."

The theme of Israel's origins as they are reflected in J's treatment of Yahweh as the creator and the establishment of a historical continuity between this creator deity and the election and blessing of the patriarchs, the origins of the people, provides the new basis for Second Isaiah's message. It is failure to see the juxtaposition of J's historical construction and Second Isaiah's message that has obscured the prophet's references to the people's origins. This was perhaps all the

---

[35] Von Rad, "Das theologische Problem des alttestamentlichen Schöpfungsglaubens", in: *Gesammelte Studien zum Alten Testament* (TB, 8), München 1958, 136-47.

[36] See esp. the useful critique by Harner, "Creation Faith", 298-307.

more important because of Ezekiel's prior denegration of such origins (Ezek. 16).

However, it is not just concerning Israel's origins that Second Isaiah employs the language of creation. The subject of Yahweh as the one and only creator and therefore the one that is in control of all of the affairs of humankind is the major concern of the disputation speeches. Second Isaiah uses arguments having to do with the proof of prophecy and the misrepresentation of the creator by the use of idols as the work of men's hands to deny that any other god but Yahweh can claim to be the one creator deity. I will not elaborate on these well-known arguments, but focus rather on two other points that are of interest for my topic.

The first is the way in which the prophet uses the divine name. As in Ezekiel and in J, Yahweh acts for his name sake to preserve his honor (Isa. 48:9-11). For this reason Yahweh was long suffering and would not let his name be profaned or yield his glory to another god. This becomes the reason for his deliverance from the exile, just as it was in his prior rescue in the wilderness, according to J. Similarly, the extended remarks about Cyrus in Isa. 45:1-7 are actually an *Erweis-wort*: "so that you may know that I am Yahweh" (v. 3), and, "so that from the east to the west all may know there is none besides me: I am Yahweh" (v. 6). There is also constant reference to the declaration of identity: "I am Yahweh", both in the context of judgment but also directed at Israel as a word of salvation.[37]

This statement of identity, however, is developed in a number of interesting ways by this prophet. Thus, the statement in Isa. 41:4: "I am Yahweh, the first one, and with the final ones I am he", contains a certain play upon the meaning of the declaration formula, "I am Yahweh". Here it is paralleled with the phrase, "I am he (אֲנִי הוּא). The same kind of language play occurs in 42:8; 43:10-13, 25; 46:4; 48:12; 51:12. Closely associated with this identification, "I am he", is the claim to being the one supreme being. Ackroyd sees in this usage of אֲנִי הוּא "a phrase which strongly suggests an attempt at theological explanation of the divine name as being equivalent to the personal pronoun, so that just as Exod. 3:14 provides us with the interpretation אֶהְיֶה (I am), Second Isaiah appears to understand the divine name Yahweh as meaning 'He', i.e., 'The one' or 'He who is'."[38]

---

[37]See also the remarks of Zimmerli, "Erkenntnis Gottes", 69-71; Idem, "Der Wahrheitserweis Jahwes nach der Botschaft der beiden Exilspropheten", in: *Studien zur alttestamentlichen Theologie und Prophetie* (TB, 51), München 1974, 192-212.

[38]Ackroyd, *Exile and Restoration*, 133.

We can, in fact, go even further and say that in Exod. 3:14-15 J makes two assertions about the name of Yahweh which Moses is to present to the people as the basis for their hope in the imminent deliverance. The one is that the name Yahweh means the one deity who exists, 'he who is', and is the one who sent Moses to them. The second is that Yahweh is the god of their ancestors, Abraham, Isaac and Jacob. This same revelation of the divine name in these two aspects is what we also find in Second Isaiah and not earlier.

Also of special interest here is Second Isaiah's use of the term אֵל for Israel's deity, because there was a strong tradition in the Levant that El was a creator deity, and the connection with creation is explicitly made in Isa. 42:5. The references to the term אֵל are rather sparse in the earlier prophets. In Ezekiel it occurs only in conjunction with the oracles against Tyre (Ezek. 28:2, 9) where it could be understood to refer to the principal Phoenician god El. In Second Isaiah the term אֵל appears in the self-declaration formula: "I am El" (43:12; 46:12) in statements that are parallel to those that use the other declaration formulas: "I am Yahweh" or "I am he". This can only suggest that an identity is being made between Yahweh and El as the supreme and sole creator deity.

The identity between Yahweh and El is also reflected in a number of texts in J of Genesis and in the past this has been given a variety of explanations in terms of Israel's religious history. We need not review these here.[39] They all rest upon the early dating of J which I would reject. Furthermore, it is quite clear from the Balaam oracles that J identifies Yahweh with El, where the names occur side by side. There is, however, an interesting use of the term אֵל in the Jacob story that calls for some comment here. In a closely related series of texts J uses the designation, with the article (Gen. 31:13; 35:1, 3; 46:2) where in the parallel accounts the name of Yahweh is otherwise used. Taken together it seems clear that J is making an identity between 'the El' and Yahweh. The assignment of these Genesis texts to an E source has been quite misleading and has completely obscured this identity.

Now, it seems to me significant that in Isa. 42:5, in the introduction to an oracle we find:

> "Thus says the El (הָאֵל), Yahweh, who created the heav-
> ens and stretched them out, who fashioned the earth and
> whatever grows up on it, who gives breath to the people
> upon it and spirit to those who walk on it."

---

[39] See J. van Seters, "The Religion of the Patriarchs in Genesis", *Bib.* 61 (1980), 220-33.

Here we have the same identity between הָאֵל and Yahweh that we
have in J in Genesis. The meaning of this identity is clear. The term
הָאֵל means the one supreme being, the creator deity who is also the
god of the patriarchs, the god of Jacob and Israel's god. The reference
to this god in Second Isaiah as the one who gives 'breath' (נְשָׁמָה) to
the people is a clear allusion to Gen. 2:7 in which God inspires Adam
with the breath of life.

Now it may be noted that Second Isaiah uses the term ברא as
a favorite term for the act of creation, along with יצר and עשׂה, and
this is not a term used in J's account of creation. Nevertheless, it is
not a term unknown before Second Isaiah, since it is used in Ezek.
21:35; 28:13, 15; Deut. 4:32 and even elsewhere in J, Exod. 34:10;
Num. 16:30. The usage in J is particularly significant in that ברא suggests the intervention by divine activity in human affairs of something
completely new. This comes out in Exod. 34:10:

> "Yahweh said to Moses (LXX): 'I am about to make a
> covenant, In front of all your people I will perform a won-
> der that has not been created (ברא niph.) in all the earth
> or among any peoples. And all the people in whose midst
> you are living will see the work of Yahweh, for it is an
> awesome thing that I am doing with you'."

This same use of ברא in Second Isaiah can be seen in 48:6-7:

> "From now on I am announcing to you new things, hidden
> things that you did not know. Now they are created (ברא
> niph.) and not formerly, before today you had not heard
> of them."

And the new event referred to is the miraculous deliverance of the
people in their wilderness journey in which all their needs will be
provided for as outlined in 41:17-20 which concludes with the *Erweiswort*:

> "So that they (everyone) may see and know, and set it
> down and understand that the hand of Yahweh has done
> this, the Holy One of Israel its creation (ברא)."

It is clear from these texts that the J text in Exod. 34:10 belongs
to the same set of ideas and the same form of speech and language
as that of Second Isaiah. For J the renewal of the covenant after the
apostasy of the calf will be the newly created wonder and a direct

parallel to his own situation. The reference to "all the people (sg.) amongst whom you are living" must mean J's current environment in the Babylonian exile.

The treatment of the exodus and wilderness wanderings tradition in Second Isaiah is altogether different from that of Ezekiel, because Second Isaiah wants to accentuate the positive as the model for his portrait of the new deliverance. Even so he alludes to details that are drawn from J's account of the exodus. In the various references to the exodus Second Isaiah is emphatic that the new exodus will be far different from, and far superior to, the previous event and much of his description is meant to contrast with the portrayal in J. This can be seen in Isa. 52:11-12:

> "Depart, depart, leave from there (Babylon), do not touch anything unclean. Leave from its midst, keep yourselves pure, you who are to carry the vessels of Yahweh. For you will not leave in haste, nor go as fugitives, because Yahweh will go before you and the God of Israel will be your rearguard."

There are several points of contact with J's version of the exodus here. In J's story the Israelites did leave with silver and gold vessels belonging to the Egyptians (Exod. 12:35-36), and it may be that Second Isaiah wants to avoid a similar occurrence among the departing exiles for fear that the objects may be 'unclean' and a temptation to apostasy. The reference to haste and flight in Second Isaiah is also found in J in the same context in Exod. 12:31-34, 39. For Second Isaiah there will be no need for such flight because of the divine protection. Yet J too emphasizes the theme of divine protection in the form of the pillar of cloud and fire which formed the guide and protection before them (Exod. 13:21-22) and in the sea story could also serve as their rearguard (14:19-20). The pillar of cloud and fire in J is also a kind of travelling theophany, and such a theophanic presence is also assumed to accompany the exiles on their journey in Second Isaiah.

3 Conclusion

I have argued in this brief sketch that Ezekiel and Second Isaiah can be used as a controlling framework of concerns and perspectives in the exilic period into which the work of the Yahwist can be fitted. For this purpose we may investigate the 'intertextuality' among these various works and establish the appropriate diachronic relationship

within this group in the same way, for instance, that one can explain
the literary connection between Jeremiah and Ezekiel. Our results
suggest that Ezekiel shows no knowledge of the J history, although
he is aware of some of the traditions, such as an Abraham story,
that lie behind J. The Yahwist, however, makes use of themes, motifs
and literary forms taken directly from Ezekiel in the formation of his
own work. J also seems to respond to a number of critical theological
issues raised by Ezekiel. Second Isaiah, for his part, is quite aware of
the specifics of the J version of early history and has been influenced
to a major extent by it. Much of the difference between Ezekiel and
Second Isaiah, therefore, can be accounted for by the assumption that
the Yahwist's work was an authoritative presentation of the early
history from creation to the conquest, written in the exilic period.

The relationship of these texts to each other is a literary, 'intertextual' one. This does not deny the possibility that J and Second
Isaiah were contemporaries and therefore J's presentation could have
been influenced by Second Isaiah as well. Nevertheless, there are quite
specific literary connections that strongly point to the use of specific
texts as a basis for later compositions. In my view, therefore, Ezekiel
is the *terminus post quem* and Second Isaiah the *terminus ante quem*
for the location of J in the exilic period.

With such a chronological control established for J, the rich theological reflection of this work could add a great deal to our understanding of this period. I agree with Von Rad,[40] and against Rendtorff,[41]
that the Yahwist is a theologian as well as historian and that his
work is full of theological narratives that address the great issues of
his day. The issues of divine justice and mercy, of sin and forgiveness,
of obedience to the divine demands and the problem of individual and
collective consequences, are all treated in J. There is a presentation of
the deity who as creator is both supreme and universal in his activity
and at the same time deeply committed to a particular people for

---

[40]See Von Rad, *Das formgeschichtliche Problem des Hexateuchs* (BWANT, 78),
Stuttgart 1938; reprinted in *Gesammelte Studien zum Alten Testament*, 1 (TB, 8),
München 1958, 9-86. However, this theologian does not belong to the Solomonic
era as Von Rad supposed.

[41]See R. Rendtorff, "Der 'Jahwist' als Theologe? Zum Dilemma der Pentateuch-
kritik", in: *Edinburgh Congress Volume* (VT.S, 28), Leiden 1975, 158-66; and in an
English version as "The 'Yahwist' as Theologian? The Dilemma of Pentateuchal
Criticism", *JSOT* 3 (1977), 2-10. See the discussion of this article in the same
volume by various scholars, including my own: "The Yahwist as Theologian? A
Response", 15-9. As in Rendtorff's work, it is the traditio-historical and redaction-
critical methodologies that have completely destroyed the theological coherence
and integrity of J's work.

their ultimate good. There is a simplicity about religious form and ethical demand, about what it means to do good and to obey God on the one hand, while still maintaining the absolute demand of loyalty to Yahweh by his people on the other hand. All these and many more topics and issues in J need to be understood and spelled out within the particular context of the Babylonian exile.

This is not to suggest a simple evolution of religion from Ezekiel to J to Second Isaiah. We have become wary of evolutionary schemes because it was an evolutionary scheme that misled Wellhausen and his contemporaries into placing J in a primitive period of Israel's history, based on J's apparent religious simplicity. The simplicity is the context of the exile without elaborate cult and only a temporary sanctuary. Yet one can recognize within these exilic authors a certain diversity of perspective. Ezekiel and his school represent a priestly tradition which has close affinities with some of the material in the Holiness Code and ultimately with P. J and Second Isaiah seem to stand in a tradition where there is little need for cult and priesthood, although the latter certainly looks forward to the rebuilding of the temple and the return of Yahweh's 'glory' to Jerusalem. While J has also borrowed heavily from the Dtr tradition, he should not be viewed as one more exilic Dtr anymore than should Ezekiel and Second Isaiah. On many important theological and ethical issues of the day J takes a quite different position from that of Deuteronomy and DtrH.[42] We need to recover this important theological voice from the wilderness of the Babylonian exile.

---

[42] J. van Seters, "The Theology of the Yahwist: A Preliminary Sketch", in: I. Kottsieper *et al.* (eds.), *"Wer ist wie du, Herr, unter den Göttern?" Studien zur Theologie und Religionsgeschichte Israels für Otto Kaiser zum 70. Geburtstag*, Göttingen 1995, 221-8.

Marjo C.A. Korpel   *Utrecht – The Netherlands*

Second Isaiah's Coping with the Religious Crisis:
Reading Isaiah 40 and 55

1 Introduction

During the conference workshops were organized devoted to reading biblical texts illustrating the necessity to reinterpret theological traditions in the light of the catastrophe of 586 BCE[1] and its aftermath. It was my task to introduce the reading of Second Isaiah for which I chose to concentrate on the first and last chapters (Isa. 40 and 55).[2] Together the two chapters contain evidence of some important switches in the theology of Second Isaiah as compared to various established theological concepts of the pre-exilic period. The chapters were distributed among the participants in a special layout (Appendices I and II at the end of this article).[3]

The prophet who is commonly designated as Second Isaiah or Deutero-Isaiah lived among the exiles in Babylonia, but his message was also directed at the sorry remnants of Judah still living in Palestine and suffering under Neo-Babylonian oppression.[4] The prophet had to face a threefold theological challenge,[5]

---

[1] According to other scholars the destruction of Jerusalem and the temple took place in 587. I follow the chronology of G. Galil, *The Chronology of the Kings of Israel and Judah* (SHANE, 9), Leiden 1996, 108-23.

[2] I would like to thank my colleagues Bob Becking and Johannes de Moor for their comments on an earlier draft of this article, and the participants in the workshop for their suggestions which I will quote as seems expedient.

[3] The texts are printed as they appeared in a book on the structure of Second Isaiah: M.C.A. Korpel, J.C. de Moor, *The Structure of Classical Hebrew Poetry: Isaiah 40-55* (OTS, 41), Leiden 1998. The definition of structural units is derived from ancient manuscripts, as indicated in the text. Obviously it was not my intention to discuss the structure itself during the workshop.

[4] This view is opposed by H.M. Barstad, *The Babylonian Captivity of the Book of Isaiah: Exilic Judah and the Provenance of Isaiah 40-55*, Oslo 1997. In my opinion, however, a Babylonian domicile still seems the most plausible option. It would take too much space to elaborate this view here. To some extent the question to which of the two locations the prophet transported himself mentally may be called academic.

[5] Cf. C. Westermann, *Das Buch Jesaja Kapitel 40-66* (ATD, 19), Göttingen 1966, 228; Y. Kaufmann, *The Babylonian Captivity and Deutero-Isaiah*, New York 1970, 19; R.N. Whybray, *Isaiah 40-66* (NCBC), Grand Rapids 1975, 32-3; W. Grimm, K. Dittert, *Deuterojesaja, Deutung – Wirkung – Gegenwart* (Calwer Bibelkommentare), Stuttgart 1990, 17-22.

- The apathy of those who asked themselves whether God had rejected his people for ever.

- The apostasy of those who chose to worship the deities of their mighty opponents.

- The seemingly definitive end of the Davidic dynasty.

As Renkema in particular has shown, pre-exilic theology did not provide satisfactory answers to these new challenges.[6] It was the aim of my workshop to discover by comparative readings how the prophet tried to develop a new theology in response to the radically different situation of his time.

2 Intertextual Reading of Isaiah 40

2.1 Isaiah 40:1-2

Apparently Second Isaiah is addressing here the theology of Lamentations, a theology of merciless retribution for past sins. In the first chapters of Lamentations Zion complains time and again, אֵין מְנַחֵם "there is no comforter" (Lam. 1:2, 9, 16, 17, 21; 2:13).[7] Some of those who acutely realized that the predicament they were in was their own fault feared that God would never forgive them, נַחְנוּ פָשַׁעְנוּ וּמָרִינוּ אַתָּה לֹא סָלָחְתָּ "We have transgressed and rebelled, and thou hast not forgiven" (Lam. 3:42), and לָמָה לָנֶצַח תִּשְׁכָּחֵנוּ "Why do you forget us for ever?" (Lam. 5:20). Indeed this was the everlasting doom the prophets had announced, וְהַעֲבַדְתִּיךָ אֶת־אֹיְבֶיךָ בָּאָרֶץ אֲשֶׁר לֹא־יָדָעְתָּ כִּי־אֵשׁ קְדַחְתֶּם בְאַפִּי עַד־עוֹלָם תּוּקָד "and I will make you serve your enemies in a land which you do not know, for in my anger a fire is kindled which shall burn *for ever*" (Jer. 17:4).

In an oracle probably belonging to the work of the First Isaiah, Isa. 22:14,[8] it had been announced that Israel's עָוֹן would not be forgiven until the sinning Jerusalemites would have died. Obviously this was what had happened now. Made this the verdict of the faithful pre-

---

[6]Cf. J. Renkema, *'Misschien is er hoop ...': De theologische vooronderstellingen van het boek Klaagliederen*, Franeker 1983, 267-342; Idem, *Klaagliederen vertaald en verklaard* (COT), Kampen 1993, 40-9; Idem, *Lamentations* (HCOT), Leuven 1998.

[7]In the course of our workshop, Dr. Antti Laato drew our attention to Isa. 22:4, where the prophet urges his audience not to comfort him for the destruction of Zion.

[8]H. Wildberger, *Jesaja*, Bd. 2: Jesaja 13-27 (BK, 10/2), Neukirchen 1978, 811.

exilic prophets an absolute truth? Obviously Second Isaiah had to answer that question.[9]

The term צבא Second Isaiah uses should be construed as a reference to the Neo-Babylonian ṣābu, the compulsory work prisoners of war had to do.[10] It seemed as if Jeremiah's words "I will make you serve your enemies in a land which you do not know" had become all too true (see also Lam. 1:3) and would never be taken back. YHWH himself had executed his people (Lam. 1:1, 20; 2:4, 17, 20, 21; 3:43).

This is what Second Isaiah wants to deny. He admits Zion's sins (עונה, חטאתיה, v. 2; see also 42:24-25; 43:24, 27-28; 43:12; 55:7), but enough is enough. The "double" which Zion has paid for her sins seems to match Jeremiah's prophecy that God would repay his people double for their iniquity and sins (Jer. 16:18).[11] In view of the idiomatic expression לקח מיד, Second Isaiah may also allude to Jeremiah's prophecy concerning the cup of wrath which Zion and her allies had to take from the hand of YHWH (Jer. 25:15-29) and which he has now taken from her hand (Isa. 51:22).

The reason for this optimism is found in the unbreakable nature of the covenant between God and his people. The pair אלהיכם || עמי (v.1) is an obvious pointer to the covenant formula "You will be my people and I will be your God" (Exod. 6:7; Lev. 26:12; Deut. 29:13, etc.).[12]

2.2   Isaiah 40:3-5

The inclusion of the poetical unit vv. 3-5 by the voice calling (3aA) and the statement that it is the mouth of the YHWH that has spoken

---

[9]Cf. H.G.M. Williamson, *The Book Called Isaiah: Deutero-Isaiah's Role in Composition and Redaction*, Oxford 1994, 106.

[10]See *CAD* Ṣ, 53-4. For the metathesis of quantity (*ṣab'u → ṣābu) see Von Soden, *GAG*, §15b.

[11]Already observed by F. Delitzsch, *Commentar über das Buch Jesaia*, Leipzig 1889, 409. According to W.L. Holladay, *Jeremiah* (Hermeneia), vol. 1, Philadelphia 1986, 478, one must assume that because of the different word for "double" in Isa. 40:2, the text of Jer. 16:18 must have been a secure part of the lore to which Second Isaiah had access. See also Ezek. 21:19, the sword against Jerusalem has to be doubled, כפל.

[12]Cf. E.J. Young, *The Book of Isaiah*, vol. 3, Grand Rapids 1972 (repr. 1996), 20; W.A.M. Beuken, *Jesaja* (PredOT), deel 2/A, Nijkerk 1979, 18-19; J.L. Koole, *Isaiah* (HCOT), vol. 3/1, Kampen 1997, 50-1; J.N. Oswalt, *The Book of Isaiah: Chapters 40–66* (NICOT), Grand Rapids 1998, 49.
The theology of the covenant is pre-exilic. In this connection it is irrelevant whether it arose in the earliest phase of Israel's history (so e.g. J.C. de Moor, *The Rise of Yahwism* (BEThL, 91A), Leuven ²1997, 364-68) or in the seventh century only (so e.g. E. Otto, "Die Ursprünge der Bundestheologie im Alten Testament und im Alten Orient", *ZAR* 4 (1998), 1-84).

(5bB) reveals that it is the prophet himself who has spoken in v.3. The "voice calling" reminds us of Isa. 6:4, where the voice belongs to God.[13]

Although he is evidently referring to the Exodus for the first time here,[14] he does so in terms totally different from the well-known passages describing this event. In my opinion it is possible that the prophet interpreted Psalm 68:5 סֹלּוּ לָרֹכֵב בָּעֲרָבוֹת as referring to the journey through the desert, even though this interpretation is erroneous according to modern opinion.[15] In most cases the verb סלל designates the building of a ramp or the levelling of a road by stamping.[16] In any case it is important that it is expected of the Israelites that they themselves will do the preparatory work. If they are courageous enough to make a start, miracles will happen, because the LORD himself will take over. As in the First Exodus, human mediators will be necessary, but the decisive act will be God's. Compare Isa. 49:11 וְשַׂמְתִּי כָל־הָרַי לַדָּרֶךְ וּמְסִלֹּתַי יְרֻמוּן "And I will make all my mountains a way, and my highways shall be raised up".

The memory (the remembrance of Gods deeds in the past) is an important source of hope for Second Isaiah, and as in the wilderness, he expects the LORD to reveal his glory (v. 5, cf. Exod. 14:4, 17; 16:7; 24:17; 40:34-35; Lev. 9:6-7, 23-24; compare Exod. 13:21-22).[17] Again the text reminds us of Isa. 6. In Isa. 6:3 too, there is an emphasis on the revelation of the glory of God to the whole world.[18]

2.3   Isaiah 40:6-8

The "voice of someone saying" reminds us of Isa. 6:8 but the structure of the text prevents us from interpreting verses 3 and 6 in the same way as in Isa. 6:4, 8. In view of the fact that v. 6aA doubtlessly echoes the beginning of the preceding canticle (v. 3aA, responsion) the imperative "Cry!" can only be understood as a summons to proclaim

---

[13]Cf. Williamson, *The Book Called Isaiah*, 38.

[14]Cf. J. Blenkinsopp, "De herinterpretatie van de Exodus-traditie in Deutero-Isaias 40–55," *Concilium* 2 (1966), 40-9; H. Simian-Yofre, "Exodo en Deutero-isaías", *Bib.* 61 (1980), 530-53; Beuken, *Jesaja*, deel 2/A, 20; D.W. Watts, *Isaiah 34-66* (WBC, 25), Waco, TX 1987, 80-1, with more literature on Second Isaiah and the Exodus theme.

[15]See S.I.L. Norin, *Er spaltete das Meer: Die Auszugsüberlieferung in Psalmen und Kult des alten Israel*, Lund 1977, 161-4; De Moor, *The Rise of Yahwism*[2], 171-90.

[16]Cf. *HALAT*, Bd. 3, 715; *DBHE*, 532.

[17]Thanks are due to Prof. Van Seters for suggesting a few of these Exodus texts during the workshop.

[18]Cf. Williamson, *The Book Called Isaiah*, 38.

a message similar to the one the prophet himself just uttered. Indeed קְרָא is frequently a summons to a prophet to speak up.[19]

However, the apathy of the victims of the Babylonian oppression was so deep that they did not believe their more optimistic fellow-victims anymore. It has been observed many times that Second Isaiah saw himself as a prophet like Moses who would like to play a major role in their new Exodus (see especially 49:1-6). But like Moses, he encountered much unbelief and opposition among his own countrymen (49:4, see also 53:3-5, etc.),[20] who had learned the bitter lesson that no faithfulness[21] can be expected from men who are too exhausted to fight anymore. It sounds as if they subtly remind the prophet of words of the First Isaiah, words spoken to the king of Assyria which in their opinion had become true in their own days, וְיֹשְׁבֵיהֶן קִצְרֵי־יָד חַתּוּ וַיֵּבֹשׁוּ הָיוּ עֵשֶׂב שָׂדֶה וִירַק דֶּשֶׁא חֲצִיר גַּגּוֹת וּשְׁדֵפָה לִפְנֵי קָמָה "their inhabitants, shorn of strength, are dismayed and confounded, and have become like plants of the field, and like tender grass, like grass on the housetops – blighted before it is grown" (2 Kgs 19:26 = Isa. 37:27).[22]

Contrasting this scepticism with the eternal reliability of God's word (8aC), Second Isaiah implicitly refers to God's irrevocable promises of covenantal faithfulness (חסד).[23] In this respect he shares the hope of the author of Lam. 3:2 חַסְדֵי יְהוָה כִּי לֹא־תָמְנוּ כִּי לֹא־כָלוּ רַחֲמָיו "The faithfulness of the LORD never ceases, his mercies never come to an end" (see also Lam. 3:32).

Two voices have spoken up, the voice of God (vv. 1-2) and that of the prophet (vv. 3aA, 6aA). Since it requires three witnesses to make a word stand (עַל־פִּי שְׁלֹשָׁה־עֵדִים יָקוּם דָּבָר, Deut. 19:15), the prophet is

---

[19] Jer. 11:6; Joel 3:9; Jon. 1:2; 3:2; Zech. 1:14, 17.

[20] Whybray, *Isaiah 40-66*, 32; Grimm, Dittert, *Deuterojesaja*, 319.

[21] I do not see any reason to adopt an exotic meaning for חסד in this verse. Cf. N.H. Snaith, "The Exegesis of Is. 40:5-6", *ET* 52 (1940-1), 394-6; L.J. Kuyper, "The Meaning of ḥsdw in Is. xl 6", *VT* 13 (1963), 489-92; Whybray, *Isaiah 40-66*, 51; Watts, *Isaiah 34-66*, 81-2; Oswalt, *The Book of Isaiah*, 53.

[22] Of course the vocabulary of Isa. 40:6-8 also resembles that of Ps. 103:15-16, אֱנוֹשׁ כֶּחָצִיר יָמָיו כְּצִיץ הַשָּׂדֶה כֵּן יָצִיץ כִּי רוּחַ עָבְרָה־בּוֹ וְאֵינֶנּוּ וְלֹא־יַכִּירֶנּוּ, "As for man, his days are like grass; he flourishes like a flower of the field; for the wind passes over it, and it is gone, and its place knows it no more", as Prof. Hugh Williamson pointed out during the workshop. See also Williamson, *The Book Called Isaiah*, 196. Most scholars however consider Ps. 103 as a post-exilic Psalm reflecting thoughts of Second Isaiah. Cf. H.-J. Kraus, *Psalmen 60-150* (BK, 15/2), Neukirchen-Vluyn 51978, 873; L.C. Allen, *Psalms 101-150* (WBC, 21), Waco, TX 1983, 20-1; K. Seybold, *Die Psalmen* (HAT, 1/15), Tübingen 1996, 402.

[23] Cf. Gen. 9:8-16; Lev. 26:44; Deut. 7:9, 12; 1 Kgs 8:23; Ps. 89:1-4; 103:17-18; see also M. Weinfeld, ברית, *ThWAT*, Bd. 1, Stuttgart 1973, 799; G.A.F. Knight, *Servant Theology: Isaiah 40-55*, Grand Rapids 1984, 14; J.L. Koole, *Jesaja II* (COT), dl. 1, Kampen 1985, 33.

actually asking the third speaker, the disillusioned voice of vv. 6aB-7aB, to bear witness of his confidence in the prophet's message of hope. Second Isaiah himself is convinced that God will confirm his testimony (מֵקִים דְּבַר עַבְדּוֹ, Isa. 44:26).

2.4   Isaiah 40:9

Again Second Isaiah is refuting the theology of Lamentations. "How lonely sits the city" (Lam. 1:1), "her fall is terrible" (Lam. 1:9), "the Lord has trodden as in a wine press the virgin daughter of Judah" (Lam. 1:15), "he has brought down to the ground in dishonor the kingdom and its rulers" (Lam. 2:2), "her gates have sunk into the ground" (Lam. 2:9), "The elders of the daughter of Zion sit on the ground in silence . . . the maidens of Jerusalem have bowed their heads to the ground" (Lam. 2:10). Instead of remaining seated in the dust, nourishing her grief, Zion has to climb on a high mountain again. In contrast to Zion, Babylon will have to sink down in the dust, רְדִי וּשְׁבִי עַל־עָפָר בְּתוּלַת בַּת־בָּבֶל "Come down and sit in the dust, O virgin daughter of Babylon" (Isa. 47:1). Again we note the emphasis on the active role Zion itself has to play in meeting God's salvatory work (see vv. 3-5 above).

Fortunately, we know for certain where Second Isaiah found inspiration for this message of hope which he repeats in a slightly different form in Isa. 52:7 (see also 41:27). It is the work of Nahum which he is taking up here (Nah. 2:1, tr. 1:15).[24] Anybody acquainted with the latter's joyful announcement of the fall of the Assyrian empire will have understood the hint: Babylon will fall just as well! Zion itself however has to believe in this message. She herself has to become a messenger of good tidings. In recasting pre-exilic theology, Second Isaiah rejects some elements of the message of his predecessors, but adopts and modifies other prophetic traditions.

2.5   Isaiah 40:10-11

It is generally agreed that the theme of the second Exodus crops up here again. Instead of the customary "strong hand" (יָד חֲזָקה, Exod. 3:19; 6:1; 13:9, etc.) the prophet seems to presuppose זְרוֹעַ חֲזָקה "strong arm" (cf. Jer. 21:5). The image of God as a Shepherd is fairly old[25] and is often applied to the Exodus (e.g. Ps. 78:52-53). In v. 11bA and Isa. 49:10 the same verb נהל "to lead gently" is employed as in

---

[24]For the dependence of Second Isaiah on Nahum see B. Becking, *Nahum* (VveB), Kampen 1986, 38-9; K. Spronk, *Nahum* (HCOT), Kampen 1997, 79-80.

[25]Cf. M.C.A. Korpel, *A Rift in the Clouds: Ugaritic and Hebrew Descriptions of the Divine*, Münster 1990, 448-53, with bibliography; K. van der Toorn, "Shepherd", in: *DDD*, 1457-9, [2]*DDD*, 770-1.

Exod. 15:13. Ezekiel had put special emphasis on God's decision to take over as a Good Shepherd because of the failure of Jerusalem's leadership (Ezek. 34).[26]

The text reminded some scholars in the workshop of Gen. 15:1, where God summons Abraham not to fear, and promises him to be his shield and to give him a very great שָׂכָר which later turns out to be a metaphor for Abraham's offspring. However, in my opinion this connection is too uncertain to be pursued.

2.6   Isaiah 40:12-14

Countering the complaint that it was the רוח יהוה which had blown away Israel (v. 7aB) the prophet questions the ability of man to comprehend the רוח יהוה (v. 13aA). Against the complaint that God neglected Israel's משפט (v. 27bB) and did not know the exhausting road the exiles had to go (v. 27bA), or would even have blocked their way deliberately (Lam. 3:9, 11), the prophet maintains that it is impossible for man to understand God's ways (v. 14). He bases this conviction on man's failure to comprehend the magnitude of God's work of creation (v.12). The images Second Isaiah uses to describe the latter are not derived from Gen. 1, but from more archaic creation accounts, describing God as the *builder* of the universe (cf. Amos 9:6; Hab. 3:6).

2.7   Isaiah 40:15-17

But the prophet derives yet another argument from his reference to God the Creator: to him who weighed the mountains in a balance (v.12b) the mighty nations must be nothing but specks of dust on a balance (v.15aB). Thus the bitter complaints about the seemingly invincible גוים who had defiled and destroyed the temple (Jer. 22:8; Lam. 1:10; Ps. 79:6, etc.) are countered by the conviction that nothing is impossible with the almighty Creator. It is not Israel that is blown away (v. 7aB), but the foreign nations and their rulers (vv. 15bA, 17aA, 23-24). In describing them as תהו (v. 17aB, see also vv. 23) the prophet underlines that God the Creator can do whatever he wants with them (cf. Gen. 1:2).

V. 16 is somewhat enigmatic and might be a reaction to the theology of those who expected that lavish sacrifices might be needed to atone for the sins of the past (cf. Mic. 6:7 "Will the LORD be pleased with thousands of rams?").[27] But Second Isaiah does not believe that restoration of the sacrificial cult is a necessary preliminary to making

---

[26]Thanks are due to Prof. Hans Barstad for this reference.

[27]Cf. Koole, *Jesaja II*, dl. 1, 59; Grimm, Dittert, *Deuterojesaja*, 69.

peace with the LORD: "I have not burdened you with offerings, or wearied you with frankincense" (Isa. 43:23), "You have not ... satisfied me with the fat of your sacrifices" (Isa. 43:24). In this respect Second Isaiah agrees with the prophets of doom who had denounced this kind of blind faith in the efficacy of sacrifices (e.g. Hos. 6:6; Amos 5:22; Isa. 1:11; Jer. 6:20; 7:22; 14:12).

2.8   Isaiah 40:18-20

The passages in which Second Isaiah attacks the makers of images are often regarded as later insertions in the book.[28] Like Spykerboer, I am not convinced by the arguments adduced for this thesis.[29] In Isa. 40:18-20, for example, the cosmic work of God the Creator of the universe and the almost comic activities of the makers of idols are deliberately contrasted. The use of the verb רקע in v. 19aB evokes the רקיע of Gen. 1 (see also Isa. 42:5; 44:24; Ps. 136:6 רקע הארץ "who spread out the earth"). In my opinion here too Second Isaiah sets forth the tradition of the prophets of doom who had denounced the making of idols.[30]

2.9   Isaiah 40:21-24

Reiteration of the argument we discussed already under vv. 12-17.

2.10   Isaiah 40:25-26

Again the prophet invokes the incomparability of God the Creator, but this time he alludes also to the Exodus tradition, suggesting that

---

[28] Cf. Westermann, *Das Buch Jesaja: Kapitel 40-66*, 41, 46-8; K. Elliger, *Deuterojesaja* (BK, 11/1), Neukirchen-Vluyn 1978, 73-81; R.P. Merendino, *Der Erste und der Letzte: Eine Untersuchung von Jes 40-48* (VT.S, 31), Leiden 1981, 572 *et passim*; R.G. Kratz, *Kyros im Deuterojesaja-Buch: Redaktionsgeschichtliche Untersuchungen zu Entstehung und Theologie von Jes 40-55* (FAT, 1), Tübingen 1991, 192-206; J. van Oorschot, *Von Babel zum Zion: Eine literarkritische und redaktionsgeschichtliche Untersuchung* (BZAW, 206), Berlin 1993, 312-8.

[29] See H.C. Spykerboer, *The Structure and Composition of Deutero-Isaiah: With Special Reference to the Polemics against Idolatry*, Meppel 1976, esp. 185. See also K. Holter, *Second Isaiah's Idol-Fabrication Passages*, Frankfurt a.M. 1995; A. Berlejung, *Die Theologie der Bilder: Herstellung und Einweihung von Kultbilder in Mesopotamien und die Alttestamentliche Bilderpolemik* (OBO, 162), Fribourg & Göttingen 1998, 370-5.

[30] Amos 5:26; Jer. 10:14; Ezek. 7:20; Nah. 1:14, etc. On the antiquity of the objections against images in Israel, see De Moor, *The Rise of Yahwism*[2], 53-4, 264-5, 350-1, 358. The circumstance that private family effigies disappear completely from the archaeological record of Israel after the destruction of the temple, as indicated by Prof. Stern in his contribution to this volume (pp. 245-55), can only mean that they had been denounced beforehand and for that reason were seen as an important cause of the catastrophe.

the one who is able to bring out the heavenly hosts (צבאם ... המוציא,
v. 26aC) will be able to bring out the people of Israel again (והוצאתי
את־צבאותי, Exod. 7:4; see also 12:17, 51). After the defeat by the Babylonian armies people complained that the LORD had not gone out with
the hosts of Israel to deliver them and feared that he would never do
so again (Ps. 44:9; 60:12 = 108:12).[31]

2.11 Isaiah 40:27-31

With regard to v. 27, see our comments on vv. 12-14. Obviously the
Creator "who is great in forces and mighty in strength" (v. 26bB)
and the "God of eternity" (cf. Gen. 21:33)[32] cannot grow tired (v.
28), even though the Israelites had tried to tire him with their sins
(Isa. 43:22-24). The Israelites who are toiling for the Babylonians are
too tired and faint to embark upon the new Exodus advocated by
Second Isaiah. Even the prophet himself may have felt so occasionally (Isa. 49:4), yet he finds the strength to speak a consoling word
to his fellow-sufferers (Isa. 50:4). It was one of the complaints of the
time that especially young people had to suffer undeservedly for the
sins of their fathers.[33] Lam. 5:13 states that young men were stagger-
ing (כשל) under the heavy loads of wood they had to carry for their
oppressors. As in vv. 7bA-8, Second Isaiah admits that this complaint
is legitimate. But he points to the inexhaustible source of power that
may be found in the almighty Creator.

Waiting for the LORD (v. 31aA), however, is no excuse for passiv-
ity. Only when one starts running, the tiredness will disappear (v.
31b). Whereas during the First Exodus God had carried Israel like
an eagle on his wings (Exod. 19:4; see also Deut. 32:11), they now
must grow wings themselves (v. 31aB, Hiphil!). Again the necessity
for self-activity as an expression of trust in the wondrous acts of God
is stressed.[34]

---

[31] Prof. Barstad referred to the Holy War theme which forms the background
for the imagery in v.26; see also H. Niehr, "Host of Heaven", in: *DDD*, 811-4,
[2]*DDD*, 428-30.

[32] On the eternal God, cf. A. de Pury, "El Olam", in: *DDD*, 549-55, [2]*DDD*,
288-91; De Moor, *The Rise of Yahwism*[2], 362, n.289.

[33] Jer. 31:29; Ezek. 18:2; Lam. 5:7.

[34] During the workshop Prof. Williamson pointed to Ps. 103:5 תִּתְחַדֵּשׁ כַּנֶּשֶׁר נְעוּרָיְכִי
"so that your youth will renew itself like that of eagles". It is significant, however,
that this post-exilic Psalm (see above, n. 22) changes the personal subject into an
abstract one (cf. *HALAT*, 282; *DCH*, vol. 3, 165), if the meaning is not a passive
(cf. *HAHAT*, 327).

3 Intertextual Reading of Isaiah 55

3.1 Isaiah 55:1-3

It has long been observed that the first and last chapters of Second Isaiah are connected in many ways.[35] First of all by the imperatives in the second person masculine, meant to exhort all who keep to their faith in the LORD to become active agents in his great work of salvation.

The everlasting covenant with Israel (v. 3bA) picks up a theme dear to the Priestly Code (Gen. 9:12, 16; 17:7, 13, 19, etc.). The Davidic dynasty had claimed this privileged position for itself (2 Sam. 23:5 and especially Ps. 89:28, לְעוֹלָם אֶשְׁמוֹר־לוֹ חַסְדִּי וּבְרִיתִי נֶאֱמֶנֶת לוֹ "My faithfulness I will keep for him for ever, and my covenant will stand firm for him").[36]

It was one of the bitter complaints in the Exile that God had renounced this covenant with his anointed, נֵאַרְתָּה בְּרִית עַבְדֶּךָ "Thou hast renounced the covenant with thy servant" (Ps. 89:40). And v. 50, אַיֵּה חֲסָדֶיךָ הָרִאשֹׁנִים אֲדֹנָי נִשְׁבַּעְתָּ לְדָוִד בֶּאֱמוּנָתֶךָ "Where is thy faithfulness of old, o Lord, which by thy trustfulness thou didst swear to David?"

Lam. 4:20 sadly refers to the exalted royal epithets that were once used of the Davidic king in the Jerusalemite cult, רוּחַ אַפֵּינוּ מְשִׁיחַ יְהוָה נִלְכַּד בִּשְׁחִיתוֹתָם אֲשֶׁר אָמַרְנוּ בְּצִלּוֹ נִחְיֶה בַגּוֹיִם "The breath of our nostrils, the LORDs anointed, was taken in their pits, he of whom we said, 'Under his shadow we shall live among the nations'."[37] Obviously this refers to Jehoiachin who was taken prisoner and transported to Babylonia. Some Judaeans hoped that he would return and be re-installed, even after Zedekiah had become a vassal ruler (Jer. 28:2-4). But when Amel-Marduk died in 560 BCE without having restored Jehoiachin to the throne and when the latter himself died shortly afterwards (Jer. 52:34, cf. Jer. 22:24-26), it became clear that there was little hope of a restoration.

Apparently Second Isaiah too does not see any possibility for restoration of the Davidic dynasty. He breaks away radically from the

---

[35] R.F. Melugin, *The Formation of Isaiah 40–55* (BZAW, 141), Berlin 1976, 86-7; T.N.D. Mettinger, *A Farewell to the Servant Songs: A Critical Examination of an Exegetical Axiom*, Gleerup 1983, 21-2; Koole, *Isaiah*, vol. 3, 14.

[36] Like many others, I regard Psalm 89 as a composite Psalm, part of it belonging to the pre-exilic royal cult, part of it an early exilic complaint about the breakdown of this royal ideology.

[37] See Renkema, *'Misschien is er hoop...'*, 288-94; Idem, *Lamentations*, 555-9. For צל "shade" as a designation of the king see F. Crüsemann, *Der Widerstand gegen das Königtum*, (WMANT, 49), Neukirchen 1978, 21-2.

old theologoumenon of the elected royal anointed and transfers this status to all faithful of Israel.[38] As we have seen, the re-establishing of the covenant links Isa. 55:3 to 40:1.

The invitation to come and buy free food and drink becomes an invitation to come to the LORD in v. 3a. Isa. 44:3 renders it more than likely that it is God's Spirit that will be poured on the thirsty. It is as if the prophet deliberately alludes to Amos 8:11, הִנֵּה יָמִים בָּאִים נְאֻם אֲדֹנָי יְהוִה וְהִשְׁלַחְתִּי רָעָב בָּאָרֶץ לֹא־רָעָב לַלֶּחֶם וְלֹא־צָמָא לַמַּיִם כִּי אִם־לִשְׁמֹעַ אֵת דִּבְרֵי יְהוָה, "The days are coming," declares the LORD, "when I will send a famine through the land – not a famine of food or a thirst of water, but a famine of hearing the words of the LORD".

3.2   Isaiah 55:4

As David had been a נגיד 'leader' (1 Sam. 9:16; 10:1; 13:14; 25:30; 2 Sam. 5:2; 6:21; 7:8), faithful Israel must now assume leadership. It is not immediately clear why David is also called a witness to the nations.[39] One might think, however, of his brave testimony when he confronted Goliath, a testimony which ended with the phrase וְיֵדְעוּ

---

[38] See on this 'democratization' of the promises once made to the Davidic dynasty, M.C.A. Korpel, "Metaphors in Isaiah LV", *VT* 46 (1996), 43-55 (49), with bibliography. I remain unconvinced by Laato's attempt to play down the radical meaning of Isa. 55:3-5. Cf. A. Laato, *The Servant of* YHWH *and Cyrus: A Reinterpretation of the Exilic Messianic Programme in Isaiah 40–55* (CB.OT, 35), Stockholm 1992, 244-5. It is hardly convincing to refer to the resurgent messianic hopes under Zerubbabel to define Second Isaiah's theology. It is not Second Isaiah but Haggai who contradicts Jeremiah's sweeping rejection of the exalted royal epithet "the signet ring on the hand of YHWH" (Jer. 22:24 ⟷ Hag. 2:23).

Whether or not Second Isaiah was adopting deuteronomistic theology here (cf. Deut. 7:9, 12, with E. Nielsen, *Deuteronomium* [HAT 1/6], Tübingen 1995, 98) remains a moot question as long as we do not know precisely which of the two came first. In any case it was this reformulated theology which prevailed afterwards (cf. Dan. 9:4; Neh. 1:5; 9:32).

[39] W.A.M. Beuken, *Jesaja*, deel 2/B, Nijkerk 1983, 285-6, takes v. 4a as a new commission for 'David', and in his opinion the theme of the king as witness was part of the royal ideology, with reference to J.H. Eaton, "The King as God's Witness", *ASTI* 7 (1970), 25-40. According to J.L. Koole, *Jesaja II* (COT), dl. 2, Kampen 1990, 328-9, not David but the Servant of the LORD is meant here. He refers to Isa. 43:10 for the Servant as a witness. Whybray, *Isaiah 40-66*, 192, refers to Ps. 18:43-50; Exod. 15:14-16 and Josh. 2:9-11 for the idea that the conquest of nations by the people of Israel constituted a witness to them of the power of the LORD. Oswalt, *The Book of Isaiah: Chapters 40–66*, 437-40, opts for the classic individualistic interpretation, the Servant as Davidic Messiah, but he admits, "To be sure, insofar as Israel accepts the Servant and identifies itself with him, the statements of v. 5 would apply to it as well". If the Servant is seen as a 'corporate personality' – a view to which I adhere – some of these approaches do not exclude each other.

כָּל־הָאָרֶץ כִּי יֵשׁ אֱלֹהִים לְיִשְׂרָאֵל "that all the earth may know that there is a God in Israel" (1 Sam. 17:46). Possibly Second Isaiah connected this with the pre-exilic part of Ps. 89 where the Davidic king is compared to the moon as "a reliable witness in the clouds" (וְעֵד בַּשַּׁחַק נֶאֱמָן, Ps. 89:38; so already the LXX). The idea of Israel witnessing of its faith among the nations was dear to Second Isaiah who was living among many foreign peoples (see also 43:10, 12; 44:8). Of course, his hope that foreign nations might embrace Yahwism has everything to do with the fact that the Persians were worshipping Ahura Mazda whose henotheistic and aniconic cult[40] may have appealed to Second Isaiah and may even have encouraged him to hope that the Persians could be converted to the 'monotheistic' faith of Israel. In this sense he expected Cyrus to be a worthy successor of David (Isa. 45:1) if, and only if, he would recognize his vocation by the sole God of Israel (45:3-7).

3.3   Isaiah 55:5

In my opinion, this too could be a transfer of the promises to the Davidic king to the faithful of Israel. In 2 Sam. 22:44 David praises God because nations whom he did not know came to serve him, תִּשְׁמְרֵנִי לְרֹאשׁ גּוֹיִם עַם לֹא־יָדַעְתִּי יַעַבְדֻנִי "thou didst keep me as the head of the nations; people whom I had not known served me".[41] However, the adhortation to actively call the unknown nations to the service of the God of Israel would seem to be a new theological approach. This so-called universalism of Second Isaiah[42] is without parallel and must be the answer to the actual situation of the moment. It is so different from the approximately contemporaneous calls for merciless revenge on the unknown nations (Jer. 10:25; Ps. 79:6) that it might well represent a stance deliberately taken.

3.4   Isaiah 55:6-9

As long as the temple stood on Zion, it was easy to seek and find God there (Ps. 63:2-3;[43] Deut. 4:29; 12:5). Now that the temple has been

---

[40]Cf. M.A. Dandamaev, *Persien unter den ersten Achämeniden*, Wiesbaden 1976, 215-41.

[41]Many commentators noted the clear reference to 2 Sam. 22:44/Ps. 18:44, cf. Delitzsch, *Commentar über das Buch Jesaia*, 542; Westermann, *Das Buch Jesaja. Kapitel 40-66*, 229; Koole, *Jesaja II*, dl. 2, 331; Kratz, *Kyros im Deuterojesaja-Buch*, 132; Van Oorschot, *Von Babel zum Zion*, 271, with n. 169.

[42]J. Blenkinsopp, "Second Isaiah – Prophet of Universalism," *JSOT* 41 (1988), 83-103; R. Albertz, *Religionsgeschichte Israels in alttestamentlicher Zeit* (GAT, 8/2), Göttingen 1992, 439-40.

[43]Because of the supplicant who "sees" God in his sanctuary (v. 2), probably pre-exilic, cf. Korpel, *A Rift in the Clouds*, 91-4.

destroyed, the prophet emphasizes the notion that God can be found in any place. Wherever there are people seeking Him,[44] He will be found. Obviously this was a theological view soon to be opposed by others (Haggai for example). But as W.H. Schmidt has shown convincingly, Second Isaiah is merely transforming old cultic and prophetic traditions here.[45]

As in Isa. 40:2 (see also 43:25; 44:22), Second Isaiah emphasizes God's willingness to forgive (v.7) and it seems not unlikely that he is not only reacting to the people who resigned themselves to the idea that God did not pardon his people (Lam. 3:42), but also to Jeremiah's message again. In Jer. 5:7 God cries out indignantly to Jerusalem, אֵי לָזֹאת אֶסְלוֹחַ־לָךְ "How can I pardon you?". But Jer 5:1 and Jer. 36:3 show that Jeremiah too reckoned with the possibility that God would forgive his people if they repented, and it is in this line that Second Isaiah says that God will forgive them if they repent.[46] The idea of seeking God as a first step to repenting is definitely pre-exilic (Hos. 3:5; Ps. 78:34) and was also picked up again by others after the catastrophe (2 Chron. 7:14).

The next two verses which form a sub-canto with vv. 6-7 develop this thought further in apparent contrast to Jer. 18:(8), 11; 26:3; 36:3. According to McKane 18:11 is a Deuteronomic modification of Jer. 18:1-6.[47] Others, like Bright, take it to be a word spoken by Jeremiah himself.[48] Whatever the truth in this respect, the theme probably belonged to the Jeremianic tradition as Second Isaiah received it.[49] The mere fact that the message about the evil YHWH was thinking

---

[44]Note that the seeking of the LORD is no longer a condition of the finding of the LORD in the colometry we believe to be intended.

[45]W.H. Schmidt, " 'Suchet den Herrn, so werdet ihr leben': Exegetische Notizen zum Thema 'Gott suchen' in der Prophetie", in: C.J. Bleeker et al. (eds.), Ex Orbe Religionum: Studia G. Widengren, vol. 1, Leiden 1972, 127-40.

[46]Note the remarkable resemblance between Jer. 36:3 and Isa. 55:7. There are some commentators who see evidence of Deuteronomistic editing in Jer. 36, but there seems no reason to deny Jeremiah verse 3, cf. A. Weiser, Das Buch Jeremia: Kapitel 1-25,14 (ATD, 20), Göttingen 1981, 322; W.L. Holladay, Jeremiah (Hermeneia), vol. 2, Minneapolis 1989, 253-4, with literature.

[47]W. McKane, A Critical and Exegetical Commentary on Jeremiah (ICC), vol. 1, Edinburgh 1986, 425-6.

[48]J. Bright, Jeremiah (AncB, 21), Garden City, NY 1965, 126; P.C. Craigie, P.H. Kelley; J.F. Drinkard, Jr., Jeremiah 1-25 (WBC, 25), Dallas, TX 1991, 243, with literature. See also W.L. Holladay, Jeremiah (Hermeneia), vol. 1, Philadelphia 1986, 514, who takes the verse as an authentic report by Jeremiah, but believes it to be added at a later time.

[49]The thought itself – YHWH thinking up evil as an answer to the evil thought up by the Jerusalemites – is not even original to Jeremiah. He borrowed it from Micah, Mic. 2:3, see Mic. 2:1.

up against Judah – an evil which could be averted only if the men of
Judah abandoned their evil ways in time – is repeated at least three
times in the book of Jeremiah indicates that in some form or other it
belonged to Jeremiah's own oracles of doom. Since the men of Judah
did *not* repent (cf. Jer. 18:12), many thought they had spoiled their
only chance to escape from Jeremiah's oracle of doom. In contrast to
this pessimism Second Isaiah now states that it is never too late to
repent and implicitly calls it evil to think so because it puts limits to
God's sovereignty.[50]

3.5   Isaiah 55:10-11

True, it had been the word of God which Jeremiah spoke and therefore
the resigned observation of Lam. 3:38 is understandable, מִפִּי עֶלְיוֹן לֹא
תֵצֵא הָרָעוֹת וְהַטּוֹב "Is it not from the mouth of the Most High that good
and evil come?" Taking up the imagery of abundant water and bread
again from the first canticle, Second Isaiah emphasizes that it is the
saving word of God for which Israel must long (cf. Deut. 8:3). I have
elaborated this elsewhere and will not repeat it here.[51]

3.6   Isaiah 55:12-13

The theme of a new Exodus is resumed in these verses. Just as during
the first Exodus, the people will go out in joy and singing.[52] Second
Isaiah linked up chapter 40 with chapter 55 by this imagery of God
leading his people out of the country of their oppressors (cf. 40:11).

By the transformation of thorns and thistles into beautiful plants
and trees Second Isaiah reverses the effect of the earlier oracles of the
First Isaiah.[53] In the Song of the Vineyard it was announced that the
choice vines of Israel would be destroyed. Thorns and thistles would
grow in their place and no rain would fall on them anymore (Isa. 5:6).
In a later Isaianic expansion[54] this is said to apply to the nobles of
Jerusalem who will be parched with thirst (Isa. 5:13). Now this curse
will be reversed and fine trees will replace the thorns again.

The phrase לְאוֹת עוֹלָם לֹא יִכָּרֵת (v. 13) apparently refers to the
reestablished covenant again. It reminds us of Exod. 31:17 בֵּינִי וּבֵין בְּנֵי

---

[50]For another late refutation of Jer. 18:11; 26:3; 36:3, see Jer. 29:11-14. Ps.
103:11 (on the dating of this Psalm see n. 22, above) seems to elaborate on Isa.
55:9.

[51]Korpel, "Metaphors in Isaiah LV", 50-55.

[52]Cf. Exod. 15:1 and the post-exilic Ps. 105:43. See also Isa. 48:20; 51:11; 54:1.

[53]For the metaphorical interpretation of these verses see my, "Metaphors in
Isaiah LV", 51-52.

[54]Cf. M.C.A. Korpel, "Structural Analysis as a Tool for Redaction-Criticism:
The Example of Isaiah 5 and 10:1-6", 53-71 (58-60).

יִשְׂרָאֵל אוֹת הוּא לְעֹלָם "It is a sign for ever between me and the people of Israel" (see also ברית עולם in v. 16).[55] The 'it' is the sabbath which comes after 6 days of hard labour. It seems not impossible that in this veiled manner Second Isaiah wanted to refer to the period of rest which can start now that the period of forced labour has come to an end (again linking up with Ch. 40: cf. 40:2). At least this veiled allusion was not lost to Trito-Isaiah who obviously picks it up in the text of 56:1-9.

4   Conclusions

On the basis of only two chapters of the Book of Second Isaiah few firm conclusions can be drawn. For that a study of the theology of the book as a whole would be necessary and probably we should take into account the elements of Second Isaiah in the First Isaiah too. However, a few observations were made at the end of our workshop.

- Second Isaiah refuses to accept the pessimistic theology of Lamentations and other bitter complaints heard after the fall of Jerusalem (40:1, 9, 14, 15, 30; 55:3, 7).

- He introduces the theme of a Second Exodus (Isa. 40:3-5, 6-8, 10-11, 25-26; 55:12-13).

- In contrast to the seemingly invincible גוים he refers to God as the Creator to whom nothing is impossible (40:15-17). Second Isaiah, however, seems to ignore the creation theology of the Priestly Code. Instead, he emphasizes the old concept of a *creatio continua* which enables him to stress that God may create totally new solutions to the problems of his days.

- The theology of Zion is rejected and modified. The people must leave Babylon and return to Zion in joy and singing, but the temple is not strictly necessary to meet God (Isa. 55:6) and the bond between Zion and the Davidic dynasty is given up. The eternal covenant now concerns Israel as a whole (Isa. 55:3-5, 13; see also 40:1, 8).

- The message of the prophets who had announced the downfall of Jerusalem as a result of Israel's sins is accepted as justified (Isa. 40:2; 55:7; also the idol-passages, 40:18–20 and parallels), but their threat that God would reject his people for ever is negated

---

[55]The verse belongs to an older stratum which was inserted by P at this point, cf. C. Houtman, *Exodus*, dl. 3: Exodus 20-40 (COT), Kampen 1996, 571-2.

(40:2; 55:7). The calls for merciless revenge on the unknown nations (Jer. 10:25; Ps. 79:6; Lam. 1:21-22; 3:64-66; 4:22, etc.) is replaced by a message of hope for all nations, if they accept the God of Israel as the Only One (55:4).

Appendix I: The Structure of Isaiah 40

פ <ס> – סֹ – 1Q^a – 4Q^b – 𝔊^{SBAQ} – 𝔖^{abcde} _____

A.i.1 (Isa. 40:1–2a)

נַחֲמוּ נַחֲמוּ עַמִּי	1aA	Comfort, comfort my people,
יֹאמַר אֱלֹהֵיכֶם:	1aB	says your God.
דַּבְּרוּ עַל־לֵב יְרוּשָׁלַ͏ִם	2aA	Speak to the heart of Jerusalem
וְקִרְאוּ אֵלֶיהָ	2aB	and cry to her

A.i.2 (Isa. 40:2b–c)

כִּי מָלְאָה צְבָאָהּ	2bA	that her forced labour is fulfilled,
כִּי נִרְצָה עֲוֺנָהּ	2bB	that her iniquity has been repaid,
כִּי לָקְחָה מִיַּד יְהוָה	2cA	that she has taken from the LORD's hand
כִּפְלַיִם בְּכָל־חַטֹּאתֶיהָ:	2cB	double for all her sins.

ס – 1Q^a – 𝔊^{SBAQ} – 𝔖^{abcde} . . . .

A.ii.1 (Isa. 40:3)

קוֹל קוֹרֵא בַּמִּדְבָּר	3aA	A voice of someone crying in the desert:
פַּנּוּ דֶּרֶךְ יְהוָה	3aB	Prepare the way of the LORD,
יַשְּׁרוּ בָּעֲרָבָה	3bA	make straight in the bare valley
מְסִלָּה לֵאלֹהֵינוּ:	3bB	a highway for our God!

A.ii.2 (Isa. 40:4)

כָּל־גֶּיא יִנָּשֵׂא	4aA	Every valley will be lifted up,
וְכָל־הַר וְגִבְעָה יִשְׁפָּלוּ	4aB	and every mountain and hill will be made low,
וְהָיָה הֶעָקֹב לְמִישׁוֹר	4bA	and the rough terrain will become level,
וְהָרְכָסִים לְבִקְעָה:	4bB	and the rocky places a plain.

A.ii.3 (Isa. 40:5)

וְנִגְלָה כְּבוֹד יְהוָה	5aA	And the glory of the LORD will be revealed.
וְרָאוּ כָל־בָּשָׂר יַחְדָּו	5bA	And all flesh will see it together,
כִּי פִּי יְהוָה דִּבֵּר:	5bB	for the mouth of the LORD has spoken.

ס <פ> – 1Q^a – 𝔊^{SBAQ} – 𝔖^{be} . . . .

A.iii.1 (Isa. 40:6)

קוֹל אֹמֵר קְרָא	6aA	A voice of someone saying: Cry!
וְאָמַר מָה אֶקְרָא	6aB	But it is said: "What should I cry?
כָּל־הַבָּשָׂר חָצִיר	6bA	All flesh is grass,
{𝔊^A} וְכָל־חַסְדּוֹ כְּצִיץ הַשָּׂדֶה:	6bB	and all their loyalty is like a flower of the field.

A.iii.2 (Isa. 40:7–8)

יָבֵשׁ חָצִיר נָבֵל צִיץ	7aA	The grass withers, the flower fades,
כִּי רוּחַ יְהוָה נָשְׁבָה בּוֹ	7aB	when the spirit of the LORD blows upon it ..."
אָכֵן חָצִיר הָעָם:	7bA	Surely, the people is grass,
יָבֵשׁ חָצִיר נָבֵל צִיץ	8aB	the grass withers, the flower fades ...
וּדְבַר־אֱלֹהֵינוּ יָקוּם לְעוֹלָם:	8aC	But the word of our God will stand to eternity!

ס <פ> – 1Qª – 𝕲ˢᴮᴬᵠ – ꜱᵃᵇᵈᵉ ....

A.iv.1 (Isa. 40:9a–b)

עַל הַר־גָּבֹהַ עֲלִי־לָךְ	9aA	Climb on a high mountain,
מְבַשֶּׂרֶת צִיּוֹן	9aB	O Zion, heraldess of good tidings!
הָרִימִי בַכֹּחַ קוֹלֵךְ	9bA	Lift up your voice with strength,
מְבַשֶּׂרֶת יְרוּשָׁלִָם	9bB	O Jerusalem, heraldess of good tidings!

A.iv.2 (Isa. 40:9c)

הָרִימִי אַל־תִּירָאִי	9cA	Lift it up, do not fear!
אִמְרִי לְעָרֵי יְהוּדָה	9cB	Say to the cities of Judah,
הִנֵּה אֱלֹהֵיכֶם:	9cC	Behold your God!

𝕲ᴬ ....

A.v.1 (Isa. 40:10)

הִנֵּה אֲדֹנָי יְהוִה בְּחָזָק יָבוֹא	10aA	Behold, the Lord GOD will come as a mighty one,
וּזְרֹעוֹ מֹשְׁלָה לוֹ	10aB	and his arm will rule for him.
הִנֵּה שְׂכָרוֹ אִתּוֹ	10bA	Behold, his wages are with him,
וּפְעֻלָּתוֹ לְפָנָיו:	10bB	and his recompense before him.

A.v.2 (Isa. 40:11)

כְּרֹעֶה עֶדְרוֹ יִרְעֶה	11aA	Like a shepherd he will shepherd his flock,
בִּזְרֹעוֹ יְקַבֵּץ טְלָאִים	11aB	in his arm he will gather the lambs,
וּבְחֵיקוֹ יִשָּׂא	11aC	and in his lap he will take them up,
עָלוֹת יְנַהֵל:	11bA	the nursing ewes he will lead gently.

ס <פ> – 1Qª – 𝕲ˢᴬ – ꜱᵃᵇᵈᵉ _____

B.i.1 (Isa. 40:12)

מִי־מָדַד בְּשָׁעֳלוֹ מַי* יָם*	12aA	Who measured the waters in the hollow of his hand
וְשָׁמַיִם בַּזֶּרֶת תִּכֵּן	12aB	and staked out the heavens with a span,
וְכָל בַּשָּׁלִשׁ עֲפַר הָאָרֶץ	12aC	and filled out a three–cup with the dust of the earth?
וְשָׁקַל בַּפֶּלֶס הָרִים	12bA	And weighed the mountains in scales
{𝕲ᴬ} וּגְבָעוֹת בְּמֹאזְנָיִם:	12bB	and the hills in a balance?

B.i.2 (Isa. 40:13–14)

מִי־תִכֵּן אֶת־רוּחַ יְהוָה	13aA	Who staked out the spirit of the LORD
וְאִישׁ עֲצָתוֹ יוֹדִיעֶנּוּ:	13aB	and which man made his counsel known to him?
אֶת־מִי נוֹעָץ וַיְבִינֵהוּ	14aA	Whom did he consult that he would have made him understand,
וַיְלַמְּדֵהוּ בְּאֹרַח מִשְׁפָּט	14aB	and would have taught him the path of what is right,
{וַיְלַמְּדֵהוּ דַעַת}	14aC	{and would have taught him knowledge,}
וְדֶרֶךְ תְּבוּנוֹת יוֹדִיעֶנּוּ:	14aD	and would have made known to him the way of deep understanding?

𝔊^{SA} . . . .

B.ii.1 (Isa. 40:15)

הֵן גּוֹיִם כְּמַר מִדְּלִי	15aA	Behold, the nations are like a drop from a bucket,
וּכְשַׁחַק מֹאזְנַיִם נֶחְשָׁבוּ	15aB	and are accounted as particles of dust on a balance.
הֵן אִיִּים כַּדַּק יִטּוֹל:	15bA	Behold, he lifts up the islands like powder.

B.ii.2 (Isa. 40:16)

וּלְבָנוֹן אֵין דֵּי בָּעֵר	16aA	And the Lebanon will not suffice for fuel,
{וְחַיָּתוֹ אֵין דֵּי עוֹלָה: <פ>}	16aB	and its beasts will not suffice for a burnt offering.

B.ii.3 (Isa. 40:17)

כָּל־הַגּוֹיִם כְּאַיִן נֶגְדּוֹ	17aA	All nations are as nothing to him,
מֵאֶפֶס וָתֹהוּ נֶחְשְׁבוּ־לוֹ:	17aB	they are accounted by him less than non-existent and void.

𝔊^{SA} − ꞩ^{abde} . . . .

B.iii.1 (Isa. 40:18–19)

וְאֶל־מִי תְּדַמְּיוּן אֵל	18aA	And to whom you would liken God?
וּמַה־דְּמוּת תַּעַרְכוּ לוֹ:	18aB	And which likeness would you arrange for him?
הַפֶּסֶל נָסַךְ חָרָשׁ	19aA	An idol? A craftsman casts it,
וְצֹרֵף בַּזָּהָב יְרַקְּעֶנּוּ	19aB	and the goldsmith overlays it with gold,
{וּרְתֻקוֹת כֶּסֶף צוֹרֵף: 𝔊^A}	19aC	and with soldering of a goldsmith's silver.

B.iii.2 (Isa. 40:20)

הַמְסֻכָּן* תְּרוּמָה	20aA	He who shapes the pedestal
עֵץ לֹא־יִרְקַב יִבְחָר	20aB	chooses wood that does not rot.
חָרָשׁ חָכָם יְבַקֶּשׁ־לוֹ	20bA	He seeks out a skilful craftsman
לְהָכִין פֶּסֶל לֹא יִמּוֹט:	20bB	to set up an idol that will not topple.

<ס> − 𝔊^S . . . .

B.iv.1 (Isa. 40:21)

הֲלוֹא תֵדְעוּ הֲלוֹא תִשְׁמָעוּ 21aA Don't you know? Didn't you hear?

הֲלוֹא הֻגַּד מֵרֹאשׁ לָכֶם 21aB Has it not been told to you from the beginning?

הֲלוֹא הֲבִינֹתֶם מוֹסְדוֹת 21aC Don't you understand the foundations

הָאָרֶץ: {𝔊ᴬ} of the earth?

B.iv.2 (Isa. 40:22)

הַיֹּשֵׁב עַל־חוּג הָאָרֶץ 22aA It is he who is dwelling on the circle of the earth

וְיֹשְׁבֶיהָ כַּחֲגָבִים 22aB and its dwellers are like grasshoppers.

הַנּוֹטֶה כַדֹּק שָׁמַיִם 22bA It is he who stretches out the heavens like a membrane

וַיִּמְתָּחֵם כָּאֹהֶל לָשָׁבֶת: 22bB and spreads them like a tent to dwell in.

𝔊ᴬ ....

B.v.1 (Isa. 40:23)

הַנּוֹתֵן רוֹזְנִים לְאָיִן 23aA It is he who is bringing princes to nothing,

שֹׁפְטֵי אֶרֶץ כַּתֹּהוּ עָשָׂה: 23aB he makes the judges of the earth void.

B.v.2 (Isa. 40:24)

אַף בַּל־נִטָּעוּ אַף בַּל־זֹרָעוּ 24aA Scarcely are they planted, scarcely are they sown,

אַף בַּל־שֹׁרֵשׁ בָּאָרֶץ גִּזְעָם 24aB scarcely their stem has rooted in the earth,

וְגַם־נָשַׁף בָּהֶם וַיִּבָשׁוּ 24bA when he blows upon them, and they wither,

וּסְעָרָה כַּקַּשׁ תִּשָּׂאֵם: 24bB and the storm carries them off like chaff.

ס <פ> – 1Qᵃ – 4Qᵃ – 𝔊ˢᴬᵠ – ςᵃᵇᶜᵉ _____

C.i.1 (Isa. 40:25)

וְאֶל־מִי תְדַמְּיוּנִי וְאֶשְׁוֶה 25aA And to whom will you liken me, that I would be his equal?

יֹאמַר קָדוֹשׁ: 25aB says the Holy One.

C.i.2 (Isa. 40:26)

שְׂאוּ־מָרוֹם עֵינֵיכֶם וּרְאוּ 26aA Lift up your eyes on high, and see:

מִי־בָרָא אֵלֶּה 26aB Who did create those over there?

הַמּוֹצִיא בְמִסְפָּר צְבָאָם 26aC He who brings out their army in number!

לְכֻלָּם בְּשֵׁם יִקְרָא 26bA All of them he calls by name;

מֵרֹב אוֹנִים וְאַמִּיץ כֹּחַ 26bB because of him who is great in forces and mighty of strength,

אִישׁ לֹא נֶעְדָּר: 26bC not one of them is missing.

ס <פ> – 1Qᵃ – ςᵇᵉ ....

C.ii.1 (Isa. 40:27)

לָמָּה תֹאמַר יַעֲקֹב	27aA	Why do you say, O Jacob,
וּתְדַבֵּר יִשְׂרָאֵל	27aB	and speak, O Israel:
נִסְתְּרָה דַרְכִּי מֵיהוָה	27bA	"My way is hidden from the LORD,
{𝔊ˢ} וּמֵאֱלֹהַי מִשְׁפָּטִי יַעֲבוֹר׃	27bB	and my right is neglected by my God?"

C.ii.2 (Isa. 40:28)

הֲלוֹא יָדַעְתָּ אִם־לֹא שָׁמַעְתָּ	28aA	Don't you know? Or didn't you hear?
אֱלֹהֵי עוֹלָם ׀ יְהוָה	28aB	The LORD is a God of eternity,
בּוֹרֵא קְצוֹת הָאָרֶץ	28aC	the Creator of the ends of the earth.
לֹא יִיעַף וְלֹא יִיגָע	28bA	He does not become exhausted and does not grow weary,
אֵין חֵקֶר לִתְבוּנָתוֹ׃	28bB	it is impossible to trace his understanding.

𝔊ᴬ ....

C.iii.1 (Isa. 40:29)

נֹתֵן לַיָּעֵף כֹּחַ	29aA	He is giving strength to the exhausted,
וּלְאֵין אוֹנִים עָצְמָה יַרְבֶּה׃	29aB	and increases the vigour of him who has no force left.

C.iii.2 (Isa. 40:30)

וְיִעֲפוּ נְעָרִים {𝔊ˢ} וְיִגָעוּ	30aA	Yes, youths may become exhausted and grow weary,
{𝔊ᵠ} וּבַחוּרִים כָּשׁוֹל יִכָּשֵׁלוּ׃	30aB	and young men may stagger terribly,

C.iii.3 (Isa. 40:31)

וְקוֹיֵ יְהוָה יַחֲלִיפוּ כֹחַ	31aA	but those waiting for the LORD will renew their strength,
יַעֲלוּ אֵבֶר כַּנְּשָׁרִים	31aB	they will grow new pinions, like eagles.
יָרוּצוּ וְלֹא יִיגָעוּ	31bA	They will run and will not grow weary,
יֵלְכוּ וְלֹא יִיעָפוּ׃	31bB	they will walk and will not become exhausted.

פ \<ס\> – 1ℚᵃ – 𝔊ˢᴮᴬᵠ – ꜱᵃᵇᶜᵈᵉ _____

Appendix II: The Structure of Isaiah 55

ס – 1Q^a – 4Q^c – 𝕲^{SBAQ} – ܦ^{abcde} _____

A.i.1 (Isa. 55:1)

הוֹי כָּל־צָמֵא לְכוּ לַמַּיִם	1aA	Ho, all who are thirsty, come to the waters,
וַאֲשֶׁר אֵין־לוֹ כָּסֶף	1aB	and he who has no silver,
לְכוּ שִׁבְרוּ וֶאֱכֹלוּ	1bA	come, buy and eat,
וּלְכוּ שִׁבְרוּ בְּלוֹא־כֶסֶף	1bB	yes, come, buy without silver,
וּבְלוֹא מְחִיר יַיִן וְחָלָב:	1bC	and without price, wine and milk!

A.i.2 (Isa. 55:2)

לָמָּה תִשְׁקְלוּ־כֶסֶף בְּלוֹא־לֶחֶם	2aA	Why do you weigh out silver for that which is not bread?
{𝕲^{S}ܦ^b} וִיגִיעֲכֶם בְּלוֹא לְשָׂבְעָה	2aB	and your labour for that which does not satisfy?
שִׁמְעוּ שָׁמוֹעַ אֵלַי וְאִכְלוּ־טוֹב	2bA	Hearken diligently to me, and eat what is good,
{𝕲^{BA}} וְתִתְעַנַּג בַּדֶּשֶׁן נַפְשְׁכֶם:	2bB	and let your soul delight in fatness.

A.i.3 (Isa. 55:3)

הַטּוּ אָזְנְכֶם וּלְכוּ אֵלַי	3aA	Incline your ear, and come to me;
{𝕲^Q} שִׁמְעוּ וּתְחִי נַפְשְׁכֶם	3aB	hear, that your soul may live!
וְאֶכְרְתָה לָכֶם בְּרִית עוֹלָם	3bA	And let me make with you an everlasting covenant,
חַסְדֵי דָוִד הַנֶּאֱמָנִים:	3bB	the steadfast testimonies of loyalty for David.

𝕲^{SA} – ܦ^{abe} ....

A.ii.1 (Isa. 55:4)

הֵן עֵד לְאוּמִּים נְתַתִּיו	4aA	Behold, I made him a witness to the nations,
נָגִיד וּמְצַוֵּה לְאֻמִּים:	4aB	a leader and commander to the peoples.

A.ii.2 (Isa. 55:5)

הֵן גּוֹי לֹא־תֵדַע תִּקְרָא	5aA	Behold, a nation that you know not you shall call,
וְגוֹי לֹא־יְדָעוּךָ אֵלֶיךָ יָרוּצוּ	5aB	and a nation that does not know you shall run to you,
לְמַעַן יְהוָה אֱלֹהֶיךָ	5bA	because of the LORD your God,
וְלִקְדוֹשׁ יִשְׂרָאֵל{𝕲^S} כִּי פֵאֲרָךְ:	5bB	and of the Holy One of Israel for he has glorified you.

ס<פ> – 1Q^{ab} – 4Q^c – 𝕲^{SBAQ} – ܦ^{bce} _____

B.i.1 (Isa. 55:6)

דִּרְשׁ֥וּ יְהוָ֖ה	6aA	Seek the LORD,
בְּהִמָּצְא֑וֹ קְרָאֻ֖הוּ	6aB	call upon him while he may be found,
בִּהְיוֹת֥וֹ קָרֽוֹב׃	6aC	while he is near.

B.i.2 (Isa. 55:7)

יַעֲזֹ֤ב רָשָׁע֙ דַּרְכּ֔וֹ	7aA	Let the wicked abandon his way
וְאִ֥ישׁ אָ֖וֶן מַחְשְׁבֹתָ֑יו	7aB	and the unrighteous man his thoughts.
וְיָשֹׁ֤ב אֶל־יְהוָה֙ וִֽירַחֲמֵ֔הוּ	7bA	Let him return to the LORD and he will have mercy on him,
וְאֶל־אֱלֹהֵ֖ינוּ כִּֽי־יַרְבֶּ֥ה לִסְלֽוֹחַ׃	7bB	and to our God, for he will abundantly pardon.

<σ> – 1Q^a – 𝔊^Q ....

B.ii.1 (Isa. 55:8)

כִּ֣י לֹ֤א מַחְשְׁבוֹתַי֙ מַחְשְׁב֣וֹתֵיכֶ֔ם	8aA	For my thoughts are not your thoughts
וְלֹ֥א דַרְכֵיכֶ֖ם דְּרָכָ֑י	8aB	neither are your ways my ways,
נְאֻ֖ם יְהוָֽה׃	8aC	declares the LORD.

B.ii.2 (Isa. 55:9)

כִּֽי־גָבְה֥וּ שָׁמַ֖יִם מֵאָ֑רֶץ	9aA	For as the heavens are higher than the earth,
כֵּ֣ן גָּבְה֤וּ דְרָכַי֙ מִדַּרְכֵיכֶ֔ם	9bA	so are my ways higher than your ways,
וּמַחְשְׁבֹתַ֖י מִמַּחְשְׁבֹתֵיכֶֽם׃	9bB	and my thoughts than your thoughts.

<σ> – 1Q^a – 𝔊^AQ _____

C.i.1 (Isa. 55:10a)

כִּ֡י כַּאֲשֶׁ֣ר יֵרֵד֩ הַגֶּ֨שֶׁם {וְהַשֶּׁ֜לֶג} מִן־הַשָּׁמַ֗יִם	10aA	For as the rain comes down {and the snow} from heaven,
וְשָׁ֙מָּה֙ לֹ֣א יָשׁ֔וּב	10aB	and does not return thither,

C.i.2 (Isa. 55:10b-c)

כִּ֚י אִם־הִרְוָ֣ה אֶת־הָאָ֔רֶץ	10bA	but waters the earth
וְהוֹלִידָ֖הּ וְהִצְמִיחָ֑הּ	10bB	making it bear and sprout,
וְנָ֤תַן זֶ֙רַע֙ לַזֹּרֵ֔עַ	10cA	giving seed to the sower
וְלֶ֖חֶם לָאֹכֵֽל׃ {𝔊^Q}	10cB	and bread to the eater,

C.i.3 (Isa. 55:11)

כֵּ֣ן יִֽהְיֶ֤ה דְבָרִי֙ אֲשֶׁ֣ר יֵצֵ֣א מִפִּ֔י	11aA	so shall my word be that goes forth from my mouth:
לֹֽא־יָשׁ֥וּב אֵלַ֖י רֵיקָ֑ם	11aB	It shall not return to me empty,
כִּ֤י אִם־עָשָׂה֙ אֶת־אֲשֶׁ֣ר חָפַ֔צְתִּי	11bA	but it accomplishes that which I want,
וְהִצְלִ֖יחַ אֲשֶׁ֥ר שְׁלַחְתִּֽיו׃	11bB	and makes succeed what I send it for.

<σ> – 1Q^a – 𝔰^b ....

C.ii.1 (Isa. 55:12)

כִּי־בְשִׂמְחָ֣ה תֵצֵ֔אוּ	12aA	For you shall go out in joy
וּבְשָׁל֖וֹם תּוּבָל֑וּן	12aB	and in peace be led forth.
הֶהָרִ֣ים וְהַגְּבָע֗וֹת	12bA	The mountains and the hills
יִפְצְח֤וּ לִפְנֵיכֶם֙ רִנָּ֔ה	12bB	shall break forth into singing before you,
וְכָל־עֲצֵ֥י הַשָּׂדֶ֖ה יִמְחֲאוּ־כָֽף׃	12bC	and all the trees of the field shall clap their hands.

{𝔊ᴬ}

C.ii.2 (Isa. 55:13)

תַּ֤חַת הַֽנַּעֲצוּץ֙ יַעֲלֶ֣ה בְר֔וֹשׁ	13aA	Instead of a camel thorn shall come up a juniper,
וְתַ֥חַת הַסִּרְפָּ֖ד יַעֲלֶ֣ה הֲדַ֑ס	13aB	and instead of a nettle shall come up a myrtle.
וְהָיָ֤ה לַֽיהוָה֙ לְשֵׁ֔ם	13bA	And it shall be a name for the LORD,
לְא֥וֹת עוֹלָ֖ם לֹ֥א יִכָּרֵֽת׃	13bB	an everlasting sign which shall not be cut off.

ס <פ> – 1𝔔ᵃᵇ – 𝔊ˢᴮᴬᏎ – 𝔖ᵇᵉ _____

Meindert Dijkstra   *Utrecht - The Netherlands*

The Valley of Dry Bones:

Coping with the Reality of the Exile in the Book of Ezekiel[*]

1 Introduction

The image of the Valley of Dry Bones is certainly one of the most impressive metaphors for the Babylonian captivity and the crisis of Israelite religion in the sixth century BCE. Religion under stress is the theme of this conference and, indeed, much stress and despair is contained in the book of Ezekiel in general and this vision in particular. Even so, the same vision expresses the ultimate hope for the future of Judea Capta. How do texts cope with reality and how do their spokesmen make a message of ultimate hope out of a vision of utter despair? How did the Jews in Babylon cope with reality, according to the book of Ezekiel? What were the questions? What were the answers given? The Golah, the Jewish communities in the diaspora, developed views on their Jewish identity. They even made the priest, Ezekiel, son of Buzi, their spokesman. Ultimately, they accepted his grim existence as that of a prophet in their midst (Ezek. 3:15; 8:1; 24:27; 33:33). Close reading of the book of Ezekiel does not intend to reveal only the prophet in person, his whereabouts and any *ipsissima verba*. Though large parts of the book of Ezekiel go back to the life and work of the priest-prophet of that name, the present book reflects mainly the concerns and expectations of those diaspora Jews who wanted to follow the *sunna* of this prophet.[1]

In this paper, I should like to discuss some texts to show what the creative tradition of the Ezekiel School made of its protagonist Ezekiel: a theology of captivity searching for a new religious and cultural identity, if not a new *status confessionis*. It was in the reinterpretation of his prophecies that the exiled Jews of Babylon taught themselves how to cope with the present situation and what to believe about the future. The present situation with its predicaments was dominated by questions about the present and future relation-

---

[*]Texts and other parts of this contribution were used for reading texts from Ezekiel in a workshop at the symposium. I would like to thank all those who participated in my workshop, and offered useful additions and also critical remarks to some of my ideas *in statu nascendi*.

[1]Why I use of the Islamic term *sunna* in this paper, I will explain later.

ship between Jerusalem and the diaspora communities, in particular in the light of a growing antagonism between the exiles and those living in Palestine.

2 The Golah-Oriented Redaction of Ezekiel

What I intend to do is to read the book of Ezekiel backwards. This does not mean reading the book in reverse order starting with the last chapter, but to read it according to its development of thought in the history of its redaction. Even if we cannot immediately read the book of Ezekiel as a source of history, we may assume that the book itself is history and that its sequence of redaction reflects something of the problems of the 'School of Ezekiel', if not the Jewish communities dispersed in the valley between the rivers, the valley of dry bones.[2] Scholarship agrees that Ezekiel's book passed through several revisions, connected with the development of the Jewish communities in the diaspora in relationship to their countrymen left behind in Palestine. This sequence of redactions gave rise to two editions, which were later standardized in the textual versions of MT and LXX, the LXX representing the shorter and older edition.[3] In his commentary Zimmerli showed convincingly how the book of Ezekiel goes back to the oral preaching of this prophet-priest, but that its present form is the result of a literary *Nachinterpretation* and *Fortschreibung* by a group of reform priests in the light of historical developments in post-exilic Palestine and the Babylonian diaspora.[4]

Pohlmann and others introduced the idea of a Golah-oriented redaction of the book of Ezekiel.[5] He assumed that after a first collection of prophetic lamentations and other pronouncements in an announcement–fulfilment scheme, the first major Golah-oriented revision of this initial *vita prophetae* assigned a special role to the exiles of 597 in the restoration and reform of the Jewish community both in the land and exile. Members of this first deportation assembled around

---

[2]By the 'School of Ezekiel', I mean the group of people defined as "...eine priesterliche Reformgruppe ..., die sich um den 597 BCE deportierten Priester-Propheten Ezechiel (Ezek. 1,3) und seine literarische Hinterlassenschaft gebildet hatte", R. Albertz, *Religionsgeschichte Israels in alttestamentlicher Zeit*, Bd. 2 (GAT, 8/2), Göttingen, 1992, 446.

[3]E. Tov, *Textual Criticism of the Hebrew Bible*, Minneapolis 1992, 333-4.

[4]W. Zimmerli, *Ezechiel 1-24*, (BK, 13/1), Neukirchen-Vluyn 1969, 106*-14*.

[5]K.-F. Pohlmann, *Ezechielstudien: Zur Redaktionsgeschichte des Buches und zur Frage nach den ältesten Texten* (BZAW, 202), Berlin & New York 1992, 3-45, 247; Idem, *Der Prophet Hesekiel/Ezechiel Kapitel 1-19* (ATD, 22/1) Göttingen 1996, 27-33. Pohlmann identifies this group with the Zerubbabel group, Idem, *Der Prophet Hesekiel*, 131.

the priest-prophet, and revised the מְגִלַּת־סֵפֶר, a kind of 'Urrolle', which they literally put into the mouth of the prophet (Ezek. 2:9–3:3), in order to stress the special position of the Golah in contrast to unfaithful Jerusalem. In this conception, no role is envisaged as being played by the captives of the second deportation, let alone by the Israelites left behind (Ezek. 2:3-5; 33:23-29). A further diaspora-oriented redaction, however, moderates this exclusive position in favour of the wider community of the exiled Jews. This theological reflection does not restrict itself to the conflict between the first exiles and the citizens of Jerusalem left behind, but tries to develop a vision of the purpose and meaning of the exile (under the theme of exile and return, diaspora and restoration) as part of God's plan for Israel.[6]

Though one may doubt whether Ezekiel was redacted in such sharply circumscribed stages related to clearly defined factions in the diaspora,[7] I agree with Pohlmann *et al.* that the book of Ezekiel as a whole was written by a reformist group assembled around the legacy of a certain prophet-priest Ezekiel. From the perspective and expectations of the exilic community, this group focused Ezekiel's literary heritage on the position and future role of the Golah in both the diaspora and the land of Israel. The book is less a biography of the prophet-priest Ezekiel than the literary legacy of a group which saw YHWH's presence among them as מִקְדָּשׁ מְעַט, '*the lesser sanctuary*' (Ezek. 11:16). It focused Ezekiel's legacy not only on the religious survival of the Judahite Golah but also on the restoration of the land and its central sanctuary as laid down in the draft of the new temple and its institutions (Ezekiel 40–48). It is not so much the *ipsissima verba* as the *Nachinterpretation* of Ezekiel's prophecies which formulates a new vision of the fate of the exiles in relation to their countrymen left behind at home in Jerusalem and Judah.

It was perhaps the same reformist group, presumably of Zadokite background, which was also responsible for the Zadokite revision of the new temple statute (Ezek. 40–48) in Jerusalem after the Zadokites had again established their leading and privileged position among the clergy of the new temple.[8] A last revision, building on an earlier ver-

---

[6] Pohlmann, *Ezechielstudien*, 120-34, 247-9.

[7] See C.R. Seitz, "The Crisis and Interpretation over the Meaning and Purpose of the Exile: A Redactional Study of Jeremiah xxi-xliii," *VT* 35 (1985), 78-97, on K.-F. Pohlmann, *Studien zum Jeremiabuch*, (FRLANT, 118), Göttingen, 1978. Though Pohlmann clearly sets the date of the Golah-oriented redaction of Jeremiah in the time of the composition of Chronicles, he is vague about the redactions of Ezekiel, suggesting a general post-exilic date beginning with the Zerubbabel group.

[8] M. Dijkstra, *Ezechiël*, dl. 2, (T&T), Kampen 1989, *sub loco* 42:1-14; 43:18-19; 44:10-16; 45:1-8; 45:19-20.

sion from the 'School of Ezekiel', reflected the compromise worked out
between the Zadokite priesthood in exile, to which Ezekiel possibly
also belonged (1 Chron. 24:16),[9] and the non-Zadokite priests-levites
who claimed better treatment and a more respected position in the
Temple than before the exile. The oppositions in the book of Ezekiel
are observable not only in the tense relationship between the exiled
Judaeans, or diaspora Jews and those left behind in the land, but
also in the views elaborated on the function of the old (deserted, but
still to be restored) central sanctuary in Jerusalem for the new 'lesser
sanctuary' of the diaspora (Ezek. 11:16).

3 The Text and Redaction of Ezekiel 25:25-27 + 33:21-22

The question has often been discussed where the prophet Ezekiel performed his duty, in Babylon, in Jerusalem, in both places, or even
somewhere else – in Phoenicia. A modern literary approach to the
book of Ezekiel makes such deliberations less relevant, for irrespective
of the prophet's domicile or provenance and settlement, it can hardly
be doubted that the place and time of the present book of Ezekiel was
the 'School of Ezekiel' in Babylon, a reformist group that ascribed to
its master the role of founding father to the Jewish community after
the exile. The most telling episode for this in the life of the prophet
which formed the basic material of the Golah-oriented book is Ezek.
24:25-27 in combination with 33:21-22. The text forms the closing
passage of an account about the sudden death of the prophet's wife
and its symbolic explanation. At the same time, it marks the opening
of the announcement and report of a following symbolic action concerning the theme of prophets as a model, a sign of God's presence
and plan among the exiled Jews.

The connecting words between Ezek. 24:12-26 and the chronistic
report in 33:21-22 are often considered to be the work of the redaction
which incorporates chapters 25:1–32:32 and, perhaps, also 33:1-20 as
the introduction to the third section in the final collection of Ezekiel.[10]
The text is indeed not without problems. Firstly, it is noteworthy that
the words בְּיוֹם קַחְתִּי מֵהֶם אֶת־מָעוּזָם in 24:25 correspond (or actually do
not correspond) with the doubled phrase בַּיּוֹם הַהוּא in vv. 26-27, while,

---

[9]H. Gese, *Der Verfassungentwurf des Ezechiel (Kap. 40–48) traditionsge-
schichtlich untersucht* (BHTh, 25), Tübingen 1957; W. Zimmerli, *Ezechiel 25-48*
(BK, 13/2), Neukirchen-Vluyn ²1979, 1240-9; Albertz, *Religionsgeschichte Israels*,
Bd. 2, 446-59.

[10]Zimmerli, *Ezechiel 25-48*, 579-81, 797; H.F. Fuhs, *Ezechiel II 25-48* (NEB.
AT), Würzburg 1988, 135; Pohlmann, *Ezekielstudien*, 4, 32-3.

secondly, the present text suggests a remarkable, if not impossible, coincidence between the fall of Jerusalem and the arrival of the fugitive and eye-witness. To remove these difficulties, one may assume that v. 26 was interpolated as a rather clumsy attempt to harmonize the text with the report of Ezek. 33:21-22.[11] But leaving out this verse makes the contradiction even more apparent, since Ezek. 24:25, 27 suggest that the speech impediment or ban on speech[12] was lifted when Jerusalem fell, whereas Ezek. 33:21-22 clearly states that this happened half a year after the fall on the arrival of the fugitive and eye-witness.

Other scholars assume that the fragments Ezek. 24:25-27 and 33:21-22 originally formed one text-unit. Similarly, from a redactional point of view the Golah-oriented revision could be based on an initially created *vita prophetae* consisting of prophecies of doom and symbolic actions in which our text formed the original transition to the prophecies of salvation and restoration.[13] Either way, it was the closing section of another series of symbolic actions dealing with the siege and fall of Jerusalem. Typically for this genre, it shows the pattern of announcement and fulfilment, which was characteristic also of the original prophetic book according to Pohlmann.[14] In addition, Vogt suggested that the seeming contradiction between the two parts of the pericope was not the result of a clumsy harmonization, but was caused by the loss of a piece of text in the textual tradition. In his opinion the announcement of the loss of speech as found in 3:25ab-26a should be included after the first בַּיּוֹם הַהוּא.[15] The emendation is ingenious, but perhaps too far-fetched. If the problem is indeed a result of a textual lapse, it is more probable that because of *homoioteleuton* after the phrase בַּיּוֹם a few words dropped out, in which it was announced that the prophet would become silent. I should like to suggest a restoration of the fourfold parallel structure of the announcement as follows:[16]

---

[11]Zimmerli, *Ezechiel 1-24*, 577-8; E. Vogt, *Untersuchungen zum Buch Ezechiel* (AnBib, 95), Rome 1981, 96-7.

[12]It is still a matter of debate whether the prophet suffered from a speech impediment, or whether his silence was the result of a ban on speech. See B. Lang, *Ezechiel* (EdF, 153), Darmstadt, 1981, 57-74; see recently D.J. Halperin, *Seeking Ezekiel: Text and Psychology*, University Park, PA 1994.

[13]Vogt, *Untersuchungen*, 95-102; Pohlmann, *Ezekielstudien*, 24-5, 32-4.

[14]Pohlmann, *Ezechielstudien*, 21-34.

[15]Vogt, *Untersuchungen*, 97-102.

[16]Dijkstra, *Ezechiël*, dl. 2, 21-3.

ואתה בן־אדם הלוא ביום קחתי מהם את־מעוזם
משוש תפארתם את־מחמד עיניהם ואת־משא נפשם בניהם ובנותיהם
ביום >ההוא תאלם<
>וביום< בוא הפליט אליך להשמעות אזנים
ביום ההוא יפתח פיך[17] [את־הפליט] ותדבר ולא תאלם עוד
והיית להם למיפת וידעו כי־אני יהוה

I should translate the restored text Ezek. 24:25-27+33:21-22 as follows:

> And you, son of man, on the day I take away their stronghold,
> their joy and glory, the delight of their eyes, their heart's desire, and
> their sons and daughters as well,
> on <that> day <you will become silent.
> And on the day> the fugitive shall come to you to tell you the news personally,
> on that day your mouth will be opened [...] and you will speak and
> will no longer be silent.
> So you will be a sign to them, and they will know that I am the LORD.
> In the twelfth year of our exile, in the tenth month on the fifth day,
> a fugitive came to me and said: "The city has fallen!"
> Now the evening before the man left, the hand of the LORD had
> come upon me[18]
> and he opened my mouth when the man came to me in the morning.
> So my mouth was opened and I was no longer silent.

If this reconstruction is correct, the text leaves no doubt that the prophet was situated amongst the people in exile and also that this tradition formed part of the original Life of the Prophet which in turn most probably retained some historically credible recollection of the prophet's experiences in exile. These experiences of the sudden loss of his wife and his speech impediment were understood symbolically, perhaps already by the prophet himself and, in any case, by the author(s) of his *vita*. It was the silence of God in the catastrophe befalling Jerusalem that was symbolically expressed and made visible in the prophet's personal fate. Once more let me repeat, however, that this literary event in its present form no longer necessarily expresses only the personal experience of the prophet who may have been known as person suffering from a speech impediment, but is

---

[17]Presumably an explanatory gloss, see BHS and the commentaries of G. Fohrer, *Ezechiel* (HAT), Tübingen [2]1955, Zimmerli *et al., sub loco.*

[18]A case of a narrative flashback ('Nachholende Erzählung'), literally: the night before he was coming, that is, started on his way in the night of Jerusalem's fall (2 Kgs 25:4; Ezek. 12:1-16), Dijkstra, *Ezechiël*, dl. 2, 21-3, 102-4; B. Maarsingh, *Ezechiël*, dl. 3 (POT, 23/1), Nijkerk 1991, 17.

now part of his school biography. It expresses the large spiritual gap in time and place between Jerusalem and the Golah. It became symbolically a *rite de passage* closing the chapter of unfaithful Israel in the land and opening a new chapter between the LORD and faithful Israel in captivity. The concrete distance in time and place reflects by metaphor the religious and spiritual gap. This deep gap becomes even more apparent in the prophecy which follows the report, in which the ban on speech is lifted (Ezek. 33:23-29).

4   Antagonism Between the People in Israel and the Golah

A salient feature in this text is the quotation put in the mouth of the people left behind in the land of Israel. There is no need to deal here with the question of whether it involves here and elsewhere in the book of Ezekiel real or fictive quotations.[19] Even if it is a fictive quotation, it is revealing for the state of mind among the exiles and serves the literary purpose of bringing clarity to the situation of guilt, despair and expectation among the diaspora. It is the *sunna* of the prophet, the tradition of his school that helps in coping with reality and in wresting meaning and purpose out of their existence in captivity. It helps the Jews of the diaspora to understand their situation and their future role in God's plan for Israel. The quotations in Ezekiel, in particular, provide interesting parameters to quantify the growing antagonism between those who lived in Palestine and the communities of the exile. Such positions about the mutual *status quo* are quoted in Ezek. 11:2-3, 15; 33:10, 24 and 37:11. Thus, the statements of the people from the land of Israel about themselves and their exiled countrymen:

> Son of man, these are the men who are plotting evil and giving wicked advice in this city, "This is not the time to build houses. This city is a cooking pot and we are the meat." (Ezek. 11:2-3)

> Son of man, it is your brothers, not only your own blood relatives, but also the whole house of Israel,[20] of whom the people of Jerusalem say, "They are far away from the LORD; this land was given to us as our possession!" (Ezek. 11:15)

---

[19] H.W. Wolff, *Das Zitat im Prophetenspruch* (BEvTh, 4), München 1937, 28-51 = *Gesammelte Studien zum Alten Testament* (TB, 22), München 1973, 54-75.

[20] The singular expression 'your brothers' is explained, perhaps by a redactor, as not only the kinshipgroup of the prophet responsible for his redemption, but the entire exilic community; see, for instance, Ezek. 33:10.

> Son of man, the people living in those ruins in the land of Israel are
> saying, "Abraham was only one man. Yet he possessed the land. But
> we are many. Surely the land has been given to us as our possession!"
> (Ezek. 33:24)

More frequently, we find desperate statements and questions posed
by members of the diaspora community:

> Son of man, what is this proverb you have in the land of Israel, "The
> days go by and every vision comes to nothing?" (Ezek. 12:22)

> What do you mean by quoting this proverb from the land of Israel,
> "The fathers eat sour grapes and the children's teeth are set on
> edge?" (Ezek. 18:2)

> You say, "We want to be like the nations, like the peoples of the
> world, who serve wood and stone." (Ezek. 20:32)

> Son of man, say to the house of Israel: This is what you are saying,
> "Our offences and sins weigh us down so that we are wasting away
> because of them. How then can we live?" (Ezek. 33:10)

> Yet your countrymen say, "The way of the LORD is not just." (Ezek.
> 18:25, 29 ‖ 33:17, 20)

> Son of man, these bones are the whole house of Israel. They say,
> "Our bones are dried up and are hope is gone; we are totally cut off
> (from the land of the living)!" (Ezek. 37:11)[21]

In these quotations, we witness an optimistic pro-land position in
clear tension with the critical questions and laments of despair of the
exilic community. In the latter, the exilic community is trying to understand its own fate in the Babylonian diaspora in contrast to the
self-satisfied view of those who continue to live in the land after the
first deportation and the fall of Jerusalem. They made the prophet
spokesman not only of their despair but also of the interpretation of
their captivity and their role in the future life of Israel. Chapters 11
and 33 especially seem to emphasize the nature of this conflict and its
development. In the subsequent oracles, which they appropriated, interpreted and revised, we are confronted with the self-contained view
of those who remained in the land and we gain a broader perspective
on the struggle by the exiles to wrest meaning from their existence

---

[21] Perhaps in this context of psalm-like language, meaning being cut off from
the land of the living (see, for instance, Isa. 53:8), but, in the broader context of
the vision, referring also to the home country.

in the diaspora. This interpretational development is strongly apparent in the complicated redaction of texts such as Ezek. 11:14-22 and
33:23-29. Let us take a closer look at the latter text.

> Then the word of the LORD came to me, "Son of man, the people
> living in the ruins of the land of Israel are saying, 'Abraham was
> only one man. Yet he possessed the land. But we are many. Surely
> the land has been given to us as our possession.'
> [Therefore say to them, "This is what the Lord GOD says,
> 'You eat meat with the blood still in it[22] and look up to your idols,
> you shed blood and take the land in possession.[23]
> You rely on your sword and do detestable things,
> each of you defiles his neighbour's wife and you take the land in
> possession.'"]
> This you will say to them, "This is what the Lord GOD says,
> 'As surely as I live, those who are left in the ruins will fall by the
> sword,
> those out in the country I will give to the wild animals to be de-
> voured,
> and those in the strongholds and caves will die of a plague.
> I will make the land a desolate waste, and their proud strength will
> come to an end,
> and the mountains of Israel will become desolate so that no one will
> cross them.
> Then they will know that I am the LORD, when I have made the
> land a desolate waste,
> because of all the detestable things they have done.'"

This text unit shows clear signs of redactional activity. Verses 25-
26 are not present in the LXX nor in some witnesses of the Vetus
Latina. Though *homoioteleuton* is often assumed here, it may be one
of the instances where the LXX has preserved the shorter edition.
In any case, the introduction of v. 27 looks like the beginning of the

---

[22]Some would emend the text reading עַל־הֶהָרִים as in 18:6 and 22:9, but the
expression is well established in Lev. 19:26, 1 Sam. 14:32-33 and beside the usual
expression אָכַל דָּם (Lev. 17:10-12) is long known to describe a fundamental ritual
offence in the Bible, Judaism, Early Christianity and Islam. See recently J. Milgrom, "Ethics and Ritual: The Foundations of the Biblical Dietary Laws", in: E.B.
Firmage *et al.* (eds.), *Religion and Law: Biblical – Judaic and Islamic Perspectives*, Winona Lake 1990, 160-9; P.J. Tomson, *Paul and the Jewish Law: Halakha in
the Letters of the Apostle to the Gentiles* (CRI, 3/1), Assen 1990; also H.L. Strack,
P. Billerbeck, *Kommentar zum Neuen Testament aus Talmud und Midrasch*, Bd.
2: Das Evangelium nach Markus, Lukas und Johannes und die Apostelgeschichte,
München 1924, 733-9.

[23]Many translations and commentaries read the last phrase of vv. 25-26 as a
rhetorical or ironic question, but the sentence is not marked as such. Perhaps the
intention of the text was to express ironically the taking of the land in possession
as a final act of violence instead of being a gift, as is said in the pious-sounding
words of the people living in the ruins. See Dijkstra, *Ezechiël*, dl. 2, 104.

original oracle after the quotation of the people in the ruins. But later redaction clearly missed a stronger motivation than the 'bad theology' in the quoted words: clear ritual and social offences that make the possession of the land more the result of criminal activity than a sign of election of the true offspring of Abraham.

This obvious insertion in the original oracle requires further scrutiny in its historical and religious ramifications. First of all, it is noteworthy that the offences mentioned all belong to the fundamentals of the Jewish *status confessionis*, the prohibition of idolatry, illicit sexual behaviour, eating of blood and bloodshed, none to be ever transgressed by a Jew even at the cost of his life. Each of them would become an axiomatic commandment and a basic concern in the development of many halakhot and even complete tractates in the Mishnah.[24] Each of them would later be listed among 'the commandments of the sons of Noah' (Gen. 9:3-6), the first law for humanity in the Bible and Judaism as early as P and the 'School of Ezekiel'. Though only the prohibition of eating animal blood and bloodshed are mentioned in Gen. 9:3-6, idolatry and illicit sexuality were included at some very early stage[25] among the commandments incumbent on righteous people among all mankind (e.g. Acts 15:20).[26] It is possible that idolatry here originally related to ancestor worship only,[27] but abstinence from any form of idolatry became the foremost commandment of the Noahite prescriptions.[28] Together with the illegal claims of the promised land and bloodshed these basic offences are subsumed, under 'detestable things', that is ritual offences, suggesting that violation of ritual law in the Bible's view is no less than any moral offence. On the contrary, ritual law may serve as the very basis of ethics as, for instance, suggested in the commands to Noah and his sons.[29] First of all, these commandments as put forward in Gen. 9:3-6 and implied

---

[24] See, for instance, on idolatry, Tomson, *Paul and the Jewish Law*, 154-68.

[25] The expression 'not defile the neighbour's wife' (also Ezek. 18:6, 15; 22:11) implies more than πορνεια, since fornication was forbidden anyhow and at all times. The context of Lev. 20:10-12 and Ezek. 22:10-11 clearly implies any form of incest. In similar vein, Acts 15:20 was understood and implemented on the basis of Lev. 18:6-18 in the early Church. See Strack, Billerbeck, *Kommentar*, 729-30.

[26] Strack, Billerbeck, *Kommentar*, 729-39.

[27] In my opinion, the expression 'lifting up the eyes to the idols' (especially Ezek. 14:1-8) referred initially to ancestor worship and consulting the dead. Compare also how the expression 'sacrifices to the dead' (Ps. 106:28) becomes the general expression for idolatry in Tannaic tradition, Tomson, *Paul and the Jewish Law*, 157.

[28] Strack, Billerbeck, *Kommentar*, on 1 Cor. 8:1; 10:20-21; Tomson, *Paul and the Law*, 155, 177-8.

[29] Milgrom, "Ethics and Ritual", 160.

in Ezek. 33:25-26 serve as the basic standards of humanity for Israel itself, but one wonders at what early stage the same commandments were also thought to be incumbent upon all mankind, or at least upon the peoples amidst whom Israel lived.

From this set of fundamental ritual and moral offences, one may learn that the countrymen in the ruins of Judah did not even keep the most basic prescriptions that should keep a Jew Jewish – prescriptions which, if taken as Noahite commandments, would even make proselytes and gentiles who do not know the law acceptable in the eyes of the Lord. It is of interest to discover a positive attitude to the righteous non-Israelite in the book of Ezekiel, thus a beginning of real diaspora theology. The hardest reproach the prophet (and apparently also his 'School' in Babylon) could make against Jerusalem was that it had not only rebelled against the LORD's laws and decrees, but also against the standards of the nations round about (Ezek. 5:7). Unfortunately, the prophet does not specify what these standards of the nations were, but if we are permitted to understand them also as basic standards for, or required from, the nations, the implications of such a universalistic understanding of this rather late insertion of Ezek. 33:25-26 into this pericope are indeed remarkable.

5 Basics of Humanity

The diaspora seems to have been developing ideas about basic standards and perhaps we find them, or some of them, formulated in this text. Abraham alone was indeed a father of many; he was even the most ecumenical patriarch of Israel.[30] It cannot be a coincidence that he is mentioned in this context of antagonism between the Golah and Jerusalem. The figure of Abraham indeed gained emphasis during the Babylonian captivity.[31] Whereas the people left in the land emphasized their claims for possession of the land against the exiles by referring to the promise of Abraham, the Golah considered itself the true seed of Abraham, seeing him as the model of their own predicament and of their future return to the promised land. It is in this period that he, the ancestor of Israel and of many other nations (Gen. 17), also became the ancestor called from Ur Kasdim, the fiery furnace of Babylon.

From the perspective of the Babylonian Jews, someone claiming to be one of the many who inherited Abraham's legacy must also be ready to obey at least the basics of humanity as laid down in Israelite

---

[30]M. Dijkstra, "Abraham", in: *DDD*, 8-9, [2]*DDD*, 3-5.

[31]Albertz, *Religionsgeschichte Israels*, Bd. 2, 419-21.

law. The original prophecy, which announced ultimate doom for the people left after the fall of Jerusalem because of their false belief in their special election to survive the catastrophe, was turned into a judgement because of the detestable things they had done (last part of 33:29). The people in the ruins were no longer considered to be descendents of Abraham. In the eyes of the diaspora community they had become completely foreign to the basic commandments of Jewish law. Even worse, the listing of the set of ritual and moral offences implies that they could not even be considered righteous aliens living in the land of Israel since they had not observed the basic standards required for Jews and gentiles alike.

Such criticism and harsh judgement hardly reflects the immediate aftermath of Jerusalem's fall but projects us into the sphere of the Jewish remnant that had survived the exile and, possibly, had returned to Jerusalem amidst the people of the land (even amidst the ruins of the land of Israel) whom they no longer considered to be Israelites, let alone Jews. It may reflect the antagonism of the time of governor Nehemiah, in which the remnant of the Jews separated themselves from the neighbouring peoples for the sake of the law of God (Neh. 10:28, see also Ezra 9:1; 10:11). Viewed this way, this pericope along with others provides an example of how the 'School of Ezekiel' coped with the historical reality of the animosity between Jerusalem and Babylon in the exilic period and also after the return of the Jews who survived the exile. That reality helped to create a new Jewish identity in opposition to the people of the land. Whatever their actual ethnic descent, from the perspective of Jewish law, they were seen as Ammonites (Tobiah, the Ammonite!) and Moabites, who were no longer to be admitted into the assembly of God. The diaspora community developed a theology in which some basic *torot d'entrée* helped to draw the boundary of their new *status confessionis*. Some of the other quotations, especially those from the mouth of the exilic community, range from utter despair (Ezek. 20:32, 37:11) and criticism of God's sound judgement (Ezek. 33:17-20) to repentance and a quest for a new religious life and laws they could live by (33:10, 15 decrees that give life). They give us insight into this process. Many of these questions and remarks form part of discussions which seem to mark the beginnings of a new halakhic interpretation of ancient Israelite law on foreign soil (Ezek. 18:1-20 and 18:21-32 || 33:10-20).

6   Text and Redaction of Ezekiel 4:9-17

The second textual unit that I would like to discuss, Ezek. 4:9-17, raises even more strongly the question of the development of new halakhot for the people in exile. Large parts of the laws and the interpretation of law developed in the diaspora were also applicable in the life of those Jews who returned from exile. Much of the effort in reforming the religious communities in Judah involved the application of the newly developed 'Law of Moses' in the diaspora. Most of the laws and prescriptions about ritual purity belong to the latest parts of the Pentateuch. This part of ancient Israelite tradition may have received new attention in the diaspora. It gained new impetus and meaning in order to separate the exilic communities from their foreign environment and pagan milieu. Post-exilic changes in the celebration of the sacred festivals of Passover[32] and Tabernacles also originated in the diaspora, as did the stricter rules about intermarriage, exacting of usury and keeping the sabbath.[33] The prohibition on marriage with Canaanites was extended in and after the exile to exclude all non-Israelites (Ezra 9–10; Neh. 13; Jub. 30:7-17; TLevi 9:10), though it remained a disputed issue (Gen. 28:6-9). All these new decrees and laws were also applicable in Palestine and even as far away as Elephantine. Still one may ask whether specific laws were also developed about Jewish lifestyle in the diaspora, laws that reflect specific conditions of living on unclean foreign soil for the Golah in Babylon and elsewhere. The fear and the threat of dying on unclean foreign soil is as old as prophecy or its Deuteronomistic revision (1 Sam. 26:19-20; Amos 7:17; Hos. 9:3), but the idea of the impurity of gentile territory became more doctrinal in the Second Temple Period.[34]

In Ezek. 4:9-17 we may find, in my opinion, a passage that deals with the problems of preparing and eating clean and unclean food in the exile:

---

[32]TAD A4.1 = Cowley, No. 21 (419 BCE); *ANET*, 491; P. Grelot, *Documents araméens d'Égypte*, Paris 1972, 383-6, the Passover letter from Hananyah on the authority of Arsames, satrap of Egypt, to the Jews of Elephantine, implies the authorization of the Jewish festival of Pesach and unleavened bread according to Pentateuchal law (Exod. 12:15-20; Lev. 23:5-8).

[33]It is hardly coincidental that the major problems of intermarriage, exacting usury, keeping the sabbath and ritual purity, which were the concerns of life in the diaspora according to the book of Ezekiel, were also the major concerns of the exilic Jews Ezra and Nehemiah in their efforts to reform the Jewish communities of Palestine.

[34]Tomson, *Paul and the Jewish Law*, 153 n.12.

Take for yourself wheat and barley, beans and lentils, millet and
spelt;
put them in a bowl and use them to make bread for yourself.
You are to eat it during the 190[35] days you lie on your side.
Weigh out twenty shekels of food each day and eat it at set times.
Also measure out a sixth of a hin of water and drink it at set times.
<And the LORD said:>[36]
"A round cake of barley you are going to eat
and she[37] will prepare it in the sight of the people
using human excrement for fuel.
In this way, the people of Israel will eat defiled food
among the nations where I will drive them."
And I said: "Not so Lord GOD! I have never defiled myself.
From my youth until now, I have never eaten anything found dead
or torn by wild animals.
No unclean meat has ever entered my mouth."
"Very well", he said to me, "I give you permission to use cow dung
instead of human excrement
for you to prepare your food on it."

Some scholars assume that the mixture of wheat, barley and so on
was forbidden, referring to the prohibition to plant a field with two
kinds of seed or to weave clothing of two kinds of material (Lev. 19:19;
Deut. 22:9-11). Though that may be precarious, it is apparently not
this mix that evokes the prophet's protest. Later Jewish sources do
not mention such a prohibition.[38] The mixture seems to express a
dearth of food in the besieged city. The prophet is asked to gather
up the remnants from his stores and prepare himself for a long siege
and put himself on carefully limited rations of food and water. This
symbolic act is clearly part of the original pantomime, acting out the
impending siege and fall of Jerusalem.[39] Its explanation is found in

---

[35] MT has 390 days; 190 days according to the LXX.

[36] The words ויאמר יהוה fit better at the beginning of v. 12, rather than having
v. 13 introduce the dialogue after the instruction.

[37] About the verbal form, see H. Bauer, P. Leander, *Historische Grammatik der
hebräischen Sprache* (Olms Paperback, 19), Hildesheim 1965, 404; *HALAT* 751.
The personal pronoun 3d p. fem. suggests reading the verbal form as a 3d p. fem.,
presumably referring to the anonymous wife of the prophet, who is supposed to
bake the bread publicly outside the house. For the expression לעיניהם, see also
Ezek. 12:3 *passim*. M. Greenberg, *Ezekiel 1-20* (AncB, 22), New York 1983, 126,
takes the expression that has no clear antecedent as another sign of interpolation.

[38] For instance, in the tractate Kilayim of the Mishnah. See Zimmerli, *Ezechiel
25-48*, 125; Maarsingh, *Ezechiël*, dl. 1, 59. In *bErubin 81a*, a bread of lentils is
permitted. It is not prohibited on the basis of Ezek. 4:9-10, since the prohibition
there concerns the use of human excrement.

[39] B. Lang, "Street Theater, Raising the Dead and the Zoroastrian Connection
in Ezekiel's Prophecy", in: J. Lust (ed.), *Ezekiel and his Book* (BEThL, 74),
Leuven 1986, 297-316.

4:16-17, now prefaced, however, by a new introduction in direct speech and by the well known address of the prophet.

This last feature is a clear indication that the text was extended by a second instruction to eat a particular round cake of barley prepared on fuel made of human excrement, followed by an unusual dialogue between the LORD and the silenced(!) prophet.[40] Most modern commentaries assume that this dialogue about eating defiled and unclean prepared food[41] is an exilic or post-exilic extension. The perspective of the text has changed. No longer is the situation of the besieged city implied, but the present and future predicament of Israel in captivity. Why the redaction included this particular *sunna* of the prophet in this series of symbolic actions about besieged Jerusalem one can only guess – presumably, as an eloquent linkage of the harsh conditions of captivity with the depths to which the people trapped in Jerusalem would sink.[42] Though such a dialogue cannot be deemed impossible in the mouth of the prophet, the 'School of Ezekiel' probably made the prophet spokesman of one of its major concerns: How to keep oneself pure on impure soil.[43] The early prophets already envisaged the emotional and practical difficulties of a 'clean' Israelite lifestyle on 'unclean' soil (Amos 7:17; Hos. 9:3). However, not only does the story of Daniel 1 tell us about practical solutions to avoid ritual impurity in a foreign context,[44] but also this passage from Ezekiel reveals that practical solutions were tried and discussed.

---

[40] The Targum translates ללחם in v. 9 למיכל 'for food', which suggests that the cake of barley in v. 12 was prepared and eaten in addition to the first mentioned food, see M. Eisemann, *Yechezkel: The Book of Ezekiel*, vol. 1: A New Translation with a Commentary Anthologized from Talmudic, Midrashic and Rabbinic Sources, New York 1977, 113-4. The majority of Jewish mediaeval and later commentaries like Rashi, Radak etc. suggest that with the cake of barley the same bread mix is meant and that either the main ingredient was to be barley, or that it concerns a less appetising method of preparation (*Rashi*) or type of bread (*Midrash Vayikra Rabbah 28:6*).

[41] This passage has received surprisingly little attention in halakhic and midrashic sources. See, for instance, *bErubin 81a*; *Midrash Vayikra Rabbah 28:6*. As far as I know, only Eliezer of Beaugency suggests that ritually unclean food may be meant. In exile, one might expect the Jews to be forced to transgress their dietary laws, but Rashi suggests that 'unclean' in this text does not refer to ritual unsuitability of food, but to its disgusting manufacture, cf. Eisemann, *Yechezkel*, 114.

[42] Also Greenberg, *Ezekiel 1-20*, 125-6, sees a secondary editorial linkage between Ezekiel's lying on his side 'bearing iniquity' (representing the paralysis of the exiles) and eating unclean food (during the period of lying).

[43] See, for instance, Maarsingh, *Ezechiël*, dl. 1, 59; Pohlmann, *Der Prophet Hesekiel* (ATD, 22/1), 92.

[44] About Dan. 1:8-9, see K. Koch, *Daniel* (BK, 22), Neukirchen-Vluyn 1986, 58-63; Tomson, *Paul and the Jewish Law*, 156 with other examples from Judith and Tobit.

In this respect, the short dialogue is an interesting example of what Islamic tradition would call a *sunna*, a tradition of the prophet. Of course, it lacks one of the most conspicuous and important aspects of such a *sunna*, the *isnad al-hadith*, the chain of traditors supporting the tradition from the School of Ezekiel, but this kind of *isnad al-hadith*, which itself appears to follow the rabbinical methods of establishing a chain of tradition,[45] is a later development. What I want to grasp and define by this somewhat anachronistic genre term *sunna* is an example taken from the lifestyle of the prophet and the early diaspora, which sets a standard for future life in exile. Precisely, by the symbolic actions of Ezekiel 24:24, 27, he becomes an 'ayatollah', a sign of God's will for future Israel. We may also compare such halakha – establishing stories from the rabbinical sources, the gospels and occasionally the letters of St. Paul, for instance the paradosis or tradition about the resurrection of Christ (1 Cor. 15:3-8) and the paradosis about the Last Supper (1 Cor. 11:23-26).

7   Sunna of the Prophet About Unclean Food

What is old and what is new in this text? The role of the prophet as an intermediary is not new. Amos acts as an intermediary in praying to God for forgiveness when he sees in a vision how the LORD is preparing disaster for Israel and God relents as a result of his intercession (Amos 7:1-8; Jer. 37:3; 42:2-4). Of Moses, something similar is told (Exod. 32:30-32 // 33:1-6), while on the other hand YHWH sometimes forbids a prophet from acting as intercessor, even by silencing him (Jer. 7:16; 11:14; 14:11; Ezek. 3:25-26). It is, however, new for such an intercession to set an example of a new lifestyle. As such, the prophet indeed becomes an 'ayatollah': Ezekiel will be a sign to you; you will do just as he has done (Ezek. 24:24).[46] The difference is the difference observable in the symbolic acts in 4:9-17. Accepted as the prophet who acted out the impending doom and the fall of Jerusalem, he was also accepted as the prophet of a new religious life-style by the Jews of the diaspora.

The result of this intercession seems trivial. The prophet and so the people of Israel in exile are allowed to use dung as fuel. Though the rule has apparently something to do with ritual purity and the eating of ritually clean food in the diaspora, it is not easy to detect

---

[45]See H.L. Strack, G. Stemberger, *Introduction to the Talmud and Midrash*, Edinburgh 1991, 6, 42-3.

[46]Pohlmann, *Der Prophet Hesekiel*, 93-4 "Indem zugleich gezeigt wird, daß es einem Ezechiel möglich ist und ermöglicht wird, ..., kommt dem Propheten Vorbildcharakter zu."

the new element in this ruling. Understandably, the prophet rejected the use of human excrement as fuel not only as revolting, but also as causing ultimate defilement. The only law that reflects desacration and ritual impurity from such contact with human excrement (like contact with dead bodies and so on) is the law on relieving oneself outside the camp (Deut. 23:12-15).[47] In general, it may be said that having uncontrolled, sickly body effluents and contact with such human secretions renders people unclean according to Levitical law (Lev. 11-15).[48] Human faeces and urine are not mentioned as such, presumably because the existence and proper use of latrines in the houses[49] or else convenient patches and cesspits called a יָד 'outside the camp' (Deut. 23:13), or מַחֲרָאוֹת (2 Kgs 10:27)[50] for communal use, should keep the community clean from defilement by them. Craigie and Labuschagne, however, rightly remark with respect to the expression כֹּל דְּבַר רָע 'anything impure' in Deut. 23:10 that it may include all kinds of nightly incontinence.[51]

It is remarkable how little we know about hygienic conditions and sanitary provision in ancient Israel.[52] However, from the reaction of

---

[47]So already in mediaeval Jewish commentaries. See Eisemann, *Yechezkel*, 114; "Hygiene", in: B.C. Roth, G. Wigoder (eds.), *EJ* 8, Jerusalem 1971, 1140-1. Desacration by human excrement is also implied in 2 Kgs 10:27 where the place of the demolished Baal temple was used as a latrine. Whether we may think here of a kind of public lavatory as in the soil of a convenient patch of waste ground (J.A. Thompson, *Handbook of Life in Bible Times*, Leicester 1986, 274-6) is uncertain. Individual latrines with cesspits are known from Israel in the eight-seventh century BCE, but also from Late Bronze Ugarit (n. 50). Eating one's own human faeces, drinking urine and falling into one's own dung and urine were seen as acts of utter despair and disgrace (2 Kgs 18:27; *KTU* 1.114:20-22), and this may be true also for using it as fuel during a siege. The text about alleged dove's dung in 2 Kgs 6:25 is far from certain.

[48]R. Hink, "Rein und Unrein", in: *RGG*, Bd. 5, 941; F. Heiler, *Erscheinungsformen der Religion* (Religionen der Menschheit 1), Stuttgart 1961, 185-93; M. Lurker, *Wörterbuch der Symbolik*, Stuttgart [3]1985, 96-7. Such effluents are powerful essences. They are considered to be unclean if they leave the body uncontrolled. It may be noted, however, that blood, spittle and urine as such can also be applied in purification rituals!

[49]See Y. Shiloh, *Excavations at the City of David I (1978-1982)* (Qedem, 19), Jerusalem 1984, 10 Area E3; Pl. 16:2; 18 Area G, locus 789, Pl. 31:1; C.H.J. de Geus, *De Israelitische stad*, Kampen 1984, 68; H. Weippert, *Palästina in vorhellenistischer Zeit* (HdA, Vorderasien 2/1), München 1988, 596-7; J.C. Courtois, "L'Architecture Domistique à Ugarit au Bronze Recent", *UF* 11 (1979), 113; M. Yon, "Ugarit: The Urban Habitat", *BASOR* 286 (1992), 29.

[50]The Qere מוֹצָאוֹת is obviously a euphemism, see 2 Kgs 18:27.

[51]P.C. Craigie, *The Book of Deuteronomy* (NICOT), Grand Rapids 1976, 299; C.J. Labuschagne, *Deuteronomium*, dl. 2 (POT), Nijkerk 1990, 233.

[52]See "Hygiene", *EJ* 8, 1140-1; Thompson, *Handbook of Life in Bible Times*, 275-6.

the prophet we may surmise that even the thought of bringing food into open contact with (dried?) human faeces is repulsive.[53] Bread ovens (תַנּוּר) and open fires for cooking and heating (מְדוּרָה, e.g. Ezek. 24:9-10) usually burned wood (e.g. Num. 15:32-36; Jer. 7:18; Ezek. 24:10) and other dried vegetable material (grass, straw, stones of fruits).[54] In areas with a dearth of wood, such as Egypt and Mesopotamia, even today cakes of camel and cow dung mixed with straw, are stored on the roofs of the village houses and used for fuel. Considering the usual construction of conical bread ovens, in which physical contact between dough and fuel is not always avoidable even for a skilled baker, the prophet from his priestly perspective imagines defilement. Moreover, the oven was also considered as a kind of vessel. If it was touched by carrion of an unclean animal, it became unclean and had to be broken up (Lev. 11:35). Human excrement was seemingly in the same category as unclean, detestable substances. But why then allow the use of animal dung? Our text explicitly mentions cow dung. It may suggest that other kinds of dung, for instance from donkeys, camels and so on,[55] were excluded, because they were unclean animals (Lev. 11:4, Deut. 14:7).

Many of the commentaries suggest that the passage is an eloquent statement about the depth of despair to which Israel was going to sink, but also a promise that living conditions in exile would not be as extreme as feared, i.e. that the Jews would be forced to transgress ritual laws for preparing food and personal hygiene. A symbolic example of this is that the prophet and his fellow countrymen were permitted to use the common type of fuel in a country deficient in firewood: cow dung. But what is the halakhic background of this particular ruling, if it is assumed that all the terms that the prophet uses in his anguished reaction have halakhic significance?[56] Dalman made a significant comment on our text by remarking that permission to use cow dung would seem to be unusual for baking bread in a תַנּוּר

---

[53] The word *גֵּל, plural גְּלָלִים 1 Kgs 14:10; Ezek. 4:12-15; Zeph. 1:17; Job 20:7, is only used for human excrement in the Old Testament, but this may be accidental, for in later Hebrew, Aramaic and also Arabic (*gillah*; *geˡēlē*) it is also used for animal manure, see G. Dalman, *Arbeit und Sitte in Palästina*, Bd. 4, Gütersloh 1928-42, 18-21; *HALAT* 182, 186.

[54] Dalman, *Arbeit und Sitte*, Bd. 4, 1-18; M. Kellermann, "Ofen", *BRL*, Bd. 2, 240-1.

[55] Dalman, *Arbeit und Sitte*, Bd. 4, 18.

[56] For instance, Eisemann, *Yechezkel*, 115. The Sages, of course, read the passage in its full halakhic meaning (*bKhullin*, 37b), but even if we cannot assume that all halakhic sanctions existed in Ezekiel's time for him as a priest, the text may have had early halakhic significance in the ensuing Second Temple Period.

or otherwise both in antiquity and in recent times.[57] If use of dung
for baking bread was not the norm in ancient or modern Palestine,
where wood was always the main source of fuel, permission to use
cow dung would seem more appropriate for the Babylonian exile. As
such, the text could be a specimen of ensuing scholarly discussion
intended to work out new living conditions for the Jews in the diaspora of Mesopotamia. Living in an unclean country poses also the
question whether certain habits on foreign soil, which were formerly
seen as unclean, could be accepted for better or worse. The halakhic
ruling restricting animal dung to cow dung may then be a somewhat
trivial example of coping with reality and a transformation of ritual
tradition and dietary laws. Indeed, the pericope explores the possibilities and limits of diaspora existence to the extreme. The extreme
proposition – let us suppose circumstances force us to use human faeces as fuel – is annulled with the help of a *sunna*, an experience of
the prophet. He rejected it as utterly intolerable by comparing it to
eating carrion, trefa and other unclean meat. But the custom of using dung as fuel in the same way that the Mesopotamian peoples did
is permitted, though it was restricted to cow dung, since a cow is a
clean animal. Understood this way, the pericope may reflect an early
scholarly discussion about a specific halakhic problem of the diaspora
community.

8   Conclusion

Such a story (actually only a short dialogue) is an early and, as far as
I can see, an extremely rare example of a Jewish halakhic discussion
about the preparation and eating of kosher food. No other examples
are known to me from the Old Testament, though one could refer to
such halakhic stories as the stoning of the blasphemer of mixed descent (application of the principle that you are to have the same law
for the alien and the native-born, Lev. 24:10-23) and the story of the
Sabbath-breaker (Num. 15:32-36), showing that gathering wood on
Sabbath is not allowed. But there is other evidence of school activity
and scholarly discussion in Ezekiel. The most interesting example is
his teachings following the *quaestio* stated in Ezek. 33:10: "If our offences and sins weigh us down and we are wasting away because of
them, how then can we live?". They not only contain an emotional
appeal for repentance, but also continue with a halakhic exposition

---

[57]Dalman, *Arbeit und Sitte*, Bd. 4, 20, 30, 32. Also the Sages mention dung as
a type of fuel to be used for a cooking fire (מְדוּרָה), only if no other kind of fuel is
available, *jShabbat*, 4b-5a.

of what it means for the righteous to follow the decrees that give life. These teachings are found in the book of Ezekiel in two slightly different versions (Ezek. 18:21-32 // 33:10-20). It is plausible to suppose here that the same teaching by the prophet was memorized by two different students and applied in two slightly different contexts of school discussion.[58] These discussions and the new insights and rules derived from them date mainly from the post-exilic period, but are presented as the *sunna* of the prophet Ezekiel, as the *sunna* of Moses and even of the patriarchs. An interesting example from the Priestly tradition is also the mitigation of the rule, 'Do not marry a Canaanite woman' (Gen. 26:34-35, 27:46–28:9, esp. 28:1, 6), which is presented as a patriarchal *sunna*. One wonders how many stories of the patriarchs were rewritten by exilic and post-exilic authors in the light of the experiences of the diaspora community, but that is another story.

---

[58] Dijkstra, *Ezechiël*, dl. 2, 100-1.

Christoph Uehlinger   *Fribourg – Switzerland*

'Powerful Persianisms' in Glyptic Iconography of Persian Period Palestine*

1 Introduction

"Religion under stress" – the title of the Utrecht conference makes it plain that the historical study of Palestine, particularly of nascent (proto-?)Judaism, during the Persian period generally concentrates on religious history viewed through the particular lenses of biblical literature. The latter stresses the hardships of exile, the difficulties met by those who returned from exile, were in charge of the re-organization of Yehud and had to face both a sometimes reluctant local population and hostile neighbours. Critical history writing during the last years has deconstructed a number of elements that build up this general picture of religious and socio-political stress, among them the very concept of 'exile' which serves as fundamental period marker in biblical literature and biblical studies alike.[1] At the end of the Utrecht conference, some would raise the question whether there was any stress at all in Persian period Palestine, or more adequately, whether 'stress' should be a leading concept for understanding the religious and socio-political developments of the time.

The only way to test the reliability of biblical historiography, and ultimately to understand it properly even if it might prove unreliable

*I am grateful to Bob Becking, Harm van Grol and Marjo Korpel for their kind invitation to the Utrecht symposium and much patience with a belated contributor. Baruch Brandl (Jerusalem), Linda Bregstein (Philadelphia), Pierre Briant (Toulouse), Elspeth R. Macintosh Dusinberre (Boulder, CO), Mark B. Garrison (San Antonio, TX), Haim Gitler, Ya'akov Meshorer, Tallay Ornan and Ephraim Stern (all Jerusalem) kindly shared with me portions of their own research, partly unpublished. Not all aspects of it could be integrated in the present article, but I am most grateful to each of them. None should of course be held responsible for opinions expressed in this article.

Some of the following arguments are based on the personal study of the original objects, notably the bullae from Samaria and Wadi ed-Daliyeh, during a stay in Jerusalem on 14-16 September, 1998. I would like to thank Mrs. Hava Katz, Chief curator at the Israel Antiquities Authority, Michal Dayagi-Mendels, Chief curator at the Israel Museum, and Ornit Ilan, Curator at the Rockefeller Museum, for permission to udy the material under their custody.

[1]H.M. Barstad, *The Myth of the Empty Land: A Study in the History and Archaeology of Judah During the 'Exilic' Period* (SO.S, 28), Oslo 1996; L.L. Grabbe (ed.), *Leading Captivity Captive: 'The Exile' as History and Ideology* (ESHM, 2; JSOT.S, 278), Sheffield 1998.

in terms of critical history writing, is to confront it with extra-biblical sources and to contextualize it within the overall cultural and social history of the Persian empire.[2] Primary sources are provided by archaeology, epigraphy and iconography; secondary sources by contemporary writers (e.g., Pseudo-Scylax or Herodotus); tertiary sources by traditions known to later historians (such as Flavius Josephus). Method demands that our reconstruction starts with the primary sources. Do they confirm our biblical view that exile was indeed the fundamental period marker of Palestine's, or for that matter, Yehud's history between the 6th and 4th century? To put it shortly, while archaeology unquestionably witnesses an important crash in the material culture of the coastal plain of Palestine, and a considerable economic recession in the central highlands, it cannot support the idea of a general exile nor mass return. 'Exile' and 'return' were essential coordinates for a minority group. The religious ideology of these founders of Yehud would never have had the impact it ultimately gained were it not closely linked, through the גּוֹלָה and the Persian administration, to Babylonian prosperity and to the centres of political power both in Babylon and Susa.

The archaeological heritage of Persian period Palestine has been collected in a masterly synthesis by E. Stern twenty years ago.[3] His overview remains the mandatory starting point for any new study of the period, although a thorough updating would be more than welcome.[4] Whoever tries to take up the task experiences stress, if anything, when he or she starts to assemble the relevant primary source material. As a matter of fact, a number of findings discussed by Stern in 1982 have still not been properly published; part of them have simply disappeared; and much more material has surfaced in the meantime and remains to be properly analysed and published.[5]

---

[2] P. Briant, *Histoire de l'empire perse: De Cyrus à Alexandre*, Paris 1996; Idem, "Bulletin d'histoire achéménide (I)", in: M.-F. Boussac (ed.), *Recherches récentes sur l'Empire achéménide* (Topoi, Suppl., 1), Lyon 1997, 5-127.

[3] E. Stern, *Material Culture of the Land of the Bible in the Persian Period 538-332* BC, Warminster & Jerusalem 1982; Idem, "The Persian Empire and the Political and Social History of Palestine in the Persian Period" and "The archaeology of Persian Palestine", in: W.D. Davies, L. Finkelstein (eds.), *The Cambridge History of Judaism*, vol. 1, Cambridge 1984, 70-87, 88-114; Idem, "Between Persia and Greece: Trade, Administration and Warfare in the Persian and Hellenistic Periods (539-63 BCE)", in: T.E. Levy, *The Archaeology of Society in the Holy Land*, London 1995, 432-45.

[4] Most recent handbooks on the archaeology of Palestine/Israel stop shortly before the period under concern, but cf. H. Weippert, *Palästina in vorhellenistischer Zeit* (HdA, Vorderasien 2/1), München 1988, 682-718.

[5] Stern is to be praised for the swift preliminary or even final publication of his own findings at Tel Dor.

The Persian period is still a very poor parent in the archaeology of Palestine. One of the consequences of this state of affairs is that we are still largely unable to distinguish clearly between material remains of Iron Age III (the period of Babylonian overlordship) and those of the early Persian period (in turn, this might indicate a very smooth transition from one to the other, with Persian administration remaining in fact 'Babylonian' for quite some time). Another stressful consequence is that we generally treat the Persian period as a single time unit although for Palestine, the roughly two centuries of Achaemenid history would require at least a tri-partite subdivision according to changing administrative policies and influences under varying political and economic conditions. In this respect, the impact of Egypt on Palestine during the 5th and particularly the 4th century, which is obvious to anyone who considers iconographical sources (esp. scarabs and bronzes[6]), is too often disregarded in historical treatments of the period, which tend to concentrate on the relations of Palestine with Persia and Greece, i.e. the centres of two competing 'world systems', and with the Phoenician cities who were among the dominant economic powers in the area.[7]

The following essay aims at nothing more than making a first step and preliminary contribution to what should become a multidisciplinary research project in the future: the study of iconography as a supplementary means, in addition to archaeological, textual, and general historical research, to analyse the cultural and socio-political constituents, economical and cultural relations and religio-ideological streams of tradition that shaped the history of the southern Levant during the 6th-4th centuries BCE.[8] Ideally, we should assemble and map all the iconographical sources according to object genres, provenance, influence or inspiration, distribution within the various regions and polities of Palestine, etc., in order to get a reasonably differenti-

---

[6] The recent suggestion of L.E. Stager to redate a 4th-century hoard of bronzes from Ashkelon (J.H. Iliffe, "A Hoard of Bronzes from Askalon", *QDAP* 5 [1936], 61-8) to the 7th cent. or 26th dynasty on the sole basis of some new (but typologically different) finds from his own excavations ("The Fury of Babylon: Ashkelon and the Archaeology of Destruction", *BAR* 22,1 [1996], 56-77, esp. 61) is unconvincing as long as a thorough typological discussion is not provided. A number of bronzes recently found at Miṣpe Yamim (R. Frankel, R. Ventura, "The Miṣpe Yamim Bronzes", *BASOR* 311 [1998], 39-55) and parallels from Egypt support the 5th-4th century dating.

[7] K.G. Hoglund, *Achaemenid Imperial Administration in Syria-Palestine and the Missions of Ezra and Nehemiah* (SBL.DS, 125), Atlanta, GA 1992, an exception to the rule, is exclusively concerned with the mid-5th century.

[8] For a recent synthesis, which unfortunately makes no use of iconography, see E.-M. Laperrousaz, A. Lemaire (eds.), *La Palestine à l'époque perse*, Paris 1994.

ated and realistic picture of Persian, Egyptian, Phoenician, Cypriot, or Greek influence or impact on the local symbol systems. This picture should then be compared to analogous evidence in Egypt, Phoenicia and Inner Syria,[9] Asia Minor[10] and Babylonia[11]. Within the limits of this paper, I can but declare an intention and engage a first preliminary sounding into a small, precisely defined set of evidence, namely glyptic displaying 'explicit Persianisms', i.e. clear iconographical references to Persia and the Achaemenid empire.

Important progress has been achieved during the past two decades in the interpretation of Achaemenid royal iconography, which is today understood as a consciously coined reflection of a distinctive imperial ideology.[12] The fundamental outlines of this ideology were defined during the reign of Darius I. It stressed the multi-ethnic and multi-cultural constitution of an empire of many peoples and speeches. In addition to highlighting military prowess in battle and the violent suppression of revolting enemies, it insisted on the free support offered by subject peoples to the divinely elected Persian king, who in turn recognized the cultural and religious diversity of his subjects as a legitimate expression of various local, or regional, identities. 'Pluralism', 'pluri-culturalism' and 'polycentrism' are among the salient concepts used in recent studies of Achaemenid imperial iconography and ideology. Some of these studies have also influenced recent debates on the history of Yehud during the Persian period, e.g. in relation to the province's organization around the temple of Jerusalem, and they have been used to shape and support theories related to biblical lit-

---

[9] A. Nunn, *Kontinuität und Wandel im Motivschatz Phöniziens, Syriens und Transjordaniens vom 6. bis zum 4. Jahrhundert v. Chr.: Vorderasiatische, ägyptische und griechische Bilder im Widerstreit* (Habil. Universität München 1996; a revised version will appear shortly in OBO Series archaeologica).

[10] O. Casabonne, "Présence et influence perses en Cilicie à l'époque achéménide: Iconographie et représentations", *Anatolia Antiqua* 4 (1996), 121-45; D. Kaptan, "Common Treats on Seals and Coins of the Achaemenid period in an Anatolian Context", in: O. Casabonne (ed.), *Mécanismes et innovations monétaires dans l'Anatolie achéménide: Numismatique et histoire* (Varia Anatolica, 10), Istanbul & Paris 1998 (forthcoming).

[11] Cf. L.B. Bregstein, *Seal Use in Fifth Century* BC *Nippur, Iraq: A Study of Seal Selection and Sealing Practice in the Murašû Archive* (unpubl. PhD diss. University of Pennsylvania, Philadelphia 1993; a revised version is planned for publication in the OBO series); Idem, "Sealing Practices in the Fifth Century BC Murašû Archive from Nippur, Iraq", in: M.-F. Boussac, A. Invernizzi (eds.), *Archives et sceaux du monde hellénistique* (BCH Suppl., 29), Paris 1996, 53-63.

[12] M.C. Root, *The King and Kingship in Achaemenid Art: Essays on the Creation of an Iconography of Empire* (AcIr, 19), Leiden 1979, and numerous studies by the same author published since, e.g. in the Achaemenid History series.

erature, such as the formation of the Torah as an officially authorized 'constitution' of a semi-autonomous province.[13]

This is not the place to discuss the pertinence of such historical and literary-historical reconstructions, which are assessed by other contributors in the present volume. In terms of interdisciplinary dialogue, one should of course welcome the mutual interaction and cross-fertilization of iconology, history, and biblical studies. However, we cannot discuss the impact of Persian/Achaemenid imperial ideology on Palestine without asking how, through what media and in what form this ideology would actually be transmitted, received and known in Palestine. With regard to the particular field of iconography, it is legitimate and necessary to start an analysis of the visual language of imperial ideology from the royal monuments in the centre of the empire (i.e. mainly Bisotun, Susa, and Persepolis).[14] But when comparing this set of evidence with others, e.g. from Asia Minor or Egypt, one recognizes that imperial iconography must have been mediated to the provinces in a highly complex process of interaction in which the Persian administration, local policy experts, workmen who were partly brought in from abroad and thus used to central codes, and locals were involved.[15] The generalities of this process are more easily perceived and reconstructed in areas where monumental iconography of the Persian period has survived, such as in Egypt, in Asia Minor, or at Sidon. In Palestine, unfortunately, no monumental iconography of Persian/Achaemenid inspiration has been preserved if it ever existed.

What images of Persian power could inhabitants of Palestine then actually see in their own country? For sure, there *are* such images from Palestine that either represent Achaemenid iconography or betray a definite Persian impact: seals and sealings, and coins, to name the two most prominent categories. It is to the former that we shall turn in this paper and ask how they reflect the symbolism of Persian Achaemenid power.

---

[13]E.g. K. Koch, P. Frei, *Reichsidee und Reichsorganisation im Perserreich* (OBO, 55), Fribourg & Göttingen [2]1996.

[14]Cf. C. Uehlinger, *"Figurative Policy*, Propaganda und Prophetie", in: J.A. Emerton (ed.), *Congress Vol. Cambridge 1995* (VT.S, 66), Leiden 1997, 297-349.

[15]See in general, A.C. Gunter (ed.), *Investigating Artistic Environments in the Ancient Near East*, Washington, DC 1990; for a case study cf. E.R.M. Dusinberre, *Satrapal Sardis: Aspects of Empire in an Achaemenid Capital* (unpubl. PhD diss. University of Michigan, Ann Arbor 1997). Cf. Briant, "Bulletin d'histoire achéménide (I)" (n. 2), 64-7, 98-104.

2 Seals and Sealings

Several scholars have studied the glyptic heritage of Persian period Palestine in recent years. Ephraim Stern, in his magisterial overview mentioned above,[16] distinguished four groups of imported (Babylonian, Achaemenid, Egyptian and Greek) from locally produced seals, either anepigraphic or inscribed, and discussed "official seals of the provinces of Judah and Samaria" as a separate group. The relative importance, numerical proportions and chronological variation of the various groups were neither tabulated nor treated in detail by Stern, but his basic distinctions remain valid. Several observations are important also for our purpose, e.g. his observation that typically Babylonian faceted quartz conoids showing a worshipper in front of divine symbols (usually those of Marduk and Nabû) continued to be used in Palestine – probably by members of the Perso-Babylonian administration – well into the 5th cent. BCE. On a particular type of seal impressions on jar handles which show a roaring lion standing on his hind legs, dated by Stern to the late 6th-5th centuries, he recognized some influence of Achaemenid Court style glyptic.[17] In more recent studies, Stern stressed aspects of continuity from the Assyrian, Babylonian through Persian periods, and also drew attention to some common features of glyptic and numismatic iconography.[18] Both his initial synthesis and recent studies are important for our concern, although their conclusions remain often rather general and are at times based on a somewhat superficial iconographical analysis.

---

[16] Stern, *Material Culture* (n. 3), chap. VII (196-214, 274-6).

[17] Stern's type B (*ibidem*, 211-3); cf. O. Keel, C. Uehlinger, *Gods, Goddesses, and Images of God in Ancient Israel*, Minneapolis & Edinburgh 1998, 386-7 (§ 223). Since the lion sealings cannot be considered to represent 'explicit Persianisms', they have been excluded from the present discussion. Note that they have been re-dated to the late Persian or even early Hellenistic period by F. Bianchi, "I sigilli anepigrafi della Giudea achemenide: una nuova datazione", *SEL* 13 (1996), 79-90. The problem would need reconsideration in the light of both new archaeological evidence from Transjordan and Jerusalem and iconographical connections of the lion series with Samarian coinage. These issues are beyond the limits of this article but would strengthen the late Persian dating.

[18] E. Stern, "Notes on the Development of Stamp-Glyptic Art in Palestine during the Assyrian, Babylonian and Persian Periods", in: M. Heltzer *et al.* (eds.), *Studies in the Archaeology and History of Ancient Israel (Fs. M. Dothan)*, Haifa 1993, 111-22 (Hebr.), 21* (Engl. summ.); Idem, "Notes on the Development of Stamp-Glyptic Art in Palestine during the Assyrian and Persian Periods", in: L.M. Hopfe (ed.), *Uncovering Ancient Stones: Essays in Memory of H. Neil Richardson*, Winona Lake, IN 1994, 135-46; Idem, "Assyrian and Babylonian Elements in the Material Culture of Palestine in the Persian Period", *Trans* 7 (1994), 51-62.

In an article published in 1992, Martin G. Klingbeil discussed 52 seals attributed to the Persian period.[19] He expressed some doubts about the pertinence of Stern's division between imported and locally made seals and concentrated his own analysis on iconographical motifs alone, acknowledging "the individual origin/origins of a particular image" (i.e., archaeological provenance?) rather than the ultimate origin of production of various seal types.[20] In my opinion, this approach not only ignores the potential of technical formalities (such as material, shape, and style) for workshop studies, and of workshop location for the study of the economic and cultural history of the area. It also represents a step backwards in the analysis of glyptic iconography which can only be properly understood when both place of manufacture and place of use are considered, although this must often be done in a tentative way. To illustrate my point with an example, to term the typically Babylonian faceted quartz conoids showing a worshiper in front of Babylonian divine symbols "Syro-Palestinian seals" as Klingbeil did is simply misleading. His study is nevertheless valuable for some of its iconographical interpretations. He also makes interesting comments on the diffusion within Palestine of various iconographical repertoires. For instance, he notes more 'conservative' tendencies in the glyptic of central Palestine, where he says the majority of iconographic motifs attested have "an eastern or Mesopotamian origin", in contrast to the glyptic of the northern coastal plain where Phoenician iconography presents a fusion of influences from many different areas. To Klingbeil, "this tendency towards fusion of different iconographic traditions may reflect the historical situation of the northern coastal region of Syro-Palestine which enjoyed a degree of independence from the Persian administration".[21] I am generally sympathetic with these observations (especially as they link central Palestine to Babylonia), but I doubt that we can draw socio-political conclusions from glyptic evidence and iconographical data as such, regardless of seal typology and other technicalities, and without specifying the social context in which different types of seals were used.

During the Persian period, seals could travel along the ways of business without regard for politics or religion, and they were often of a more private rather than public character. Klingbeil's putative

---

[19] M.G. Klingbeil, "Syro-Palestinian Stamp Seals from the Persian Period: The Iconographic Evidence", *JNSL* 18 (1992), 95-124. His catalogue does not include Stern's lion sealings. A forgery (No. 36) however and some items which antedate the Persian period (e.g., his Nos. 7, 20, 24, 30, 32?, 51) are included.

[20] Note esp. his comment, *ibidem*, 101-2, n. 22.

[21] Klingbeil, *ibidem*, 117-8.

conservative character of Persian period Samaria has found a dramatic disclaimer in the recent publication of two important groups of mid-4th century bullae, the vast majority of which have been sealed with seal stones and finger-rings displaying rather 'modern' and fashionable Greek iconography.[22] Mary J.W. Leith's recently published presentation of the Wadi ed-Daliyeh bullae has greatly advanced the study of Persian period glyptic from Palestine and set a new standard for future research concerned with Persian period glyptic from Palestine.[23] Leith analyses and discusses every seal design at length and draws together numerous parallels from many different regions. Moreover, her interpretation is informed by recent studies of Mark B. Garrison on sealings from Persepolis[24] and of Linda M. Bregstein on sealings from Nippur,[25] two authors who have analysed in depth seal use and sealing practices, distribution of seal types and iconographical motifs among various classes of seal owners, etc., within well-defined and well-dated archival contexts.

Pioneer work has also been accomplished by Astrid Nunn who brings together all kinds of image-bearing objects (except coins) from Persian period Lebanon, Syria and Transjordan in her recent Munich *Habilitationsschrift*, a study which will eventually provide the necessary companion to Stern's dissertation on Palestine/Israel.[26] Material gathered by Nunn is mentioned below wherever it contains close parallels to items excavated in Palestine.

Finally, recent studies by Elspeth R. McIntosh Dusinberre on so-called Graeco-Persian seals and coinage from Anatolia[27] are also rel-

---

[22] M.J.W. Leith, *Wadi Daliyeh*, vol. 1: The Wadi Daliyeh Seal Impressions (DJD, 24), Oxford 1997; E. Stern, "A Hoard of Persian Period Bullae from the Vicinity of Samaria", *Michmanim* 6 (1992), 7-30 (Hebr.), 41* (Engl. summ.).

[23] A personal inspection on 14–16 September 1998 of those bullae from Wadi ed-Daliyeh which are relevant to this study has confirmed that Leith's drawings are generally reliable and the photographs of a very high quality. Some drawings published in this article include a few minor improvements.

[24] See esp. M.B. Garrison, *Seal workshops and artists in Persepolis: A study of seal impressions preserving the theme of heroic encounter on the Persepolis Fortification and Treasury Tablets* (unpubl. PhD diss. University of Michigan, Ann Arbor 1988); Idem, "Seals and the Elite at Persepolis: Some Observations on Early Achaemenid Persian Art", *ArsOr* 21 (1992), 1-29; Idem, "The Identification of Artists and Workshops in Sealed Archival Contexts", in: Boussac, Invernizzi (eds.), *Archives et sceaux* (n.11), 29-51.

[25] Cf. Bregstein, *Seal Use* (n.11).

[26] Nunn, *Kontinuität und Wandel* (n. 9), esp. "Die Glyptik" (pp. 126-93).

[27] E.R.M. Dusinberre, "Imperial Style and Constructed Identity: A 'Graeco-Persian' Cylinder Seal from Sardis", *ArsOr* 27 (1997), 99-129; Idem, "King or God? Imperial Archaeology and the 'Tiarate Head' Coins of Achaemenid Anatolia", *Near Eastern Archaeology* 61 (1998), 154-68.

evant for our inquiry since they consider these media as "part of an interregional symbolic system in the Achaemenid empire that served to signify and legitimate the new sociopolitical order. The variable in this symbolic system was a multitude of local styles."[28] We shall ask whether the situation observed in Palestine conforms with these conclusions based on material from Asia Minor, especially from satrapial Sardis.

The following pages provide an overview on Persian Period stamp and cylinder seals and sealings from Palestine that display explicit 'Persianisms', i.e. iconographical motifs which are distinctly related to Persian Achaemenid iconography. The selective nature of this choice should always be kept in mind when reading along the following pages. Still, our presentation increases the number of relevant items (defined by our 'Persianism' criterion) referred to by all earlier authors.[29] It also tries to improve their iconographical description wherever possible. The number of 30 seals and sealings discussed here should be put against a total database of c. 250 items. Representing c. 12% of the presently available data from Palestine, these objects should be taken into account by anyone studying the impact of the Achaemenid empire and its ideology on the area. The seal images vehiculate certain notions of Persian power, particularly but not exclusively royal Achaemenid power, that were definitely known to members of the seal-owning upper class in 5th- and 4th-century Palestine, particularly in Samaria.

The seals and sealings are listed below in the form of an object inventory.[30] Technical discussions that are not directly related to our topic have been kept to a minimum but could not be totally avoided. Such an inventory list may seem out of place in a conference volume that aims at synthetical treatments. However, I am convinced that no iconographical study, and no synthetical treatment, can dispense

---

[28] Dusinberre, *ibidem*, 99.

[29] To compare with Klingbeil's study (which appeared before the final publication of the Wadi ed-Daliyeh bullae), while we consider only 5 out of his 52 seals because we concentrate on 'explicit Persianisms', we count some 25 additional items within this category which are absent from his discussion.

[30] The description of seals and sealings will proceed in the following order: Obj = object, material description (* pertains to measurements of partly damaged, fragmentary objects); Icon = iconography; Prov = archaeological provenance, with date based on archaeological context; Orig = probable location of original production, with suggested date of manufacture, based upon parallels; Loc = present location; Bib = bibliography of earlier publications and studies mentioning the object, not comprehensive but aiming at the most useful titles for reference and discussion. '–' indicates that no relevant information was available to me at the time of writing.

itself from dealing with the most basic and factual technicalities of the primary source material. With regard to seals particularly, the technicalities alone allow for questions about access to raw material and technology, style, workmanship, workshop location, circulation etc., questions which are fundamental and preliminary to any thesis on impact, influence and reception of ideological matters.

2.1   Scenes of 'Heroic Encounter'

Scenes of 'heroic encounter' or 'heroic control'[31] have a long history both in Mesopotamian and Levantine iconography. On Persian period seals from Palestine, they appear in several groups and variants which represent clearly distinct cultural traditions. One may roughly distinguish a Syro-Mesopotamian tradition, where the hero is usually bare-headed and clad in a short kilt, which may also be worn under a long robe (*figs. 1-2*); a 'Syro-Phoenician' tradition where the hero's role is taken by the god Bes (*fig. 3*); a Persian tradition where the hero wears the typically folded *kandys* robe and as a rule the dentate or crenellated crown (*kidaris*) which accounts for his designation as Persian *royal* hero (see below); and a Greek (and Cypriot) tradition which identifies the 'Master of lions' with Heracles (*fig. 4*). In the present context, only the first and third group are relevant for our discussion.

1   Obj: Scaraboid, agate, 19.3 x 14.3 x 6.6 mm. Modeled style, fine rendering of details (e.g. drapery and wingfeathers); neither border nor ground line. Icon: Bearded male, whom headgear (crenellated? crown, i.e. *kidaris*) and costume (*kandys*) characterise as Persian 'royal hero', facing right, holding at their horns a pair of winged monsters (leonine? or rather bovine[32] body, bearded human-head, ibex-horns), both with their head turned outwards; below crouching winged monster of unidentifiable nature (bull- or human-headed?[33]); above winged sun-disk, with wings roughly following the contours of the sealing surface, bird's tail and two band-like protrusions;[34] a rhomb-like addition in the field obscures one of the bands and may result from a makeshift correction.

---

[31] The terminology is adapted from Garrison, *Seal workshops and artists in Persepolis* (n.24).

[32] The photograph of the cast does not allow for differentiation, but the tails and general type recall the mixed creatures on a more readable cylinder seal in the Louvre, cf. D. Collon, *First Impressions: Cylinder Seals in the Ancient Near East*, London 1987, No. 659.

[33] Cf. B. Buchanan, P.R.S. Moorey, *Catalogue of Ancient Near Eastern Seals in the Ashmolean Museum*, vol. 3: The Iron Age stamp seals (c. 1200-350 BC), Oxford 1988, Nos. 459-60 for human-headed examples.

[34] On this, cf. D. Parayre, "Les cachets ouest-sémitiques à travers l'image du disque solaire ailé (perspective iconographique)", *Syr.* 67 (1990), 269-301, esp. 278, 293, Nos. 42-3, 71-2, 81-2.

Seals Nos. **1-8**: Scenes of 'Heroic Encounter'

Prov: Gezer, 'Philistine grave' 2; mid-5th cent. BCE. Among the associated finds, a cylinder seal "with a conventional Assyrian pattern" was found but stolen from the field.[35] Judging from the whole group of tombs, the people buried in the 'Philistine graves' must have been members of the Persian administration based in Gezer, with connections to Babylonia and possibly Egypt.

Orig: Levantine workshop, derivative of Achaemenid Court Style, probably central or southern Syria;[36] 5th cent. BCE. The seal has been compared by N. Avigad[37] and others to the seal of Pamin, a biconvex agate (not onyx as Avigad had it) scaraboid of slightly larger dimensions but with an almost identical layout of the sealing surface (except the inscription) and a similar iconography (royal hero mastering two lions, crouching gazelle, winged sun), bought in the 50's on the Jerusalem antiquities market.[38] D. Parayre suggested a common origin in a Palestinian workshop and was even more specific ("un artisan de Gezer") in a later paper.[39] However, both her typological classification (which, as far as the Gezer item is concerned, depends entirely on Macalister's drawing) and her iconographical interpretation are somewhat problematic (the band-like feature is misunderstood by Parayre as a pair of hanging uraei, whereas it is a non-Egyptian feature characteristic of Assyrian and Achaemenid winged disks). Since one seal with attested provenance cannot locate a workshop (no other relatives are known from the Gezer area), her suggestion is too specific to commend itself. Agate was rarely available to Palestinian workshops.[40] The orthography of the Pamin inscription which must be part of the originally planned design, point to the Phoenico-Aramaean area north of Palestine, while the owner's Egyptian name[41] might favour the coastal area. A close comparison of photographs confirms the probability of related origin for the Gezer seal, although the latter is distinguished from the Pamin seal by a more common flat sealing surface and a more sophisticated iconography and quality of workmanship. Other slightly more removed Achaemenid

---

[35] Cf. R.A.S. Macalister, *The Excavation of Gezer. 1902-1905 and 1907-1909*, London 1912, vol. 1, 291-2, vol. 3, pl. LV; Stern, *Material Culture* (n. 3), 73-5.

[36] The possibility that the seal was imported from Mesopotamia (Stern, "Assyrian and Babylonian Elements" [n. 18], 53; Idem, "Notes" [n. 18], 138) can be excluded.

[37] N. Avigad, "Three Ornamented Hebrew Seals", *IEJ* 4 (1954), 236-8, esp. 237-8.

[38] Cf. N. Avigad, B. Sass, *Corpus of West Semitic Stamp Seals*, Jerusalem 1997, No. 1097, where the item ranges among the "Phoenician or Aramaic (or Ammonite) seals".

[39] Parayre, "Les cachets ouest-sémitiques" (n.34), 278; Idem, "A propos des sceaux ouest-sémitiques: le rôle de l'iconographie dans l'attribution d'un sceau à une aire culturelle et à un atelier", in: B. Sass, C. Uehlinger (eds.), *Studies in the Iconography of Northwest Semitic Inscribed Seals* (OBO, 125), Fribourg & Göttingen 1993, 27-51, esp. 39 with figs. 57-8.

[40] Cf. O. Keel, *Corpus der Stempelsiegel-Amulette aus Palästina/Israel: Einleitung* (OBO.SA, 10), Fribourg & Göttingen 1995, 145 §§ 377-8.

[41] Cf. Avigad, Sass, *West Semitic Stamp Seals* (n. 38), 544.

Court Style parallels[42] should also be taken into account before postulating a Palestinian origin.

Loc: present whereabouts unknown (Istanbul?); cast in London, Palestine Exploration Fund, no reg. No.

Bib: R.A.S. Macalister, "Thirteenth Quarterly Report on the Excavation of Gezer", *PEQ* (1905), 309-327, esp. 319 with fig. 1; Idem, *Excavation of Gezer* (n. 35), vol. 1, 292 with fig. 153; Avigad, "Hebrew Seals" (n. 37), 238; K. Galling, "Assyrische und persische Präfekten in Geser", *PJ* 31 (1935) 75-93, esp. 91-2; Stern, *Material Culture* (n. 3), 199; Idem, "Assyrian and Babylonian Elements" (n. 18), 53-4, 59, fig. 1c; Idem, "Notes" (n. 18), 137-9, with fig. 4; Keel, Uehlinger, *GGG* (n. 17), 375-6, with fig. 361a.

2 Obj: Scaraboid, opaque white stone, base damaged on both sides and at the top hole, 16 x 13 x 7 mm. Flat and plain engraving, no border line, ground line, exergue left empty.

Icon: 'Master of animals' facing left, holding at the bend of their horns a pair of upright winged, ibex-horned monsters, both turned outwards with their head looking back towards him; above winged sun (disk not specified), with wings roughly following the contours of the sealing surface, bird's tail and two band-like protrusions.

Prov: Tell eṣ-Ṣafi, mixed context (rubbish heap over the southern city wall).

Orig: Levantine workshop, possibly Palestine, derivative of provincial Court Style imitations (such as No. **1** above), 5th cent. BCE.

Loc: Jerusalem, Rockefeller Museum, PAM-IAA J. 378 (not seen); cast in London, Palestine Exploration Fund, no reg. No.

Bib: F.J. Bliss, "Second Report on the Excavations at Tell es-Sâfi", *PEQ* (1899), 317-33, esp. 332, pl. 6:9; Idem, R.A.S. Macalister, *Excavations in Palestine During the Years 1898-1900*, London 1902, 40, 152, Pl. 83:5; Keel, Uehlinger, *GGG* (n. 17), 375-6 with fig. 361c.

Seal No. **1** is remarkable for its quite exquisite workmanship and complex iconography. In contrast to all other depictions of 'heroic encounter' from Palestine (but cf. No. **12** below), the royal hero is here placed on a crouching winged being which serves as a kind of pedestal to the scene. This refers to the Assyrian tradition of *Mischwesen* which accompany the higher gods, acting both as pedestal animals, guardians, and helpers for their divine patron and emphasizing the latter's might since with all their fierceness they are submitted to the god's power. There is thus no doubt that the hero on seal No. **1** can considered to be of divine nature. At the same time, the outspread wings of the heavenly disk make it clear that he enjoys the protection of higher powers in heaven. While his costume relates him to Achaemenid royalty, the figure is probably not the king in person (the Persian king was not considered of divine nature, and Achaemenid iconography could clad the major deities in royal costume).

---

[42]Cf. J. Boardman, "Pyramidal Stamp Seals in the Persian Empire", *Iran* 8 (1970), 19-45, Nos. 99, 114.

However, the hero's royal qualities are so evident that an interplay of meaning is probably intended. As we shall see, certain seal engravers would stress the royal features of the hero to such an extent that he must be perceived as generally embodying Achaemenid royalty, and sometimes as a depiction of the king in person. Representing "a polysemic symbol of king and hero, king and god"[43] the hero's triumphant image functioned as a visual metaphor for cosmic stability being related to Persian royalty.

The presence of such a remarkable seal at Gezer calls for futher comment. Bregstein's study of the sealings in the Murašû business archive from Nippur (dated 454-404 BCE) has shown that no strict correlation exists between office holders or private individuals and the iconography of their seals. Seal selection seems to have been by and large a matter of personal choice and preference.[44] Garrison has observed considerable freedom in seal selection even among the highest-ranking members of the imperial administration and palatial environment at Persepolis.[45] However, the situation in far-off provincial Palestine (as probably in Inner Syria as well) must have been different in more than one respect. Seal designs displaying explicit Persian symbolism were quite common in Babylonia, let alone the Persian heartland, but they were not current in Palestine, and Levantine workshops seem to have taken time to adopt Achaemenid Court Style conventions, to say the least (see below). An individual owning such an elaborate seal in 5th-century Palestine must therefore have had particular reasons or opportunities for that, since he clearly did not choose or own what was commonly represented on the local Levantine market.

Interestingly, the complex design of seal No. 1 remains quite unique among the seals and sealings from Palestine displaying 'explicit Persianisms'. Sealing No. 12 comes closest by featuring another pedestal animal, a so-called 'royal sphinx'. Focussing specifically on such pedestal animals, Dusinberre has noted that these "were initially portrayed in central Achaemenid glyptic art used only by a select group of people", namely high-ranking members of the imperial adminis-

---

[43] Dusinberre, "Imperial Style" (n.27), 105; in "King or God?" (n. 27), the same author discusses other images that may have served to sustain the notion not of a divine Persian king, but of the quasi-divine character of Achaemenid kingship.

[44] Cf. Bregstein, *Seal Use* (n. 11), 206-7; Idem, "Sealing Practices" (n. 11), 59.

[45] Garrison, "Identification of Artists" (n. 24), 44-5. But note his particular comments on the Achaemenid Court Style, which at Persepolis displays a tightly controlled iconography reflecting "a unified program of visual imagery of empire" designed during the last two decades of the 6th century under Darius I (Garrison, "Seals and the Elite" [n. 24], esp. 13-20).

tration.[46] Furthermore, according to the evidence from Persepolis, pedestal animals were produced "only in the styles most intimately connected with Persepolitan imperial art".[47] Only "by the end of the fifth century, (...) the use patterns of seals with pedestal animals had apparently changed, so that the image, previously restricted in its circulation, was available to a wider portion of society. (...) At the beginning of Achaemenid hegemony, pedestal animals were clearly associated with individuals of very high social status, but by the last quarter of the fifth century, this distinction seems to have been somewhat blurred. But, importantly, even in the Murashu archive the people using these pedestal-animal seals were all officials acting in official capacity."[48] Dusinberre's observations seem to confirm our impression based on the particular archaeological context that seal No. **1** must have belonged to a non-local official of the imperial administration, who may have acquired his seal in Syria.

If one looked for a 'heroic encounter' design in Palestine, it would have been much easier to find a version of the 'Syro-Mesopotamian' hero, be it on an expensive Phoenician greenstone scarab such as one found at Samaria (*fig. 5*)[49] or on a simpler scaraboid such as seal No. **2**. Towards the middle of the 5th century, mould-made glass stamps (scaraboids and conoids) became available. They were mass-produced and must have sold relatively cheap. Glass scaraboids of the kind showing 'heroic encounter' scenes have been found, e.g., at Dor (*fig. 2*).[50] Interestingly, they maintain the 'Syro-Mesopotamian' hero in the central position. On other glass seals from Gezer, where the hero apparently does not fight *Mischwesen* but lions, he also wears a kind of cap and is again reminiscent of the 'Syro-Mesopotamian'

---

[46]Dusinberre, "Imperial Style" (n. 27), 103.

[47]*Ibidem*, 113.

[48]*Ibidem*, 108.

[49]J.W. Crowfoot *et al.*, *The Objects from Samaria (Samaria-Sebaste, No. III)*, London 1957, 87 No. 22, pl. 15:22; Klingbeil, "Syro-Palestinian Stamp Seals" (n. 19), 99, 105-6, 124 No. 34; Keel, *Corpus Einleitung* (n. 40), 144 § 371; Keel, Uehlinger, *GGG* (n. 17), 375-6 with fig. 361b. For the workshop's location in Phoenicia (Byblos?), cf. Nunn, *Kontinuität und Wandel* (n. 9), 148-50.

[50]Two items, cf. most conveniently E. Stern, *Dor: Ruler of the Seas*, Jerusalem 1994, 190-2 with fig. 124 (first and second row); Idem, "Assyrian and Babylonian Elements" (n. 18), 55, 60 fig. 2:c-d. For selected parallels, cf. M.V. Seton-Williams, "The Excavations at Tell Rifa'at, 1964", *Iraq* 29 (1967), 16-33, esp. 25-6, pl. 10:4; M.-L. Vollenweider, *Musée d'Art et d'Histoire de Genève, Catalogue raisonné des sceaux-cylindres et intailles I*, Genève 1974, Nos. 44-5; D. Barag, *Catalogue of Western Asiatic Glass in the British Museum*, vol. 1, Dorchester 1985, Nos. 102-4. For a similar stamp seal from Persepolis, cf. E.F. Schmidt, *Persepolis*, vol. 2: Contents of the Treasury and Other Discoveries (OIP, 69), Chicago 1957, pl. 5:11.

rather than the Persian hero.[51] Only few glass seals tend to depict the headgear almost as a crown (but cf. *figs. 6-7!*), e.g. the following item from Samaria:

3 Obj: Conoid, blue glass, base slightly convex, upper end of cone missing, ⌀ 15 x 11* mm; mass-produced (probably cast) from a stamped matrix mould; borderline(?), no baseline.
Icon: Bearded male hero facing left, wearing a cap with long robe leaving bare the advancing leg, mastering a pair of upright horned quadrupeds turned towards him with their heads looking back outwards; above possibly a winged sun.
Prov: Samaria, Qy (acropolis, c. 490N/740E, near the Hellenistic round tower), reg. No. 2; unstratified.
Orig: Local Phoenician mass production, possibly Sidon; first or second degree derivative from Achaemenid Court Style; 5th/4th cent. BCE. Closer dating may depend on the identification of the quadrupeds. While the drawing makes one think of caprids (note particularly horn and lack of tails),[52] Crowfoot describes them as lions.[53] If correct, close parallels would include items from al-Mina (str. 3),[54] Ras el-Bassit,[55] Ras Shamra (house I, 2nd half 4th cent. BCE)[56] and unprovenanced seals from Syria and Lebanon (one bought in Sidon[57]) in various collections[58] which show a certain degree of variation in the rendering of the hero's headgear (from hair through cap to almost *kidaris*).
Loc: –
Bib: Crowfoot *et al.*, *Objects* (n. 49), 88 No. 26, 393 fig. 92:80; Klingbeil, "Syro-Palestinian Stamp Seals" (n. 19), 99, 105, 124 No. 35; Stern, "Notes" (n. 18), 140, 142 fig. 6; Idem, "Assyrian and Babylonian elements" (n. 18), 54, 60 fig. 2b.

---

[51] Two items, cf. Macalister, *Excavation of Gezer* (n. 35), resp. vol. 2, 347; vol. 2, pl. 214:29 and vol. 2, 295 fig. 437:8, 347.

[52] Cf. H. Keel-Leu, *Vorderasiatische Stempelsiegel: Die Sammlung des Biblischen Instituts der Universität Freiburg Schweiz* (OBO, 110), Fribourg & Göttingen 1991, No. 167, which clearly shows ibexes and for which the Samaria item is cited as a very close parallel.

[53] Describing a close parallel, P.R.S. Moorey comments: "they look rather like lions, but the hand positions suggest he [scil., the hero] may be grasping horns" (Buchanan, Moorey, *Ashmolean*, vol. 3 [n. 33], 68, No. 452). The same observation, which perfectly fits Achaemenid flavour, applies to the Samaria stamp.

[54] L. Woolley, "Excavations at Al Mina, Sueidia", *JHS* 58 (1938), 1-30, esp. pl. 15:MN134.

[55] P. Courbin, "Rapport sur la Xème et dernière campagne à Ras el Bassit", *AAAS* 36-37 (1986-7), 107-20, esp. 119 fig. 15.

[56] R. Stucky, *Ras Shamra – Leukos Limen* (BAH, 110), Paris 1983, 65, pl. 27:7.

[57] L. de Clercq, *Collection De Clercq: Catalogue méthodique et raisonné*, T. 2, Paris 1903, No. 57.

[58] Cf. Barag, *Western Asiatic Glass* (n. 50), No. 100; H.H. von der Osten, *Altorientalische Siegelsteine der Sammlung Hans Silvius von Aulock* (Studia Ethnographica Upsaliensia, 13), Uppsala 1957, Nos. 200-1; Vollenweider, *Catalogue raisonné* (n. 50), Nos. 41-3 (ex-Pereire); Keel-Leu, *Stempelsiegel* (n. 52), No. 168 (ex-Matouk).

Syro-Phoenician glass stamps of the 5th-4th centuries (scaraboids and conoids) are very typical for the Persian period and enjoyed a wide circulation all over the Levantine coast. The fact that they do not conform the hero's depiction to the Achaemenid royal image, looks as if they consciously denied Persian royalty to take over the quasi-divine position that was traditionally held by the 'Syro-Mesopotamian' hero or deity (who may well be Ninurta/Nimrod[59] or one of his successors).

The picture looks completely different in another group of seals, or rather sealings: The Persian royal hero is recognized as 'Master of lions' – which is not the same as a 'Master of *Mischwesen*'! – on a number of sealings from 5th/4th-century Jericho and Samaria (Wadi ed-Daliyeh). Most of them have been impressed with imported cylinder seals[60] related to the Achaemenid Court Style.

4 Obj: Sealing from a cylinder seal on a sherd (or jar stopper?), 38* x 38* x 6 mm (according to published scale; H 19 mm according to Hammond), lower and right part missing.
Icon: Persian 'royal hero' or king looking left with *kidaris* (and probably *kandys*), a quiver hanging over his back, both arms slightly bent and raised to grasp a (pair of) lion(s) held upside down at a hindleg, the forepart twisted back expressing dramatic movement, with one paw pointing outwards; the lower parts of the hero and the left animal are missing. The position of the lion's forepaws seems best to correspond to No. **5** rather than Nos. **6** or **7**. The most distinctive elements on this item, if correctly identified, are the quiver and the winged sun (with disk?) above the royal hero.
Prov: Jericho, trench II, square LXXVII, pit cutting into Iron Age II levels, reg. No. 1255.
Orig: Achaemenid court style, probably 5th cent. BCE.
Loc: Amman or Jerusalem?; cast in London, PEF, or Jerusalem, BSAJ.
Bib: K.M. Kenyon, T.A. Holland, *Excavations at Jericho*, vol. 4: The Pottery Type Series and Other Finds, London 1982, 558, 560 fig. 227:7; P.C. Hammond, "A Note on Two Seal Impressions from Tell es-Sulṭan", *PEQ* (1957), 68-9, esp. 69, pl. 17.

5 Obj: Sealing (12 x 14 mm) of a cylinder seal on bulla (17 x 22 mm), string preserved.
Icon: Persian 'royal hero' or king looking left with *kidaris* and *kandys*, both arms raised to grip a pair of lions held upside down at a hindleg, their foreparts twisted back expressing dramatic movement, with one paw pointing to the hero and the other in the opposite direction; only parts of the left animal are visible on the impression.
Prov: Wadi ed-Daliyeh, relation to preserved documents unknown; c. 332 BCE.

---

[59] Cf. C. Uehlinger, "Nimrod", in: ²*DDD*, 627-30.

[60] That a sealing on a clay bullae originates from a cylinder rather than stamp seal may be detected by several criteria, e.g. a straight base and/or even top line, traces of caps which held the original seal, the layout of the design preserved on the sealed surface, or a convex upper surface of the sealed bulla.

Orig: Achaemenid Court Style, 4th cent. BCE. Provenanced parallels come from Nippur, Ur and Persepolis;[61] the Chiha collection has a comparable cylinder seal from a probably North Syrian workshop, with a secondary terminal motif (a cock on a tree).[62] The suggestion that the cylinder seal was produced by a local workshop at Samaria (Leith, *Wadi Daliyeh*, 29) can be excluded, which indirectly is confirmed by the third quality parallels on Samarian coinage.
Loc: Jerusalem, Rockefeller Museum (IAA), J. 968.
Bib: F.M. Cross, "The Papyri and their historical implications", in: P.W. Lapp, N. Lapp, *Discoveries in the Wâdî ed-Dâliyeh* (AASOR, 41), Cambridge, MA 1974, 17-29, esp. 28, pl. 62:f; Stern, "Notes" (n. 18), 138-40 with fig. 5; Idem, "Assyrian and Babylonian elements" (n. 18), 54, 60 fig. 2a; Leith, *Wadi Daliyeh* (n. 22), 209-12, No. WD 17, pl. 17:1.[63]

6   Obj: Sealing (16 x 18 mm), probably from a cylinder seal, on bulla (18 x 19 mm), string preserved; ground line.
    Icon: Cf. No. **5**. By contrast to the latter and No. **4**, both paws of the lion(s) rest on the ground; of the left animal only its free hindleg is visible on the impression.
    Prov: Wadi Daliyeh, relation to preserved documents unknown; c. 332 BCE.
    Orig: Achaemenid Court Style, 4th cent. BCE; not from the same seal as Nos. **5** or **7**. That the cylinder seal was produced by a local workshop at Samaria (Leith, *Wadi Daliyeh*, 29) can be excluded (cf. No. **5**).
    Loc: Jerusalem, Rockefeller Museum (IAA), J. 748.
    Bib: Cross, "The Papyri" (cf. No. **5**), 28-9, pl. 62:g; Leith, *Wadi Daliyeh* (n. 22), 209-12, No. WD 51, pl. 17:3.

7   Obj: Sealing (17 x 15 mm), probably from a cylinder seal, on bulla (22 x 18 mm), string preserved; ground line.
    Icon: Cf. No. **5**. By drawing the royal hero turned right, Leith has clearly misunderstood the details which are corrected in our drawing according to a close inspection of the published photographs and autopsy of the sealing. As on No. **6**, both paws of the lion(s) rest on the ground; nothing of the left animal is visible on the impression.
    Prov: Wadi ed-Daliyeh, relation to preserved documents unknown; c. 332 BCE.
    Orig: Achaemenid Court Style, 4th cent. BCE; not from the same seal as **5** or **6**.[64] The surmise that the cylinder seal was produced by a local workshop

---

[61] Not all the parallels cited by Leith, *Wadi Daliyeh*, 210 n. 7, are equally pertinent since they mix up winged and unwinged, upright and hanging lions. For good parallels see Bregstein, *Seal Use* (n. 11), Nos. 7, 9-12 for No. 5, *ibidem*, Nos. 13, 52 for Nos. **6** and **7** (but the hero always faces right and his arms are generally bent).

[62] C. Doumet, *Sceaux et cylindres orientaux: la collection Chiha* (OBO.SA, 9), Fribourg & Göttingen 1992, No. 192.

[63] Note that the large numbers added in brackets to WD-Nos. on Leith's plates are the *negative* (not PAM-IAA inventory) numbers of the relevant items.

[64] Leith has a curious remark on the relationship of Nos. **6** and **7** which according to her "look very similar. In their current state of preservation, if the hero's head were not facing in different directions on the two bullae it would be tempting to assign them to the same seal" (Leith, *Wadi Daliyeh* [n. 22], 210). However,

at Samaria (Leith, *Wadi Daliyeh*, 29) can be excluded (cf. No. **5**).
Loc: Jerusalem, Rockefeller Museum (IAA), J. 733.
Bib: Leith, *Wadi Daliyeh* (n. 22), 209-12, No. WD 36, pl. 17:2.

8 Obj: Sealing on bulla, string preserved, probably from a scaraboid or conoid (no published measurements); horizontal layout.
Icon: "Still faintly visible in the smoothly worn impression are the Persian Hero's left arm raised in the characteristic manner to grip the head or hind leg of an opponent and a piece of the vertical line of the hero's cloak. Traces of an indeterminate type of animal, probably winged, appear on the right side of the bulla. The presence of an animal on the left can be assumed on the basis of the hero's central placement in the composition" (Leith's description based on a photograph). Although the published drawing is more explicit than the photograph, the hero's cloak is clearly the Persian *kandys* and he faces left. That the animal is winged seems doubtful to me; the photograph instead allows for a reading of both animals as lions held upside down, with traces of the hindlegs, tail, body and twisted head for the right-hand animal, as well as traces of the tail and possibly body of the left-hand one.
Prov: Wadi ed-Daliyeh, bulla attached to papyrus 14 (recording a lease or sale of storechambers); c. 332 BCE.
Orig: Probably Levantine (North Syria?), but derivative of Achaemenid Court Style; 4th cent. BCE. Neither the bad state of preservation nor the potential parallels (conoid with horizontal layout) from Egypt and the Aleppo market[65] allow for a more precise workshop definition.
Loc: Jerusalem, Rockefeller Museum (IAA?; not seen there), J. 779.
Bib: Leith, *Wadi Daliyeh* (n. 22), 213 No. WD 3B, pl. 18:1.

The 'Master of lions' on these seals is almost certainly the Persian king. It is significant that four out of these five sealings were made with cylinder seals. Cylinders are very useful for sealing on plain clay tablets, but not on tiny bullae. Original cylinders of the Persian period are not found very often in the Western provinces.[66] In contrast to earlier periods, there was no real market, and consequently neither local production nor regular trade for them in the southern Levant. Why then should three different individuals among the Wadi ed-Daliyeh seal owners use a cylinder for sealing – each seal showing the same design? How could these people have acquired their

---

that Nos. **6** and **7** originate from the same seal is not only excluded because of iconographical differences in detail (these are somewhat difficult to evaluate because of the unprecise handling of the seals during the impressing process, particularly in the case of cylinders rolled over a bulla), but also by the two sealings' sheer dimensions which do not correspond.

[65] Buchanan, Moorey, *Ashmolean*, vol. 3 (n. 33), Nos. 448-9.

[66] Note however the 'heroic encounter' scene on a well-known seal from Tell el-Heir: E. Oren, "The 'Migdol' Fortress in North-Western Sinai", *Qad.* 10, Nos. 38-9 (1977), 71-76, esp. 76 (best published photo of impression); Stern, *Material Culture* (n. 3), 196 fig. 316, 198; Collon, *First Impressions* (n. 32), No. 423.

seals? That all three got their seals by coincidence from a trader from abroad seems improbable. Were they in regular contact with business partners in North Syria, Mesopotamia or beyond so that they would regularly operate in a cuneiform environment? This could definitely not explain their using cylinder seals, since in the second half of the 4th century, not even in a totally cuneiform environment would a transaction necessarily require a cylinder seal. As a matter of fact, we know of hundreds of stamp or ring sealings on cuneiform tablets of the 5th and 4th centuries. Should our hypothetical Western clients have been guided by practical arguments alone, they would certainly have preferred to buy a stamp seal or a metal finger-ring.[67]

The most plausible explanation is that these citizens of Samaria used their conspicuous cylinder seals not only in their primary function, but also regarded them as powerful status symbols and markers of loyalty. Neither Greeks, nor Egyptians, nor, for that matter, Phoenicians produced or used cylinder seals at that time. Fashion rather tended to prefer Greek gems and finger-rings (which make up the bulk of the Wadi ed-Daliyeh bullae). To use a cylinder seal in 4th-century Samaria must by itself have been a demonstration of one's affinity to Babylonia, or Persia, all the more if the actual seal design related as closely as the ones discussed here to Achaemenid imperial ideology. The designs on sealings Nos. **5-7** are so closely related, almost identical, although from three different seals, that they probably come from one workshop. It is tempting to assume that they belonged to a series produced in a Mesopotamian or Persian workshop and that they had been brought to the West by government officials. In provincial Samaria, they would then have been offered to loyal subjects by the Persian governor or another official.

It can hardly be coincidental that contemporaneous coins from Sidon and Samaria display the same version of the Persian king's 'heroic encounter' with two lions (see below).

2.2   Scenes of 'Heroic Combat'

'Heroic combat' is distinguished from 'heroic encounter' or 'heroic control' in two respects: the hero faces only one opponent; the confrontation is more violent, since the hero is usually armed with a dagger. The hero's identity is again variable according to cultural traditions and seal workshops. For our purpose, we shall once more restrict

---

[67] To take the example of the Nippur Murašû archive, its 657 impressions divide equally into cylinder (204), stamp (227) and metal ring (217) sealings (Bregstein, "Sealing Practices" [n. 11], 55).

ourselves to seals that display 'explicit Persianisms':[68] on these, the hero generally wears the *kidaris* and is thus characterized as 'royal hero', and his opponent is always a *Mischwesen*.

> **9** Obj: Scaraboid, greenstone facies, lower quarter of base lost, 24.1 x 19.5 x 9.2 mm; cut style, with hatchings for interior details; border line.
>
> Icon: Bearded male hero wearing *kidaris* and short kilt to the left; that the upper part of the body is naked (Keel) is possible but difficult to ascertain. With one arm the hero holds a dagger, with the other he grasps by the horn a winged bull turned left (i.e., fleeing outwards), looking back toward him; above crescent moon.
>
> Prov: Tell Keisan, surface, field No. 3.668.
>
> Orig: While the material is typical of the so-called Tharros production of the 6th-5th cent. BCE, the seal must have been produced at a Levantine workshop since it combines typically Persian features (such as the crown) with totally un-Persian ones (such as the short kilt); early 5th cent. BCE.[69]
>
> Loc: Jerusalem, Ecole Biblique et Archéologique Franaise.
>
> Bib: O. Keel, "La glyptique", in: J. Briend, J.-B. Humbert (eds.), *Tell Keisan (1971-1976): Une cité phénicienne en Galilée* (OBO.SA 1), Freiburg & Göttingen 1980, 257-99, esp. 277-8 No. 21, pl. 89:21 = O. Keel *et al.*, *Studien zu den Stempelsiegeln aus Palästina/Israel*, Bd. 3 (OBO 100), Freiburg & Göttingen 1990, 231-2, No. 21, pl. 8:21; Klingbeil, "Syro-Palestinian Stamp Seals" (n. 19), 98, 106, 124 No. 4; Stern, "Notes" (n. 18), 144-5 with fig. 17; Keel, Uehlinger, *GGG* (n. 17), 375-6 with fig. 360b.

Seal No. **9** clearly perpetuates the Assyrian theme of a divine hero battling against a winged bull, which on Neo-Assyrian cylinder seals is frequently accompanied by astral symbols (echoed on our seal by the crescent) and may itself have definite astral connotations. A 'royal hero' fighting a bull and various monsters also appears on apotropaic door reliefs in Persepolis (cf. *fig. 6*). The hero generally holds his opponent at a horn – the horn thus becoming a major feature of the opponent's image.[70] This is a typically Persian period feature common to both the monumental rendering of 'heroic combat' at Persepolis and on numerous seals.

---

[68] Two glass seals from 5th-century contexts from Abu Ghosh (W.R. Taylor, "Recent Epigraphic Discoveries in Palestine", *JPOS* 10 [1930], 16-22, esp. 21-2, pl. 2:B) and Bet-Guvrin (Barag, *Western Asiatic Glass* [n. 50], No. 96) and a sealing recently found in Jerusalem (City of David excavations, courtesy D.T. Ariel), all of which may ultimately go back to one and the same master stamp, could also be considered in this section. However, as the Dor scaraboids mentioned in n. 50, they seem to show a 'Syro-Mesopotamian' rather than the Persian royal hero. Since an extensive study on them by Baruch Brandl is in press for vol. 5 of the City of David Final Reports (forthcoming in the Qedem series), I chose not to treat them in detail here.

[69] For iconographical parallels from Nippur, cf. Bregstein, *Seal Use* (n. 11), Nos. 96-9.

[70] Cf. Uehlinger, *"Figurative policy"* (n. 14), 340.

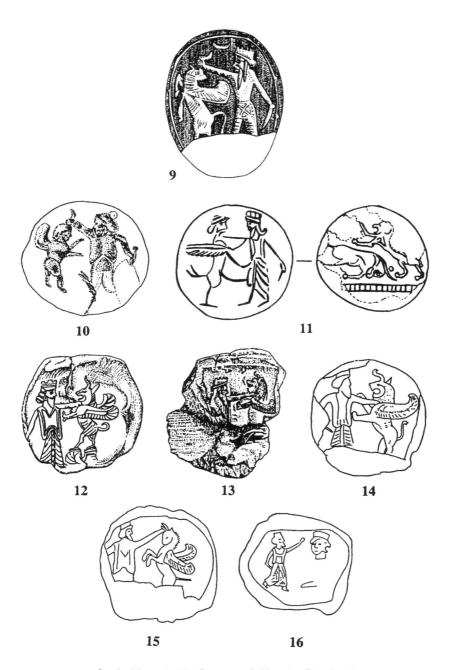

Seals Nos. **9-16**: Scenes of 'Heroic Combat'

While the Persepolis hero's costume conforms to Persian court etiquette, our figure is rather a variant of the traditional 'Syro-Mesopotamian' hero. He, however, is brought somewhat up to date and 'Persianized' by his crenellated crown.

10 Obj: Conoid, dark blue glass, base slightly convex, fairly big chip broken out, ⊘ 16 x 18.5 mm; mass-produced (probably cast) from a stamped matrix mould; no ground line.
Icon: Bearded male hero facing left, bare-headed but wearing a (rather short) *kandys*; one arm holding a dagger, the other grasping by the horn a rampant winged monster (human-headed, feline body, lion tail) facing him.
Prov: Gezer, tomb 153, 5th cent. BCE. (not Samaria as stated by Culican).
Orig: Local Phoenician mass production, possibly from Sidon; the master stamp used to produce the mould could have been of Anatolian or North Syrian origin, derivative from Achaemenid Court Style; 5th cent. BCE.
Loc: Jerusalem, Rockefeller Museum, J. 491 (not J. 767 as stated by Culican[71]); cast in London, Palestine Exploration Fund, no inv. No.
Bib: R.A.S. Macalister, "Ninth Quarterly Report on the Excavation of Gezer", *PEQ* (1904), 320-354, esp. 336 with fig. 5; Idem, *The Excavation of Gezer* (cf. n. 35), vol. 1, 359 with fig. 186; W. Culican, "The iconography of some Phoenician seals and seal impressions", *AJBA* 1/1 (1968), 50-103, esp. 52 (= Idem, *Opera selecta: From Tyre to Tartessos* [SMA Pocket-book, 40], Göteborg 1986, 211-64, esp. 213) pl. I top left.[72]

11 Obj: Truncated cone (or weight stamp), one side convex, opaque white stone (chalcedon?), base chipped and damaged, ⊘ 16.2/18 x 15.1 mm; modeled style.
Icon: Face A: Lion to the right attacking a bull falling in the opposite direction;[73] double ground line with ladder hatchings, exergue left empty.
Face B (convex): Persian 'royal hero' wearing *kidaris* and *kandys* to the left; with one arm he holds a dagger, with the other he grasps by the throat a rampant winged monster (human-headed, feline body, eagle claws and probably bird's tail) facing him, standing on one foot while 'kicking' him with the other. No ground line.

---

[71] Culican's error derives from a confusion of this item with a broken conical glass seal from Samaria that was once kept in the same showcase. Registered as J. 767 in the Rockefeller Museum's *Gallery Book for Visitors*, it is described as showing a "Man holding lion and dog (?) with his outstretched hands". I have not been able to locate this seal which may well belong to the 'heroic encounter' group.

[72] That Macalister's piece from Gezer and the conoid shown on Culican's plate and said to come from Samaria are one and the same item could be established during a short visit to the Israel Antiquities Authority and the Rockefeller Museum on 14 September 1998. I am grateful to Mrs. Hava Katz, Chief curator of IAA, for permission to study the object; Mrs. Ornit Ilan, Curator of the Rockefeller Museum, and Ms. Alegre Savariego, IAA staff member, for practical assistance.

[73] An astronomical interpretation of this widespread motif has been suggested by W. Hartner, "The Earliest History of the Constellations in the Near East and the Motif of the Lion-Bull Combat", *JNES* 24 (1965), 1-16.

Prov: Samaria, surface(?) 1914.
Orig: Achaemenid Court Style derivative, possibly of Anatolian (Lydian or Cilician?) origin; later 5th/4th cent. BCE.
Loc: Formerly Jerusalem, YMCA, Clark coll. No. 116; present location not reported.
Bib: Unpublished.

Unfortunately seal No. **10** is much worn and almost illegible (but compare our drawing to Macalister's). Material and manufacture clearly relate it to a group that circulated along the Phoenician coast, although the design has not yet found exact iconographical parallels in the area and may be based on a stamp imported from further north. The hero retains the bare-headed appearance of the 'Syro-Mesopotamian' hero, but he wears the Persian folded court robe and his attitude of holding the monster by the base of a horn is another typical adaptation. The horn alone allows one to distinguish the monster from a Levantine cherub, which would not fit this role as opponent.

No. **11** is another interesting witness of a long-distance import. The seal shape (which relates to weights) and the much-worn design on the base belong to the sphere of North Syrian glyptic. The hero is now clearly defined by royal attributes. The monster comes again close to a cherub. It is held by the throat. This minor detail relates the seal to the following series of sealings from Samaria that show the Persian royal hero (or the heroic king) battling against a horned, winged lion monster.

12 Obj: Sealing (c. 16* x 14* mm) of a cylinder seal on bulla (20.5 x 19.8 x 5.9 mm); modeled style.
Icon: Male, bearded 'royal hero' facing right, wearing *kidaris* and *kandys*; with one arm he holds a dagger (not preserved), with the other he grasps by the throat a rampant winged lion-monster (horned, lion's body, eagle's feet) facing him; the monster stands on the wing and (horned?) crenellated crown of a crouching Persian 'royal sphinx'; the left-hand and lower end of seal design are not visible on the sealing.
Prov: Samaria, Qf (northern slope, below the Augusteum, c. 540N/600E), reg. No. 1149; unstratified (pre-Herodian deposits, Qf level VIa according to PAM-IAA inventory).
Orig: Achaemenid Court Style, 5th/4th cent. BCE. More simple parallels without the additional royal sphinx include sealings from Daskyleion,[74] Nippur,[75] and Persepolis.[76]
Loc: Jerusalem, Rockefeller Museum, PAM-IAA 32.2282 (exhibit).[77]
Bib: Crowfoot *et al.*, *Objects* (n. 49), 88 No. 42, pl. 15:42; Stern, "Notes"

[74]K. Balkan, "Inscribed Bullae from Daskyleion-Ergili", *Anat.* 4 (1959), 123-8, esp. 124-5 and pl. 33:a-b.
[75]Bregstein, *Seal Use* (n. 11), Nos. 89-90.
[76]Schmidt, *Persepolis*, vol. 2, (n. 50), pl. 13:60.
[77]The drawing by I. Haselbach (Fribourg) published here reflects a personal

(n. 18), 144-5 with fig. 14; Keel, Uehlinger, *GGG* (n. 17), 375-6 with fig. 360a (to be replaced by the present drawing); Leith, *Wadi Daliyeh* (n. 22), 215.

13 Obj: Sealing (no published measurements) of a cylinder seal (H c. 20 mm according to the excavator) on fragmentary tablet (!, no published measurements); modeled style.
   Icon: Almost identical to No. **12**, but the loss of the design's lower part and the bad quality of the published photograph make it difficult to be more specific.[78] It is not clear whether one or both wings of the monster were depicted. The left, right and lower end of the seal design are not preserved.
   Prov: Samaria, acropolis, strip 8, under corridor 814 of Hellenistic building, reg. No. 4496.
   Orig: Achaemenid Court Style, 5th/4th cent. BCE.
   Loc: Cambridge, MA, Harvard Semitic Museum?
   Bib: G.A. Reisner *et al.*, *Harvard Excavations at Samaria*, Cambridge, MA 1924, vol. 1, 378; vol. 2, pl. 57h:1-2; J. Nougayrol, *Cylindres-sceaux et empreintes de cylindres trouvés en Palestine* (BAH, 33), Paris 1939, 61 No. 126, pl. 6; Stern, "Notes" (n. 18), 144-5 with fig. 15; Leith, *Wadi Daliyeh* (n. 22), 215.

14 Obj: Sealing (19 x 14* mm) of a cylinder or stamp seal, on bulla (19 x 17 mm), broken into several pieces, string preserved; modeled style.
   Icon: Cf. No. **13**, but clearly from a different seal. The monster was not shown standing on another *Mischwesen*, and only one wing is depicted. The second foreleg which apparently crosses the royal hero's outstretched arm has no parallel in the other sealings.
   Prov: Wadi ed-Daliyeh, relation to preserved documents unknown; c. 332 BCE.
   Orig: Achaemenid Court Style, 4th cent. BCE. That the cylinder seal was produced by a local workshop at Samaria (Leith, *Wadi Daliyeh*, 29) can be ruled out (cf. No. **5**).
   Loc: Jerusalem, Rockefeller Museum (IAA), J. 959.
   Bib: Leith, *Wadi Daliyeh* (n. 22), 214-7, No. WD 4, pl. 18:2.

The three sealings which may or may not be contemporary (Nos. **12-13** could be slightly earlier), were certainly made with imported hardstone cylinder seals and are again late representatives of the Court Style. All features are Persian Achaemenid. No. **12** is reminiscent of No. **1** because of the additional *Mischwesen* shown under the feet of

---

inspection of the object on 14/16 September 1998 in the Rockefeller Museum, Jerusalem. I thank Mrs. Hava Katz, Chief curator of IAA, for permission to study the object, Mrs. Ornit Ilan, Curator of the Rockefeller Museum, for practical assistance.

[78] Our two drawings present considerable differences, but these are partly dependent on the different quality of our Vorlagen. No. **13** was published by Reisner as a quite indistinct photograph, Nougayrol's pencil drawing is of no help, and I have not seen the original. As a rule, bullae and similar flat impressions of such minute and delicately cut seals should be photographed and published twice with different lighting in order to allow one to recognize the details.

the lion monster. A detailed study would be necessary to determine the precise significance of the 'royal sphinx' in this position and of its relationship to the royal hero and to the monster standing on it. But clearly this additional sphinx enhances the mythological character of the scene. Seal designs with two crouching royal sphinxes are well attested on cylinder seal versions of 'heroic encounter', but precise parallels with only one additional *Mischwesen* placed underneath the opponent in a 'heroic combat' composition are extremely rare.

Together with the winged bull (see below, No. **14**), the winged lion monster (*anzû* in the Mesopotamian tradition) represents one of the most typical and traditional symbolic rendering of chaotic forces in Achaemenid glyptic. The motif of heroic combat against this monster appears at Persepolis (cf. *fig. 7*) although with a few minor differences, the most notable being that the hero wears typically royal attributes on the sealings but not on the reliefs. While he is clearly some sort of apotropaic genius in the palatial environment of Persepolis, the seals and sealings stress his royal identity. A western provincial would almost certainly identify this hero either with the Persian king himself or, in a more abstract manner, with Achaemenid kingship in general, for which the image claims irresistible capacity to keep the world under control and to assure cosmic order.[79] The overlapping of history and meta-history, politics and mythology reminds one of a characteristic mood of early apocalypticism.

I have already referred to Dusinberre's recent hypothesis that during the first half of the Persian period, seals of this kind which put particular stress on the meta-historical quality of Persian Achaemenid power belonged to people who were closely related to the Persian imperial administration.[80] Among the c. 300 sealings from Daskyleion, a collection which comes from the satrapial administration, 87 show a 'heroic combat' scene comparable to our Nos. **6-7**.[81] A few of them even include a royal owner's claim ("I am Xerxes, the king"), and most have a palm tree as terminal.[82] Our sealings from Samaria represent somewhat simpler versions. However, that one of them comes from a tablet found at Samaria is significant and points to official use, although not even fragments of a related text survived. Moreover, the

---

[79] "What the Achaemenid commissioners of these seals may have wanted to imply then, would be the new concept that the Persian king was simultaneously the human king as well as the super-human hero of Assyrian scenes with fantastic animals" (Leith, *Wadi Daliyeh* [n. 22], 217).

[80] See above, discussion of seal No. **1**.

[81] Cf. Balkan, "Inscribed Bullae" (n. 74), 125.

[82] Both features appear at the time of Darius I together with 'heroic encounter'.

provenance of all three items from Samaria or its vicinity conforms
to the fact that the design is well attested on 4th-century Samarian
coinage but apparently absent from other contemporary coinage of the
area (Sidonian coinage has only the lion as opponent). Consequently,
the three sealings should be related to the Persian provincial administration and to locals working in close cooperation with the latter.
They should be considered alongside Nos. **5-7** for which we already
suggested a more indirect link with the Persian administration.

We may conclude that as far as miniature media are concerned,
the image of the Persian royal hero – which western provincials would
easily identify either with the king or with Achaemenid kingship in
general – must have been the most powerful and renowned among the
visual expressions of Persian imperial ideology in Palestine.

15 Obj: Sealing (15* x 18* mm) of a concave stamp (Leith) or cylinder seal on
bulla (19 x 20 mm), string and papyrus fragments preserved on the reverse;
modeled style.
Icon: Male, bearded 'royal hero' facing right, wearing *kidaris* and *kandys*;
in one hand he holds a dagger (not preserved), with the other he grasps by
the horn a rampant winged bull facing him, with scissor-like open wings.[83]
Prov: Wadi ed-Daliyeh, relation to preserved documents unknown; c. 332
BCE.
Orig: Achaemenid Court Style, 4th cent. BCE; "perhaps an import to
Samaria from farther east" (Leith, contradicting her suggestion, *Wadi Dali-
yeh*, 29, that the cylinder seal was produced by a local workshop at Samaria,
a possibility which can be safely excluded; cf. No. **5**).
Loc: Jerusalem, Rockefeller Museum (IAA), J. 963.
Bib: Leith, *Wadi Daliyeh* (n. 22), 218-9, No. WD 8, pl. 18:3.

16 Obj: Sealing (8 x 9 mm) of a metal finger-ring on bulla (12 x 13 mm),
string and papyrus fragments preserved on the reverse; modeled style; no
ground line.
Icon: Male, bearded 'royal hero' facing right, wearing *kidaris* and *kandys*;
in one hand he holds a dagger; the other arm is outstretched in the usual
manner although in this instance it does not lead to an opponent's horn
or throat but rather reminds of a menacing (or even greeting?) gesture.
The entity facing the hero on the right is difficult to understand. Leith
suggested it to be a lying sphinx and noted a few comparanda – including
a nondescript oval stamp seal from Susa – that, on second look however, are
all too different in style and iconography to support this suggestion.[84] My
own inspection of the bulla, unfortunately under somewhat poor lighting
conditions, could not confirm Leith's interpretation. What she drew as
the putative sphinx's forelegs has no physical relation to the head on the

---

[83]The bull almost resembles a horse such as the (unwinged) animal on an unprovenanced stamp seal in Paris: L. Delaporte, *Catalogue des cylindres orientaux
et des cachets assyro-babyloniens, perses et syro-cappadociens de la Bibliothèque
Nationale*, Paris 1910, No. 639.
[84]Leith, *Wadi Daliyeh* (n. 22), 226 with n. 3-4.

upper right. This head is easier to recognize, but it seems to be an isolated feature suspended in the field: since it ends neatly at the bottom of the throat, it cannot belong to some larger figure. The unbearded face is clearly human and probably female. It would be tempting to restore it as a bifacial janiform head, with a leonine face to the right such as appear on sealings from Ur and elsewhere and on Philisto-Arabian coinage,[85] but one must admit that details are almost indistinct on this feature measuring hardly 3 mm in height.

Prov: Wadi ed-Daliyeh, relation to preserved documents unknown; c. 332 BCE.

Orig: 'Graeco-Persian'?, 4th cent. BCE.

Loc: Jerusalem, Rockefeller Museum (IAA), J. 970.

Bib: Leith, *Wadi Daliyeh* (n. 22), 226-8, No. WD 19, pl. 20:1.

The two sealings just mentioned may enlarge our perception of the 'Achaemenid Court Style' group of sealings. The winged bull already seen on No. **9** continued to be represented as the royal hero's opponent until the very end of the Persian period. Sealing No. **16** is interesting since it shows a kind of free variation on a time-honoured motif on behalf of seal engravers who must have been acquainted with the iconography of contemporary coinage. The scene however remains enigmatic and cannot be confidently interpreted at the present.

It is puzzling that no example of 'heroic combat' scenes showing the king battling against a lion has yet turned up in the glyptic heritage of Palestine, but this may be due to the hazards of archaeological discovery. Seals with this motif – which actually perpetuates the Assyrian royal (or palace) stamp seal – are very current in Persian period glyptic from other areas. That the scheme was known in Palestine too is amply demonstrated by coinage (particularly from Sidon and Samaria). An unprovenanced ivory plaque in the Hecht Museum in Haifa, which may originate from Samaria, is unfortunately too fragmentary as to allow a precise identification of the king's leonine opponent (*fig. 8*).[86]

To conclude this section, it seems obvious that the theme of 'heroic combat' showing the Persian royal hero battling against a *Mischwesen*, which belonged to the official repertoire of Achaemenid state

---

[85] Cf. H. Gitler, "Achaemenid Motifs in the Coinage of Ashdod, Ascalon and Gaza from the Fourth Century BC", *Trans* 17? (1999) [in press]; Mildenberg, "Imagery" (below n. 115), 14-5; D. Collon, "A Hoard of Sealings from Ur", in: Boussac, Invernizzi (eds.), *Archives et sceaux* (n.11), 65-84, esp. 75-6 and pl. 22.

[86] E. Stern, "Four Phoenician Finds from Israel", in: K. van Lerberghe, A. Schoors (eds.), *Immigration and Emigration within the Ancient Near East* (Fs. E. Lipiński; OLA, 65), Leuven 1995, 319-34, esp. 328-32. Cf. an Achaemenid ivory from Susa which shows the lion in the role of the opponent: P. Amiet, "Les ivoires achéménides de Suse", *Syr.* 49 (1972), 167-91, esp. 186 fig. 17:b.

iconography, was known as such and understood as a powerful visual metaphor for Achaemenid kingship and Persian imperial ideology in Palestine, and particularly in Samaria. Among the many seal images featuring 'explicit Persianisms', the 'heroic combat' scenes and the depictions of the royal hero as 'master of lions' stand out as quite an impressive group. Taken together, they may be viewed as the most significant visual translations of what the power of the Persian empire should have meant to western provincials: mastering of chaos, ordering of the world. Both series appear almost exclusively on seals that had been imported from elsewhere. Local glyptic production apparently refrained from adopting these 'powerful Persianisms' into their own repertoire.

The glyptic evidence from Palestine does not reflect other models of official Achaemenid state art (such as, e.g., the 'king on high' compositions). The latter should thus not be over-estimated in an assessment of the impact of visually mediated Persian imperial ideology on Palestine. While the image of the king sitting on his throne and giving an audience is well attested on bullae from Daskyleion,[87] where it is certainly related to the satrapial administration, it does not (yet?) appear on sealings from the Levant (but on coins, see below).[88] Another peaceful image, this one prominent in Sidonian coinage, namely the king appearing in a processional chariot (cf. *fig. 9*), is also absent from the contemporary glyptic of Palestine.[89] On seals from Palestine, vigorous and extremely dramatic metaphors of Persian power clearly prevail. Persian power, they claim, is essentially founded upon the strength of heroic kingship.

2.3   Antithetical *Mischwesen* Compositions

Mischwesen do not only appear in menacing postures on Persian period glyptic from Palestine, they may also feature in symmetrical compositions as peaceful pairs facing each other. In contrast to the afore-mentioned scenes whose essence is the suppression of menace or revolt, these compositions convey a strong sense of 'law and order'. Clearly, these *Mischwesen* are not the same as the ones who are

---

[87]Cf. D. Kaptan, "The Great King's Audience", in: F. Blakolmer *et al.* (eds.), *Fremde Zeiten (Fs. J. Borchhardt)*, Bd. 1, Wien 1996, 259-71. "Within the mechanism of imperial propaganda, the audience scene (...) stresses the power of central administration which required the absolute loyalty to the king from the highest Persian official in the province, *khshahthrapavan*, to the people under the control of the Achaemenid empire" (*ibidem*, 268).

[88]Note, however, the provincial variant on coins from Samaria (below, sect. 4).

[89]Contrast, e.g., an agate seal in Berlin bought at Luxor, cf. L. Jakob-Rost, *Die Stempelsiegel im Vorderasiatischen Museum Berlin*, new ed. Berlin 1997, No. 473.

fought by the royal hero. Instead of menacing, they rather embody the peaceful stability of Persian power.

17-21 Obj: Five different sealings (c. 8 x 15 mm) probably of a metal finger-ring with oval bezel, on five bulla (see Leith for details); horizontal layout, modeled style; irregular border of tiny dots, no ground line.
Icon: Two recumbent bearded, winged sphinxes wearing the Persian dentate crown (thus 'royal sphinxes'), facing each other, flanking a male figure facing left clad in a short kilt, one hand raised in a gesture which may denote respectful veneration rather than menace.[90]
Prov: Wadi ed-Daliyeh, originally attached to at least three different documents, among them payrus Nos. 14 (lease or sale of storechambers) and 1 (slave sale), the latter dated March 19, 335 BCE. Since "Yehônûr" is the only name appearing on all three documents, the seal employed was probably the personal seal of this individual.
Orig: Cyprus or Phoenicia, 4th cent. BCE.
Loc: Jerusalem, Rockefeller Museum (IAA), J. 762, 763, 765, 965, 921.
Bib: Cross, "The Papyri" (cf. No. **5**), 29, pl. 63:j-m; Leith, *Wadi Daliyeh* (n. 22), 220-4, Nos. WD 3A, 10A, 11B, 12, 24, pl. 19:1-3.

Although it is impossible to identify the human figure on these tiny sealings who must be a hero of some kind, Leith's interpretation of the scene as a variant of 'heroic encounter' (see above, 2.1.) does not commend itself. Leith herself recognizes that a heroic encounter or combat against 'royal sphinxes' would be a very odd concept. Furthermore, neither the hero's attitude nor the sphinxes' recumbent position fit the usual scenario of 'heroic encounter' compositions. The 'royal sphinxes' cannot be considered as the hero's opponents but enhance his centrality and appear almost as his guardians.[91]

22 Obj: Sealing (6 x 10 mm) probably of a metal finger-ring, on bulla (11 x 17 mm), string preserved, papyrus imprint; horizontal layout, modeled style; dot border.
Icon: Pair of seated, winged 'royal sphinxes' facing each other.
Prov: Wadi ed-Daliyeh, relation to preserved documents unknown; c. 332 BCE.
Orig: While the motif may relate the seal to Lydia, iconographical parallels come from regions as diverse as Egypt, Sardis, Kerch (Russian Crimea), Nippur and Persepolis. None of these features the dot border which is typical of Phoenician – including Samarian – glyptic and coinage. 4th cent. BCE.
Loc: Jerusalem, Rockefeller Museum (IAA), J. 945.
Bib: Leith, *Wadi Daliyeh* (n. 22), 237-8, No. WD 48, pl. 21:2.

---

[90] Leith, *Wadi Daliyeh*, 222, considers the gesture to be menacing but points out contra Cross that the figure does not hold any weapon.
[91] On close inspection of the minute original, the hero figure reminded me of the Heracles as 'Master of lions' on a 'Greek' sealing from Wadi ed-Daliyeh (cf. Leith, *Wadi Daliyeh*, 162-4 No. WD 47; our *fig. 4*).

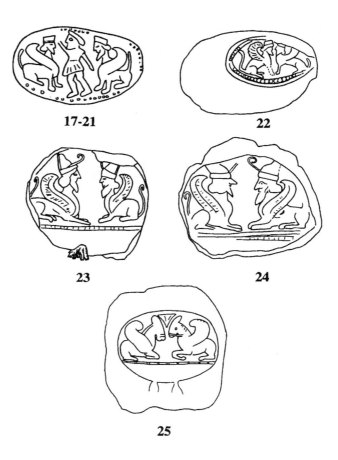

17-21   **22**

23   **24**

25

Seals Nos. **17-25**: Antithetical *Mischwesen* compositions

23 Obj: Sealing (15 x 17 mm) of a circular (conical?) stamp seal (truncated cone?), on bulla (15 x 17 mm), string preserved, papyrus fibres on front and back; modeled style; ground line with ladder hatchings (cf. No. **11**), exergue left empty.
Icon: Pair of recumbent, winged sphinxes wearing the double crown of Egypt, facing each other.
Prov: Wadi ed-Daliyeh, relation to preserved documents unknown; c. 332 BCE.
Orig: Phoenicia?, 4th cent. BCE.
Loc: Jerusalem, Rockefeller Museum (IAA), J. 966.
Bib: Leith, *Wadi Daliyeh* (n. 22), 231-4, No. WD 13, pl. 20:2.

24 Obj: Sealing (15 x 17 mm) of a circular (conical?) stamp seal (truncated cone?), on bulla (16 x 17 mm), string preserved; modeled style; double version of ground line with ladder hatchings (cf. No. **23**, or due to improper sealing), exergue left empty.
Icon: cf. No. **23**.
Prov: Wadi ed-Daliyeh, relation to preserved documents unknown; c. 332 BCE.
Orig: Phoenicia?, 4th cent. BCE.
Loc: Jerusalem, Rockefeller Museum (IAA), J. 938.
Bib: Leith, *Wadi Daliyeh* (n. 22), 231-4, No. WD 41, pl. 20:3.

25 Obj: Sealing (10 x 13 mm) of a stone stamp seal (scaraboid?), on bulla (17 x 17 mm), string preserved; modeled style; ground line with ladder hatchings (cf. No. **23**), exergue left empty.
Icon: Pair of recumbent winged horses, apparently wearing bridles and reins, facing each other;[92] possibly lotus flower between their heads.
Prov: Wadi ed-Daliyeh, relation to preserved documents unknown; c. 332 BCE.
Orig: Achaemenid Court Style with possible Phoenician mediation, 4th cent. BCE.
Loc: Jerusalem, Rockefeller Museum (IAA), J. 969.
Bib: Leith, *Wadi Daliyeh* (n. 22), 199-201, No. WD 18, pl. 16:1.

Within the limits of the present inquiry, we may ignore other symmetrical *Mischwesen* compositions of Babylonian origin (such as human-headed scorpion monsters) or Greek inspiration (sphinxes and other winged beings shown in more vivid, less heraldic postures) among the bullae from Wadi ed-Daliyeh. Within the group displaying 'explicit Persianisms', 'royal sphinxes' appear more often than other *Mischwesen*. Their peculiar appearance with an Egyptian double crown on

---

[92] "The pose of the horses with forelegs tucked under their chests may be an Achaemenid trait. The joined animal foreparts which acted as decorative column capitals at Persepolis and Pasargadae fold their forelegs under their chests in exactly the same way; and while many of these capitals seem to have been in the form of bulls, at least one capital fragment, found at Pasargadae, was of a horse. (...) Seal engravers presumably had first-hand exposure to such examples of large-scale Achaemenid sculpture" (Leith, *Wadi Daliyeh*, 200).

sealings Nos. **23** and **24** undoubtedly has more than aesthetic implications. Since the royal sphinxes can be regarded as symbolic embodiments of Persian imperial power, it echoes and visualizes the renewed Persian claim to dominion in Egypt at the time of Artaxerxes III.

2.4 Hunting Scenes

Scenes of hunting on foot or in a chariot appear long before the Persian period in Palestinian glyptic. Hunting on horseback is attested from the late Neo-Assyrian period onwards. There are a few hunting scenes in Persian period glyptic from Palestine. With the exception of one group of glass scaraboids, however, the evidence is not very consistent – a striking contrast, e.g., to 'Graeco-Persian' glyptic where the subject matter was familiar.

> **26** Obj: Sealing (no published measurements) of a cylinder seal (*pace* Stern), on a relatively large bulla (c. 25 x 25 mm); modeled style.
> Icon: Male hero (unbearded?) running in *Knielauf* to the right, wearing striated hat (not *kidaris*) and long 'Babylonian' robe over a short kilt, quiver on the back, bow drawn against a recumbent *Mischwesen*, probably a winged lion with a quite distinct mane, which is partly visible on the left side of the bulla (*pace* Stronach); cross-like winged sun-disk as terminal. I am not acquainted with any precise parallel, but the subject seems to have been more current in Babylonia and Elam than elsewhere.[93]
> Prov: Tell el-Balaṭa/Shechem, area II "outside the ruined house" (Toombs); post-str. V (525-480 BCE), not stratified.
> Orig: Babylonia?; 5th-4th cent. BCE.
> Loc: Amman, National Archaeological Museum, J. 7207.
> Bib: G.E. Wright, *Shechem – the Biography of a Biblical City*, New York & Toronto 1965, 168, fig. 94; L.E. Toombs, "The Second Season of Excavation at Biblical Shechem. Part 2: The Archaeological Results", *BA* 20 (1957) 92-105, esp. 101 fig. 11, 104; K. Jaroš, *Sichem: Eine archäologische und religionsgeschichtliche Studie, mit besonderer Berücksichtigung von Jos 24* (OBO 11), Freiburg & Göttingen 1976, 57, Abb. 156; Stern, *Material Culture* (n. 3), front cover, 197 with fig. 317; D. Stronach, "Early Achaemenid Coinage: Perspectives from the Homeland", *IrAnt* 24 (1989), 255-79, esp. 271; T. Ornan, *Studies in Glyptics from the Land of Israel and Transjordan: Assyrian, Babylonian and Achaemenid Cylinder Seals from the First Half of the First Millennium* BCE (unpubl. MA thesis, Hebrew University, Jerusalem 1990), 41-2, No. 31.[94]

---

[93]Cf. Collon, *First Impressions* (n. 32), Nos. 419, 426; L. Legrain, *The Culture of the Babylonians from their Seals in the Collections of the Museum* (PBS 14), Philadelphia 1925, No. 993 (Nippur).

[94]I am grateful to my colleague Dr. Jürg Eggler (Fribourg) for having made an impression from the original bulla located by him at Amman. The drawing by Noga Ze'evi (Jerusalem), published here with the kind permission of Tallay Ornan, has been slightly corrected according to the impression.

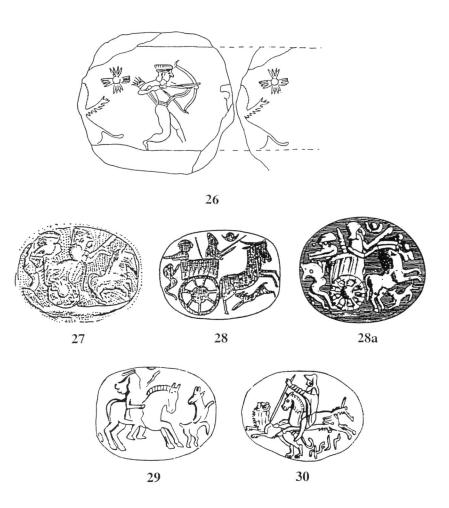

26

27   28   28a

29   30

Seals Nos. **26-30**: Hunting Scenes

The hunting figure on this sealing was identified with as Persian king by the excavators, followed by Stern, who considered the design to be common in Persian glyptic. Both statements call for comment. The hunter's headgear is clearly not the royal *kidaris*, and the robe puts him into to the tradition of the Babylonian hero rather than the Persian royal archer. Furthermore, while royal hunt on lions and other wild animals is indeed quite well attested, shooting with a bow against one or several monsters is not. In my opinion, No. **26** is not a depiction of royal hunt but rather of a divine or semi-divine hunter hero (cf. Ninurta/Nimrod referred to in sect. 2.1).

27 Obj: Scaraboid, bluish glass, worn, no published measurements (c. 26 x 21.5 x – mm according to published drawing); no border line; mass-produced (probably cast) from a stamped matrix mould.
Icon: Chariot drawn by a single horse running to the right; the charioteer wears a kind of triangular hat and a stick; another person (probably of royal status) stands at the back of the chariot, turned to the left, and kills with a dagger(?) an apparently falling animal, probably a lion.
Prov: Dor, surface find, reg. No. 5174.
Orig: Phoenician mass production, possibly from Sidon or further south; c. 450-370 BCE. In addition to the somewhat more elaborate following items, there are unprovenanced parallels in several museum collections, e.g. in the British Museum.[95] A comparable piece (showing only the driver in the chariot, but no hunt) in the Ashmolean Museum may have been acquired in Jerusalem.[96]
Loc: Naḥšolim, Center of Nautical & Regional Archaeology, reg. No.?
Bib: E. Stern, "Two Phoenician Glass Scarabs from Tel Dor", *JANES* 16-7 (1984-5), 213-6, esp. 215-6; Idem, *Dor: Ruler of the Seas*, Jerusalem 1994, 190-1 with fig. 124 (third row); Idem, *Excavations at Dor: Final Report*, vol. 1/B: Areas A and C: The Finds (Qedem Reports, 2), Jerusalem 1995, 475-8 with fig. 10.1:2 and photo 10.2.

28 Obj: Scaraboid, bluish glass, worn, no published measurements (c. 19 x 14 x – mm according to published drawing); no border line; mass-produced (probably cast) from a stamped matrix mould.
Icon: cf. No. **27**; among the most notable differences, a dog running to the left is shown under the horse, an astral symbol (disk in crescent) appears in the field above the horse, and a spear seems to stand between the two men in the chariot. Bliss's drawing should be interpreted according to the following exact parallel from Kamid el-Loz.
Prov: Tell ez-Zakariye/Azeka.
Orig: Phoenician mass production, from Sidon or further south; c. 450-370 BCE.
Loc: –
Bib: F.J. Bliss, "Third Report on the Excavations at Tell Zakarîya", *PEQ* 31 (1899), 170-87, esp. 187, pl. 7:11; O. Keel, *Corpus der Stempelsiegel-Amulette aus Palästina/Israel: Katalog* (OBO.SA, 13), Bd. 1, Fribourg & Göttingen 1997, 726-7, No. 4.

[95]Barag, *Western Asiatic Glass* (n. 50), No. 97
[96]Buchanan, Moorey, *Ashmolean*, vol. 3 (n. 33), No. 513.

28a Obj: Scaraboid, bluish glass, 18 x 16 x 7 mm; no border line; mass-produced (probably cast) from a stamped matrix mould.
Icon: cf. No. **28**.
Prov: Kamid el-Loz, cemetery, tomb 2; 450-370 BCE.
Orig: Phoenician mass production, from Sidon or further south; c. 450-370 BCE.
Loc: Beirut, National Museum?
Bib: R. Poppa, *Kāmid el-Lōz*, Bd. 2: Der eisenzeitliche Friedhof, Befunde und Funde (SBA, 18), Bonn 1978, 63 No. 3, 74 No. 8, pl. 3:2-3; E. Gubel, "Phoenician Seals in the Allard Pierson Museum, Amsterdam (CGPH 3)", *RSF* 16 (1988), 145-163, esp. 162, pl. 32:b; Nunn, *Kontinuität und Wandel* (n. 9), 167, 169, 186 No. 238, pl. 63:238.

Stern has compared the seal from Dor to the well-known series of Sidonian coins showing the Persian king in a processional chariot accompanied by an acolythe who follows the chariot (*fig. 10*). He noted a number of differences between the two scenes, but nevertheless concluded that they were basically identical, arguing further that the Dor seal "should probably be interpreted as the property of a high-ranking official, perhaps even the Sidonian king's representative in the city of Dor, who used it to seal documents with the emblem of Sidon, just as the king of Sidon did, as shown on its coins".[97] Attractive at first glance, the theory looks doubtful to me. A lion hunt scene (seals) has a completely different meaning than a processional scene (coins). Moreover, the Azeka item (apparently overlooked by Stern) clearly shows that the diffusion of these seals extended beyond Sidonian territory and that it was not linked to the Sidonian administration. While we cannot exclude that Sidon was indeed the centre of production of these glass scaraboids, other places further south cannot be ruled out. Finally one should remember that seals used for authentification of public or otherwise official documents required a fairly clear impression in order to be recognized. As a rule, they would thus be preferably made of some hardstone material rather than friable glass which does not produce a very clear relief even on a carefully executed sealing. In my opinion, the rather common and cheap glass scaraboids mentioned in this section are unlikely to have fulfilled an official administrative function. They are mevertheless interesting for our purpose since they apparently imply that below the level of the Persian imperial administration, seal carvers would not care much for the imperial etiquette that may have reserved the slaying of lions for the Great King alone. The lion hunter in the chariot may be a local ruler; nothing indicates that he should be identified with the Persian king.[98]

---

[97] Stern, *Dor Final Report*, vol. 1/B (cf. No. 27), 477.

[98] Conversely, if the seal engravers meant the lion-slayer to be the Persian king, this would mean that they did not care for vestimentary etiquette.

Persian hunters seem however to be depicted on the last two seals
to be included in our discussion.

29 <u>Obj</u>: Scaraboid, blue glass, slightly damaged on the sides, surface worn, 16
x 12 x 9 mm; no border line; modeled style.
<u>Icon</u>: Riding horseman to the right hunting a caprid, erect with head turned
back.
<u>Prov</u>: Tell eṣ-Ṣafi, unstratified.
<u>Orig</u>: Palestine?; 5th-4th cent. BCE.
<u>Loc</u>: present whereabouts unknown (Istanbul?); cast in London, Palestine
Exploration Fund, no reg. No.
<u>Bib</u>: Bliss, "Second Report ... Tell es-Sâfi" (cf. No. **2**), esp. 332, pl. 6:10.

30 <u>Obj</u>: Scaraboid, sealing surface slightly convex, yellow hardstone, 22 x 17
x – mm; no border line, no perforation; modeled style.
<u>Icon</u>: Riding horseman in typically Persian costume to the left spearing a
running lion with head turned back. Phoenician inscription: *tyln*.
<u>Prov</u>: allegedly from Rišon le-Ṣion, bought in Jaffa at the beginning of the
century.
<u>Orig</u>: 'Graeco-Persian', Cilicia?; 5th cent. BCE.
<u>Loc</u>: formerly Jerusalem, German Protestant Instit.; present whereabouts
unknown.
<u>Bib</u>: G. Dalman, "Epigraphisches und Pseudepigraphisches", *MNDPV* 9
(1903), 17-32, esp. 31; K. Galling, "Beschriftete Bildsiegel des ersten Jahrtausends v. Chr. vornehmlich aus Syrien und Palästina: Ein Beitrag zur
Geschichte der phönizischen Kunst", *ZDPV* 64 (1941) 121-202, esp. 194
No. 145, pl. 12:145; Avigad, Sass, *West Semitic Stamp Seals* (n. 38), No. 852.

Riding horsemen were perhaps the most widespread and well-known
ambassadors of 'Persianism' throughout the empire. 'Persian riders' –
as they are usually called – appear on various visual media throughout
the empire. They form an important group among the terracotta figurines found, e.g., in favissae and other contexts in southern Palestine
and along the coastal plain.[99] A 5th-century ivory comb recently excavated at Ashkelon shows a rider on horseback over a reclimbing ibex
(*fig. 9*).[100] With regard to glyptic, however, images of Persian riders
are comparatively rare. Except for the quite peculiar seal No. **29**,
local Palestinian workshops do not seem to have adopted the motif.

The last observation is important when one comes to study the
iconographic repertoire of Persian period coinage from Palestine, particularly from Samaria. Together with many other motifs, the images
of Persian riders attested there do apparently not reflect the repertoire
of local Palestinian seal workshops but rather derive from Cilician or
other 'Graeco-Persian' prototypes.

---

[99] Cf. Stern, *Material Culture* (n. 3), 167 fig. 285, 168, 179, 181; on the meaning
of these figurines which perpetuate an earlier Iron age tradition, cf. C. Uehlinger,
"Riding Horseman", in: ²*DDD*, 705-7.
[100] For Achaemenid parallels from Susa, cf. Amiet, "Ivoires achéménides" (n. 86),
187 No. 8 with pl. 3:5, 189 with figs. 22-3.

3 Synthesis

Summing up our preliminary inventory of 'powerful Persianisms' in
glyptic iconography from Palestine,[101] we may draw the following conclusions:

1. Seals and sealings featuring 'explicit Persianisms' do not represent a very large group within Persian period glyptic found in
   Palestine. They constitute a relatively *small corpus* especially
   when compared to other groups, e.g. the much more numerous
   Egyptian, Phoenician, Babylonian, or Greek seals and sealings
   of the period. The impact of Persian iconographical schemes
   on Palestine must have been very limited for reasons of sheer
   quantity. Taste and market preferences clearly went in other
   directions and took their models from elsewhere.

   When we consider *chronology*, the bulk of seals and sealings
   discussed belongs to the second half or even last third of the
   Persian period, which makes the potential for Persian impact in
   the late 6th and earlier 5th centuries BCE even slimmer.

2. The influence of Persian Achaemenid figurative schemes on the
   locally produced Palestinian or locally distributed Egyptian and
   Phoenician glyptic seems to have been very limited. One may
   recognize one or the other vestimentary *aggiornamento*, or ad-
   aptations of *Mischwesen* to new conventions. But when we remember that such modifications concern a handful out of c. 250
   seals and sealings from Palestine, their importance is marginal.

   This overall picture is in marked contrast to the one which can
   be observed in Asia Minor and which is characterized conven-
   tionally by the label 'Graeco-Persian art'. Evidence mainly from
   satrapial Sardis has recently been reassessed by Dusinberre. According to her conclusions, "Achaemenid imperial programs promoting ideologies of empire were translated into regional artistic
   compositions to make them intelligible to local viewing audi-
   ences in widely disparate parts of the empire. This adaptation

---

[101] For reasons of space, I do not discuss motifs which have no direct relation
to the concept of Persian power although they betray a kind of 'Orientalizing
fascination' on behalf of their authors and probably the seal owners as well; cf.,
e.g., the Greek-inspired 'Perseries' represented by bullae from Wadi ed-Daliyeh
showing a Persian couple in conversation (cf. Leith, *Wadi Daliyeh* [n. 22], 151-61,
whose comparison of the scene with 'heroic combat' compositions looks far-fetched
to me).

of images had a self-reflexive function as well [i.e., for the Persian patrons], for the appropriation and manipulation of local iconographies and styles signified the incorporation of these areas into the empire."[102] While this theory may adequately interpret the situation in Anatolia and possibly Egypt, it does not fit the glyptic evidence from Palestine surveyed in this paper. Dusinberre's threefold process of signifying Achaemenid imperial power ("spreading imperial ideology to distant parts of the empire, asserting power over those areas, and incorporating local imagery into official imperial art")[103] did apparently not operate with regard to Palestine. In great contrast to other imperial administrations that had ruled in Palestine during earlier periods (Middle and New Kingdom Egypt and to some extent Assyria), the Achaemenid imperial administration apparently did *not* interfere in any way in the local seal production, certainly not in the engravers' choices regarding the composition of their figurative repertoire.

Two main reasons may explain this contrast: basically, Persian interest and involvement must have been much more intense in Asia Minor than in far-off Palestine which was 'Third World' to the Achaemenids not worthy for investment. (As for Persian interest and involvement in Egypt, this has to be considered separately: neither did it produce something even remotely comparable to 'Graeco-Persian' art nor did it necessarily have an impact on Palestine.) To the extent that the physical presence of people of Persian origin was probably limited to military officers and administrators, Persian culture remained a largely foreign element in Palestine. Granted that we interpreted the incomplete evidence correctly, we could even observe a certain reluctance or reservation on behalf of Phoenician seal engravers to adopt Persian Achaemenid (even royal) figurative models, an attitude which is in strong contrast to the same craftsmen's openness to integrate schemes from Egypt, Cyprus or Greece. For those who could choose between different models and for their clients, the Persian Achaemenid schemes apparently did not look attractive enough to be followed. Another plausible rationale for the absence of the king on locally produced glyptic could be that royal iconography was controlled and limited to seal workshops related to the Persian administration.

---

[102]Dusinberre, "Imperial style" (n. 27), 114.
[103]*Ibidem*, 114; cf. Idem, "King or God?" (n. 27), 154.

3. When we consider the *provenance* of the seals and sealings discussed in this article, we may notice a few items found in the northern coastal area (Keisan, Dor), some more in the southern Shephelah (Gezer, Tell eṣ-Ṣafi, Azeka), and quite a large number found in Samaria (Samaria, Wadi ed-Daliyeh, Shechem). The hoard of bullae from Wadi ed-Daliyeh clearly distorts the picture, since it represents one half of the items considered. However, it also gives a telling testimony to the limited impact of Achaemenid iconography on glyptic used in Palestine in the later Persian period, since the 'explicit Persianisms' in that hoard alone are relatively small in number. The geographical unbalance and the numerical *prominence of finds from Samaria* may not be totally fortuitous. As a matter of fact, Achaemenid iconography and other 'Persianisms' figure much more prominently on coins from Samaria than from anywhere else in the country (see below). If anywhere in Palestine, it was thus in Samaria that Achaemenid iconography could have a certain impact according to our present documentation.

As far as I can see, the markedly different impact of Persia and the Achaemenid imperial administration on Samaria and Yehud has not always been appreciated in historical research devoted to Persian period Palestine. One reason may be that because of the relative abundance of biblical and later Jewish sources, this research has for a long time – and somewhat unduly – privileged Yehud, giving it a more important place in the region than what material culture would reflect. As far as our topic is concerned, it is striking that except for one item from Jericho, Yehud is not represented at all in our survey on iconographical Persianisms.[104] The same holds true for Transjordan. One could of course quibble over the concept of 'explicit Persianism' and include one or another individual item from Transjordan in our survey.[105] The overall picture would still not look very different: if anything, Transjordanian glyptic of the Persian period reflects the influence of Babylonian glyptic.

---

[104] Cf. n. 17.

[105] As far as glyptic is concerned, one should particularly note a cylinder and a stamp seal from Tell el-Mazar: K. Yassine, "Ammonite Seals from Tell el-Mazar", in: Idem, *Archaeology of Jordan: Essays and Reports*, Amman 1988, 143-155, esp. 145 No. 201, 147 No. 204; Nunn, *Kontinuität und Wandel* (n. 9), 185 No. 260, 187 No. 320, pls. 62:234 and 65:270. Cf. also the survey of D. Homès-Frédericq, "Influences diverses en Transjordanie à l'époque achéménide", *Trans* 11 (1996), 63-76. The Babylonian influences in 5th-4th century Transjordan are much stronger than the Achaemenid ones which show up only in the Jordan valley and the Amman region.

Finally, the absence of the southern coastal plain from our survey of 'powerful Persianisms' is particularly noteworthy. Surprising as it may seem at first sight, it is confirmed by the sheer absence of explicit visual references to the Achaemenid empire both from the coinage of the southern cities (Gaza, Ashkelon, Ashdod) and from the so-called 'Philisto-Arabian' coinage. One may perhaps conclude that Gaza and the Arab tribes were not an integral part of the Persian empire but enjoyed a largely autonomous status of their own.

4. With regard to the *origin* of the seals considered (i.e., workshop location inferred from material and style), our corpus clearly falls into two equal parts, one being formed by Achaemenid Court Style seals (actually mostly cylinder sealings), the other by Phoenician seals, with only a very few representatives of other groups (Syrian and local). While the latter and the Phoenician seals are evenly distributed in all the areas represented, the Court Style items clearly concentrate in Samaria. This again confirms our impression that Persian Achaemenid influence was more strongly felt there than anywhere else in Palestine.[106]

Persian officials would have been the prime mediators of this process, since they probably used Achaemenid Court Style seals for official purposes. That the Court Style items are almost only sealings is probably more than an accident of discovery. It shows that these seals really played their primary role in the context of administrative matters. In addition to the primary use, however, we also suggested that Persian officials may have offered such seals to reward local subjects on special occasions. Used as a means to strengthen the loyalty of people whose cooperation the imperial administration wanted to rely upon, the seals would then also become a marker of status and allegiance for a tiny minority among the seal-owning elite of the local population of Samaria.

5. Looking back at the *iconographic repertoire* of the seals and sealings featuring some 'explicit Persianisms' – and particularly the Achaemenid Court Style items –, we may notice in passing the

---

[106]It may be more than an accident of discovery that fragments of a Persian throne – which must have belonged to a high-ranking state officer – were found in Samaria; cf. M. Tadmor, "Fragments of an Achaemenid Throne from Samaria", *IEJ* 24 (1974), 37-43. Fragments of another throne are known from a shipwreck discovered near Athlit: A. Raban, "A Group of Objects from a Wreckage Site at Athlit", *Michmanim* 6 (1992), 31-53 (Hebr.), 41*-2* (English summ.).

total lack of specifically 'religious' subject matter other than 'heroic combat' or 'encounter', such as cult (worship or offering) scenes, representations of deities, divine symbols or the like, which contrasts neatly with Egyptian, Assyrian and Babylonian glyptic and their respective influence on Palestinian glyptic in earlier periods. This observation confirms the commonly accepted opinion that the Persian administration generally did not interfere with the religious beliefs of their subjects, certainly not by imposing nor even publicizing the worship of Persian deities, but rather aimed at favouring cultic normality in pacified provinces.[107] The great majority of images reviewed here relate to the control and suppression of chaotic forces, embodied in monsters and lions, by the Persian royal hero or king. It seems doubtful that those who used the seals showing scenes of 'heroic encounter' or 'heroic combat' would always operate a neat distinction between the royal hero and the heroic king. It is notable, however, that seals or sealings with military subject matter related to particular victorious campaigns (another characteristic feature of Persian period glyptic) are also lacking from the repertoire attested in Palestine. The one common notion which is emphatically stressed by a great proportion of seals and sealings is the *heroic character of Persian kingship*.[108]

4   An Outlook on Coinage: The Power of a New Medium

During the Persian period, coinage became the most important and most widely distributed medium for iconography in Palestine, relegating glyptic to the second rank for the first time since the 18th century BCE. No study concerned with the impact of the Persian Achaemenid empire and its political ideology on Palestine can thus ignore the numismatic evidence. While it is impossible to enter a discussion of 'powerful Persianisms' in the coinage of Persian period Palestine within the limits of this article, I may be allowed to make

---

[107] Cf. P. Bedford, "Early Achaemenid Monarchs and Indigenous Cults: Toward the Definition of Imperial Policy", in: M. Dillon (ed.), *Religion in the Ancient World: New Themes and Approaches*, Amsterdam 1996, 17-39 for a recent assessment.

[108] An intriguing Babylonian cylinder seal in the British Museum shows a 'heroic encounter' composition with the Persian hero mastering two lions on a pedestal, i.e. as if it were free-standing statuary, besides the cultic symbol of Marduk venerated by a worshiper, i.e. as if it were itself a venerable entity: Collon, *First Impressions* (n. 32), No. 418.

a few summary observations and draw some perspectives by way of conclusion.[109]

It is well-known and can be demonstrated in detail that glyptic iconography and coinage were closely related during the Persian period, seals and coin stamps being sometimes produced in the same workshops.[110] It thus comes as no surprise that almost all the iconographical schemes discussed above are also attested on coins from 4th-century Palestine. However, while the glyptic evidence included sealings made from Achaemenid Court Style seals which had probably been imported from the centre of the empire, the numismatic evidence does not know such a thing as a Persian stamp being used for minting in Palestine (the only coinage which may be called Persian imperial, i.e. the gold Darics and silver sigloi with the royal archer,[111] is only marginally attested in the area).[112] The numismatic evidence from Palestine, except imported Greek money, comes from local mints that operated either in Palestine proper or in Phoenicia.

The coinage of Persian period Palestine is usually divided into four categories. These show remarkably different attitudes with regard to iconographical 'Persianisms'. The coinage of the Phoenician cities, of which only Tyre and Sidon are relevant for our purpose, presents a differentiated picture. While Tyre stressed local mythology (Melqart on the hippocamp) and claimed mediatorship between Athens and Egypt (owl with flail and crook), Sidon – the seat of a satrap – on the

---

[109]For sake of brevity, I may omit an extensive bibliography and simply refer to the recent survey by H. Gitler, "The Levant", in: C. Morrisson, B. Kluge *et al.* (eds.), *A Survey of Numismatic Research, 1990-1995* (IAPN.SP, 13), Berlin 1997, 101-13. Note also U. Hübner, "Die Münzprägungen Palästinas in alttestamentlicher Zeit", *Trumah* 4 (1994), 119-145 (not mentioned in Gitler's survey), and now of course L. Mildenberg's *Vestigia Leonis: Studien zur antiken Numismatik Israels, Palästinas und der östlichen Mittelmeerwelt* (NTOA, 36), Fribourg & Göttingen 1998.

[110]Fine examples, though not directly related to our topic, are discussed by E. Gubel, "La glyptique et la genèse de l'iconographie monétaire phénicienne - 1", in: T. Hackens, G. Moucharte (eds.), *Numismatique et histoire économique phéniciennes et puniques* (Studia Phoenicia, 9; PHAA, 58), Louvain-la-Neuve 1992, 1-11; and see Kaptan, "Common Treats" (n.10).

[111]On these, see M. Alram, "Dareikos und Siglos: Ein neuer Schatzfund achaimenidischer Sigloi aus Kleinasien", in: R. Gyselen (ed.), *Circulation des monnaies, des marchandises et des biens* (Res Orientales, 5), Bures-sur-Yvette 1993, 23-51. In a recent reassessment of the latter, Stronach, "Early Achaemenid Coinage" (cf. No. **26**), 278, concluded that "the 'archer' coins may have sought to depict the king (in line with an ethical message which has been recognised in the Achaemenid royal inscriptions) as a constant warrior in defence of the values of 'order-truth' (*arta*)".

[112]Hübner, "Münzprägungen Palästinas" (n. 109), 123-4 and Abb. 4.

one hand emphasized her military strength and naval power (fortified town on the sea, galley), on the other demonstrated its allegiance to the Achaemenid king by visual metaphors featuring the Persian king such as the royal procession in the chariot (*fig. 10*), the royal archer,[113] or 'heroic combat' scenes showing the royal hero battling against the lion.

In striking contrast, the coinage of the autonomous south-Palestinian towns of Gaza, Ashkelon and Ashdod remained almost unaffected by Achaemenid iconographical schemes.[114] These towns were independent enough that they did not need to bother for Persian schemes, and the Persian administration neither could nor tried to prevent them from not doing so. The same holds true for the second group, the so-called 'Philisto-Arabian' coinage, which shows a blend of Egyptianizing, Phoenician, Greek and other influences and autochtonous images, with a particular flavour for Bes and hybrids, but no concern whatsoever for Persian Achaemenid iconography.[115]

The fourth category is provincial coinage – mostly small denominations – such as the one minted in Samaria and the other in Yehud (Jerusalem).[116] Yehud coinage, generally of rather poor minting quality, shows very few 'Persianisms', but also no particular dependency on Phoenician models. The royal heads on a few third or fourth quality issues[117] are remarkable insofar as they constitute a kind of direct link to the Great King, but they remain quite exceptional. In contrast, Samarian coinage[118] is literally full of 'Persianisms', surpassing

---

[113] This motif was taken over from the Persian darics and sigloi.

[114] But note the forthcoming discussion by H. Gitler, "Achaemenid Motifs" (n. 85). Gitler is concerned with hybrid heads which cannot be regarded as Achaemenid and appended animal protomai, some of which are reminiscent of Achaemenid monumental column capitals. I doubt that these features relate to issues of imperial ideology alongside the arguments developed by M.C. Root, E.R.M. Dusinberre and others. Hybrid heads are not attested in Achaemenid iconography. They could however have been inspired by Lydian and Lycian glyptic and coinage.

[115] Cf. L. Mildenberg, "On the Imagery of the Philisto-Arabian Coinage – A Preview", *Trans* 13 (1997), 9-15, esp. 13.

[116] Cf. L. Mildenberg, "*yehūd* und *šmryn*: Über das Geld der persischen Provinzen Juda und Samaria im 4. Jahrhundert", in: *Geschichte-Tradition-Reflexion (Fs. M. Hengel)*, Bd. 1: Judentum, Tübingen 1996, 119-46.

[117] Cf. Mildenberg, "*yehūd* und *šmryn*", Nos. 4, 5(?) and 10.

[118] The study of Samarian provincial coinage will be considerably enhanced with the forthcoming publication of a new corpus by Y. Meshorer and Sh. Qedar which will replace their former publication *The Samarian Coinage*, New York 1991. I thank Prof. Ya'akov Meshorer, Chief curator at the Israel Museum, Jerusalem, for the permission to see a provisional draft of the new book. However, since the latter is not yet available for reference and close study, the following treatment

178 CHRISTOPH UEHLINGER

by far any other mint of the region in this respect. This confirms and emphasizes our conclusion based on the glyptic evidence, namely that Persian iconographical models and Achaemenid royal ideology had a particularly strong impact on 4th-century Samaria.[119]

Since Samaria seems to have stood in a kind of double dependency both from the Persian king and from Sidon, one can easily understand that her coins should feature all the 'Persianisms' known from Sidonian money: the royal archer (SC 17, 22, 52, 56-57; *fig. 11*); 'heroic combat' scenes showing the royal hero battling against the lion (SC 16, 44-45, 48-51; *fig. 12*). Only the royal chariot procession which emblematically signified the particular relationship binding the king of Sidon (the acolythe) to the Persian king (*fig. 10*) had to be modified and figures on Samarian coins only in a simplified version (SC 48; *fig. 13*). But the Samarian minters did not content themselves with replicating the Sidonian models, they added even more Persian Achaemenid iconography. Heroic scenes also include the Persian king or hero fighting against the winged leonine monster (SC 3; *fig. 14*), a human-headed leonine monster,[120] a bull (SC 19, 31-33; *fig. 15*), or horses;[121] the Persian king as 'Master of lions' (SC 59-60; *fig. 16*). Further royal scenes include depictions of the king (or the local deity??) enthroned, holding staff and flower (SC 18, 21, 33, 36-38; *fig. 17*), or the king standing with his staff (SC 37; *fig. 18*); the king in a chariot drawn by two running horses (SC 35); the royal head (SC 41-42; *fig. 19*). Still other coins feature a typically Persian four-winged deity wearing the royal crown (SC 14, 21, cf. 36; Mithra?), a pair of Persian royal heroes (?, SC 54), a Persian rider (SC 35, 38, 57; *fig. 20*), occasionally even riding over a fallen Greek soldier,[122] Persian guardsmen (SC 89-90) and numerous depictions of high-ranking Persian dignitaries, generals and officers; and finally the royal sphinx.[123] The evidence for 'powerful Persianisms' is impressive.

Obviously these depictions are not all an expression of Samarian loyalty to the Achaemenid king and to the Persian imperial administration. One should rather suspect that the unusual emphasis betrays propaganda which may have intended to cover particular tensions in real life. The many 'portraits' of Persian officers point to a strong

---

will be very short and cannot offer more than a few preliminary observations.
[119] For the sake of brevity, the following paragraph refers to the catalogue in Meshorer, Qedar, *Samarian Coinage*, 45-63 by citing the relevant entry numbers.
[120] Meshorer, Qedar, *Samarian Coinage* [forthcoming], Ms. pl. 21:146.
[121] *Ibidem*, Ms. pl. 10:66.
[122] *Ibidem*, Ms. pl. 18:123-4.
[123] Cf. R. Deutsch, M. Heltzer, "Numismatic Evidence from the Persian Period from the Sharon Plain", *Trans* 13 (1997), 17-20, Nos. 13-4.

Persian military presence at Samaria. Many of these issues must have been minted by order of Persian officials stationed in the province, or of some higher authority such as Mazday the satrap.[124] A number of issues were apparently struck with imported stamps, or with third quality local stamps copied from Sidonian, Cilician and other models. Coins inscribed with names of local dignitaries show that these could stress 'Persianism' more or less according to political choice, necessity or taste.

In sum, one cannot ignore that more than any other repertoire of the area, the coins of Samaria emphatically claim strong allegiance of the province to the Great King and his representatives. Consequently, the glyptic and numismatic evidence from Samaria and Yehud should be considered when we come to read the books of Ezra and Nehemiah and other literature of Persian period Palestine. This, however, is another story.

---

[124]It is probably not an accident that the only cuneiform signs hitherto found on coins figure on coins issues from Samaria. Although the meaning of the signs cannot yet be fully appreciated, they witness to at least some sort of contact of dye cutters working in and for Samaria with cuneiform-writing people, probably working in the higher administration of the Persian empire. Cf. A. Lemaire, F. Joannès, "Premières monnaies avec signes cunéiformes: Samarie, IVème s. av. n. è.", *NABU* (1994, No. 4), 84-6 § 95.

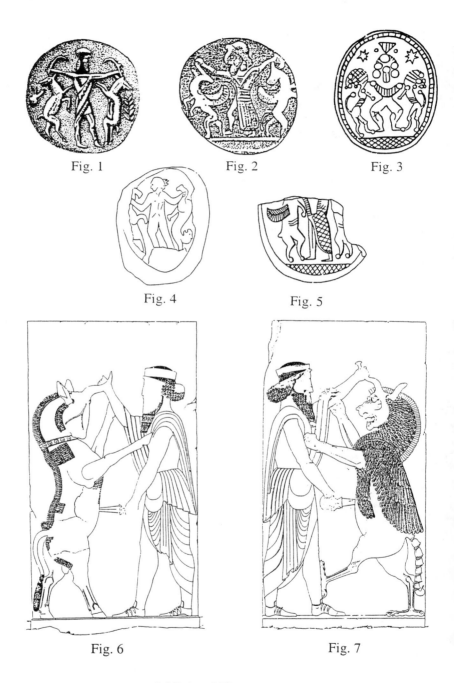

Fig. 1

Fig. 2

Fig. 3

Fig. 4

Fig. 5

Fig. 6

Fig. 7

Additional Figures 1-7

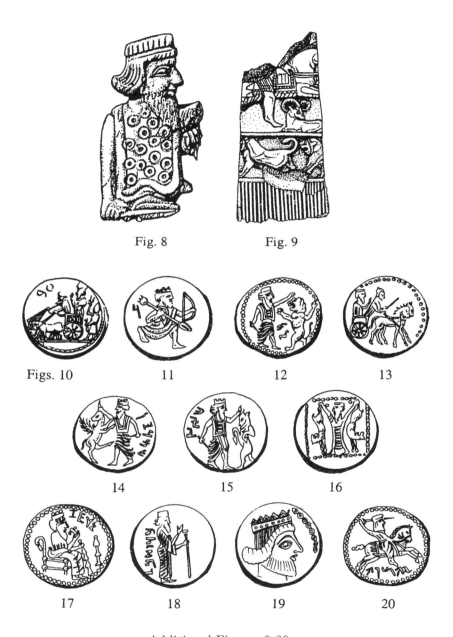

Fig. 8   Fig. 9

Figs. 10   11   12   13

14   15   16

17   18   19   20

Additional Figures 8-20

Sources of Figures

Seals and sealings: list of figures (* drawings by Inés Haselbach, Fribourg).

1* After photograph of cast (courtesy PEF, London). **2** Keel, Uehlinger, *GGG* (n. 17), 375 fig. 361c. **3** Crowfoot *et al.*, *Objects* (n. 49), 393 fig. 92:80. **4** P.C. Hammond, *PEQ* (1957), 69, pl. 17:b. **5** Leith, *Wadi Daliyeh* (n. 22), pl. 17:1 (corrected). **6** *Ibidem*, pl. 17:3. **7** *Ibidem*, pl. 17:2 (corrected). **8** *Ibidem*, pl. 18:1. **9** Keel, Uehlinger, *GGG* (n. 17), 375 fig. 360b. **10*** After W. Culican, *AJBA* 1/1 (1968), 52, pl. I top left; photograph of cast (courtesy PEF, London), and impression of original (courtesy Israel Antiquities Authority, Jerusalem). **11*** After photographs and impression of the original (courtesy O. Keel, Fribourg). **12*** After Crowfoot *et al.*, *Objects* (n. 49), pl. 15:42. **13*** After Reisner *et al.*, *Harvard Excavations at Samaria*, Cambridge, MA, 1924, vol. 2, pl. 57h:2. **14** Leith, *Wadi Daliyeh* (n. 22), pl. 18:2 (corrected). **15** *Ibidem*, pl. 18:3 (corrected). **16** *Ibidem*, pl. 20:1 (corrected). **17-21** *Ibidem*, pl. 19:1. **22** *Ibidem*, pl. 21:2 (corrected). **23** *Ibidem*, pl. 20:2. **24** *Ibidem*, pl. 20:3. **25** *Ibidem*, pl. 16:1. **26** T. Ornan, *Studies in Glyptics from the Land of Israel and Transjordan. Assyrian, Babylonian and Achaemenid Cylinder Seals from the First Half of the First Millennium* BCE. (unpubl. MA thesis, Hebrew University, Jerusalem 1990), No. 31; drawing Noga Ze'evi (Jerusalem), slightly corrected. **27** E. Stern, *Excavations at Dor: Final Report*, vol. 1/B: Areas A and C: The Finds (Qedem Reports, 2), Jerusalem 1995, 476 fig. 10.1:2 (reversed). **28** F.J. Bliss, *PEQ* 31 (1899), pl. 7:11 (reversed). **28a** R. Poppa, $K^{\bar{a}}mid$ el-$L^{\bar{o}}z$, Bd. 2: Der eisenzeitliche Friedhof, Befunde und Funde (SBA, 18), Bonn 1978, pl. 3:2 (reversed). **29*** After photograph of cast (courtesy PEF, London). **30*** After Avigad, Sass, *WSS* (n. 38), No. 852.

Additional figures (* drawings by Inés Haselbach, Fribourg).

1 K. Yassine, *Archaeology of Jordan* (n. 105), 150 No. 302. **2** Stern, *Dor* (n. 50), 191 fig. 124, first row left. **3** Keel, Uehlinger, *GGG* (n. 17), 379 fig. 366a. **4** Leith, *Wadi Daliyeh* (n. 22), pl. 12:2. **5** Keel, Uehlinger, *GGG* (n. 17), 375 fig. 361b. **6** F. Lajard, *Introduction à l'étude du culte public et des mystères de Mithra en Orient et en Occident*, Paris 1847, pl. 14. **7** *Ibidem*, pl. 21. **8*** Stern, "Four Phoenician Finds" (n. 86), 330 fig. 9. **9*** L.E. Stager, *Ashkelon Discovered: From Canaanites and Philistines to Romans and Moslems*, Washington, DC, 1991, 30. **10** D. Baramki, *Phoenicia and the Phoenicians*, Beirut 1961, 82 fig. 6 (obv.). **11** Meshorer, Qedar, *The Samarian Coinage* (n. 118), 54 No. 52 (rev.). **12** *Ibidem*, 47 No. 16 (rev.). **13** *Ibidem*, 53 No. 48 (obv.). **14** *Ibidem*, 45 No. 3 (rev.). **15** *Ibidem*, 48 No. 19 (rev.). **16** *Ibidem*, 55 No. 59 (obv.). **17** *Ibidem*, 51 No. 38 (obv.). **18** *Ibidem*, 51 No. 37 (rev.). **19** *Ibidem*, 52 No. 41 (obv.). **20** *Ibidem*, 51 No. 38 (rev.).

Helen Schüngel–Straumann   *Kassel - Deutschland*

Paritätische Modelle von männlich und weiblich am Anfang und Ende der Priesterschriftlichen Schöpfungserzählung (Gen. 1:1–2:4a)

Die folgenden Ausführungen beschäftigen sich mit dem Schöpfungsbericht der Priesterschrift, Gen. 1:1–2:4a. Dieser Text hat seinen Entstehungsort im Babylonischen Exil und danach, also im 6. (und 5.) Jh. v. Chr. Es geht zunächst um die Situation, in der er entstanden ist, dann um die "gender"spezifischen Aspekte am Anfang und am Ende des Textes, schließlich um die Frage, warum die Priesterschrift gerade *diese* Akzente gesetzt hat.

1   Situation

Die Krise, die mit dem Verlust des Landes, der Hauptstadt, des Tempels, des Königtums, mit einem Wort, der gesamten Eigenständigkeit, eingetreten ist, kann gar nicht überschätzt werden. Politisch, sozial und religiös muß sich Israel vollständig umstellen. Jerusalem ist nur noch eine periphere Größe, die Jahwe–Religion lediglich eine unter vielen. Wie kann Israel in dieser Zeit seine eigene Identität finden und bewahren? Aufgrund dieser neuen und aufregenden Situation hat natürlich eine Erzählung wie Gen. 1 nicht in erster Linie die Aufgabe, Belehrung über die Entstehung der Welt und der Menschen zu geben, sondern die eigene Glaubenssituation zu stärken, sich seiner Identität zu versichern, neue Grundlagen für das Leben in der Diaspora zu erarbeiten. Das Ziel des Berichtes von Gen. 1 ist dann auch nicht der Mensch, wie vielerorts zu lesen ist, sondern der *Sabbat*. Der siebte Tag, auf den der ganze Text hin konzipiert ist, will eine neue Orientierung geben für diese Zeit der Krise, einen festen Punkt, an dem sich der fromme Jude/die gläubige Jüdin in Zukunft ausrichten kann. Gerade weil im Exil die rein nationalen Aspekte nicht mehr ausreichen, wird nun der Sabbat in der Schöpfung begründet, um dann zu einem Unterscheidungsmerkmal zwischen Juden und Heiden zu werden.

Aus dem gleichen Grund der Versicherung und Stärkung der gläubigen Existenz redet der Text dann auch nicht nur vom Israeliten, sondern grundsätzlich von *allen* Menschen (אדם). Im Blick ist beim letzten der Schöpfungswerke der Mensch/die Menschheit schlechthin; der Verfasser hat also ein übernationales, ganz universales Konzept, wenn er in der Krisenzeit des Exils vom Menschen schlechthin spricht.

2 "Gender"spezifische Aspekte am Anfang und Ende von Gen. 1

2.1 Gen. 1:26-28

Gen. 1 spricht vom Menschen immer als אדם. Dieser Begriff, der nur im Singular vorkommt, ist ein Kollektiv, einen Plural davon gibt es nicht. Vor allem aber ist אדם in allen Erzählungen der Urgeschichte (Gen. 1–11) nie ein Individuum, und vor allem kein Eigenname, wie er sich aus einer falsch verstandenen Interpretation der Erzählungen von Gen. 2–3 ("Adam" und "Eva" in der Spätzeit [ab dem 2. Jh. v. Chr.]) entwickelt hat.[1]

Am Ende der Schöpfungswerke von Gen. 1, am sechsten Tag, steht die Erschaffung von אדם. Diese wird – anders als bei den übrigen Schöpfungswerken – mit einem expliziten Entschluß Gottes eingeführt:

26   a   Und אלהים (Gott) sagte:
     b   "Laßt uns Menschen machen als unser Bild: etwa in
         unserer Gestalt,
     c   damit sie herrschen über die Fische des Meeres,
         über die Vögel des Himmels und über das Vieh
         und über alles wilde Getier auf der Erde und
         über alles Kriechgetier, das auf der Erde kriecht."

In diesem Vorsatz spricht Gott im Plural ("Lasst uns ... "). Mit אדם sind eindeutig alle Menschen gemeint, die Fortsetzung spricht von ihnen dann auch im Plural. In einem Finalsatz wird deutlich, wozu diese Erschaffung als Bild Gottes dient: die Menschen sollen herrschen.

Nur in V. 26 wird die Aussage vom 'Bild Gottes'[2] mit zwei verschiedenen Begriffen ausgedrückt, es stehen hier die beiden Ausdrücke צלם (Bild, Gestalt, Standbild, etwa eines Königs) und zusätzlich דמות ("etwas in der Ähnlichkeit wie"). Die vorsichtige Formulierung "als unser Bild: etwa in unserer Gestalt" heißt auch, daß dem Verfasser

---

[1]Zur Wirkungs– und Rezeptionsgeschichte der Texte von Gen. 1–3 vgl. den ersten Teil von H. Schüngel–Straumann, *Die Frau am Anfang: Eva und die Folgen*, Freiburg 1989, Münster ²1997; K.E. Børresen (ed.), *Image of God and Gender Models in Judaeo-Christian Tradition*, Oslo 1991.

[2]Vgl. dazu W. Gross, "Die Gottebenbildlichkeit des Menschen im Kontext der Priesterschrift", *ThQ* 161 (1981), 244-64, sowie den Überblick (nur männliche Auslegungen!) von Idem, "Die Gottebenbildlichkeit des Menschen nach Gen. 1:26, 27 in der Diskussion des letzten Jahrzehnts", *BN* 68 (1993), 35-48. Zur feministischen Interpretation vgl. Ph.A. Bird, "Sexual Differentiation and Divine in the Genesis Creation Texts", in: Børresen, *Image of God*, 11-31.

eigentlich die Worte fehlen, um das auszudrücken, was er meint. Den gleichen Ausdruck דמות verwendet z.B. der Prophet Ezechiel, wenn er seine Visionen beschreibt. Damit bringt er zum Ausdruck daß ihm letztlich die passenden Worte gar nicht zur Verfügung stehen: "Ich sah etwas, das aussah wie ... das ähnlich war wie ..." (vgl. Ez. 1:5, 16, 22, 26).[3]

Der Priesterschrift liegt ja das Bilderverbot vor.[4] Von Jahwe, dem Gott Israels, darf kein Bild gemacht werden, so bestimmen Ex. 20:4 und Dtn. 5:8. Diese Verbotssätze verwenden jedoch andere Termini für "Bild" als Gen. 1:26-27. Zudem spricht der Schöpfungsbericht hier auch nicht von einem Bild *Jahwes*, sondern von einem Bild אלהים. Für eine Einschränkung sorgt dann zusätzlich noch der Plural: die Priesterschrift schließt hier wohl אלהים/Gott mit dem himmlischen Hofstaat zusammen ("Laßt uns ..."). Dem Göttlichen entspricht der Mensch, und zwar in seiner Ganzheit.

Der Mittelteil gibt die Ausführung an:

27 a Und es erschuf Gott אדם als sein Bild
    b als Bild אלהים erschuf er *ihn*,
    c männlich und weiblich erschuf er *sie*.

In dieser dreiteiligen Ausführung wird der Mensch in den ersten beiden Zeilen im Singular bezeichnet, in der dritten Zeile steht ein Plural, wobei hier grammatisch eine gewisse Spannung entsteht. Zweimal fällt hier das Wort צלם (Bild). Die Ausführung des göttlichen Vorsatzes ist kürzer geschildert als der Entschluß. Neu ist der Zusammenhang der Aussage "männlich und weiblich erschuf er sie" mit der Erschaffung als "Bild". Damit kommt der Satzteil "männlich und weiblich erschuf er sie" genau in die Mitte der Sätze über die Menschenschöpfung zu stehen. Ganz zentral ist somit auch hier – wie in Gen. 2, wo die Erschaffung der Frau in den Garten, in die gute Ordnung Gottes gehört – die Differenzierung der menschlichen Geschlechter in die Schöpfung eingebunden. Sie gehört zu der persönlich von Gott ausgeführten Schöpfung, wie sie in diesem Vers dreimal mit dem Verb ברא = erschaffen ausgedrückt wird; dieses Verb wird ausschließlich vom voraussetzungslosen Schaffen Gottes gebraucht. Wie in Gen. 2

---

[3]Über diese beiden hebräischen Begriffe informiert sehr klar S. Schroer, *In Israel gab es Bilder* (OBO, 74), Fribourg/Göttingen 1987, bes. 322-32. Für die ältere Interpretation vgl. G.A. Jónsson, *The Image of God: Genesis 1,26-28 in a Century of Old Testament Research* (CB.OT, 26), Lund 1988. Vgl. auch die Ausführungen bei Gross, "Gottebenbildlichkeit" (1993), über die neuesten Funde aus Tell Fekheriye in dem oben (Anm. 2) zit. Überblick, 40-5.

[4]Vgl. hierzu Chr. Dohmen, *Das Bilderverbot: Seine Entstehung und seine Entwicklung im Alten Testament* (BBB, 62), Bonn 1985.

Gott ausdrücklich selbst feststellte, daß es nicht gut sei für אדם, daß
er allein sei, so gehört bei P die Bestimmung "männlich und weiblich"
in die gute Ordnung Gottes. Sie gehört nicht nur in die Schöpfung,
sondern noch enger in die Abbildlichkeit Gottes hinein. "Männlich
und weiblich" bezieht sich auf den *ganzen* Menschen. Eine Aufteilung des Menschen in Geist und Körper oder etwa eine Beschränkung
der Gottbildlichkeit auf die Seele hätten die Verfasser von Gen. 1
gar nicht verstanden, weil diese griechische Aufteilung des Menschen
dem hebräischen Denken fremd war. Der Mensch *als Ganzes*, in seiner
weiblichen und männlichen Ausprägung, ist Bild Gottes.

Der dritte Teil bringt die Folgen dieser Erschaffung, den Segen
Gottes:

28 a Und es segnete sie אלהים,
    b und es sprach zu ihnen אלהים:
    c "Seid fruchtbar und werdet zahlreich
    d und füllet die Erde
    e und unterwerft sie
    f und herrscht über die Fische des Meeres
       und die Vögel des Himmels
       und über alles Getier, das auf der Erde kriecht."

Die Aussagen dieses prägnanten Textes sind insgesamt nicht auf dem
Hintergrund einer langen und einseitigen Interpretationsgeschichte,
sondern zunächst in ihrem *eigenen* altorientalischen Kontext zu lesen. Die Priesterschrift will nicht metaphysische Aussagen über den
Menschen machen, sondern sie gibt Stellung und Aufgabe des Menschen auf dem Hintergrund altorientalischer Welt- und Menschenvor-
stellung an. Dabei sagt der Text selbst, was unter "Bild Gottes" zu
verstehen ist: der Finalsatz in V. 26 gibt das *Herrschen* an, und dies ist
am Schluß, in V. 28, wiederholt (wobei hier die Aufzählung der Tiere
kürzer ist). Die Priesterschrift hat die altorientalische Königsideologie
im Blick wo der König als Stellvertreter der Gottheit auftritt. Solche
Vorstellungen waren vor allem in Ägypten ausgeprägt. König oder
Königin traten dort als Repräsentanten der Gottheit auf. In Ägypten
wird der König als Bild (*ḥntj*) eines Gottes bezeichnet, weil er als dessen "lebendiges Kultbild" gilt. "Ursprünglich bezeichnet es eine Statue, und zwar sowohl von Privatpersonen als auch von Königen und
von Göttern, speziell die in der Prozession getragene Statue. Es besagt
also zunächst, daß der König die öffentliche, sichtbare Erscheinungs-
form Gottes sei, die er auf Erden gegeben hat. Das Wort *ḥntj* wird
in dieser Verwendung auch gern mit dem Attribut 'lebend' versehen.
So heißt Hatschepsut auf ihrem nördlichen Obelisken in Karnak 'Sein

lebendes Bild, König von Ober- und Unterägypten, Makare, das Gold
der Könige'; in Deir el Bahari nennt Amun sie: 'Mein lebendes Abbild auf Erden' und gibt späterhin Amenophis II. die gleiche Bezeich-
nung."[5] Dies wird auch durch neuere Untersuchungen neu bestätigt.
Boyo Ockinga gibt weitere Beispiele in deutscher Übersetzung aus einer Inschrift Amenophis IV., wo der Gott Amun zum König spricht:

> "Dieses Land habe ich in seiner Länge und Breite
> geschaffen um auszuführen,
> was mein Ka wünscht;
> Dir habe ich gegeben /// meine //// insgesamt;
> Du beherrschst es (das Land) als König, so wie (zu der
> Zeit) als ich König von
> Ober- und Unterägypten war;
> Du bewirtschaftest es für mich aus liebendem Herzen,
> denn du bist mein geliebter Sohn, der aus meinem Leibe
> hervorgegangen ist,
> mein Abbild, das ich auf Erden gestellt habe.
> In Frieden lasse ich dieses Land regieren,
> indem du die Häupter aller Fremdländer tilgst."[6]

Interessant ist, wie die Priesterschrift mit diesem vorgegebenen Material umgeht. Entscheidendes ist uminterpretiert: Während es sich
in Israels Umwelt um herausragende Einzelpersonen handelt, ist für
die Priesterschrift der Mensch *als Mensch* Stellvertreter Gottes. Dies
wird besonders darin deutlich, daß das Herrschen als die besondere
Füllung dieser Aussage zu sehen ist. Nicht in seinem "Geist", auch
nicht in seiner "Seele" oder in seiner "aufrechten" ist der Mensch Bild
Gottes, sondern in seiner Funktion als Verwalter/in der Welt. Dieses
Verwalten oder Herrschen wird bereits in der altorientalischen Tradition gern mit dem Bild des Hirten dargestellt. Auch in Israel ist
der gute König/die gute Königin Hirte des Volkes, so wie Jahwe, der
sein Volk leitet und schützt (vgl. Ps. 23). Solches "Herrschen" bedeutet somit nicht willkürliches Verfügen – dem steht gerade entgegen,
daß die Menschen in der priesterschriftlichen Schöpfungsgeschichte die

---

[5] E.K. Otto, "Der Mensch als Geschöpf und Bild Gottes in Ägypten", in: H.W.
Wolff (ed.), *Probleme biblischer Theologie, Gerhard von Rad zum 70. Geburtstag*,
München 1971, 335-48, hier 345.
[6] B. Ockinga, *Die Gottebenbildlichkeit im Alten Ägypten und im Alten Testament* (ÄAT, 7), Wiesbaden 1984, 146. Weitere Beispiele und eine Auseinandersetzung mit den beiden Begriffen צלם und דמות im ägyptischen Kontext finden
sich hier 148ff.

Tiere nicht verzehren dürfen; dies ist erst nach der Sintflut erlaubt[7] –, sondern es heißt Verantwortung übernehmen: Die Menschen als Stellvertreter Gottes sind für die Geschöpfe zuständig wie Gott für die Schöpfung insgesamt.

Wie sieht nun Gen. 1 die Aufgabe des Menschen? Da im Abbild das Abgebildete selbst präsent ist, ist somit Gott im Menschen anwesend, *wenn* dieser in Verantwortung seinem Gott gegenüber die Schöpfung leitet wie ein Hirte seine Herde. Wichtig ist zu betonen, daß hier die Menschen nur über die übrige Schöpfung herrschen, also nicht über andere Menschen! Das Herrschen über Menschen – wie es auch die altorientalischen Könige tun – ist Gott allein vorbehalten. Der Verfasser von Gen. 1 hat somit Vorstellungen, die er aus seiner Umwelt übernommen hat, in gezielter Weise verschoben: einmal ist das Herrschen über Menschen ausgeschlossen, weiter sind die Menschen klar als männlich und weiblich qualifiziert. Damit ist in dieser Aussage auch die Herrschaft des Mannes über die Frau ausgeschlossen! Daß dies bis heute nie explizit ausgesprochen wurde, ist mehr als erstaunlich. Eine genaue Analyse der Formulierung von Gen. 1:26-28 ergibt nämlich genau dies: Mann und Frau beherrschen/leiten die übrige Schöpfung, und dies schließt überaus deutlich ein, daß sich keines der beiden Geschlechter die Herrschaft über das andere anmaßen darf.

Bei der Redeweise "der Mensch" oder "die Menschen" gerät häufig aus dem Blick daß es sich immer um *beide* Geschlechter handelt, von denen hier die Rede ist. Ausdrücklich wird von der Priesterschrift *beiden* diese Leitungsfunktion übertragen, Mann und Frau. Die letzte Zeile des Mittelstücks ("männlich und weiblich erschuf er sie") ist nicht nur für den Fruchtbarkeitssegen notwendig. Hier ist freilich die Frau unverzichtbar, aber der Auftrag des Herrschens wird in V. 28,

---

[7]E. Zenger, *Gottes Bogen in den Wolken: Untersuchungen zu Komposition und Theologie der priesterschriftlichen Urgeschichte* (SBS, 112), Stuttgart 1983, macht in seiner 2. Auflage (1987) darauf aufmerksam, daß hier eine archaische gesellschafts- oder herrschaftskritische Dimension nachwirkt. Tatsächlich aßen ja die Menschen zur Zeit der P nicht vegetarisch. P postuliert hier also ein Ideal, eine Utopie. Jürgen Ebach, hatte darauf aufmerksam gemacht: "Vegetarisch zu leben bedeutet in der Tradition des Altertums, sich der mit dem Fleischverzehr gesetzten Hierarchie zu enthalten ... Im Anteil am Fleisch manifestiert sich die Stellung eines Menschen in der gesellschaftlichen Hierarchie – in der Verteilerfunktion die Herrschaft." Cf. J. Ebach, *Ursprung und Ziel: Erinnerte Zukunft und erhoffte Vergangenheit: Biblische Exegesen, Reflexionen, Geschichten*, Neukirchen 1986, 33. Analog zu dieser utopischen Vorstellung der vegetarischen Ernährung haben die Aussagen von der Gottebenbildlichkeit von Mann und Frau ebenso hierar-chie*kritische* Funktion: die Herrschaft des Mannes über die Frau wird als nicht schöpfungsgemäß abgelehnt.

und zwar im Plural, wiederholt! Mann und Frau haben somit *gemeinsam* den Auftrag, die Welt verantwortlich zu leiten und sich zu vermehren, die (noch) leere Erde anzuffüllen. Dies heißt aber auch – betrachtet man dies von der anderen Seite –, daß Mann und Frau nur dort als Repräsentanten, als Bild Gottes fungieren, wo sie gemeinsam die Verantwortung tragen. Dies ist nicht individuell gemeint, als könnten die Menschen nur noch paarweise ihren Kulturauftrag ausführen, sondern grundsätzlich. Wenn ein Geschlecht allein die Welt be*herr*scht, kommt es zu einer Perversion der gemeinten theologischen Aussage. Die allgemeine Redeweise vom Herrschaftsauftrag an den Menschen hat jedoch häufig praktisch nur für den Mann Wirkungen gezeigt.[8]

Bevor ich die Frage stellen will, wie die Priesterschrift zu einer so paritätischen Aussage in der Gender-Frage kommt, möchte ich noch kurz den Anfang des Berichts in den Blick nehmen.

2.2 Die schöpferische רוח am Anfang der Schöpfung (Gen. 1:2)[9]

Nicht nur beim letzten Schöpfungswerk hat die Priesterschrift eine Symmetrie zwischen männlich – weiblich hergestellt, auch am Anfang bringt sie betont einen femininen Begriff in den Text, der in den altorientalischen Parallelen bei der Chaosschilderung fehlt. Wie in manchen Psalmen gehört רוח zur Schöpfungssprache einer relativ späten Zeit (vgl. Pss. 33:6; 104:3 u.a.). Gen. 1 steht sie betont am Anfang als Klammer zwischen überkommener Chaosschilderung und der Schöpfung durch das Wort (ab V. 3).

> 1:1 Als Anfang hat Gott den Himmel und die Erde geschaffen.
>
> 1:2a Und die Erde war Wüste und Leere, und Finsternis (war) über (der) Urflut.[10]

---

[8]Die Interpretation der (männlichen) Exegeten geht so gut wie nie auf die feministischen Interpretationen dieser Stelle ein. So stehen sie fast wie zwei verschiedene Welten nebeneinander. Auch der neueste (1993) Überblick von Gross (s.o. Anm. 2) geht auf keine einzige feministische Interpretation ein. Dies beklagt inzwischen Johannes de Moor, wenn er auf die erste diesbezügliche Bemerkung von Elisabeth Cady Stanton eingeht: "Unfortunately, Stanton's approach was simply ingnored by the male majority of exegetes and theologians of the last century", J.C. de Moor, "The Duality in God and Man: Gen. 1:26-27 as P's Interpretation of the Yahwistic Creation Account", in: Idem (ed.), *Intertextuality in Ugarit and Israel* (OTS, 40) Leiden 1998, 112-25, hier: 113.

[9]Vgl. dazu ausführlich H. Schüngel-Straumann, *Rûah bewegt die Welt: Gottes schöpferische Lebenskraft in der Krisenzeit des Exils* (SBS, 151), Stuttgart 1992.

[10]Übersetzung Zenger, *Gottes Bogen*, 185.

Nach 1:2a folgt:

> Und die רוח אלהים schwebte/flatterte (מרחפת) über den Wassern.

Erich Zenger hat diesen Versteil einer Nachinterpretation zugewiesen, dem ursprünglichen Konzept der Priesterschrift somit abgesprochen, weil dieser Satz wie ein Fremdkörper in der Gesamtkomposition liege.[11]

Der Satzteil mit der רוח אלהים gehört jedoch nicht zur Chaosschilderung von V. 1f., vielmehr steht diese in Paranthese und bezieht sich auf die Chaosschilderungen der Umwelt, die hier in Klammer aufgenommen sind. Daher muß Gen. 1:1-2 so übersetzt werden:

> a   Am Anfang hat אלהים den Himmel
> und die Erde erschaffen
> b   – die Erde aber war (noch) wüst und leer, und Finsternis
> (lag) über der Urflut –,
> c   und die רוח אלהים schwebte (dafür) über den Wassern.

רוח אלהים gehört unbedingt zur Aussage über das Erschaffen אלהִים, die Gottesbezeichnung der ersten Zeile wird dafür wieder aufgenommen. Das *erste Subjekt* in der Bibel überhaupt wird in dieser Struktur wieder aufgenommen im Zusammenhang mit רוח, das dadurch einen besonderen Stellenwert erhält. Damit wird das Erschaffen als exklusives Werk dieses Gottes Israels vorgestellt, die überlieferte Chaosschilderung wird gerahmt durch die Aussage über das Wirken dieses Gottes.[12] Daß von der Sache her kein Widerspruch zwischen רוח (f.) und דבר (m.) besteht, beweisen zahlreiche Psalmstellen, die beide Vorstellungen parallel benutzen.[13] Von der Bildvorstellung ist ja auch die Nähe schon dadurch gegeben, daß beides, רוח und דבר, aus dem

---

[11]Für Zenger ist dieser Versteil am ehesten eine theologische Kommentierung von Pˢ, der Grundschrift Pᵍ will er ihn jedoch absprechen, weil er "wie ein Fremdkörper in der ansonsten planvollen Gesamtkomposition" stehe, vor allem dann, wenn der Satz als Teil der Chaosschilderung interpretiert wird (*Gottes Bogen*, 81, Anm. 97).

[12]Daß die Aussagen der Chaosschilderung nicht von der gleichen Hand stammen können wie die Zeile mit רוח אלהים, dürfte schon daran deutlich werden, daß unterschiedliche Begriffe für 'Wasser' verwendet werden. In Zeile b wird תהום für die bedrohliche Urflut gebraucht, Zeile c dagegen bringt den Plural מים für die Wasser, über die Gottes רוח schwebt. Dieser Begriff wird dann im folgenden Text auch wieder aufgenommen, so ab V. 6 für die Scheidung der Wasser; er gehört somit zu P, während der Begriff תהום in Gen. 1 nicht wieder aufgenommen wird.

[13]Pss. 33:6, 147:18, 148:8 u.a. Zwar kommt דבר als Substantiv in Gen. 1 nicht vor, wohl aber das Verb. Es geht hier um die Vorstellung, nicht um den grammatischen Begriff.

Munde Gottes hervorgeht. Für alttestamentliches Denken ist es charakteristisch, komplizierte Zusammenhänge nicht terminologisch säuberlich zu trennen, sondern eher durch einander ergänzende Begriffe anschaulich zu machen. So stehen hier die schöpferische רוח und das bewirkende Wort in einem ausgewogenen Gleichgewicht. Der רוח-Begriff darf nun allerdings nicht isoliert, sondern muß im Zusammenhang mit dem verwendeten Verb interpretiert werden. רחף, das nur dreimal im AT vorkommt, ist ein Verb der Bewegung und kann mit "schweben", "flattern", auch "zittern", "sanft bewegen", "beben", evtl. auch "brüten" übersetzt werden. Die nächste Parallele zu Gen. 1:2 ist Dtn. 32:11, wo Jahwe mit einem Adler verglichen wird, der über seinen Jungen schwebt. Von daher ist die schützende, Leben wahrende Funktion dieses Verbs deutlich. Gen. 1:2 schwebt die weiblich vorgestellte רוח אלהים über den Wassern als eine Kraft, die sich bewegt und dabei ist, anderes in Bewegung zu setzen. Sie ist die potenziert vorgestellte Schöpferkraft Gottes, die ansetzt, die geordnete Welt zu erschaffen.

Wie am Ende der Schöpfungswerke von Gen. 1 haben wir auch am Anfang bei P den Versuch, ein Gleichgewicht herzustellen zwischen männlichen und weiblichen Vorstellungen. Sicher ist dies nicht zufällig. Wie kommt der Verfasser der Priesterschrift dazu, solche paritätischen Modelle zu entwickeln?

3 Das Gleichgewicht bei P

Es ist noch die Frage zu klären, wie die Aussagen zur "gender"-Problematik in die Zeit des Exils einzuordnen sind. Wie kommt P dazu, den Schöpfungsbericht am Anfang der Bibel mit so betont grammatisch feminin strukturierten Vorstellungen zu rahmen? Am Anfang und am Ende der Schöpfungswerke gibt es ein Gleichgewicht, eine Parallelität von männlich – weiblich, die auffallend sind. Die Aussage der Gottebenbildlichkeit von Mann *und* Frau ist singulär in einer Zeit, die sicher nicht frauenfreundlicher war als die israelitische Königszeit. Denn die priesterschriftliche Quelle denkt in anderen Bereichen streng hierarchisch, z.B. in den verschiedenen Kultordnungen. An zahlreichen Stellen, z.B. bei den Reinheitsvorschriften, steht die Frau an zweiter oder untergeordneter Stelle. Von einer Gleichheit *in der Praxis* kann wohl nicht die Rede sein.

In Gen. 1 hat P dagegen versucht, ein Idealbild, eine Utopie dessen zu entwerfen, wie die Welt in der Absicht Gottes gestaltet ist. Wie bei einem komplizierten Uhrwerk zeigt P das gesamte damalige Wissen über Gestirne, Pflanzen, Tiere und Menschen auf, wie sie in ihrer Gesamtheit und ihrer Geordnetheit funktionieren. Bei der genauen Beobachtung der Welt in ihrer vorgefundenen Vielfalt und Gegliedertheit konnte diesen Männern nicht entgehen, wie sehr überall das Prinzip männlich – weiblich (ein typischer Ausdruck der Priesterschrift) maßgebend ist. Die Abhängigkeit der ganzen Schöpfung und allen Lebens von dieser Polarität war den priesterschriftlichen Verfassern bewußt. Die Welt erscheint ihnen als etwas Durchdachtes, Durchstrukturiertes und sehr symmetrisch Aufgebautes. Aus der genauen Beobachtung dieser Symmetrie im menschlichen Bereich konnte nicht ausbleiben, daß die Einsicht in das paarweise angeordnete Lebensprinzip auch bei der Erschaffung des Menschen am Ende von Gen. 1 zum Zuge kommt.

Wie sich diese Vorstellungen in der Praxis für die konkreten Frauen des Exils ausgewirkt haben und wo sie ihren Ort haben, ist schwer zu bestimmen. In den letzten Jahrhunderten vor der Zeitenwende ist dann eher wieder ein Rückschritt festzustellen, indem nämlich, vor allem in den Apokryphen und Pseudepigraphen, die Gottebenbildlichkeit der Frau abgewertet, der des Mannes nachgestellt oder sogar ganz bestritten wird.[14] Aber auch wenn unserem Verfasser die soziologische und theologische Tragweite seiner programmatischen Gedanken noch gar nicht voll bewußt gewesen sein sollte, so sind doch hier die Ansätze für konstruktives Weiterdenken gegeben, einfach weil sie sich aus der Beobachtung der Wirklichkeit selbst, so wie sie schon vor mehr als zweitausend Jahren betrachtet werden konnte, ergeben.[15]

In der Frage der femininen Vorstellung der רוח am Anfang von Gen. 1 ist die nachexilische Zeit eigene Wege gegangen, wenn die חכמה (Sophia) an zahlreichen Stellen den Platz der רוח von Gen. 1:2 einnimmt. Sophia wird in dieser Spätzeit eine eigene schöpferische Potenz.[16]

P gibt somit in einer leidvollen Situation Perspektiven für die Zukunft.[17] Daß der Schöpfungsbericht von Gen. 1 eine Utopie zeichnet, scheint mir sicher. אדם bezeichnet *alle* Menschen, nicht nur die Is-

---

[14]Vgl. H. Schüngel-Straumann, *Die Frau am Anfang* (Anm. 1) sowie E. Gössmann/H. Schüngel-Straumann, "Gottebenbildlichkeit", in: E. Gössmann *et al.*, *Wörterbuch der Feministischen Theologie*, Gütersloh 1991, 173-81.

[15]Bird, "Sexual Differentiation", 25, schränkt ihre Interpretation von "männlich-weiblich" auf die rein kreatürliche Ordnung ein, während P über die sozialen Konsequenzen nicht reflektiere. Aber wir müssen dies heute tun! Sie schließt die Ausführungen mit der Aussicht, daß der Text "does not establish any hierarchy within species, either of gender or function; all of its statements pertain to the species as a whole. Thus it may serve as a foundation text for a feminist egalitarian anthropology, since it recognizes no hierarchy of gender in the created order."

[16]Vgl. u.a. S. Schroer, *Die Weisheit hat ihr Haus gebaut: Studien zur Gestalt der Sophia in den biblischen Schriften*, Mainz 1996; H. Schüngel-Straumann, *Denn Gott bin ich, und kein Mann*, Mainz ²1996, 121-35, und die jeweils angegebene umfangreiche Literatur.

[17]Zenger, *Gottes Bogen*, 179.

raeliten, und es meint Mann *und* Frau. Als ersten Schöpfungsbegriff bringt P zudem רוח, ein Terminus, der auch im Alten Orient geläufig, also nicht spezifisch national ist.

Die Verwirklichung dieser Utopie steht noch aus, das spricht nicht gegen sie. Der Mensch kann wohl ohne solche Entwürfe nicht leben. So sind die "modern" anmutenden Aussagen der Priesterschrift in der "gender"-Problematik auch heute noch bedenkenswert. Auch bei einer ganz anderen Sicht der Welt können wir dem Ansatz der priesterschriftlichen Schöpfungsgeschichte in seiner Tiefenstruktur Impulse entnehmen, die alt, aber nicht veraltet sind.

Janet Tollington   *Cambridge – United Kingdom*

Readings in Haggai:
From the Prophet to the Completed Book, a Changing Message in Changing Times

1   Introduction

The book of Haggai dates the prophet's words to three specific occasions during the year 520 BCE; the first day of the sixth month, the twenty-first day of the seventh month and the twenty-fourth day of the ninth month. It also refers to activity taking place on the twenty-fourth day of the sixth month. There is no reason to doubt the year of the prophet's ministry since the message makes direct reference to the start of the programme of rebuilding the Jerusalem temple in earnest. It is commonly accepted that this work took place between 520 and 516 BCE. However, it is worth considering whether the precise dating is factual or a feature of the compiler's, or an editor's work; and whether there is theological significance in the given dates. These issues will be discussed later in this paper.

The general context for the prophet's ministry is within a community whose religion is under stress because the temple is still in ruins and there is no Davidic monarch on the throne. These were two of the main tenets of the pre-exilic faith of Judah, alongside occupation of the promised land, to which the exiles had now been able to return. The community included some who had remained in the land throughout the exile, some who had moved in from surrounding territories such as Edom during the exile and some who had returned from Babylon over the past few years.[1] Hag. 1:6 indicates that poor harvests were being experienced, there was poverty and deprivation, and hard work alone was inadequate to transform the situation. Community effort was concentrated on building up society and the economy, on establishing themselves as an identifiable people in the Persian empire. This was the priority and there were insufficient resources to

---

[1] The edict of Cyrus, 538 BCE, has generally been regarded as the event which initiated the return of the exiles cf. Ezra 1. However extant records indicate that few returned during Cyrus's reign, whilst early in the time of Darius around 45,000 went back to Jerusalem, J.L. Berquist, *Judaism in Persia's Shadow*, Minneapolis 1995, 26-7. An absence of archaeological finds in and around Jerusalem indicating Judah's connections with Persia prior to the reign of Cambyses (530-522 BCE) suggests that his conquest of Egypt in 525 BCE may have provided an impetus for the exiles to return.

do anything about the temple site, even if any among them had the inclination. I suggest that there was much disillusionment about the future; there was no prosperity and no sign of God's blessings, nor of the fulfilment of God's promises. Some of the returnees were perhaps thinking that they had been better off in Babylon.

There is no indication in the book of Haggai itself of specific conflict between the groups which comprised the community. The designation עַם הָאָרֶץ in 2:4 appears to be a neutral reference to all the gathered people rather than a pejorative term for those perceived as foreigners in Ezra 4:4, cf. Ezra 10:2, 11. Similarly the term כֹּל שְׁאֵרִית הָעָם in Hag. 1:12, 14; 2:2[2] does not distinguish one section from another but is used to refer to all those who responded to the prophet's message.[3] However, human experience of living in society suggests that communities which include native residents, migrants, returned exiles, or similar diverse groups, take several generations before they accept one another as true citizens. People feel threatened by incomers, they are suspicious of new ideas being brought in and they resent any who refuse to compromise or accommodate other views. It is improbable that the community in Jerusalem lived without serious tensions and antagonisms[4] but there is no evidence in this short prophetic book to indicate where the divisions lay. Haggai himself remains an enigma since nothing is known of his origins and personal history. It cannot be determined whether or not he had been in Babylon and therefore his association with any section of the community can only be a matter of conjecture.[5]

---

[2] The word כֹּל is omitted in Hag. 2:2 in MT although LXX reads πάντας (in all three verses).

[3] D.J.A. Clines, "Haggai's temple, constructed, deconstructed and reconstructed", in: Idem (ed.), *Interested Parties: The Ideology of Writers and Readers of the Hebrew Bible* (JSOT.S, 205), Sheffield 1995, 46-75, argues throughout that the text implies social conflict while trying to suppress it. On 70-1 and n. 62 he claims that "Only a *remnant* worked on the temple – which implies that the majority did not." He presents no evidence for this opinion that the *majority* failed to respond to the prophet. I am unconvinced by his argument that the general reference to 'people' in 1:13 must mean 'the remnant', since it is so defined by 1:12, whereas 'people' in 1:2 and 2:14 necessarily refers to the whole people, most of whom ignore Haggai's message. I note that he makes no comment about the identity of 'all you people of the land' in 2:4. According to 2:2 this is also addressed to 'the remnant' – I rather think this point deconstructs Clines' argument.

[4] Indications of tensions and divisions can be found in Ezra 3-6; Isa. 56-66 and Zech. 1-8. However some of this is prompted by external groups and it is not certain whether any or all of this material provides a true picture of Jerusalem society at the precise time of Haggai's ministry.

[5] For a brief overview of scholarly opinions see J.E. Tollington, *Tradition and Innovation in Haggai and Zechariah 1-8* (JSOT.S, 150), Sheffield 1993, 48-50.

The oracles in Haggai lack any condemnation of religious malpractice among the community. There is no reference to idolatry, nor apostasy, nor to the rejection of YHWH as God. The only criticism offered by the prophet is implied in Hag. 1:2, 4 and 2:14 where a lack of appropriate urgency and half-heartedness are the charges laid against the people suggesting that Haggai may have perceived them as nominalist Yahwists who lacked commitment to their faith. It is apparent that priests were functioning in a traditional role as interpreters of *torah*, Hag. 2:11-13, and it is probable that some pattern of sacrificial worship and regular fasting was being maintained focused on the ruined temple site, cf. Zech. 7:3. If Ezra 3:2-6 offers a reliable record then it suggests that the altar had been re-established by the first group to return from exile and that the major festivals had been observed there since that time;[6] but by what proportion of the community and how faithfully cannot be determined.

I have argued elsewhere[7] that Haggai's words were collated and set within a narrative framework by his near contemporary, the prophet Zechariah, or a close follower of Zechariah and therefore I maintain that a text of the book of Haggai existed from the very early period of the completed second temple.[8] This does not preclude the possibility that a subsequent redactor may have modified, or added the specified dates for political or theological reasons in a later period, nor that other minor additions may have arisen during the text's transmission.[9]

However, the general dating provides a clear context against which to read the prophecies. It was the period when the community in Je-

---

[6]P.R. Bedford, "Discerning the Time: Haggai, Zechariah and the 'Delay' in the Rebuilding of the Jerusalem Temple", in: S.W. Holloway, L.K. Handy (eds.), *The Pitcher is Broken: Memorial Essays for Gösta W. Ahlström* (JSOT.S, 190), Sheffield 1995, 71-94, suggests that all the claims about rebuilding associated with the temple in Ezra 1-6 should be dated to the reign of Darius I, not to the time of Cyrus.

[7]Tollington, *Tradition and Innovation*, 23 and 180.

[8]M.H. Floyd, "The Nature of the Narrative and the Evidence of Redaction in Haggai", *VT* 45 (1995), 470-90, argues that the book came into being through a single literary compositional process, which largely fabricated both Haggai's reported speech and reporting narration, as against the idea of an editorial framework being used to incorporate the prophet's oracles. His discussion of the use of patronymic details and of the comparison between other prophetic superscriptions and the narrative introductions in Haggai as evidence for this theory is not convincing in my opinion. However I note that his conclusion, that the author of the book bases the work on something concrete and writes from a prophetic self-consciousness, 483-4, would accord with my previously published suggestions about the provenance of the compiler.

[9]For example Hag. 2:5a which is widely recognised as a scribal gloss. See Tollington, *Tradition and Innovation*, 20, nn. 1-2.

rusalem was motivated by the prophet to begin the rebuilding process and it purports to relate to the first 3 or 4 months spent on preparation and actual building work. This was a turning point for the community, a time of great stress, of hopes and disappointments and undoubtedly a time when diverse opinions were to be heard among the people. The prophet's words were probably directed towards the gathered community in Jerusalem rather than the leaders; but whether in the market place or in the context of the cult is unclear. The redirection of the oracles towards Zerubbabel and Joshua which appears in the text at Hag. 1:1 and 2:2, 4, I have previously argued is the work of the compiler.[10]

2   The Message of Haggai the Prophet

The prophet proclaims a message of challenge and encouragement based on traditional Yahwistic religious understandings which uses ancient motifs and reflects Davidic and Zion theology. It expresses a desire to restore the ideals of worship as first experienced in the early years of the Solomonic temple. This is indicated in the way Haggai equates crop failure and poverty with the absence of divine blessing, 1:5-6, which resonates with the ideas of blessing and curse theology expressed in Deut. 27–28. He calls for the rebuilding of the temple to be the priority in the community, showing the importance of temple theology. The people's prevarication over this may not arise solely due to difficult social circumstances. Hag. 1:2 might suggest that they were waiting for a specific time, although it is unclear how it would be identified.[11] The temple is described in 1:8 as a place which will be pleasing to YHWH and as the location for YHWH's glory to appear.[12]

---

[10]Tollington, *Tradition and Innovation*, 19-23.

[11]The 'seventy year' motif is sometimes mentioned in this connection. It is interesting that the dedication of the second temple in 516 BCE coincides with seventy years after the destruction of the first temple. However, Jer. 29:10 refers to seventy years in relation to the promised return from Babylon for the first wave of exiles who were taken into captivity in 597/6 BCE. It makes no reference to the temple. A carefully argued interpretation of the 'time' is offered by Bedford, "Discerning the Time". His conclusion that the community's perception of Zerubbabel influenced their understanding of when any temple building would receive divine sanction, is not significantly at variance with my interpretation. Bedford offers good reasons as to why Haggai was able to persuade the community to begin rebuilding but these matters are not relevant to this paper.

[12]Clines, "Haggai's Temple", 48-52, argues that the temple is to be a *treasure house* and nothing more. It is for the reader to decide whether he is justified in rejecting the possibility that 'glory' might result from more than solely the abundance of silver and gold which YHWH will cause to be brought into the temple, Hag. 2:7.

This accords loosely with ideas from Deuteronomy, for example Deut.
12:5, and from Ezekiel, for example Ezek. 1:28; 10:4; 43:1-5.

Generally within the oracles there is a strong emphasis on the corporate nature of the community without any suggestion of individual
responsibility. All the people are jointly addressed and the only references to individual circumstances, at the end of 1:6, are comments
which typify the ways in which the whole community has been ad-
versely affected. The stress on YHWH's power over the natural world
reiterates many themes and motifs from the pre-exilic period. Hag.
1:7-11 and 2:6, 15-19 use images of poverty, drought, crop failure, the
withholding of dew, and blight as symbols of divine punishment in
much the same way as in Deut. 28:22, Amos 4:9 and Mic. 6:14-15.
The focus on YHWH's presence among the people, in Hag. 1:13; 2:4,
5b, links to the idea of Israel as the elect people and perhaps underlying all the agricultural imagery there is a link with the concept of
the land as that of promise, flowing with milk and honey, Exod. 3:17.
These allusions to the exodus traditions may account both for the substance of Hag. 2:5a and for the eventual incorporation of this scribal
gloss into the final text. All this supports a claim that Haggai was
proclaiming traditional theological ideas and calling for a continuity
of religious practice as in the era of the first temple.

Similar arguments can be presented regarding the hopes in Hag.
2:7-9 for the pilgrimage of the nations to a prosperous Jerusalem,
which express the Zion traditions of Isa. 2:2-4 (= Mic. 4:1-3); 49:22-
23. The final oracle in the text, Hag. 2:21-23, speaks clearly of the
prophet's expectation that there would be a restoration of the Davidic monarchy in the person of Zerubbabel. This is couched in the
language of traditional theology in a way that deliberately reverses
the prophecy of Jer. 22:24-30 concerning Coniah (Jehoiachin) and the
end of the Davidic dynasty by turning it into a message of restoration
and hope.[13]

In Hag. 2:11-14 issues of holiness and purity are raised and the
priests are presented as responsible for torah rulings, part of their
traditional role. The concepts about uncleanness and its contagion
reflect material in Lev. 11; 22 and Num. 19:11. It seems that Haggai
is not reiterating a specific pre-exilic tradition but drawing on general
understandings of what it meant for priests and people to be holy. The
meaning of 2:14 is somewhat obscured by the dating system and the
ordering of the oracles within the book.[14] Its basic message is that the

---

[13]For a full discussion of this oracle see Tollington, *Tradition and Innovation*,
135-43.

[14]I shall return to discuss these matters later in this paper.

laying of the temple foundation represents the cleansing process which the community needed to undergo in order to be fit to receive YHWH's blessings, which are once again expressed in agricultural terms.

This summary of Haggai's prophetic message illustrates that he did not belong to a narrow school of thought; he was not presenting a specific theology identifiable as Deuteronomistic or Priestly or any other to which a defining label can be given. Haggai was calling for a return to a true expression of Yahwism through the restoration of both the cult in the temple and the Davidic monarchy. This would lead to a new experience of divine blessings and the glory of YHWH would be revealed in the prosperity and wellbeing, the שָׁלוֹם of Israel.

3   The Message of the Book's First Edition

The text of Haggai, however, must be read against a slightly differ-ent context, that of a few years later than the prophecies, the period when the temple building was about complete and yet there was no sign of any dramatic intervention by YHWH, nor any marked trans-formation in the community's standard of living and international status. This situation would have prompted cognitive dissonance in the community and increased the tensions, highlighting the different viewpoints of specific groups. The compiler has redirected the mes-sage away from the community as a whole[15] towards two identified leaders, Zerubbabel the governor and Joshua the high priest, Hag. 1:1, 12, 14; 2:2, 4. Each time the governor is accorded priority in that he is mentioned first but this is very slight in that more emphasis appears to be on the equality of status and close relationship of the two characters.

The oracle directed solely to Zerubbabel in 2:21-23 lacks his patr-onym in the opening address as though to emphasize his political appointment by the Persians as governor rather than his Davidic des-cent. It is also possible that the use of כַּחוֹתָם *'like a signet ring'* in 2:23 rather than the definite phrase without כ functions in the same way.[16] Likewise in 2:4 Zerubbabel is mentioned only by name whereas

---

[15] Except in Hag. 1:13.

[16] If this is the case, then the possibility that the compiler has modified the original oracle away from a positive expression of monarchic hopes must be con-sidered, although I acknowledge that this will always be a matter of conjecture. What actually happened to Zerubbabel is not known. He is not mentioned in con-nection with the celebrations when the rebuilt temple was dedicated, Ezra 6:14-18, and this significant Davidic descendant disappears quietly from the stage of his-tory. The Bible's silence about his fate prohibits any reasoned comment about his status or any hopes attached to him at the time when the book of Haggai was compiled.

Joshua's legitimate status as high priest is again stressed by the inclusion of his patronym. I suggest that these variations in the text are a deliberate ploy by the compiler intended to demonstrate that YHWH had indeed chosen Zerubbabel to be a leader of the community but not to be the king. The community was not to be an independent nation but would remain under Persian rule. Nonetheless YHWH was in overall control, of Persia as well as Israel, choosing to work through the Persian administrative systems and yet still remaining faithful to the Davidic promise.

By setting these two leaders side by side the compiler indicates that both governor and high priest must share responsibility for encouraging the faithfulness and obedience of Israel towards the word of YHWH.[17] The two men must lead by example and involve themselves in the fulfilment of the divine commands and the text suggests that they are not to lord it over the people but to work alongside them in bringing about the new Israel, the whole community being enlivened and encouraged by the presence and power of YHWH in its midst, 1:12, 14; 2:4-5. There is no suggestion in the book of Haggai that the two leaders are given any privileged insight into YHWH's purposes, nor any special blessings; but together they are both representatives of the people's response to YHWH and a sign to Israel and the nations of YHWH's authority in all earthly matters temporal and spiritual, political and religious, practical and academic. Both leaders are presented as equally responsive to the prophetic word, suggesting that the compiler held a high view of the authority of prophecy.

4   The Message Conveyed Through the Dating Scheme

I have suggested that the substance of Haggai's oracles can be interpreted without difficulty given the available information concerning his historical context. Likewise I have demonstrated that the focus of the prophet's words, but not the overall message, has been redirected by means of the framework supplied by the compiler. It is now appropriate to reflect on whether the dates within the book and the ordering of both the oracles and the narrative material offer yet another level of meaning to a discerning reader.

On the basis of Zech. 1:7 which indicates the eleventh month as Shebat and the association of the seventh month with the feast of booths in Ezra 3, it is evident that the old (Babylonian) system of

---

[17]I have argued elsewhere that Zechariah prophesied the advent of a diarchy between Joshua and Zerubbabel and that this hope was expressed in the framework to the book of Haggai. See Tollington, *Tradition and Innovation*, 154-81.

numbering the months of the year is to be understood when reading the book of Haggai. The date given in the opening verse thereby indicates that Haggai's prophecies began in the month of Elul. This corresponds to a period around August/September in our calendar, when harvest was approaching; but it was also the month which was understood as the last one of the year. Since the prophet makes reference to poor harvests in the oracles which follow, this date may recall the historical reality, although Hag. 1:6, 9-11 appears to focus on the experience of the recent past rather than on the forthcoming harvest. The date which is subsequently given in the text at 1:15 suggests that the people began to build the temple twenty-three days later, indicating that they responded very promptly to the prophetic word with the intervening period being spent gathering the necessary materials as commanded.[18]

These dates have no apparent significance for the compiler as they do not relate to any known events in relation to either Zerubbabel or Joshua.[19] However if they are read theologically then their function may be to draw attention to endings and the possibility of new beginnings. In Hag. 1:2-6 the prophet reminds the people that the situation is still as though they were in exile, as though YHWH was absent. This oracle is followed by a divine command in 1:8 which offers the hope of a transformed future. If the people respond obediently and faithfully towards YHWH they will experience blessings instead of the continuing punishment, which will come to an end. Reading the dates in this way, the next one, at 1:15 symbolises the turning point that coincides with the year end. On the twenty-fourth day of the last month work on the temple is commenced and so the community can look forward to a new era breaking in as the new year begins.

---

[18]D.L. Christensen, "Poetry and Prose in the Composition and Performance of the Book of Haggai", in J.C. de Moor, W.G.E. Watson (eds.), *Verse in Ancient Near Eastern Prose* (AOAT, 42), Neukirchen–Vluyn 1993, 17-30, argues that Hag. 1:15 must be read with the following verses of text and not, as I am doing, with the preceding passage. His argument depends partly on the presence of a *petuchah* paragraph marking in MT after 1:14 and a claim that *setumah* and *petuchah* markings should be taken more seriously as division points in the text, although I note that he prefers to ignore their occurrence after Hag. 1:6 and 2:5 when they fall within the boundaries of units which he identifies as strophes. He is unable to offer a credible suggestion as to why the unit Hag. 1:15–2:9 should commence with two different dates in consecutive verses and therefore I am not persuaded by his argument.

[19]I accept that the compiler may have included some dates in the first text of Haggai. However I am suggesting that such dates were modified or expanded in a later period.

In the text the next date, the twenty-first day of the seventh month, follows immediately at Hag. 2:1. This falls during the celebration of Succoth when first fruits of the harvest were offered to YHWH in thanksgiving. According to Lev. 23:39-43 this festival extends from the fifteenth to the twenty-second day of Tishre and thus the specified date is the final day of feasting before the solemn rest which concludes the celebrations. It is conceivable that Haggai did actually prophesy during this festival at the temple site seeking to encourage the community to believe that although there was little to celebrate this year, next year would be different so long as the rebuilding work was maintained until the temple was complete. However, in view of the prevalence of agricultural imagery in Haggai's other oracles it is surprising that there is no reference to the hope of bountiful harvests in the future in this oracle if it really was proclaimed in the context of Succoth, the harvest festival.

If Ezra 3:1-6 is historically reliable it implies that all the appointed feasts were observed from the time when the exiles first returned from Babylon. This would mean that between the date when building work had begun the community had celebrated the solemn rest of New Year on the first day of Tishre and then the Day of Atonement on the tenth day and since the fifteenth had been celebrating Succoth.[20] Consequently little work could have been done and only the foundations of the temple would have been in evidence; and these may have been a discouraging sight. However the content of Haggai's oracles belies such faithful religious observance among the community and we have no positive evidence to indicate either way whether any of the festivals were celebrated in the post-exilic period prior to the re-establishment of the temple cult.

If Hag. 2:3-9 is read in isolation from its narrative context it becomes apparent that it does not pre-suppose that any work of rebuilding had begun. The words could easily have been proclaimed beside the ruins. Moreover, since the fundamental meaning of this oracle, a current discouraging situation which will be transformed into a revelation of YHWH's glory and presence through the building of the temple,[21] parallels the meaning of Hag. 1:4-11 it is feasible that

---

[20]Lev. 23:23-36 refers to the dates and the days of sabbath rest.

[21]Christensen, "Poetry and Prose", 28, suggests that וַעֲשׂוּ in Hag. 2:4, which he claims lies at the very centre of the book, should be interpreted as a command to offer sacrifice, observe the feast of Succoth, celebrate, rather than an instruction to work on the building. Although the verb is used with this meaning in Deut. 16:13, the immediate context in Hag. 2:1-9, even allowing for the fact that the passage is dated during Succoth, seems to indicate that building work is the more probable meaning here.

the prophet proclaimed them both on the same occasion. If this was the case then either the compiler or a later editor of the book would appear to have separated or re-ordered the material as well as having supplied the dates.

Again I conclude that such redaction would not have contributed to the purposes of the compiler, other than that it shows the ongoing close co-operation between Joshua and Zerubbabel in a joint leadership role. However I believe that a theological reason can be offered. By separating the oracles and dating the second one at the end of Succoth another level of meaning is given to the text. In this literary context new year has been experienced, atonement has taken place symbolising the cleansing of the community and the restoration of its relationship with YHWH, and the people are portrayed as having faithfully celebrated Succoth even though they have little to offer and for which to give thanks. Through this festival they have been reminded of when their ancestors wandered in the desert for forty years, living in booths, before entering the promised land.[22] That earlier time of hardship had been followed by the establishment of Israel as a nation and in due course God bestowed on them the monarchy and the Jerusalem temple to replace the tabernacle wherein YHWH had previously been understood to dwell. Then, for a while, they had experienced the fulness of YHWH's blessings. Remembrance of God's faithfulness in the past would offer hope for the future and encourage the community to believe that they might again have a monarch, a temple to match the splendour of Solomon's and be the recipients of divine blessings in the days that lay ahead.

I concede that this theological interpretation could apply to the historical context of the prophet Haggai but I have argued that it only arises from a reading of the redacted text which I believe derives from a later period. Such a message of hope would be applicable for the post-exilic community at other times of discouragement, not just in the period of initial restoration. I will refrain from suggesting a suitable context which may have given rise to this process of redaction until the significance of the remaining dates within the text has been discussed.

According to Hag. 2:10, 20 the remaining oracles were proclaimed just over two months later on the twenty-fourth day of the ninth month, which is Chislev, and exactly three months after the rebuilding work was commenced, 1:15a. However it should be noted that Hag. 2:20 refers to the day by number but not the month. It is the

---

[22] Lev. 23:43.

positioning in the text of this oracle addressed to Zerubbabel which leads to the interpretation that the ninth month is implied. Since the twenty-fourth day of the sixth month has been mentioned as the occasion when work began on the temple, is it feasible that 2:21-23 were the prophet's second utterance at that earlier time?[23]

Studies relating to ancient building practices and in particular rituals associated with foundation ceremonies and the role of the king[24] lead me to suggest that Zerubbabel performed a significant function when the foundations of the new temple were laid.[25] Although the text of Haggai makes no direct reference to a ceremony surrounding the laying of a foundation stone,[26] the occasion when work began could certainly be construed in a similar way. Therefore I maintain that this provides a suitable context for Haggai's prophecies regarding the monarchic status of Zerubbabel. If I am correct in this it follows that Hag. 2:20-23 originally read as a second oracle proclaimed on the day when the building work began[27] which was dated by the

---

[23] J. Nogalski, *Literary Precursors to the Book of the Twelve* (BZAW, 217), Berlin 1993, 230, acknowledges that this date is presented in a way which deviates from the general pattern of date formulae in Haggai but nonetheless attributes it to the same editor who arranged the material in chronological order. In n. 44 he argues that the occurrence of the phrase " 'a second time' locates the date quite precisely as identical with 2:10." This is valid in relation to the canonical text but it offers no evidence about the true date on which the oracle may have been uttered, nor about the possible existence of a differently ordered text at some time in the book's transmission.

[24] R.S. Ellis, *Foundation Deposits in Ancient Mesopotamia*, New Haven 1968 and A.S. Kapelrud, "Temple Building, a Task for Gods and Kings", *Or.* 32 (1963), 56-62. See also the discussion of these studies in relation to Zerubbabel and Zech. 4:7-10 in Tollington, *Tradition and Innovation*, 145-54.

[25] His role was likely to have been very similar if the original foundations of the ruined temple were to be re-used, since these would have been cleared and prepared in readiness for the new building.

[26] Hag. 2:18b refers to the laying of the foundations but not to a ceremony. There are difficulties with both the text and the interpretation of the whole of 2:18. Many scholars regard either the specific date in 18a, or the clause about the foundations being laid in 18b, or both, to be glosses which have crept into the text. Decisions about this are inevitably subjective since no external evidence is available on these matters but I am not persuaded that 2:18b should be excised.

[27] Nogalski, *Literary Precursors*, 221-6, discusses the relationship between Hag. 2:10-23 and Hag. 1:15a which specifies a date for this work. He rejects the suggestion that 1:15a refers backwards to the previous oracle and supports those who argue that the oracle which it originally introduced has been relocated. Hag. 2:20-23 was proposed as the oracle in question by P.F. Bloomhardt, "The Poems of Haggai", *HUCA* 5 (1928), 166-8, but following a discussion of this and other options Nogalski concludes, 226, that "a plausible rationale for displacing 2:20-23 has not yet been advanced." I suggest that it is possible that 1:15a originally referred backwards to the brief oracle in 1:13 and forwards to 2:20-23. Although

compiler to the twenty-fourth day of a month,[28] and that the date in
2:10, which is repeated in 2:18, was added by a subsequent redactor.
Any other explanation would require a complex process of redaction
involving rearrangement of the text which cannot be justified.

However, let us return to consider the implication of the date
which the text provides for all the material in Hag. 2:10-23. The
twenty-fourth day of the ninth month was a date without special
significance until the time of Antiochus Epiphanes (175-64 BCE). During his reign the Jerusalem temple was desecrated[29] and exactly two
years later purified and rededicated on 25 Chislev 164 BCE.[30] From
that time onwards the rededication of the temple has been celebrated
by the eight day festival of Hanukkah which begins on the twenty-fifth
day of the ninth month.[31]

Hag. 2:11-14 concerns the problem of uncleanness and the ease
with which this is transmitted from one member of the community
to another whereas holiness is not something which can be gained
merely through contact with a holy object. Haggai proclaimed this as
a comment on the impure state of the Jerusalem community before it
repented, responded to YHWH in obedience and began to rebuild the
temple. Therefore it seems improbable that these words were uttered
three months after the work had commenced. If the date was genuine to the prophet's context he would be saying that the work on the
temple was still unacceptable to YHWH because of the people's lack of
holiness; yet in 2:15-19 the oracle continues by declaring that a significant turning point has been reached in the laying of the foundations.
No longer will divine punishment be sent upon the unclean nation,
instead divine blessings will be experienced by those who have rededicated themselves to YHWH and committed themselves to the building
work. This means that there is an internal contradiction when the text
is read in the light of the specified date and it leads me to conclude
that the date has no relevance to the original prophecy. It is widely
recognised that the repetition of the same date in 2:18a disrupts the

---

I accept, with Nogalski, *Literary Precursors*, 222, that dating material usually
introduces prophetic oracles, it seems plausible that the compiler might have po-
sitioned the date between two oracles uttered on the same occasion especially
since emphasis is being given to the fact that building work actually commenced
on that day in response to the prophet's words.

[28] I note that Zech. 1:7 dates the series of visions to the twenty-fourth day, albeit
of the eleventh month in the same year. This may be no more than coincidence
but I wonder whether there was originally a closer correlation of dates between
the texts of Haggai and Zechariah.

[29] 1 Macc. 1:54-59; cf. Dan. 11:31; 12:11.

[30] 1 Macc. 4:36-56; 2 Macc. 10:1-6.

[31] 1 Macc. 4:59; 2 Macc. 10:6-8.

oracle and that it is almost certainly secondary.[32] Its inclusion in the
text may be a somewhat clumsy attempt by a scribe to overcome the
internal contradiction by implying that the twenty-fourth day of the
ninth month was in fact the date when the foundations were laid and
that oracle and event coincide. However, even this doesn't produce
a harmonious reading because in its textual setting 2:18b-19 appears
to be a reflection looking back on how things had changed since the
foundations were laid. If the date is deleted from 2:18 however it is
possible to read the remaining part of the oracle in terms of future
promise. On this reading I conclude that the whole of Hag. 2:11-19
may initially have been proclaimed on the day when the temple foundations were laid, which is the same occasion that I suggested for the
final oracles in 2:21-23.

An explanation for the date in Hag. 2:10 is now required and I believe that a theological reason can be offered if the text is read against
the background of the Maccabean era. In 164 BCE the twenty-fourth
day of the ninth month was the day before the rededication of the purified temple. According to 1 Macc. 4:36-51 an extensive programme
of cleansing and rebuilding had been undertaken in preparation for
the occasion when sacrifice would be offered again in the cleansed
sanctuary. This was to be accompanied by celebrations of thanksgiving lasting eight days in recognition of their deliverance from the
Gentiles by God. For that community in Jerusalem a new era was
about to begin with the hope that it would be a time of divine blessing and an age in which Judah would enjoy religious freedom and
some measure of independence among the nations of the world. The
parallels between this context and the time of Haggai are obvious
and so I suggest that the prophecies of Haggai were used as a source
of encouragement for the people in the period after the desecration
of the temple by Antiochus and as they embarked on the process of
cleansing and restoration. In this second century BCE context, and in
particular on the eve of the rededication ceremony, Haggai's words
about unholiness and unclean produce being offered to YHWH, Hag.
2:14, would be very powerful as they recalled the sacrilege which had
taken place in the temple in the last two years. As I have already
argued the oracle marked a turning point for its original hearers as
did this occasion for the later community in Jerusalem. I suggest that
it was in this context that a redactor added the date to the text at
2:10 emphasising the validity of the reapplication of these prophecies
to a differing situation.[33]

[32]This is the view of the editors of BHS where it is indicated as a gloss.

[33]This may have been especially important as it became apparent that the

The oracles about monarchic hopes invested in Zerubbabel can also be interpreted in this context either in terms of hopes for some kind of royal leader or as messianic expectations. Therefore it would be quite appropriate for the redactor to allow Hag. 2:20-23 to remain as the final words of the text.

5 Conclusion

I have argued that Haggai's oracles may all have been proclaimed on just two occasions. The words in 1:2-11 and 2:3-9 as oracles of challenge and encouragement intended to inspire the community to turn back to YHWH and to rebuild the temple. This probably took place in sight of the temple ruins on an unknown date during 520 BCE. Sometime later, on the day when the foundations were (re-)laid he again prophesied proclaiming the oracles which are now identified as Hag. 1:13b; 2:11-19 and 2:21-23.

Two or three years later the oracles were set in a narrative framework by the compiler who identified the year in which Haggai prophesied and supplied a date on which the rebuilding work commenced as the twenty-fourth day of a month. Whether the given day is accurate and whether it was the sixth or some other month cannot be ascertained on the evidence currently available. I suggest that the text was compiled as follows: Hag. 1:1-11 (omitting mention of the first day in v. 1); 2:1b-9 (omitting the date in v. 1a);[34] 1:12-15; 2:10b-23 (omitting the date in 2:18). In all probability Hag. 2:5a does not belong to this first text either, although it may have been written in the margin as an interpretative gloss at quite an early stage in the text's transmission.

The next stage in the development of the text interprets Hag. 2:2-9 against the background of the feast of Succoth and a redactor relocates this oracle, incorporates 2:5a into it, and supplies an introductory date for it at 2:1a. As I indicated earlier in this paper, this development could have occurred in response to a variety of situations. However I believe that the events of 164 BCE provide a context for this redaction as well as for the addition of the date in Hag. 2:10 and 18, which I

---

problems for the Jews were not in fact over and that the age of blessings had not yet arrived.

[34] This provides a solution to the problems which arise due to the juxtaposition of two different dates in Hag. 1:15 and 2:1. It is frequently argued that 1:15a should be regarded as the addition to the text, an argument which requires a reader to accept that 1:15b really belongs as the opening to chapter 2. I believe that my suggestion is more credible on the basis of the verse divisions in the text even without acceptance of my full hypothesis.

have argued above. According to 2 Macc. 10:6 the first celebration of what became the festival of Hanukkah was experienced as a stark contrast to the community's situation during Succoth a little over two months earlier. It is conceivable that the presence alongside the text of the gloss, Hag. 2:5a, and its clear association with the theme of Succoth, prompted the redactor to make all these changes at the same time. As a result Haggai's oracles of encouragement and promise were presented in the text in a sequence conforming to the series of events which had been recognised as of great religious significance in 164 BCE by the Jerusalem community. This enabled the continuing relevance of these prophecies of hope to be stressed as the text was read in subsequent years to a people who were still waiting for the fulfilment of God's word and the coming of YHWH's eternal reign.

I have presented a reading of the book of Haggai which identifies an initial oral proclamation, a literary compilation after a relatively short space of time, one instance of a gloss being appended to the text, and one level of redaction which reflects the re-application of the prophecies to a new situation in the history of God's people. I maintain that this demonstrates that prophecy remained a living tradition in the latter stages of the development of the Hebrew scriptures. It also shows how prophecy could be used as a source of inspiration in many situations of religious stress and social upheaval because it was understood as the word of the living God to the community of faith in every age.

Harm van Grol   *Utrecht – The Netherlands*

'Indeed, Servants We Are':

Ezra 9, Nehemiah 9 and 2 Chronicles 12 Compared

Servitude plays a part in Ezra 9, Nehemiah 9 and 2 Chronicles 12:1-12. A similar sequence of events occurs in these three texts. Sin is followed by punishment. Punishment is followed by mercy. Expectations are that mercy will mean restoration or the like, but in these three texts the result is "some relief" and "servitude". As far as I am aware this sequence does not occur elsewhere in the Old Testament.[1]

Ezra 9, Nehemiah 9 and 2 Chronicles 12 are roughly contemporary texts. The sequence mentioned above can be conceived as a paradigm to understand the religio-political situation after the exile: the subjection to the Persians.

But is there really so much resemblance between our three texts that we can talk of one and the same paradigm? Sara Japhet's *Ideology* cautions us against seeing too much unity and resemblance between Chronicles and Ezra-Nehemiah.[2] Especially when we deal with a theological paradigm like the one above. One may even question the analysis given above as far as 2 Chronicles 12 is concerned. Should there not be a neat balance between sin and retribution in Chronicles? There should be no 'leftover' or 'continued' punishment ...

Against this background I will compare Ezra 9, Nehemiah 9 and 2 Chronicles 12 in more detail and ask for the role political servitude plays in each of these texts.[3]

---

[1] This contribution was, of course, written before the workshop on this theme was held. The discussion in the workshop will be reflected in some notes and remarks. As far as the unique sequence concerns, it became clear that the phenomenon of partial deliverance – or, seen from the other side, restrictive punishment – also occurs in other texts, but that the combination of partial deliverance with servitude is indeed unique.

[2] S. Japhet, *The Ideology of the Book of Chronicles and Its Place in Biblical Thought* (BEAT, 9), Frankfurt a. M. 1989.

[3] This study is part of a project in which structural and intertextual aspects of Ezra-Nehemiah are being studied. This project is part of a research programme of the Catholic Theological University of Utrecht, named Tradition and Transformation. In a previous study on Ezra 9:6-7 I tried to establish to what extent Ezra joins in with traditional concepts and to what extent he takes a new course. In order to answer that question I made a hermeneutical construct, this is a collection of traditional and contemporary concepts that could be compared with that of Ezra 9:6-7. I published the results of this study in H.W.M. van Grol, "Schuld und Scham: Die Verwurzelung von Ezra 9,6-7 in der Tradition", *EstB* 55 (1997), 29-52. The next step was to test the historical value of this hermeneutical construct. Is

1   Ezra 9:6-15

1.1   Genre and Rhetoric

Ezra 9:6-15 has to be characterized as a *prayer*, but it is also a *sermon*. The story tells that there is an audience (Ezra 9:4) and that this circle increases. They even respond straightaway to what Ezra is doing (Ezra 10:1). Apparently, Ezra's prayer has the effect of a sermon. Shecaniah, the spokesman, refers to his prayer as "the counsel of my lord" (Ezra 10:3) and the community reacts in accordance with Ezra's words.

Even the phraseology itself betrays that the prayer is also a sermon. An important part of the prayer is addressed not to God, but mentions him in the third person to the audience, which is included in the inclusive 'we' (Ezra 9:7-9). The compilation of law texts is quoted in such a way that it is addressed to a group in the second person plural (Ezra 9:11-12). The three questions in Ezra 9:10-14 make more sense as part of a sermon than as part of a prayer. They are rhetorical questions. Especially the second can hardly be seen as a question to God (Ezra 9:13-14a). It is a direct exhortation to the audience: "Are we once again to break your commandments?" I think it is also important that the prayer does end not in a question to God but in a sketch of the situation (Ezra 9:15). God is not the one to react, the community is.[4]

	verse	prayer	sermon
A	6	confession: opening	
B	7-9		*expositio*: old guilt → mercy
A'	10-12	confession: deepening	
B'	13-14		*admonitio*: new guilt → destruction?!
C	15	confession: conclusion	

it present in the text of Ezra itself? Is Ezra really working with older texts and alluding to them? In a lecture for the joint meeting of OTW and SOTS (held at Wedham College, Oxford, July 1997) I analysed two cases of possible allusions in Ezra 9:6-9. I asked whether Ezra 9:6 is a realization of the call to shame in Ezekiel 36:32 or not, and whether the signs of mercy in Ezra 9:8-9 are represented as the fulfilment of 'Isaianic' promises or not. I was able to affirm the first case but remained more doubtful about the second. This lecture was published as H.W.M. van Grol, "Exegesis of the Exile – Exegesis of Scripture? Ezra 9:6-9", in: J.C. de Moor (ed.), *Intertextuality in Ugarit and Israel* (OTS, 40), Leiden 1998, 31-61. During the preparation for that paper I came across the present parallel.

[4]C.F. Keil, *The Books of Ezra, Nehemiah, and Esther*, Grand Rapids, MI 1980 (reprint; the German original was published in Leipzig 1870), 118: "Ezra does not pray for the pardon of their sin, for he desires only to bring the congregation to the knowledge of the greatness of their transgression, and so to invite them to do all that in them lies to atone for their guilt, and to appease God's wrath."

The preceding table visualizes how prayer and sermon alternate. The text starts off as a prayer. Ezra 9:6 is a first confession of the guilt of the mixed marriages, stressing its unprecedented proportions. Then Ezra changes the address and directs himself to the audience (Ezra 9:7-9). He states the actual situation of the community and its recent history. The latter he characterizes as a sequence of deep guilt and punishment followed by mercy, unexpected and only for a very short time thus far. On this exposition he will found – in the second part of his prayer – a warning, an admonition, the essence of his speech: God will react to the new, immense guilt, but not once more with punishment and mercy. He will mercilessly destroy his people.

Therefore Ezra 9:7-9 is an important moment in Ezra's sermon. Ezra emphasizes the essential sequence of guilt and mercy by making the same move twice. Once in vv. 7-8 and then again in v. 9. He enters at length into the precious, tangible signs of mercy. Only then he brings up the imminent guilt of the mixed marriages again, but now penetrating more deeply into the matter (Ezra 9:10).

1.2   The Two Paragraphs Ezra 9:7-9

The preceding analysis of genre and rhetoric is corroborated by an analysis of syntax and stylistics.[5] In the following translation the text hierarchy is marked by way of indentations.

7a "From the days of our fathers to this very day we have been deep in guilt:
7b   because of our iniquities, we have been handed over,
             [we, our kings and our priests, to the kings of the lands,
             [to the sword, to captivity, and to pillage and to shame,
                   [to this very day,
8a   but now, for a brief moment, mercy came to us from YHWH, our God,
8b   in leaving us a remnant
8c   and in giving us a stake in his holy place,
8d   so that our God has brightened our eyes
8e   and given us a little relief in our servitude.

9a   Indeed, servants we are,
9b   but in our servitude our God has not abandoned us,
9c   rather, he has extended to us (his) favour before the kings of Persia,
9d   in giving us relief
9e   to raise again the house of our God
9f   and to set up its ruins,
9g   and in giving us a wall in Judah and in Jerusalem."

---

[5] I presented this analysis in a – soon to be published – paper addressed to the OTW, in Groningen, September 1997: "Structure and Meaning of Ezra 9:6-9". I can only present some of the results here.

Ezra 9:6, 7-8 and 9 are three coherent paragraphs. The second and
the third paragraph are subordinated to the first. This difference in
textual level is marked by an asyndetic construction at the beginning
of v. 7. It interrupts the immediate succession of clauses and serves
as a kind of pause. It is an important, textual turning point. Ezra
9:7-8 and 9 are two parallel paragraphs. V. 9 – starting with כי – is
an emphatic repetition of the vv. 7-8. This repetition is not only a
matter of content – twice a sequence of guilt and mercy –, but also
of linguistics: the two paragraphs exhibit a pattern of syntactic and
semantic balance and verbal repetitions.[6]

1.3   The Place and Function of Servitude

Servitude is mentioned in the first part of this prayer, which turns
out to be a sermon. The two paragraphs Ezra 9:7-8 and 9 reflect on
the present situation of the community in Judah. As mentioned, Ezra
makes the same move twice. What does he say?

In the first paragraph Ezra takes a deep, very old, constant guilt
as his point of departure. This guilt, he says, has been the reason
for destruction and exile. But recently God is showing mercy to his
people: there is a remnant and this remnant lives again in Jerusalem.
In this way God revives the community. But Ezra's last words convey
something else: "a little relief in our servitude". The political servitude, which started with the exile, is apparently continuing. So the
following sequence is found in this paragraph:

guilt→punishment→mercy = a remnant returned/relief in servitude.

A similar line of reasoning can be found in the second paragraph. Its
starting-point is the present situation: "servants we are", which exists
already for a long time: "in our servitude". This political dependence
started with the destruction and the exile. First the subjugation by
the Babylonians, later on the subjection to the Persian kings. In this
situation God has not abandoned his people, but he favours them
through the Persian kings. This implies both "relief", so that they
could rebuild the temple, and a safe place in Judah and Jerusalem.
The sequence is here:

servitude→favour = a temple and a wall/relief in servitude.

The details of both paragraphs can be combined systematically:

- Sin: The guilt is deep, very old, and it drags on to this very day
  (Ezra 9:7a: עונות ||אשמה גדלה).

---

[6] Ezra 9:7a || 9a, 7b-8a || 9b-c, 8b-e || 9d-g. The data are presented in Van Grol,
"Structure and Meaning".

- Punishment: The guilt has been the reason for the subjection to the (Babylonian and Persian) kings, exile and destruction, and this continued up to this very day (Ezra 9:7b: נתן *nif'al* + ביד). At present it takes the shape of political servitude (Ezra 9:8e-9b: עבות, עבדים). This continuity is emphasized so strongly that it is hardly noticeable that things could have been quite different without God's mercy. The notion 'remnant' implies the possibility of total destruction (Ezra 9:13-14: עד־כלה). And this was the perspective of punishment.

- Mercy: God has not abandoned his people (Ezra 9:9b: עזב *qal*), but he has shown mercy to them, recently (Ezra 9:8a: תחנה). This mercy is – in human terms – favour before the kings of Persia (Ezra 9:9c: חסד).

- The actual shape of God's mercy: a remnant returned (Ezra 9:8b-c: שאר *hif'il* + פליטה). The mercy becomes manifest in the mere existence of a rest (*versus* total destruction) and in the return of this rest to Judah (*versus* a continuous exile). There are other tangible signs of mercy: the rebuilding of the temple and political and military safety (Ezra 9:9e-g). All this is qualified with the twice mentioned word 'relief': "a little relief" (Ezra 9:8e, 9d: מחיה מעט), and this word is ambivalent. There is no total destruction and no more exile, but the political servitude is continuing. Therefore: "a little relief in our servitude".

The writer arranged the two paragraphs in such a way that the servitude occupies the centre. The words for servitude form an *anadiplosis*. They are used again emphatically to introduce a new paragraph, which states the same things differently. In this way the tangible signs of mercy stand out against a background of servitude so that they become all the more precious. This is the message that Ezra wants to convey: one has to take special care in order to let God's mercy be continued; it is still so early and so vulnerable. In this way the mentioning of servitude is rhetorically motivated.

2   Servitude in Ezra and Nehemiah

2.1   A Survey

Political servitude has a prominent place in Ezra 9. What is the situation in the rest of Ezra and in Nehemiah? Four derivatives of the root עבד are important: the nouns עבדות, עבודה, and עבד, and the verb

עבד.[7] The noun עבדות is rare in the Bible and is only found in Ezra
9:8, 9 and Nehemiah 9:17. The noun עבודה appears in Ezra-Nehemiah
five times, but only once in the sense of political servitude: Nehemiah
5:18.[8] The noun עבד is found in Ezra-Nehemiah twenty-eight times,
but refers only twice to political servitude: Ezra 9:9 and Nehemiah
9:36.[9] The verb עבד is used only once, meaning something else.[10]

This survey shows that there are only three relevant passages:
Ezra 9, Nehemiah 5 and 9. We already discussed Ezra 9 and we are
going to discuss Nehemiah 9 in the next section. That leaves us with
Nehemiah 5. The noun עבודה is used there in a subordinate clause.

In 5:14-19 Nehemiah deals with an aspect of his behaviour as a
governor. He states that he did not what he was entitled to do: to
'eat the bread' of a governor. This would have involved laying heavy
burdens on the people and demanding bread and wine. Neither did
his servants display such a 'lordly' behaviour. His efforts were not
for profit. In fact, many others ate at his table. Nehemiah motivates
his behaviour in two ways. He says: "But I, I did not do like this,
because of the fear of God" (Neh. 5:15), and: "But even so, I did
not demand the food allowance of the governor, because *the service*
lay heavy upon this people" (Neh. 5:18). His first motive is religious;
the second reason is socio-economic, down to earth. The text reads:
כי־כבדה העבדה על־העם הזה. What does עבודה mean here? It could refer
to the assistance of the people in the reconstruction of Jerusalem's
wall, mentioned in Nehemiah 5:16. But עבודה nowhere else is used as
a reference to the reconstruction of the wall. Normally it is indicated,
as in Nehemiah 5:16, by "the work on this wall", מלאכת החומה הזאת.
In fact, our text refers to the political subjection to the Persians. The
directly preceding section – dealing with the poverty of the people
and the personal slavery within the community – suggests that this
poverty has its root in "the king's tax", מדת המלך (Neh. 5:4). The sub-
ordination to the Persians was such a heavy burden upon the people
that Nehemiah did not want to add some private tax. This political
servitude is so obvious that Nehemiah uses the definite article: "*the*
servitude".[11] So, this passage clarifies the referential meaning of the

[7]See the surveys and bibliographies in C. Westermann, "עבד", *ThHAT*, Bd. 2,
182-200, and H. Ringgren *et al.*, "עבד", *ThWAT*, Bd. 5, 982-1012.

[8]Ezra 8:20; Neh. 3:5; 5:18; 10:33, 38.

[9]Ezra 2:55, 58, 65; 4:11; 5:11; 9:11; Neh. 1:6 (2x), 7, 8, 10, 11 (3x); 2:5, 10, 19,
20; 5:5; 7:57, 60, 67; 9:10, 14; 10:30; 11:3.

[10]Neh. 9:35. The Aramaic verb with – as is well known – a completely different
meaning is used in the Aramaic parts of Ezra 4–7 thirteen times.

[11]Compare Exod. 5:9. It uses the following words to describe the slavery in
Egypt: תכבד העבדה על־האנשים. The combination of the noun עבדה and the verb

nouns עבדות and עבד in Ezra 9. Theological and political language cross each other.

2.2   Nehemiah 9

The noun עבדות in Nehemiah 9:17 refers to the slavery in Egypt, and the noun עבד in 9:36 to the current situation, the political servitude in the Persian period. We will discuss Nehemiah 9:36-37:

36a   "See, we are servants today!
36b   And as for the land which you gave to our fathers
36c   to enjoy its fruit and its good gifts –
36d   see, we are servants upon it!
37a   Its abundant produce goes to the kings
37b   whom you have set over us because of our sins.
37c   They rule over our bodies and over our cattle as they please.
37d   We are in great distress."

Nehemiah 9 contains a penitential prayer and confession of guilt (cf. Neh. 9:2-3). This prayer offers – after the opening (Neh. 9:5-6) – a long retrospective of the history of Israel, from Abram to the exile (Neh. 9:7-31). Then the prayer comes to the point (Neh. 9:32: ועתה); the summary has reached the present day. A supplication is followed by an extensive description of the current situation. Our passage is both the end and the climax of this part and the prayer as a whole (Neh. 9:36-37).

After the prayer is finished the community comes into action. They enter into a pact and so they commit themselves to keep the law of God (Neh. 10).[12] This sequence: first a confession of guilt and a penitential prayer and then a corrective action of the people, in accordance with the law, this sequence resembles that of Ezra 9–10. But there we can observe a dramatic tension – in the relation between Ezra and the community – with the central question whether the people will follow Ezra or not. Therefore, the prayer of Ezra is a sermon as well. This tension is lacking in the communal prayer of Nehemiah 9.

How does this prayer deal with the servitude? The whole passage quoted above is a description of it. And this servitude is the climactic characterization of the current situation of the community. The people are a slave in their own house (Neh. 9:36b-d). This has two sides:

כבד *qal* in one clause occurs only here and in Neh. 5:18. In 1 Kgs 12:4 ∥ 2 Chron. 10:4 the forced labour imposed by Solomon is described with the noun עבדה and the adjective כבד. There מעבדת אביך הקשה parallels מעלו הכבד.

[12]See Japhet, *Ideology*, 112-5 on the meaning of 'covenant' in 2 Chron. 29:10 and Ezra 10:3 ('oath', 'commitment').

1. Taxes and levies: Instead of enjoying the fruits and the good gifts of the land themselves, the people have to give its abundant produce to the kings (Neh. 9:37a-b: ותבואתה מרבה למלכים). In this poetic phrase one recognizes "the king's tax", מדת המלך (Neh. 5:4). Elsewhere tax in kind and heavy burdens are mentioned (Neh. 5:15: הכבידו על־העם).

2. Forced labour: Instead of the freedom to dispose of their own bodies and their own cattle, these are put at the disposal of the kings (Neh. 9:37c: ועל גויתינו משלים ובבהמתנו כרצונם).[13] This 'lordly' behaviour is also mentioned elsewhere (Neh. 5:15: שלטו על־העם).

Thus, the servitude is a political dependence which is evident from taxes and levies as well as forced labour. The texts typify this situation with the following phrases: "great distress", ובצרה גדולה, a unique collocation (Neh. 9:37d), and "all the hardship", כל־התלאה (Neh. 9:32).[14] Japhet gives the following characterization:

> "The book of Ezra-Nehemiah paints a very dark picture of the situation. In fact, de Vaux calls Nehemiah 9 'un cri de détresse,' and Kaufmann offers the following convincing perspective: 'It was a time of servitude and poverty. Nothing could be done without begging, without seeking the indulgence of foreign kings and governors ... His description ... of the period reeks of misery'."[15]

In which line of reasoning is this servitude found and which place does it occupy therein? The prayer portrays the history of the people as a continuing story of sin, punishment and mercy. The same tragedy has taken place time and again. See the following survey:

---

[13] Compare Gen. 47:18; there too the noun גויה is used in a context of forced labour; cf. Gen. 47:21 (BHS!) and 25.

[14] תלאה is found in Exod. 18:8 and Num. 20:14 as a description of the slavery in Egypt and the exodus.

[15] Japhet, Ideology, 502-3. Th. Willi, Juda – Jehud – Israel: Studien zum Selbstverständnis des Judentums in persischer Zeit (FAT, 12), Tübingen 1995, gives a rather different picture of the situation and describes Ezra-Nehemiah as a 'no-nonsense' document, e.g. 89: "Der Verlust der Eigenstaatlichkeit war längst ein fait accompli." Without comment, he contradicts his own opinion in an earlier book, Die Chronik als Auslegung: Untersuchungen zur literarischen Gestaltung der historischen Überlieferung Israels (FRLANT, 106), Göttingen 1972; e.g. 10-1: "der Verlust der Staatlichkeit war die Wunde, die ... immer wieder aufgerissen wurde".

gifts	7-15		20-25						35a
sin	16-17a	18	26	28a	29			33b-34	35b
punishment			27a	28b		30b	32		[36-37]
mercy	17b	19	27b	28c	30a	31			

The paradigm that I try to point out, is impressed upon the reader just by repetition:

- Gifts: Gifts and actions of God both start and accompany the people's history (see also Neh. 9:36b-c).

- Sin: The sins of the people are the source of all the trouble. These sins have a long history: from the journey through the desert to the present day (see also Neh. 9:37b). They can be characterized as ingratitude towards a generously giving God, as a matter of fact as a refusal to listen to the commandments (Neh. 9:34-35).

- Punishment: Sin is followed by punishment and this punishment is called: "all the hardship that has come upon us ... from the days of the Assyrian kings to this very day" (Neh. 9:32). And "on this very day" it is actually the political servitude described in Nehemiah 9:36-37 (עבדים). This state of affairs already pre-supposes mercy, because the original goal of punishment was total destruction (Neh. 9:31: לא־עשיתם כלה). So the political servitude is already a moderated punishment, beyond the mercy.

- Mercy: God did not abandon his people, but was merciful to them. So he did not finish them off (Neh. 9:31: ולא עזבתם). God's mercy is essential. This is indicated by the prayer, where the long name of God is used, as known from Exodus 34, later on summarized as, "you are a gracious and merciful God" (Neh. 9:17, 31: כי אל־חנון ורחום אתה).

The stubbornness of the people who act in defiance of the commandments, is sharply opposed to the unmotivated mercy of God. So the point is certainly that the time has come to repent and to keep the law (Neh. 9:34-35). And the community follows that suggestion in the next chapter.

What is repentance expected to bring about? In the case of Ezra 9 it means that God will not destroy his people. Such an ultimate threat is lacking in Nehemiah 9. God is merciful under all circumstances. Is an improvement of the situation expected? Nowhere in Nehemiah 9–10 something comparable is expressed. Yet this may be inferred from the emphasis on God's gifts: the hope to enjoy again the goods of the land (compare Neh. 9:36b-c).[16]

There is still another important difference between Ezra 9 and Nehemiah 9: in Nehemiah 9 nothing positive is said about the actual situation of the people. Only the negative side is discussed. No word about a returned remnant , no relief. Now, the line of reasoning of Nehemiah 9 can be formulated as follows:

$$\text{gifts} \rightarrow \text{sin} \rightarrow \text{punishment} \rightarrow \text{mercy} = \text{servitude}$$

I suppose that the two differences between Ezra 9 and Nehemiah 9 mentioned above, are linked and have something to do with the difference in rhetorical function. The function of the prayer/sermon in Ezra 9 is keep the people away from *new* sinful behaviour. Therefore it is emphasized that God has just recently been merciful to his people. This mercy is at stake. The function of the prayer in Nehemiah 9 is to sketch the background for the pact in Nehemiah 10.[17] The people will break with their *old* sinful behaviour. Therefore the hopeless history of misery and servitude is emphasized, a history in which they threw away the gifts of God.

2.3   A Contemporary Paradigm

The sequences of Ezra 9 and Nehemiah 9 are *grosso modo* similar. The differences can be noticed. The outlines are similar:

$$[\text{gifts} \rightarrow] \text{ sin} \rightarrow \text{punishment} \rightarrow \text{mercy} = [\text{relief in}] \text{ servitude}$$

This sequence constitutes a paradigm that could help the community in Judah to make sense of their current, political situation. It has to be realized – in my opinion – that the subjection of the province Judah to the Persians was not something natural. Of course, such a servitude is never wished for, humanly. My concern, however, is what is natural in a theological sense and what not. There is an abundance of texts that make very clear that after a punishment consisting of destruction and exile the people may expect forgiveness and restoration.[18] The usual paradigm seems to be:

---

[16]Cf. H.G.M. Williamson, *Israel in the Books of Chronicles*, Cambridge 1977, 67-8: "neither is there any indication that confession of sin leads to restoration (Ezr. 9, Neh. 9)".

[17]If the prayer is dated to the exilic period and situated in the land itself (cf. H.G.M. Williamson, "Structure and Historiography in Nehemiah 9", in: M. Goshen-Gottstein [ed.], *Panel Sessions: Bible Studies and Ancient Near East* [Proceedings of the Ninth World Congress of Jewish Studies, 7], Jerusalem 1986, 117-31) of course a change in perspective between the original text and the later redaction has to be accepted.

[18]Jer. 25:11-14; 30:8-9; Ezek. 34:27; 2 Chron. 36:20; compare Isa. 14:1-4; Zech. 2:11-13 [7-9].

$$\text{sin} \rightarrow \text{punishment} \rightarrow \text{mercy} = \text{restoration}$$

The story of the Exodus from Egypt is so powerful, because it deals with liberation from bondage, with the movement from exile and slavery to one's own land and freedom.[19] What is attractive about a story that moves from servitude to servitude? But that exactly is the post-exilic reality according to the texts of Ezra and Nehemiah. Destruction and exile were not followed by a complete restoration, but, on the contrary, by "a little relief" and a continuation of servitude. Actually, it is emphasized, one should be glad that God did destroy his people not completely. This is the only way to understand the meaning of mercy in this context. The current situation gives rise to a new paradigm:

$$\text{sin} \rightarrow \text{punishment} \rightarrow \text{mercy} = \text{a little relief} + \text{a continuing servitude}$$

3   2 Chronicles 12:1-12

3.1   Text and Structure

2 Chronicles 12:1-12 is a story about the raid by pharaoh Shishak into Judah and his march on Jerusalem:

A	1a	"It came to pass,
	1b	when Rehoboam had consolidated his royal rule
	1c	and had become powerful,
	1d	that he abandoned the law of YHWH, he and all Israel with him.
B	2a	It came to pass in the fifth year of king Rehoboam
	2b	that Shishak, king of Egypt, marched on Jerusalem
	2c	– because they had become unfaithful to YHWH –
	3	with twelve hundred chariots (...)
	4a	and he captured the fortified cities of Judah
	4b	and came as far as Jerusalem.
C	5a	Then Shemaiah the prophet came to Rehoboam and the leaders of Judah,
	5b	who had gathered at Jerusalem running before Shishak.
	5c	He said to them:
	5d	'Thus says YHWH:
	5e	"You, you have abandoned me
	5f	so I for my part, I have abandoned you to the hand of Shishak".'
D	6a	The leaders of Israel and the king humbled themselves.
	6c	They said:
	6d	'YHWH is just.'

---

[19]The "idea that exile and restoration paralleled Israel's bondage in Egypt and the exodus" can be found in the books of Ezekiel, Jeremiah and Second Isaiah; see Japhet, *Ideology*, 385.

C   7a   When YHWH saw
    7b   that they had humbled themselves,
    7c   the word of YHWH came to Shemaiah:
    7d   "They have humbled themselves,
    7e   so I will not destroy them;
    7f   I will give them some deliverance,
    7g   and my wrath will not be poured out on Jerusalem by
          the hand of Shishak;
    8a   but they will become his servants,
    8b   then they will learn my service and the service of
          the kingdoms of the lands."

B   9a   So Shishak, king of Egypt, marched on Jerusalem
    9b   and he took away the treasures (...).
    10-11 (the reaction of Rehoboam on a matter of detail)

A   12a   Because he had humbled himself,
    12b   the anger of YHWH turned away from him,
    12c   so as not to destroy (him) completely;
    12d   in Judah, too, good things were found."

The story is clear to a large extent. I distinguished seven paragraphs:
2 Chron. 12:1, 2-4, 5, 6, 7-8, 9-11, 12, and marked them in the layout
of the translation. The events follow one another in a logical sequence.
Only the last paragraph is reflective and looks back.[20] The text has a
more or less concentric structure:[21]

1	A			Intro
2-4		B		Shishak's march on Jerusalem
5			C	A word of God: judgment
6				D Repentance: to humble oneself
7-8			C	A word of God: mercy
9-11		B		Shishak's pillaging of Jerusalem
12	A			End

---

[20] The story runs on to 2 Chron. 12:12. 2 Chron. 12:13, the beginning of the
next passage, refers back to 2 Chron. 12:1a-c.

[21] I. Kalimi, *Zur Geschichtsschreibung des Chronisten: Literarisch-historiogra-
phische Abweichungen der Chronik von ihren Paralleltexten in den Samuel- und
Königsbüchern* (BZAW, 226), Berlin 1995, 238, says: "Der Vers 2 Chr 12,9a fun-
giert als Wiederaufnahme von V. 2b (|| 1 Kön, 14,25b), um den Einschub 2 Chr
12,2c-8 zu überbrücken". He failed to notice that this literary technique has some
stylistic quality. H.G.M. Williamson, *Ezra and Nehemiah* (OTGu), Sheffield 1987,
45, uses the term 'repetitive resumption', that marks the material in between as
a digression. He has just as little eye for the literary shape of the resulting text as
Kalimi. Cf. W.M. Schniedewind, *The Word of God in Transition: From Prophet
to Exegete in the Second Temple Period* (JSOT.S, 197), Sheffield 1995, 87 and
n. 13.

It starts with sin. Rehoboam and his people abandon the law of YHWH (2 Chron. 12:1). Punishment follows immediately. Pharaoh Shishak raids into Judah, captures the fortified cities and lays siege to the walls of Jerusalem (2 Chron. 12:2-4). Then a quick transformation takes place: prophetic statement→repentance→mercy. The prophet Shemaiah gets in touch with the king and the leaders and brings them a word of God in which he points out the connection between the events: sin→punishment. The addressees humble themselves and put YHWH in the right. God reacts by adjusting the punishment. He will not destroy Judah completely. He will give "some deliverance". There will be servitude instead of complete destruction. Judah will be subjected to Shishak (2 Chron. 12:5-8). In the fourth paragraph Shishak continues his campaign by pillaging temple and palace. In this way the servitude begins to take shape (2 Chron. 12:9-11). The last paragraph is a summary and draws the moral from this story: God spares the one who humbles himself and repents (2 Chron. 12:12).

It is worth the effort to see these events in a systematic sequence and to list the words that are used in the subsequent stages:

- Sin: Rehoboam and all Israel with him abandoned the law of YHWH (2 Chron. 12:1d: עזב *qal*), abandoned YHWH himself (2 Chron. 12:5e). So they became unfaithful to YHWH (2 Chron. 12:2c: מעל *qal* + ־ב).

- Punishment: Punishment follows immediately,[22] and adequately: they abandoned God, he abandons them to the hand of Shishak (2 Chron. 12:5f: עזב *qal*).[23] He intends in his anger (אף־יהוה) to destroy Judah completely (2 Chron. 12:12b-c: להשחית לכלה; compare 2 Chron. 12:7e). He will pour out his wrath on Jerusalem by the hand of Shishak (2 Chron. 12:7g: נתך *qal* + חמתי). So Shishak marches on Jerusalem, captures the fortified cities of Judah and is about to take Jerusalem.

- Repentance: Stimulated by the words of Shemaiah the prophet, the leaders of Israel and the king humble themselves (2 Chron. 12:6a, 7b, 7d, 12a: כנע *nif'al*). They admit: "YHWH is just" (2 Chron. 12:6c: צדיק יהוה).

---

[22] For three years everything goes well (2 Chron. 11:17). The sin of Rehoboam comes in the fourth year. Shishak's campaign follows in the fifth year. See Japhet, *Ideology*, 169.

[23] A nice play on the double meaning of the verb. Cf. Japhet, *Ideology*, 170, n. 493.

- Mercy: The story has no word for mercy.[24] The anger of YHWH turns away from Rehoboam (2 Chron. 12:12b: שוב qal + ממנו). God gives them "some deliverance"[25] (2 Chron. 12:7g: כמעט לפליטה), i.e. no complete destruction (2 Chron. 12:7e, 7g, 12c), but political servitude. They will become the servants of Shishak (2 Chron. 12:8a-b: עבודה ממלכות הארצות, עבדים), who starts off by pillaging temple and palace (2 Chron. 12:9).

This sequence resembles the paradigm of Ezra and Nehemiah, where we found:

sin→punishment→mercy = a little relief + a continuing servitude.

Here we find:

sin→punishment→repentance→mercy = some deliverance + servitude.

Moreover, the words used are mostly the same as or similar to those in Ezra and Nehemiah.[26]

3.2   An Accidental Resemblance?

Does 2 Chronicles 12 indeed exhibit the same paradigm as Ezra 9 and Nehemiah 9, or is the resemblance accidental?

The story of 2 Chronicles 12 cannot be found in the book of Kings. It belongs to the material exclusive to the book of Chronicles.[27] It can, therefore, be expected to be a typically chronistic story. Sara Japhet laid out the ideology of the Chronicler.[28] She tried to characterize the many different aspects of the chronistic realm of ideas in a systematic way. Her contribution to the field has not been surpassed yet.[29] It is possible and sensible to compare the paradigm I found in Ezra 9 and Nehemiah 9 with Japhet's chronistic ideology. There are some essential differences:

---

[24] Japhet, *Ideology*, 190, notes that "Chronicles contains only two mentions of YHWH's compassion for His people" (2 Chron. 30:6-9 and 36:15; cf. 1 Chron. 21:13 ‖ 2 Sam. 24:14).

[25] The meaning of this phrase is not exactly clear. There are two meaningful interpretations: "some deliverance", and "as a little remnant". See the discussion in Schniedewind, *Transition*, 87 n.12.

[26] These words are listed in the presentation of the sequences (§§ 1.3, 2.2 and 3.1) and can be compared easily. Moreover, the roots עזב and עבד are found collocated only in 2 Chron. 12 and Ezra 9. Another striking parallel: Ezra 9:8: ולתתנו מחיה – 2 Chron. 12:7: ונתתי להם כמעט לפליטה מעט.

[27] To be precise, 2 Chron. 12:1-12 parallels 1 Kgs 14:25-28. Thus, the Chronicler repeats what we now find in 2 Chron. 12:2a-b, 9-11, and elaborates on this with his own story; Japhet, *Ideology*, 57-8.

[28] Japhet, *Ideology* (see above, n.2).

[29] Little by little, a more fundamental criticism is now beginning to take shape, for example in Schniedewind, *Transition*, and especially B.E. Kelly, *Retribution and Eschatology in Chronicles* (JSOT.S, 211), Sheffield 1996.

1. In Ezra 9 and Nehemiah 9 sin is seen in a context of sin, a history of sin. In Chronicles this history is lacking. There can be no 'leftover' punishment or continued punishment. Chronicles shows a policy of tit for tat.[30] Sin is punished immediately and completely. Therefore, the servitude in 2 Chronicles 12 is an immediate punishment. But the servitude in Ezra and Nehemiah has started in the past and continues in the present. It is not a direct punishment but a continuing punishment.

2. There is a crisis in Ezra-Nehemiah and a need to understand the state of affairs: the destruction of Judah, the exile and the continuing servitude. Chronicles is not concerned with things like this. Chronicles is characterized by 'an overall religious system': good and bad are systematized and demonstrated in each period of the history of Judah.[31] This means that the servitude of Ezra-Nehemiah was a tangible and painful reality and that of Chronicles an ideological construct.

3. Chronicles has a balanced system of sin and punishment and there repentance gets in. Sin is punished, but punishment can be averted by repentance. Repentance is rewarded with mercy. This results in the sequence: sin→punishment→repentance→mercy. In Ezra 9 and Nehemiah 9 repentance is lacking. Mercy is free, it is gratuitous.

These three differences make it difficult to claim that 2 Chronicles 12 contains our paradigm. The resemblance between 2 Chronicles 12 on the one hand and Ezra 9 and Nehemiah 9 on the other seems to be accidental. How could the Chronicler make use of a paradigm that helps to understand the continuing servitude under the Persians?

But things are not that easy. It is not difficult to find our paradigm contradictory to chronistic ideology, but that does not explain the story in 2 Chronicles 12. In fact, the story itself is inconsistent with this chronistic ideology!

Repentance plays a central part in the story of 2 Chronicles 12. According to the chronistic ideology repentance should be rewarded with mercy. But if that is right, the story's servitude is inexplicable. After all, there was repentance! Why, for all their repentance, were king and people punished with servitude? Why is there no complete deliverance? 2 Chronicles 12 is inconsistent. Why?

---

[30] See the conclusions of Japhet, *Ideology*, 164-5; cf. Kalimi, *Geschichtsschreibung*, 165-71: "Maß für Maß", and Willi, *Chronik*, 212, n. 29.

[31] Cf. Japhet, *Ideology*, 153-6.

Japhet is unconvincing on this point. She shows that the "Chronicles' reworking of historical events" in Kings involves, among other
things, that "every success, whether personal or public, is considered
a reward. Whenever a possible reward is mentioned without the appropriate causes for it, the Chronicler provides the source of merit".
One of her examples is that "the penitence of Rehoboam and Judah
provides an explanation for the outcome of Shishak's campaign".[32]
This is only partly true.

One could, of course, say that the Chronicler could not be systematic or consistent because his *Vorlage* had already stated *expressis
verbis* the outcome of Shishak's campaign: Shishak carried off the
treasures of temple and palace. The Chronicler merely explained the
transformation of total destruction into the pillaging of Jerusalem.
And he could do so only by supposing, *casu quo* introducing, repentance. The result is a real but unavoidable inconsistency.[33]

However, who says that the originally intended punishment was
total destruction? It seems to be the Chronicler himself. He is making
up this story. He could have considered the pillaging of Jerusalem an
adequate punishment for the sin of Rehoboam and Judah.[34] He did
not need this story of total destruction and repentance! So, why did
he write it? Japhet asks herself: "Given that divine justice is speedy
and all-embracing, what place is there for human repentance? Can it
have any effect?"[35] and finds "the following principle" in Chronicles:
"a sinner must be warned and asked to repent ... Repentance has the
power to change destiny, personal and national. It can counteract the
effects of even the worst sin".[36] But if that is right, then one has to
admit that the repentance in 2 Chronicles 12 was not that effective.

My conclusion is that the *partial* deliverance in 2 Chronicles 12
cannot be explained within the chronistic system of retribution as
laid out by Japhet. It is this partial deliverance that introduces the
servitude, the heart of our paradigm. There seems to be some reason
to put Japhet's systematization of the chronistic ideology in perspective,[37] and have another look at this rather unique story of 2 Chron. 12.

---

[32] Japhet, *Ideology*, 166-7, and n. 487.

[33] This appears to be the position of R.K. Duke, *The Persuasive Appeal of the
Chronicler: A Rhetorical Analysis* (JSOT.S, 88), Sheffield 1990, 68-9, 94-5 and
131-2.

[34] Japhet, *Ideology*, 169, ignores this and plays down the pillaging: "the attack
is not all that disastrous".

[35] Japhet, *Ideology*, 175-6, and the discussion, 176-91.

[36] Japhet, *Ideology*, 190; cf. Williamson, *Israel*, 113.

[37] Kelly, *Retribution*, especially plays down the systematic side of the chronistic
ideology according to Japhet. Then he states that the book does intend not to

3.3   A Well Designed Parable

So I will henceforth assume that the Chronicler deliberately constructs a partial deliverance, and that he intends to bring up the theme of servitude in his story, and that the point of the story can be found in the motive that God himself formulates in the prophetic word: "they will become his servants, then they will learn my service and the service of the kingdoms of the lands". The theme of servitude has not been drawn from the *Vorlage*, and its presence is prominent and intentional. Are we able to understand this servitude without referring to the political servitude that was the day-to-day reality of writer and readers – a reality that also had its effect on Ezra 9 and Nehemiah 9?! William Schniedewind emphasizes the topical, homiletic function of the Chronistic stories:

> "It remains to ask, what was the Chronicler's purpose? I believe that the Chronicler saw himself in a role similar to that of his inspired messengers. The Chronicler speaks primarily to the people – that is, to the post-exilic community ... As a corpus, the speeches in Chronicles cannot be understood simply by the context of their First Temple period referents; they are primarily speeches to the post-exilic community. We may take, as an example, the prophet Shemaiah's speech ... The language of Shemaiah's speech is remarkably similar to a sermon that Ezra delivers to the post-exilic returnees (Ezra 9.6-9) and its references to a 'remnant' and 'serving the kingdoms of the world' have more relevance to the post-exilic community than to the historical context of Shishak's invasion."[38]

If the story of the Chronicler really goes into the experiences and the needs of the readers of his time, and if the Chronicler, in his story

---

show how retribution works consistently throughout history, but rather how God's *mercy* is present time and again. "There is no balance between blessing, which comes *consistently* whenever Israel 'seeks YAHWEH', and judgment, which can be mitigated or remitted entirely", Kelly, *Retribution*, 108; original italics; cf. 42 and 87.

[38]Schniedewind, *Transition*, 250-1; see 86-91 for an analysis of the story. Cf. W.M. Schniedewind, "Prophets and Prophecy in the Books of Chronicles", in: M.P. Graham *et al.* (eds.), *The Chronicler as Historian* (JSOT.S, 238), Sheffield 1997, 204-24, esp. 222.

about the servitude in the time of Rehoboam, actually deals with the contemporary servitude, what then does he mean? What is the function of his text? I suggest that the story stipulates the following:

- The contemporary servitude, experienced every day, has to be associated with mercy. It is an escape from total destruction.[39] This view can also be found in the two other texts discussed above, especially in Ezra 9.

- This time of servitude is a time of learning; learning the difference between "the service of the kingdoms of the lands" and that of God.[40] In this respect 2 Chronicles 12 goes beyond Ezra 9 and Nehemiah 9. Both other texts offer an explanation for the political servitude (i.e. sin), and offer comfort by contrasting servitude and total destruction, but this story points to a surpassing intention of God. Servitude as a process of learning! This view on servitude opens up a new perspective. It is an indirect invitation to turn away from the service of the kingdoms of the lands (and their gods) and enter into the service of God with total abandon.

- An attitude of (permanent) humility, i.e. repentance, matches this service of God. This view is not exclusive to this story but it is just one of the main themes of the book.[41]

- If one considers the subjection to the Persians as a moment of learning, then thereby a limit is set.[42] The end of this servitude lies hidden in repentance, an attitude of permanent humbling oneself, in being the servant of God. We noticed that Ezra 9 does not presuppose that the political servitude to the Persians would come to an end, and that such an end is only hoped for in

---

[39]Therefore, 'partial deliverance' is a more appropriate term then 'restrictive punishment'.

[40]2 Chron. 12:8b is unanimously read: "to learn the difference between ... and ...". See A.B. Ehrlich, *Randglossen zur Hebräischen Bibel*, Bd. 7, Hildesheim 1968 (= Leipzig, 1914), 361 and 127.

[41]Kelly, *Retribution*, 51-6, discusses the following concepts: 'seeking Jahweh' (דרש and בקש), prayer (התפלל), repentance (שוב) and 'humbling oneself' (כנע). See also Japhet, *Ideology*, 199-202 and 264.

[42]Kelly, *Retribution*, 211, seems to suggest the same: "Even if the Chronicler took a basically positive view of Persian rule ..., nevertheless the writer was keenly aware *that such a subject condition was a consequence of sin (which might be reversed by repentance)*, and that there remained a great difference between '(Yahweh's) service and the service of the kingdoms of the countries' (2 Chron. 12.8)" (my italics, HvG).

Nehemiah 9. The bitterness of Ezra 9 and especially Nehemiah 9 is absent in 2 Chronicles 12; there the termination of the political servitude is implied from the beginning.[43]

A final question: what are the reasons for the particular setting of this story (*Sitz in der Literatur*)? Throntveit states: "Thus, the pericope functions as a paradigmatic introduction to the prophetic addresses that will follow".[44] But this view is too formal and the specific details of this story are not taken into account. The story contains the first of the Chronicler's prophetic addresses after the – ideal – period of the united monarchy. The Chronicler creates a strong connection with the experiences of his own time straight away in this first speech. In this way he arranges his material so that history can function as a parable for his own time, a time that Persian rule is coming to an end.

---

[43] If the book of Chronicles has to be dated to the early Ptolemaic period (see the contribution of Sara Japhet to this volume), the story could convey the hope that political changes, i.e. the end of Persian rule, imply the forthcoming end of the political servitude.

[44] M.A. Throntveit, "The Chronicler's Speeches and Historical Reconstruction", in: Graham *et al.* (eds.), *The Chronicler as Historian*, 225-45, here 239.

Herbert Niehr *Tübingen – Germany*

Religio-Historical Aspects of the 'Early Post-Exilic' Period

1 Introduction

The definition of the 'early post-exilic' period is not as clear as it might seem at first sight. The beginnings of this period are of course given by Cyrus II's conquest of Babylon in 539 BCE. But where should one delimit the close of this period, especially in regard to Jerusalem and Judah/Yehud? As will be demonstrated below, a first important caesura is made by the ending of the Davidic dynasty around 500 BCE.

In trying to research the religio-historical aspects of the 'early post-exilic' period as so delimited, two intricate problems need first to be discussed.

The first problem lies in the sources for this period. On the one hand we have abundant archaeological material at our disposal[1] but on the other hand we have only very few and fragmentary written primary sources from Palestine itself.[2] So the main textual sources are delivered by the Old Testament, especially the books of Haggai and Zechariah. Our second problem consists in the fact that it is impossible to verify a break between the time and religion before 586 BCE and the time and religion after 586 BCE. Wellhausen's classical view, according to which after 586 BCE only "verwahrloste, ihrer Führer beraubte, halbheidnische Bauern"[3] dwelt the country, can no longer be taken as a point of departure for historical inquiry. It is preferable to reckon with long-term changes which were motivated by more then just the events of 586 BCE. So after 586 BCE the element of continuity prevails as has been clearly demonstrated by H. Barstad:

---

[1]For an archaeological overview of this period, cf. E. Stern, *Material Culture of the Land of the Bible in the Persian Period 538-332* BCE, Warminster – Jerusalem 1982; H. Weippert, *Palästina in vorhellenistischer Zeit* (HdA, Vorderasien 2/1), München 1988, 682-718; O. Keel, C. Uehlinger, *Göttinnen, Götter und Gottessymbole* (QD, 134), Freiburg 1992, 430-52; C. Uehlinger, "Figurative Policy, Propaganda und Prophetie", in: J.A. Emerton (ed.), *Congress Volume Cambridge 1995* (VT.S, 66), Leiden 1997, 297-349, esp. 332-5; H.M. Barstad, *The Myth of the Empty Land* (SO.S, 28), Oslo 1996, 47-55.

[2]Cf. the overview in Weippert, *Palästina*, 693-7.

[3]J. Wellhausen, "Die Rückkehr der Juden aus dem babylonischen Exil", *NGWG.PH*, Göttingen 1885, 166-86, esp. 184.

"The very sharp distinction made between 'before and after 586', overshadowing the fact that we are dealing with a continuous culture, is inappropriate, and should be regarded as 'mythical' rather than 'historical'. According to the sources that we do have access to, sources that are steadily growing in number and importance, there are clear indications of cultural and material continuity before and after 586, rather than an enormous gap. The gap is rather to be considered a construction of later tradition."[4]

This deconstruction of the Old Testament conception of an exile in recent scholarship forces us to admit, therefore, that the fall of Babylon in 539 BCE and the overlordship of Cyrus II did not immediately affect life and religion in Palestine. Palestine became part of the Persian orbit only under Cambyses in 525 BCE.

Our first conclusion therefore must be that immediately after 586 BCE and even after 539 BCE there was no considerable change in the religious history of Judah (or Yehud). The religio-historical aspects of the so-called 'early post-exilic' period are to be collected from various intimately connected areas of religion: Royalty – temple – theology – piety.

2   Religio-Historical Aspects of Continuity and Change

2.1   Royalty

2.1.1   Kings

The deportation of the Judahite king Jehoiachin in 597 BCE and the destruction of Jerusalem and the deportation of Zedekiah in 586 BCE did not mark the end of the Davidic dynasty as is usually believed in Old Testament scholarship.

In this context it is interesting to note that the Dtr. work closes with the report of the amnesty for king Jehoiachin (2 Kgs 25:27-30). Already in 1956 E. Janssen had pointed out correctly:

"Es ist bezeichnend, daß der Deuteronomist gerade in der Begnadigung des Jojachin den Anfang der Juda wieder zuteil werdenden Gnade Jahwes sieht und nicht in irgendeinem anderen Ereignis oder Zustand jener Zeit, etwa daß immer noch die Masse des Volkes im Lande wohnen durfte.

---

[4]Barstad, *Myth*, 8; and still important is E. Janssen, *Juda in der Exilszeit* (FRLANT, 69), Göttingen 1956.

> Daß es gerade die Begnadigung des Königs war, zeigt,
> daß das Königtum nach einer Anschauung jener Zeit in
> dem wiederhergestellten Lande seinen Platz einnehmen
> sollte."[5]

So it is important to stress that Jehoiachin was king until his death, even though he had been deported to Babylon.[6]

There are also indications that Gedaliah, who replaced Zedekiah, was made king by the Babylonians. Gedaliah's royal rank was, however, suppressed by the compilers of the Dtr. work because Gedaliah was not of Davidic offspring.[7] It was perhaps Gedaliah's assassination which made it advisable for the Babylonians to take further governors of Judah from the house of David.

When we proceed into the later history of Judah/Yehud we come upon Sheshbazzar and Zerubbabel.[8] Sheshbazzar's status is not easy to grasp; the titles of נָשִׂיא (Ezra 1:8) and פֶּחָה (Neh. 5:18) are ascribed to him in later sources. The royal status held by Zerubbabel is clearly alluded to in the book of Haggai where YHWH says to him: "I will take you, Zerubbabel son of Shealtiel, my servant, and will wear you as a signet-ring; for you it is that I have chosen." (Hag. 2:23).[9] Also the book of Zechariah alludes to the royal status of Zerubbabel who sits on a throne and reigns (Zech. 6:13). In other texts in the book of Haggai Zerubbabel is called 'governor' (Hag. 1:1; 2:12.21). According to 1 Chron. 3:17-24 Zerubbabel was of Davidic descent. This tension between Zerubbabel's twofold rank as royal figure and governor has provoked some scholars to undertake further research.

Thus historical scholarship has brought forward some interesting aspects in this context. Some years ago P. Sacchi[10] argued that the Davidic monarchy did not automatically end with the disaster of 586 BCE. Jehoiachin kept the title of 'king' and Judah remained a Babylonian province. Besides, it is important to note that Sheshbazzar was of Davidic origin as was also his successor, his nephew Zerubbabel. So Sheshbazzar and Zerubbabel were both Judaean kings and Persian

---

[5] Janssen, *Juda in der Exilszeit*, 79.

[6] Cf. P. Sacchi, "L'esilio e la fine della monarchia davidica", *Henoch* 11 (1989), 131-48, esp. 137-9.

[7] Cf. J.M. Miller, J.H. Hayes, *A History of Ancient Israel and Judah*, London 1986, 421-4.

[8] For these persons cf. esp. S. Japhet, "Sheshbazzar and Zerubbabel: Against the Background of the Historical and Religious Tendencies of Ezra-Nehemiah", *ZAW* 94 (1982), 66-98; part 2, *ZAW* 95 (1983), 218-29.

[9] Translations of Old Testament texts are taken from the New English Bible.

[10] Cf. Sacchi, "L'esilio".

governors. It was only under Darius I between 520 and 515 BCE that the Davidic monarchy came to an end by a civil war which was won by the priests.

This line of argument advanced by Sacchi was reinforced by F. Bianchi and A. Lemaire. F. Bianchi declared:

> "Les textes bibliques et une série de parallèles proche-orientaux permettent à notre avis d'affirmer que la dynastie davidique, pendant les soixante-dix années qui vont de la chute de Jérusalem (586) à la reconstruction du temple (515), a continué à gouverner en tant qu'Etat vassal de la monarchie chaldéenne, puis perse. Nous essaierons donc de démontrer que Jéchonias, Sheshbassar et Zorobabel furent des véritables rois." [11]

A. Lemaire was able to show that Ṣemach was a proper name, not a symbolical one. These names, Ṣemach and Zerubbabel, were alternatively used in two cultures. The status of Judah/Yehud up to and including the time of Zerubbabel is explained by Lemaire as a "province proche d'un royaume vassal". [12] So the status of Judah/Yehud as a province and a vassal kingdom were not mutually exclusive. It seems that Zerubbabel was succeeded by his second son and then by his son-in-law, so that only gradually was the Davidic lineage abandoned. The Davidic dynasty came to an end only around 500 BCE. Zerubbabel and his immediate successors were vassal kings who acknowledged Persian overlordship. [13]

As our sources outside and within the Old Testament are silent about the specific end of the Davidic dynasty, we cannot verify the last-mentioned points, although they seem to be very likely. This is especially so because in some parts of the Persian Empire (e.g. in Phoenicia) formerly independent kings continued their rule as vassal kings of the Persians. [14]

---

[11] F. Bianchi, "Zorobabele re di Giuda", *Henoch* 13 (1991), 133-50; Idem, "Le rôle de Zerobabel et de la dynastie davidique en Judée du VIᵉ siècle au IIᵉ av. J.C.", *Trans* 7 (1994), 153-66, esp. 154.

[12] A. Lemaire, "Zorobabel et la Judée à la lumière de l'épigraphie (Fin du VIᵉ s.av. J.-C.)", *RB* 103 (1996), 48-57.

[13] Cf. Lemaire, "Zorobabel et la Judée", 56-7.

[14] Cf. J. Elay, "The Phoenician Cities in the Persian Period," *JANES* 12 (1980), 13-28; Idem, *Sidon: cité autonome de l'empire perse*, Paris 1988, esp. 107-60; 235-56.

2.1.2   Priests

Just as the Davidic lineage was not interrupted after 586 BCE, so the
priestly lineage continued also. According to 1 Chron. 5:40-41 the high
priest Jehoshua was the grandson of the priest Seraiah who had been
deported to Ribla and was executed there (2 Kgs 25:18). Seraiah's
title had been כֹּהֵן רֹאשׁ, indicating that he was the chief priest of the
First Temple. It is not by chance that his grandson became high priest
(כֹּהֵן גָּדֹול) during the early Achaemenid period. The title of high priest
is new in the Persian period. It first occurs in the book of Zechariah;
our first primary evidence stems from the Elephantine papyri around
410/407 BCE (cf. TAD A4.7:18; A4.8:17).[15]

It can furthermore be seen from the Old Testament that there
came to be an equality between the vassal king or governor and the
high priest. According to Zech. 4:1-14 the two olive-trees standing
near the מְנֹורָה in the temple represent the two anointed ones: the
king and the high priest. In other words: the Judaean vassal kings
or governors, some of whom were of Davidic origin, had to share
their political power with the highest representation of the Jerusalem
temple, the high priest.

According to Zech. 6:13 Zerubbabel (= Ṣemach) will build the
temple of the Lord, he will assume royal dignity and he will be seated
on the throne; he will govern with a priest at his right side and they
will procure peace for the land. The crown, however, will be put on
the head of the high priest and it will remain in the temple (6:11, 14).

Here in Zech. 6:11 we have a later priestly correction of an original
crowning of Zerubbabel, because the following sentence in v. 12 is
directed towards Ṣemach (=Zerubbabel).[16]

The precise course of the transition of political power from the
house of David to the high priest remains unclear to us. "Tout laisse
croire qu'à la fin du VIe siècle, la mort de Zorobabel ne fit que mar-
quer le début du processus d'affaiblissement de la monarchie (desti-
tution progressive de la lignée davidique, non sa disparition) au profit
du sacerdoce".[17] About 100 years later there were Persian governors
in Judaea, e.g. Bagohi is attested in the Elephantine papyri (TAD

---

[15] For the edition and translation of all Elephantine texts quoted in this article
cf. B. Porten, A. Yardeni, *Textbook of Aramaic Documents from Ancient Egypt*,
Vol. 1, Jerusalem 1986.

[16] For the difficulties of this text see A.S. van der Woude, "Serrubabel und die
messianischen Erwartungen bei Sacharja", *ZAW* 100 (1988), 138-56, esp. 147-50;
P.L. Reddit, "Zerubbabel, Joshua, and the Night Visions of Zechariah", *CBQ* 54
(1992), 249-59, esp. 251-3, 256.

[17] Bianchi, "Zorobabele re", 163.

A4.7:1; A4.8:1; A4.9:1). So priesthood does not simply replace the kings of the house of David after Zerubbabel's death. But it could be that after Zerubbabel the governors were no longer of Davidic origin. They confined themselves to military and administrative duties, whereas cultic affairs were in the hands of the high priest. It remains open to mere speculation whether the honorific position of the נָשִׂיא in the temple as planned in Ezek. 40-48 ever came true in this manner.

The law of the king who is to obey the priestly administrated Torah according to Deut. 17:14-20 also fits very well into this period.[18]

In the course of time we can see the high priests replacing the Davidic kings: The high priest is anointed (Exod. 29:7; Lev. 8:12), he wears official robes (Exod. 28:1-43; 39:1-31) and a crown (Exod. 28:36-38; 39:30-31; Zech. 6:11), he sits on a throne (Zech. 6:13)[19] and he is the mediator between god and mankind (Lev. 17).

Priests were also responsible for the end of the royal cult of the dead in Jerusalem. Throughout the times of the Davidic kings we do not have available any indications of the practice of this cult in Jerusalem. Its practice is proven only by its criticism in Ezek. 43:7-9. This text tries to suppress the worship of dead kings which was originally an important element of the temple cult. This can be clearly seen in Aramean cult places like Sam'al and Guzana in Northern Syria.[20] Now by Ezekiel or his school who also belong to priestly circles the royal cult of the dead is criticized as defiling YHWH's holy name. So a rigid opposition developed between the cult of the dead kings and the cult in the temple. As concerns the date of this text, it is not likely that such a sharp criticism of the royal cult of the dead would have been possible during Zerubbabel's lifetime or even immediately after his death.[21] This critique betrays a priestly ambition to obtain a monopoly of the cult in the Jerusalem temple.

---

[18] Cf. for an overview of datings e.g. F. García López, "Le roi d'Israël: Deut. 17,14-20", in: N. Lohfink (ed.), *Das Deuteronomium* (BEThL, 68), Leuven 1985, 277-97; U. Rüterswörden, *Von der politischen Gemeinschaft zur Gemeinde* (BBB, 65), Frankfurt 1987, 50-66, 106-11.

[19] For the difficulties of this text cf. H.-J. Fabry, "כִּסֵּא", in: *ThWAT*, Bd. 4, 1982-4, 247-72, esp. 265-6.

[20] Cf. H. Niehr, "Zum Totenkult der Könige von Sam'al im 9. und 8. Jh. v. Chr.", *SEL* 11 (1994), 57-73.

[21] Contrary to most scholars, I think it is an unlikely assumption that Zerubbabel was removed from his position or that he simply disappeared; cf. Van der Woude, "Serubbabel"; Bianchi, "Zorobabele re", 161-3.

2.2 The Temple

2.2.1 Royalty and the Temple

First of all, the temple has to be seen as

> "a major political and economic institution, as well as a religious one. Together with the Judaean king and the aristocracy, the temple would have been a major landowner and an enormously important economic institution, similar to what we find in other ancient Near Eastern cultures. Besides the symbol effect, and the undoubtedly strong damaging outcome on morale and national religious pride, the destruction of the temple in Jerusalem by Nebukadnezzar must also be viewed as a means of gaining economic and political control, and as part of Nebukadnezzar's programme of imposing his own superstructure on Judaean economy and polity."[22]

Thus it is not surprising to find that the cult went on in the temple temenos even after 586 BCE, simply because the religious aspect of the temple was less subverted than the economic and political ones.

That is why it should not be judged an extraordinary decision to rebuild the temple.[23] The decisive initiative lay in royal hands, in the hands of the vassal kings or governors who perhaps sought to strengthen their influence over Jerusalem. They were, of course, supported by the priests who had a lively interest in regaining the privileged position they had enjoyed during the time of the First Temple. All over the Ancient Near East kings acted as temple-builders and the building of a temple was a royal initiative.[24] The Second Temple

---

[22]Barstad, *Myth*, 69-70.

[23]For a discussion of the Second Temple cf. esp. D.L. Petersen, "The Temple in Persian Period Prophetic Texts", in: Ph.R. Davies (ed.), *Second Temple Studies* (JSOT.S, 117), vol. 1: Persian Period, Sheffield 1991, 125-44; R.P. Carrol, "So What Do We *Know* about the Temple?", in: T.C. Eskenazi, K.H. Richards (eds.), *Second Temple Studies* (JSOT.S, 175), vol. 2: Temple and Community in the Persian Period, Sheffield 1994, 34-51; D.J.A. Clines, "Haggai's Temple Constructed, Deconstructed and Reconstructed", in: *Ibidem*, 60-87; P. Marinkovic, "What Does Zechariah 1–8 Tell us about the Second Temple?", in: *Ibidem*, 88-103; P.R. Bedford, "Discerning the Time: Haggai, Zechariah and the 'Delay' in the Rebuilding of the Jerusalem Temple", in: S.W. Holloway, L.K. Handy (eds.), *The Pitcher is Broken: Memorial Essays for Gösta W. Ahlström* (JSOT.S, 190), Sheffield 1985, 71-94; A. Sérandour, "Les récits bibliques de la construction du second temple: leurs enjeux", *Trans* 11 (1996), 9-32.

[24]On this point cf. esp. S. Lackenbacher, *Le roi bâtisseur* (EtAs, 11), Paris 1982; V. Hurowitz, *I Have Built You An Exalted House* (JSOT.S, 115), Sheffield 1992.

does not form an exception to this rule. Its foundations were laid by
Zerubbabel, a prince of Davidic origin and a vassal king of the Persians. This is clearly stressed in the book of Zechariah: "He will bring
out the former stone" (Zech. 4:7), which is to be understood as an
allusion to a temple building ritual. Then the text continues: "Zerubbabel with his own hands laid the foundation of this house and with
his own hands he shall finish it" (Zech. 4:9). Zech. 6:12-13 is comparable: "Here is a man named Semach; he will shoot up from the
ground where he is and will build the temple of the Lord. It is he who
will build the temple of the Lord, he who will assume royal dignity,
will be seated on his throne and govern, with a priest at his right side
and concord shall prevail between them." In Hag. 1 and 2 Zerubbabel
and Jehoshua, the high priest, are likewise called upon to rebuild the
temple. In later times the Aramaic narrative in the book of Ezra says
that Zerubbabel and Jehoshua had begun to build the house of God
in Jerusalem (Ezra 5:2) and that previously Sheshbazzar had set the
אֻשַּׁיָּא (foundation of the temple) in place (Ezra 5:16).

This important aspect of the royal initiative in temple-building has
sometimes already been grasped in articles which discuss the *raison
d'être* of the Second Temple.[25] As Yehud under Persian rule was still
a vassal kingdom, it needed a temple as was previously the case during the periods of Assyrian and Neo-Babylonian domination. By implication, the Second Temple was a royal building, as had been the
First Temple before. Within this context it is important to note that
neither Haggai nor Zechariah adduce a royal edict by Cyrus or Darius
as the *raison d'être* for the reconstruction of the temple. It was the
royal authority of Zerubbabel which sufficed to fulfil this task, while
conversely he needed a temple for the cultic dimensions of his royalty.

Nevertheless, the reconstruction of the temple also served the interests of the Persian overlords. In this context the above-mentioned
socio-political function of a temple in the Persian period should not
be overlooked. In his overview of "Temple and Society in Achaemenid
Judah" J. Blenkinsopp states:

> "Temples served as catalysts of economic exchange and
> promoters of social cohesion. The temple may also have
> been seen as a point of convergence for the symbolic struc-
> tures of the region, an 'emblem of collective identity',

---

[25] Cf. esp. D.L. Petersen, "Zerubbabel and Jerusalem Temple Reconstruction",
CBQ 36 (1974), 366-72; still important is K. Galling, "Serubbabel und der Ho-
hepriester beim Wiederaufbau des Tempels in Jerusalem", in: Idem (ed.), *Studien
zur Geschichte Israels im persischen Zeitalter*, Tübingen 1964, 127-48.

thereby mitigating to some extent the inevitable resentment generated by subjection to a foreign power."[26]

2.2.2 YHWH and the Temple

In the book of Haggai the well-being of the country is connected with the building of the temple:

> "You look for much and get little. At the moment when you would bring home the harvest, I blast it. Why? says the Lord of Hosts. Because my house lies in ruins, while each of you has a house that he can run to. It is your fault that the heavens withhold their dew and the earth its produce. So I have proclaimed a drought against land and mountain, against corn, new wine, and oil, and all that the ground yields, against man and cattle and all the products of man's labor." (Hag. 1:9-11; cf. 2:15-19; Zech. 1:12-17; 8:10-12).

In this text YHWH is portrayed as a weather god bringing rain and fertility to his country, but his blessings will be experienced only if his cult is performed in a ritually correct manner in his sanctuary.

As the realm of Yehud was confined to Jerusalem and its immediate surroundings the Second Temple had a fair chance of becoming the only central sanctuary for the inhabitants of Yehud. And as the royal power diminished considerably after Zerubbabel's death, the high priest got the chance of dominating this temple. So we can observe the growth of a one-temple-ideology according to which the Jerusalem temple was the only legitimate YHWH sanctuary. This can clearly be seen from independent evidence between 410 and 407 BCE when the Jews of Elephantine wanted to receive permission to reconstruct their destroyed temple (TAD A4.7; A4.8). The Jerusalem priests did not even answer their letter (TAD A4.7:17-18; A4.8:16-18). And the Persian governor allowed only meal offerings and incense, not holocausts (TAD A4.9:9-11; cf. A4.10:8-12), which seem to have been a prerogative of the temple in Jerusalem. Furthermore, the temple in Elephantine is called *bt mdbḥ'* by the respondents from Jerusalem (TAD A4.9:3) and not *'gwr'* 'temple' as in the Elephantine papyri (TAD A4.7 *passim*; A4.8 *passim*; A4.10:8; cf. A4.3:11), so denying it the same status as the Jerusalem temple.

---

[26] J. Blenkinsopp, "Temple and Society in Achaemenid Judah", in: Davies (ed.), *Second Temple Studies*, vol. 1, 22-53, esp. 26.

It is also more than likely that the *bamot* were still in existence after 515 BCE. Criticism of them in Ezekiel and Trito-Isaiah strongly points into this direction.[27]

2.3   Theology

2.3.1   YHWH's Presence in the Temple

Having discussed the aspects of royalty and temple we have to proceed to the question of YHWH's presence in the temple. How was this presence imagined in the new temple which was consecrated in 515 BCE? Compared to texts treating this topic for the First Temple a change has taken place.[28]

While the pre-exilic texts about YHWH's presence in the Jerusalem Temple are characterized by the dominance of the title יְהוָה צְבָאוֹת, which qualifies YHWH as being enthroned on the cherubim throne, texts from after 586 BCE witness to an almost complete eclipse of this epithet. This eclipse was compensated for by two new locutions which emphasized YHWH's presence in the Temple: the שֵׁם-theology of the Deuteronomistic circles and the כָּבוֹד-theology of the Priestly circles. The connection between the eclipse of the title יְהוָה צְבָאוֹת and the rise of the שֵׁם- and כָּבוֹד-theologies has been recognized and studied by T.N.D. Mettinger.[29] The שֵׁם-theology of the Deuteronomistic circles, as testified in Deuteronomy and the Deuteronomistic History, compensates for the concept of a deity present in his own cult statue. This original conception was no longer viable after 597 or 586 BCE, so that the book of Deuteronomy denies the visibility of YHWH's תְּמוּנָה (Deut. 4:12, 15-16). The conception of the שֵׁם-theology is that YHWH is enthroned in heaven and has chosen a place on earth for his name to dwell in. YHWH is thus present on earth by virtue of his name. The שֵׁם can be understood as a hypostasis of the deity. With the help of this hypostasis, the question of the presence of the deity in its cult statue was solved in a new way.

The כָּבוֹד-theology of the priestly school, found in the book of Ezekiel and in the Priestly Document, is different because of its close link to the Temple and because it recognizes the concept of a divine throne, albeit in a modified form. YHWH's כָּבוֹד fills the Temple for

---

[27] Cf. S. Ackerman, *Under Every Green Tree* (HSM, 46), Atlanta 1992, 173-94; M. Gleis, *Die bamah* (BZAW, 251), Berlin & New-York 1997, 247-52.

[28] For the following passage cf. H. Niehr, "In Search of YHWH's Cult Statue in the First Temple", in: K. van der Toorn (ed.), *The Image and the Book* (CBET, 21), Leuven 1997, 73-95, esp. 90, 94.

[29] Cf. T.N.D. Mettinger, *The Dethronement of Sabaoth* (CB.OT, 18), Lund 1982.

ever, and according to this model it replaces the missing cult statue. The 'artisan' tradition in Exod. 35–39 therefore refers only to the construction of the sanctuary and the instruments, with no word about the production of a cult statue because it had already been replaced by the כָּבוֹד. According to Ezek. 1:26-28, the כָּבוֹד "is described as having a human form". In contrast to the more abstract שֵׁם-theology, the כָּבוֹד-theology uses the concept of the divine form. During the Achaemenid period, the Temple was also referred to as the כִּסֵּא כָבוֹד, the 'throne of glory' (Jer. 17:12-13).

A further question is whether these texts concerning YHWH's presence in the Second Temple correspond to any empirical cultic reality or not. In this context a speculation about the interior of the Second Temple may be allowed.[30] As the existence of the divine image in the holy of holies of the First Temple seems clear to me, the situation in the Second Temple might differ from this.

According to Zechariah's fifth vision (Zech. 4:1-14), the seven-branched מְנוֹרָה fulfilled the function of a cult symbol of YHWH's presence in the Second Temple. In fact, the symbol of the מְנוֹרָה should be understood as proof of the existence of an earlier divine statue. The מְנוֹרָה replaces a cult statue of YHWH, destroyed or removed during the plundering of the First Temple in 586 BCE. It is significant that the seven lamps of the מְנוֹרָה were regarded as 'YHWH's eyes' (Zech. 4:10b) and that the מְנוֹרָה itself stood for YHWH (Zech. 4:14). This intimate connection between YHWH and the מְנוֹרָה becomes especially clear when one considers the role of the cultic lamp in ancient Near Eastern temples, the purpose of which was to make the divine image shine. After the divine statue had disappeared from the First Temple, the lamp remained and assumed the function of the divine statue itself, as Zech. 4:10-14 intimates.

Zechariah's visions constitute a programmatical *hieros logos* for the construction of the Second Temple. The picture of the מְנוֹרָה representing YHWH which emerges in the fifth vision (Zech. 4:1-14) demonstrates that in some theological circles the Second Temple could not be imagined without a cult symbol. The vision of the מְנוֹרָה, which occured before the dedication of the Second Temple, can be connected with the priestly data for the construction of the sanctuary, according to which a מְנוֹרָה must be placed in front of the holy of holies (Exod. 25:31-40). The priests had to take care of the מְנוֹרָה each day, a procedure which reminds us of the daily caring for the cult statue.

---

[30]For the following passage cf. Niehr, "Search", 92-3.

2.3.2   YHWH and the Other Deities

What can be said about the gods and goddesses venerated next to
YHWH in the Second Temple? Is it a reasonable view to believe that
their cult had been abolished together with the destruction of the
First Temple? Certainly not! But, unfortunately, we do not have at
our disposal any primary evidence tackling this subject. We should
not let ourselves be seduced by some texts of Deutero-Isaiah claiming
a kind of monotheism. These texts are theological statements exag-
gerating YHWH's role and denying the existence of other gods.[31] But
they cannot be taken as proof of the existence of monotheism in Yehud
from the Achaemenid period onward. Nor can any Persian influence
on the conception of YHWH or on monotheism in Yehud be made out.
This frequently discussed topic has been taken up again by G. Ahn
in an as yet unpublished *Habilitationsschrift* and has been answered
in the negative.[32]

Since continuity was the dominant feature which characterized
royalty, priesthood, temple and piety during the early Achaemenid
period, we should not expect any changes in the pantheon venerated
in the Jerusalem temple either. It is even possible that the Persian
oikumene with its enlarged trading possibilities introduced new gods
and goddesses into Judaea, in accordance with the insight that trade
routes are also routes for new gods.[33] This insight might also be valid
for the veneration of gods brought by Edomites from the South and
by Phoenicians from the North and the West. Traces of the veneration of other gods and goddesses beside YHWH can be seen from
archaeological finds (terracottas, figurines), even though we have no
epigraphical evidence for these cults.

The cultic critique advanced in the Old Testament against the
veneration of gods beside YHWH is a strong indicator of the existence
of such practices throughout the 6th and 5th cent. BCE. S. Ackerman
has collected and evaluated the relevant Old Testament material and
she is right in pursuing this track into the 5th cent. BCE. There is no

---

[31] For a convenient overview cf. F. Stolz, *Einführung in den biblischen Monotheismus*, Darmstadt 1995, 172-5.

[32] Cf. G. Ahn, *Monotheismus in Israel und Iran: Methodologische und histori-
ographische Überlegungen zur Frage nach dem Einfluß des Zoroastrismus auf das
nachexilische Judentum* (Diss. habil. Univ. Bonn), 1994. I am indebted to G. Ahn
for making this book available to me.

[33] B. Gladigow, "Mögliche Gegenstände und notwendige Quellen einer Religionsgeschichte", in: H. Beck *et al.* (ed.), *Germanische Religionsgeschichte* (RGA.E,
5), Berlin 1992, 3-26, esp. 22.

indication of a break whether after 586 BCE, or after 539 BCE, or after 515 BCE in the Second Temple.[34]

It is also very likely that Asherah, the main goddess of the Jerusalem pantheon before 586 BCE, was still venerated during the Achaemenid period.[35] To maintain that Asherah and her cult were abolished in the early Achaemenid period on the basis of Zech. 5:5-11[36] is unconvincing because Zech. 5 deals only with the abolition of personified evil.[37] The explicit exclusion of the goddess Asherah becomes clear only in the books of Chronicles.[38] So depending on the date of the books of Chronicles in ca. 380 BCE[39] or even in the 2nd cent. BCE,[40] Asherah seems to have played a role in theology, though a negative one.

If we cast a side-glance at the temple of Elephantine in Upper Egypt, it immediately becomes clear that several other gods, e.g. Anatyahu, Anatbethel and Ashambethel, were venerated here alongside YHWH.[41] It cannot be denied that the temple of Elephantine had relations with the temple of Jerusalem, because the Elephantine community tried to get permission for reconstructing their temple from the Jerusalemite high priest. Thus they regarded themselves as a branch of the Jerusalem temple. It could be that the Elephantine papyri can serve us as a kind of external evidence for the cult practised in Jerusalem until the end of the Persian period.[42] But the lack of primary sources for Jerusalem does not allow us to treat this topic in more detail.

---

[34] Cf. S. Ackerman, *Under Every Green Tree* (HSM, 46), Atlanta 1992, 5-99.

[35] Cf. C. Frevel, *Aschera und der Ausschließlichkeitsanspruch* YHWHs (BBB, 94/1), Weinheim 1995, 518-32.

[36] Cf. C. Uehlinger, "Die Frau im Efa (Sach 5,5-11)", *BiKi* 49 (1994), 93-103; Idem, "Figurative Policy" 344-347.

[37] Cf. V. Haas, "Ein hurritischer Blutritus und die Deponierung der Ritualrückstände nach hethitischen Quellen", in: B. Janowski *et al.* (eds.), *Religionsgeschichtliche Beziehungen zwischen Kleinasien, Nordsyrien und dem Alten Testament* (OBO, 129), Freiburg & Göttingen 1993, 67-8.

[38] Cf. C. Frevel, "Die Elimination der Göttin aus dem Weltbild des Chronisten", *ZAW* 103 (1991), 263-71.

[39] So S. Japhet, *I & II Chronicles* (OTL), London 1993, 23-8; I. Kalimi, "Die Abfassungszeit der Chronik – Forschungsstand und Perspektiven" *ZAW* 105 (1993), 223-33.

[40] So G. Steins, *Die Chronik als kanonisches Abschlußphänomen* (BBB, 93), Weinheim 1995, 491-9; Idem, "Die Datierung des Chronisten: Ein neuer methodischer Ansatz", *ZAW* 109, 1997, 84-92.

[41] Cf. in detail K. van der Toorn, "Anat-Yahu, some other Deities, and the Jews of Elephantine", *Numen* 39 (1992), 80-101.

[42] So a proposal by B. Diebner, "Die Bedeutung der mesopotamischen 'Exilsgemeinde' (*galut*) für die Theologische Prägung der Jüdischen Bibel", *Trans* 7 (1994), 123-42, esp. 138-9, n. 45.

The gradual disappearance of different major deities from the Jerusalem pantheon in Achaemenid times leads us to a further consideration. L.K. Handy has demonstrated that Northwest semitic panthea
of the Late Bronze and Iron ages displayed a four-tiered hierarchy
consisting of authoritative deities, major active deities, artisan deities and messenger deities. During the Achaemenid period and even
later the second and third levels of this hierarchy were gradually dis-
carded because more stress was laid on YHWH as an authoritative
deity and on the messengers as YHWH's servants.[43]

> "Thus, when Yahweh is taken as the sole deity to have any
> power in the cosmos, the messenger deities may be allowed
> to exist since they have no power at all. All other deities,
> from Asherah through the Craft-Gods, could disagree with
> Yahweh and thereby diminish the centrality of power in
> the single deity. By retaining the messenger level of the
> Syro-Palestinian pantheon, the theologians have managed
> to retain for Yahweh the full extent of divine authority
> and still allow 'the' God rule over a heavenly 'host' which
> could do nothing but what its ruler desired."[44]

Thus ancient minor gods became more and more prominent and a
new hierarchy of archangels and angels was developed. One also gets
the impression that the repertoire of demons and evil spirits increased
considerably, and that they too formed a hierarchy under Satan, who
is mentioned for the first time in the book of Zechariah (Zech. 3:1-2).

2.4   Piety

2.4.1   Domestic Cults

The insights gained from the official side (concerning royalty, temple,
theology) need to be supplemented by a look at the piety of the individual. In this regard we have to tackle the conservative character of
the domestic cults. The main evidence for the maintenance of earlier
forms is provided by the texts which denounce family ancestor figurines and their veneration, e.g. the decalogue (cf. Exod. 20:3-5; Deut.

---

[43] Cf. L.K. Handy, "Dissenting Deities or Obedient Angels: Divine Hierarchies in
Ugarit and the Bible", *BR* 35 (1990), 18-35; Idem, "The Appearance of Pantheon
in Judah", in: D.V. Edelman (ed.), *The Triumph of Elohim* (CBET, 13), Kampen
1995, 27-43; Idem, *Among the Host of Heaven*, Winona Lake 1994.

[44] Handy, "Dissenting Deities", 29.

5:7-9).[45] A certain change in domestic piety is perhaps indicated by the absence of the so-called 'pillar figurines' from the 6th cent. BCE onwards. This archaeological insight into the domestic cults of the post-exilic period, however, should not be connected too quickly with Old Testament texts denouncing other gods than YHWH.

On the other hand it seems that the pillar figurines were replaced by other types of terracottas and metal figurines, especially those representing pregnant women and women holding children. These terracottas stem from Phoenician workshops.[46]

Another aspect to be considered here is the spread of incense burners (Räucherkästchen).[47] During the Persian period the use of incense burners was no longer confined to sanctuaries and temples but is widely found in private houses. The reason for this change is the increasing commercialization of the Persian empire. So "exchange relations were established involving long-distance transport of goods."[48] As one consequence of this, frankincense became less expensive during the Persian period, so that even households could afford incense to burn. Thus one has to reckon with the possibility of domestic cults in which the use of incense had its '*Sitz im Leben*'.

Further aspects of piety which are severely criticized in the 6th and 5th cent. BCE are religious banquets, cults outside the temple, libations for the dead, eating the flesh of swine and sexual acts under sacred trees.[49] All this provides a vivid impression of a piety which did not differ from the earlier form of popular religion during the time of the kings.

3   Conclusion and Outlook

Throughout this paper a strong element of continuity after 586 and after 539 BCE has been demonstrated. The early post-exilic period (539-500 BCE) has been seen to be a period of transition but not of rapid changes. So the Second Temple was rebuilt as a royal sanctuary, but the major changes one can descern relate to the question of YHWH's presence in this temple.

It is not possible to attribute these changes to one single event in 539 BCE or in 515 BCE. The time of change seems to have come

---

[45] Cf. O. Loretz, "Das 'Ahnen- und Götterstatuen-Verbot' im Dekalog und die Einzigkeit Jahwes", in: W. Dietrich, M.A. Klopfenstein (eds.), *Ein Gott allein?* (OBO, 139), Freiburg & Göttingen 1994, 491-527.

[46] Cf. Stern, *Material Culture* , 158-82.

[47] Cf. W. Zwickel, *Räucherkult und Räuchergeräte* (OBO, 97), Freiburg & Göttingen 1990, 74-90.

[48] Blenkinsopp, "Temple and Society", 47.

[49] Cf. Ackerman, *Green Tree*, 101-212.

with the end of the monarchy around 500 BCE when the temple fell into priestly hands. A. Lemaire reckons with this change when Zerubbabel's son-in-law, who was not a Davidide by birth, was appointed governor by Darius:

> "Cette nomination du provoquer un choc idéologique grave dans les milieux traditionnels judéens qui eurent probablement du mal à accepter l'autorité d'un gouverneur non davidide. Par contrecoup, elle dut augmenter le respect populaire pour la dynastie sacerdotale représentant la continuité des traditions judéennes depuis l'époque de David. Politiquement et littérairement, le grand-prêtre semble avoir récupéré une partie de l'élan populaire suscité par la prédication prophétique en faveur de Ṣēmaḥ/Zorobabel."[50]

It has been often stated that the 5th cent. BCE, the time where tradition places Ezra and Nehemiah,[51] is a dark age. But if we have regard to the fictitious character of both Ezra and Nehemiah, and to the Hellenistic date of the books ascribed to them, this age is even darker than is often thought. It it not easy to say at what time new rules of cult and piety, which we tend to characterize as 'Jewish', were prescribed and followed. In this context it is interesting to compare the religious and cultic history of Yehud in Hellenistic times before and after the Maccabean revolt. As concerns the period before the Maccabean revolt, M. Hengel has argued for a certain laxity in religious and cultic affairs even in the circles of priests and other people who had to do with the temple.[52] But even this remark does not grasp the decisive point because there was no such thing as normative judaism at that time. This changed considerably only during and after the Maccabean revolt. So the time between the Maccabean revolt and the reign of the Hasmoneans seems to be the decisive period of change towards an orthodox judaism.

Thus, circumcision perhaps became obligatory for every male only during the Maccabean period;[53] the same insight may be valid for

---

[50] Lemaire, "Zorobabel et la Judée", 57.

[51] Cf. J.C.H. Lebram, "Die Traditionsgeschichte der Esra-Gestalt und die Frage nach dem historischen Esra", in: H. Sancisi–Weerdenburg (ed.), *Achaemenid History* 1, Leiden 1987, 104-38; Ph.R. Davies, "Scenes from the Early History of Judaism", in: Edelman (ed.), *Triumph*, 145-82, esp. 157-63.

[52] Cf. M. Hengel, *Judentum und Hellenismus* (WUNT, 10), Tübingen 1988, 486-95.

[53] Cf. K. Grünwaldt, *Exil und Identität* (BBB, 85), Frankfurt 1992, 47-56.

the taboos concerning necromancy, funerary rites and the cult of the dead,[54] and the consumption of certain animals now declared unclean.[55] The replacing of a cult image of YHWH by a holy book and a mainstream aniconism also fit well into this period.[56]

It should not be overlooked that all these aspects of so-called post-exilic judaism have their own prehistory. None of these aspects fell from heaven during the time between the Maccabean revolt and the reign of the Hasmoneans. This prehistory sometimes reaches back into royal times, e.g. circumcision and certain verdicts concerning the realm of the dead. But before the Maccabean period these rules were never normative because a normative judaism had not yet come into existence. As concerns the historical development of this final stage, an interesting suggestion has been made by Ph.R. Davies.[57] According to him:

> "the emergence of Judaism can be traced by a series of discrete historical developments and was characterized by distinct phases, beginning with the formation of cultural habits and customs, then the cultivation of those as a distinct way of life in opposition to 'Hellenism' and finally, as a set of competing and ever more religious definitions of that culture. The catalyst for the last development was the religious character that the 'Maccabean revolt' was given and the subsequent embroiling of the Hasmoneans in religious (not exclusively cultic) matters through their adoption of a religious ideology in support of their bid for power, their assumption of the high priesthood, and the lobbying of groups with whom they had been obliged to associate in their bid for power. Judaism, by which I mean the culture that all those who called themselves Judaeans adopted as their mark of identity, increasingly took on the form of a religion."

---

[54] For an overview cf. H. Niehr, "Aspekte des Totengedenkens im Juda der Königszeit", *ThQ* 178 (1998), 1-13, esp. 12-3.

[55] Cf. B. Ego, "Reinheit und Schöpfung", *ZAR* 3 (1997), 131-44.

[56] Cf. D.V. Edelman, "Tracking Observance of the Aniconic Tradition through Numismatics", in: Idem (ed.), *Triumph*, 185-225; Niehr, "Search", 94-5; K. van der Toorn, "The Iconic Book: Analogies between the Babylonian Cult of Images and the Veneration of the Torah", in: Idem (ed.), *Image*, 229-48.

[57] Davies, "Early History of Judaism", 180-1.

Ephraim Stern *Jerusalem – Israel*

Religion in Palestine in the Assyrian and Persian Periods*

1 Introduction

This paper will be divided into two parts. The first will deal with
the rather complicated picture emerging from the finds of the 7th
century BCE – the period of the Assyrian domination of the country –
and the last period of the independent Judaean kingdom down to its
destruction by the Babylonians in 586 BCE. In the second part I will
summarize the state of affairs in the Persian period (538-332 BCE)
and point out the differences between the two periods and explain
the significance of these differences.

2 The Assyrian Period

During the 7th century BCE, or the Assyrian period, seven nations
were settled in Palestine. The eighth one, i.e. the Arameans of the
kingdom of Geshur, who lived on the north-eastern border of Israel,
was deported by the Assyrians in 732 BCE and never came back. The
seven nations are from north to south: The Phoenicians along the
north coast and the Galilee, the Samaritans who replaced the people
of the destroyed Israelite kingdom in the province of Samaria, the
late Philistines who prospered in their four cities: Ashdod, Ashkelon,
Gaza and Ekron and the three nations of East Jordan: that is the
Ammonites, the Moabites and the Edomites, and finally the Judaeans.

In the Assyrian period each of these seven nations had its own
independent cult, consisting of the worship of a pair of major deities.
Each of the male gods of these nations had a distinct name. Most
of the names are mentioned in the Biblical sources, but not all of
them. Before they were destroyed by the Assyrians the Arameans had
Haddad as their chief deity, the Phoenicians had Ba'al, Dagan was the
chief god of the Philistines, Milcom of the Ammonites, Chemosh of
the Moabites, Qos of the Edomites and YHWH of the Judaeans, and
later also of the Samaritans.[1] It is interesting to observe that among
all of them, including the Philistines and even the Judaeans, the chief
female deity was the Ashtoret ('Ashtart) or Asherah.

---

*Thanks are due to Dr. Karel Vriezen – Utrecht University, for his detailed
and constructive comments on an earlier draft of this article.

[1] On these deities see the relevant entries in K. van der Toorn *et al.* (eds.),
DDD, Leiden ²1999.

It is a well-known fact by now that each of these many nations created the images of its gods in a form different from that of the others. By the 7th century BCE the representation of the different deities had been clearly consolidated and it is easy for any experienced archaeologist or specialist in ancient art to attribute at first glance a figurine to a Phoenician, a Philistine or even the Judaean cult. At the same time one of the strange results of the study of the cult objects is that despite these differences of deities and cults there exists a large amount of unity too. Except for the differing images of their gods, the various nations used the same cult objects, the same types of incense altars made of stone and clay, bronze and clay censers, cult stands and incense burners, chalices, goblets and bronze and ivory sticks adorned with pomegranates etc. It was easy to take cult vessels of one deity, for example from the sanctuary of Arad, and place them in the service of another one, as is described in the famous stele of Mesha, the king of Moab who delivered the vessels of YHWH taken from the conquered Judaean city of Nevo to the temple of Chemosh.[2]

According to recent archaeological finds we may assume that in Judah many sanctuaries dedicated to their own national god had been erected at various sites. Such a sanctuary was called: "The house of YHWH". The most important and central one was, no doubt, the sanctuary on the Temple Mount in Jerusalem. The Bible itself testifies to the existence of additional sanctuaries at Bethel, Shilo, and Beer-Sheba (1 Sam. 1:24).

Another sanctuary was erected during the 7th century BCE in Bethel by one of the priests who had survived from the kingdom of Israel. He introduced the new deportees into the secrets of the *Yahwistic* cult. And as the writer of 2 Kgs 17:41 has pointed out, perhaps in irony, "those nations worshipped the LORD, but they also served their idols". A complete Judaean sanctuary has been uncovered by Y. Aharoni in the fortress in Arad.[3] Although this sanctuary was erected long before the 7th century BCE, many scholars tend to attribute its last stages (strata VII-VI) to this period, while others tend to believe that it was destroyed already before the 7th century BCE. Whether earlier or not, this temple may serve us an example for all other Judaean temples and sanctuaries of that period. The Arad sanctuary contains three parts: '*Ulam*', '*Heichal*' and '*Debir*' and was oriented east-west. From the central unit, the '*Heichal*', one

---

[2]Cf. R.W. Suder, *Hebrew Inscriptions: A Classified Bibliography*, Londen 1984; A. Dearman (ed.), *Studies in the Mesha Inscription and Moab* (ABSt), Atlanta 1989.

[3]Y. Aharoni, "Arad its Inscriptions and Temple", *BA* 31 (1968), 20-32; D. Ussishkin, "The date of the Judaean Shrine at Arad", *IEJ* 38 (1988), 142-57.

could ascend by three steps to the holy of holies. This was a raised platform and one of its '*Masebot*' was uncovered in the destruction level, and two additional ones were found embedded in the wall of the holy of holies – these were not in use in the sanctuary's last period. On the third step two limestone incense altars have been found, with remains of burnt material on their upper part, probably incense. In the courtyard a large altar has been uncovered. Its dimensions were 2.5 x 2.3 m. and it was built of clay bricks and unhewn stones and covered with a heavy layer of plaster. According to Aharoni the plan of the house and its contents justified the assumption that "it was a Yahwistic-Judaean temple".

Apart from the sanctuary at Arad some additional cult installations have been uncovered in other Judaean fortresses of the 7th century BCE. I. Beit-Arieh, for example, recently has reported on the existence of a cult platform to which a few steps were leading close to the gates of the Judaean fortresses of 'Uza and Radum near Arad. Another '*Bamah*' was previously reported by Aharoni near the gate of another Judaean fortress at Tel-Sheba, where also a large four-horned stone altar has been found.

Recently, a similar installation has been uncovered also in the Judaean fortress of Vered-Jericho and here too the excavator, A. Eitan, claims that it was a cultic '*Bamah*'. Some stone stairs found near the gate of the fort of Mesad-Michmash, on the kingdom's north border, were also considered as leading to a sacred platform or '*Bamah*'. These new finds have strengthened Aharoni's assumption that almost all border-fortresses of the Judaean kingdom had cult centres. It should also be mentioned that in a large number of these fortresses numerous figurines, altars, and other types of cult objects have been recovered.

It may be assumed that a sanctuary for YHWH existed in Lachish, the second city in importance in Judah, as in the Lachish relief in Nineve a pair of large cultic stands are depicted as war spoil taken out by Sennacherib's soldiers after they had sacked the city. These stands belong to a type of which smaller ones have been unearthed in many of the country's towns.

It should be added here that the existence of sanctuaries dedicated to "YHWH" in various settlements outside Jerusalem was not peculiar to the 7th century BCE. Mention should be made of the famous cult site in Kuntillet-Ajrud dating to the end of the 9th century BCE and dedicated to "*Yahweh of Samaria and his Asherah*" or "*Yahweh of Teman*" and his Asherah.[4] Another one is mentioned in the Mesha

---

[4]Z. Meshel, "Did Yahweh have a Consort? The new Religious Inscriptions

stele which was even earlier, where the Moabite king claims to have
taken (from the city of Nevo) the vessels of YHWH and had laid them
before Chemosh. This means that in the Judaean city of Nevo, before
it had been plundered by the Moabites, there was also a sanctuary
dedicated to YHWH.

"A house of Yahweh" is indeed mentioned in many inscriptions
of that period. For example in one of the Arad ostraca it is said of
someone that "he is in the house of YHWH".[5] A recently published
Judaean ostracon reads, "Pursuant to the order to you of Ashyahu
the king to give by the hand of Zecharyahu silver of Tarshish to *the
house of Yahweh*, three shekels".[6] And the inscription on a small ivory
pomegranate, reads (according to the translation of Avigad), as follows, "Sacred to the priest of the house of YHWH".[7] The mention
"house of YHWH" in two ostraca has led their publishers to believe
that they alluded to the temple in Jerusalem.

However, if one takes all the information nowadays available into
consideration, it is doubtful that this assumption is necessary. A
"house of YHWH" may have been located in any settlement in Judah,
or in any area settled by Judaeans. In this respect we should add
that on ostraca in the sanctuary of Arad itself, the names of two well-
known priestly families, Meremot and Pashur, have been found who
probably served in the local "house of YHWH".

Generally, the priests who served in the YHWH sanctuaries received their posts within their families, from father to son, only seldom
they were appointed by the ruler. We do possess a few seals in which
only the title "*Cohen*" (priest), is added to the name. One of them
published recently is that of "Ianan the son of Helqiah the priest",
who may have been the father of a high priest in Jerusalem. From the

---

from Sinai", *BAR* 5,2 (1979), 28-9; J.A. Emerton, "New Light on Religion: The
Implications of the Inscription from Kuntillet 'Ajrud", *ZAW* 94 (1982), 2-20;
W.G. Dever, "Ashera, Consort of Yahweh, New Evidence from Kuntillet 'Ajrud",
BASOR 255 (1984), 21-37; P.K. McCarter, "Aspects of the Religion of the Israelite
Monarchy: Biblical and Epigraphic Data", in: P.D. Miller *et al.* (eds.), *Ancient
Israelite Religion: Essays in Honor of F.M. Cross*, Philadelphia 1987, 138-9, 143-4.

[5] Y. Aharoni, *Arad Inscriptions*, Text 18:9-10; see now J. Renz, W. Röllig,
Handbuch der althebräischen Epigraphik, Bd. 1, Darmstadt 1995, 382-4.

[6] Cf. P. Bordreuil *et al.*, "Deux ostraca paléo-hébreux de la collection Sh.
Mousaïeff", *Sem* 46 (1996), 49-76; Planches 7 et 8. On this inscription, see B.
Becking, "Does a recently Published Paleo-Hebrew Inscription Refer to the Solomonic Temple?", *BN* 92 (1998), 5-11; A. Berlejung, A. Schüle, "Erwägungen zu
den neuen Ostraka aus der Sammlung Moussaïeff", *ZAH* 10 (1998), 68-73.

[7] Cf. N. Avigad, "The Inscribed Pomegranate from the 'House of Lord'", *The
Israel Museum Journal* 8 (1989), 7-16. See also Renz, Röllig, *Handbuch*, Bd. 1,
192-3.

period of the last days of the Israelite kingdom, a seal which mentions an Israelite priest who was active in the *Yahwhistic* temple at Dor, reads, "*belonging to Zechario the priest of Dor*" (cf. "Amaziah, the priest of Bethel", Amos 7:10). And there is also the seal of "Miqnayahu servant of Yʜwʜ", which means that Miqnayahu served in the cult of one of the many Yʜwʜ temples.[8] From this data it may be concluded that someone who had the title of a priest, could serve in any of the country's temples. Also may be mentioned the evidence found in the various archaeological excavations in Judah which points to the frequent use of Yʜwʜ's name among the Judaeans of the Assyrian period. According to A. Millard, the dominance of Yʜwʜ's name among the Judaeans of that period is clear: Out of about 1200 personal names on seals and ostraca 557 are compounded with *yhwh*, 77 with *ʾl*, while only 35 (!) involve other deities.[9] Furthermore the many occurrences of the name of Yʜwʜ in the ostraca of Lachish and Arad as well as in ostraca of other Judaean sites may be mentioned.[10] The name appears in oaths and blessings such as: "I have blessed you to Yʜwʜ"; "May Yʜwʜ let hear my lord tidings of peace"; "May Yʜwʜ bless you in peace"; "May Yʜwʜ give my lord pleasant tidings"; "May Yʜwʜ give you prosperous tidings", etc.[11]

However, there is yet another inscription from Judah and from the same period, mentioning the name of the *divine couple* who were worshipped by the locals: Yʜwʜ and the Asherah. This matches their occurence in the inscriptions in the early Israelite sanctuary at Kuntillet-Ajrud and their worship by the Israelites at that time. This inscription was found in a tomb at Khirbet el-Qom (perhaps to be identified with the town of Makeda in the central mountains of Hebron). The inscription says, "blessed will be Ariyahu to Yʜwʜ and his *Asherah*". In the nearby site of Beit Loyah a Judaean tomb inscription has been uncovered which mentions Yʜwʜ as the lord of Jerusalem and the mountains of Judah.[12]

---

[8] N. Avigad, *Corpus of West Semitic Stamp Seals*, Jerusalem 1997, 59-60; nn. 27-29.

[9] A. Millard, "The History of Israel Against the Background of Ancient Near Eastern Religious History," in: T. Eskola, E. Junkkaala (eds.), *From Ancient Sites of Israel: Essays on Archaeology, History and Theology in Memory of A. Saarisalo*, Helsinki 1998, 101-17.

[10] Cf. J.H. Tigay, *You Shall Have No Other Gods: Israelite Religion in the Light of Hebrew Inscriptions*, Atlanta 1986, esp. 47-63.

[11] Y. Aharoni, *Arad Inscriptions*, Jerusalem 1981; H. Torczyner *et al.*, *The Lachish Letters (Lachish 1)*, London 1938, see also C.W. Mitchell, *The Meaning of* BRK *'to bless' in the Old Testament* (SBL.DS, 95), Atlanta, 1987.

[12] W.G. Dever, "Iron Age Epigraphic Material from the Area of Khirbet el-Kom", *HUCA* 40-41 (1969-1970), 158-69, 200-1; A. Lemaire, "Les Inscriptions de

Now, the frequent appearance of specific cultic objects unique to the Judaeans may be discussed, namely the hundreds of clay figurines which are divided over female and male types. The pagan cult in Judah, whether being of foreign origin (either Egyptian or Phoenician) or of national Judaean origin in the shape of the deities YHWH and Asherah (or 'Ashtart), is presented by quite a rich assemblage of finds. These particular finds are dated from the late 8th century down to the beginning of the 6th century BCE. These figurines are distributed all over Judah. From the Benjamin region in the north, at Bethel, Tel-Nasbeh, Gibeon, Ramot and Moza to Jerusalem, Ramat-Rahel, Beth-Zur and Tel-Rabud on the mountain's ridge, to Jericho and En-Gedi in the east and Gezer, Beth-Shemesh, Batash, Azeka, Tel-Judeida, Tel 'Erani, Tel Halif, Tel Lachish, Tel Beit-Mirsim, and others in the west. In the southern part of the country they are found at Tel Sheba, Tel Masos, Tel 'Ira, 'Aroer and Arad. They are found in large settlements or in small fortresses such as Khirbet Abu Tuwein. In short: from all parts of Judah.

In Judah, as in other kingdoms of the Assyrian era, most of the figurines are those of females, and they belong to the type known as 'pillar figurines'. This is the type with the molded heads that are similar to each other in their expression. They look somewhat stylized. The body usually is solid and handmade, in the shape of a small column, to which were added the exaggerated breasts supported by the goddesses' hands. This type of deity is usually identified with 'Ashtart, the fertility goddess. Sometimes the goddess is depicted as playing a tambourine, or holding a dove – the traditional emblem of the goddesses in all periods. Seldom this figurine is found with a hollow, round body, made in the Phoenician tradition, called 'bell shaped' body. Even rarer are those which are made as flat, impressed plaques which represent similar figures.

Another popular type are the 'Ashtart figurines with 'pinched' heads, sometimes called 'bird head figurines'. Of these the head is made by hand, just like the body, and not pressed against a mold. These figurines too portray a standing female supporting her breasts with one or two hands.

It should be pointed out that the figurines from Judah, like the rest, were painted in strong colours: white, black, red, etc. A few figurines have survived in full colour, from which it can be learned that particularly the eyes and hair were painted, and sometimes jewelry was added around the necks. The best examples came from the city

Khirbet el-Qom et l'Ashéra de YHWH", *RB* 84 (1977), 595-608; J. Naveh, "Old Hebrew Inscriptions in a Burial Cave", *IEJ* 13 (1963), 74-96.

of David in Jerusalem. There are also 'Ashtart figurines from Judah which were made of different materials, such as ivory and bone. As was mentioned before, the distribution of 'Ashtart figurines shows that their cult was practiced all over the kingdom. In the summary of his recent comprehensive study of these Judaean figurines, R. Kletter writes,

> "If we adopt the heartland of Judah concept (i.e. Judah within the borders described above), than 822 figurines (ca. 96%) were found within this area. This number is so high that there is only one possible conclusion: *these pottery figurines are Judaean.*"[13]

It should also be noted that *out of the 822* figurines found in Judah, not less than *405* (!) came from Jerusalem itself. They were found either in the excavations of Kenyon and Shiloh, and B. and A. Mazar in the city of David, or in those of N. Avigad and others in the upper city. And since Kletter's study (1996), finds of many more figurines from Jerusalem have been published: female and male figurines alike, some of them in a very short distance from the Temple Mount itself.

The *male figurines*, even though they are found by dozens in all the sites of Judah which have been enumerated above, including Gibeon and Jerusalem, are not well represented in the reports and in the scientific literature. Now that we have some results and statistical data from the cults practiced in the other parts of the country, namely from the Phoenicians, the Ammonites, the Edomites and the Philistines, it seems that also among those nations the male deities constitute an important part of the find. In this respect too Judah did not differ from its neighbours.

The male figurines there, as in other kingdoms, appeared in two forms: the more complete figurines represent *horsemen*, who, according to some scholars, are connected with the cult of 'sun chariots'

---

[13] J.B. Pritchard, *Palestinian Figurines in Relation to Certain Goddesses Known Through Literature*, New Haven 1943; T.A. Holland, *A Typological and Archaeological Study of the Human and Animal Representations in Plastic Art of Palestine During the Iron Age*, Unpublished Doctoral Thesis, Oxford 1975; Idem, "A Study of Palestinian Iron Age Backed Figurines with Special Reference to Jerusalem Cave I", *Levant* 9 (1977), 121-55; Y. Nadelman, "Iron Age II Clay Fragments from the Excavations, Appendix A", in: B. and E. Mazar, *Excavations in the South of the Temple Mount, the Ophel of Biblical Jerusalem* (Qedem, 29), Jerusalem 1989, 123-5; D. Gilbret-Peretz, "Ceramic Figurines", in: D.T. Ariel, A. de Groot (eds.), *Excavations at the City of David 1978-1985*, vol. 4 (Qedem, 35), Jerusalem 1996, 29-34; R. Kletter, *The Judaean Pillar-Figurines and the Archaeology of the Ashera*, Oxford 1996.

mentioned in the Bible, but according to some other scholars they are representing the figure of the warrior god, which is a more plausible explanation. This warrior god occurs in the cult of all other nations of the country, among Phoenicians, Ammonites, etc. (and cf. Isa. 13:4, "the lord of hosts is mustering a host of war"). The 'Judaean horsemen' have a stylistic uniqueness: their heads sometimes are made in the 'pinched' form of the 'bird's heads', in the same way as some of the heads of the Judaean 'Ashtarts (see above). The horse too has a very characteristic head: long and cut straight at its end, a head that has no analogy among the other nations' horse-figurines. The bodies of the Judaean horsemen and horses are solid and handmade.

Another type of a male figurine's head is the one crowned with a round 'turban'. This type is not familiar at all and we only posses a few dozens of the heads. The specific turban is very similar to the one worn by the Judaeans who are depicted as leaving the city on the the Lachish-relief. Identical turbans are worn by some of the Israelite male figurines of the Assyrian era from Megiddo as well as by some of the Ammonite stone sculptures. If we compare the Judaean male figurines with the more complete Ammonite examples, it seems that they too were depicted with their hands beside the body or one hand raised in blessing.

Which Judaean deities are represented by these clay figurines? We may only guess. They might represent one of the foreign deities whose cult was practiced also in Jerusalem, perhaps that of the Phoenician Ba‘al. But, it is also possible that they are pagan representations of the *national Judaean god, Yahweh and his consort 'Ashtart or Asherah*, for all these figurines – as we have seen – are Judaean and only Judaean. The combination of the archaeological finds, namely

- the mention of the name of YHWH (and that of his Asherah/ 'Ashtart) in the ostraca and other written Judaean sources of the Assyrian period,

- and the fact that many clay figurines are typical of Judah alone,

brings us to the inevitable conclusion that between the foreign pagan practices and the pure monotheism of the Judaeans, there existed a cult which may be called '*Yahwistic Paganism*'. The material collected here mainly belongs to this mixed cult. It concerns the remains of sanctuaries, '*Bamot*' (open sacred high places), as well as altars and figurines, and vessels which were in use in the sanctuaries. We shall see that with regard to the use of these artifacts there is hardly any difference between their function in the Judaean cult and in the cult of all other Palestinian nations, except for the use of the national chief god's name, which was YHWH in Judah, Qos at Edom, etc. Of course in the background there always has been the monotheistic, central cult practiced in the temple of Jerusalem by its priests, and preached by various prophets. And some of the kings of Judah from time to time made efforts to centralize the monotheistic cult in Jerusalem: in the days of Hezekiah, perhaps in the early period of Manasse and certainly during the reign of Josiah. Regarding the distribution of the cult of the *'Yahwistic paganism'* from this period, it seems that they did not really succeed. This cult was very common in Jerusalem and the rest of Judah during this entire period until the destruction of the monarchy.

3   The Persian Period

From the archaeological point of view, we almost know nothing about the cult of the next period, the *Babylonian period* which lasted from the destruction of the first temple in the year 586 BCE down to 539 BCE. I do not intend to deal with this period here but want to stress the conclusion that this period means a clear and objective vacuum. The Babylonians did not only destroy Judah but also the rest of the country. They exiled many nations, among them the Philistines who never returned, and many regions of the country were left completely devastated by them, including the previously prosperous sea coast.

In the beginning of the *Persian* period, when the curtains are lifted again, the picture is completely different. Instead of a separate national paganic cult unique to each of the individual nations of the country, new types of clay figurines appear which reflect a certain 'Koine'. This 'Koine' develops along the entire eastern coast of the Mediterranean. In Palestine this happens too. Their distribution, however, is totally different. From the Persian period all figurines are found only in the Negeb (or Edumaea, then inhabited by the Edomites), as well as along the coastal part and the Galilee, regions which in that time are inhabited mostly by the Phoenicians.

Generally, the archaeological finds of the Persian period reflect three major types of figurines that occur simultaneously in all assemblages: an adult male, represented as a king either sitting on a throne or standing, or as a warrior on a horse; a fertility goddess holding either her breasts or a child, and sometimes she is pregnant; and young boys. These figurines are made in local, Phoenician, Egyptian, Persian and Greek styles.[14]

---

[14]E. Stern, *Material Culture of the Land of the Bible in the Persian Period, 538-332* BCE, Warminster 1982, 158-82.

This is consistent with Sabatino Moscati's observation that the
Phoenician cult was composed of a 'triad of deities': "a protective god
of the city; a goddess, often his wife or companion who symbolizes the
fertile earth; and a young god somehow connected with the goddess
(usually her son) whose resurrection expresses the annual cycle of
vegetation. Within these limits, the names and functions of the gods
vary, and the fluidity of this pantheon, where the common name often
prevails over the proper name, and the function over the personality,
is characteristic. Another characteristic of the Phoenician triad is its
flexibility from town to town".[15]

Thus, Ba'al had many local names. Some were connected with
sacred mountains such as Ba'al Saphon (and perhaps Ba'al Carmel);
others were connected with geographic regions as in Ba'al Lebanon.
Mainly, however, they were related to different cities where Ba'al had
different names, such as Ba'al Eshmun in Sidon, Melqart in Tyre,
Ba'al Gebal in Byblos and Ba'al Haman in Carthage.

The same holds for the goddesses. 'Ashtart (Ashtoret) underwent
similar changes from town to town. In Byblos she was called Ba'alat
Gebal and depicted as the Egyptian goddess Isis; in Carthage she
was known as Tanit Pane Baal; and in Sarepta she was called Tanit-
Ashtoret, etc.

But all the figurines from now on were found only in areas outside
the region settled by the returning Judaean exiles. Here we continue
to find a great number of assemblages of cultic figurines – in Indumea,
Philistia, Phoenicia and Galilee – that is, in those parts of the country
still dominated by pagans. In these regions dozens of *favissae* full of
clay figurines and stone statuettes have been found, most of them
along the Mediterranean coast. Some of the largest assemblages come
from Dor.[16]

At the same time, during the Persian period, we find a very strange
phenomenon: in the areas of the country occupied by Jews, *not a
single cultic figurine* has been found! This in spite of the many excavations, as well as surveys that have been conducted in Judah, and
the same is true of Samaria. Also, archaeologists failed to locate any
sanctuaries for this period within Judah and Samaria while many have

---

[15]S. Moscati, *The World of the Phoenicians*, London 1973, 62.

[16]E. Stern, "A Favissa of the Phoenician Sanctuary from Tel Dor", in: G. Vermes, J. Neusner (eds.), *Essays in Honour of Yigael Yadin* (JJS, 33), Oxford 1982,
35-54; E. Stern, "Two Favissae from Tel Dor, Israel", in: C. Bonnet *et al.* (eds.),
Studia Phoenicia, vol. 4: Religio Phoenicia, Namur 1986, 277-87; E. Stern, "The
Beginning of the Greek Settlement in Palestine in the Light of the Excavations at
Tel Dor", in: S. Gitin, W.G. Dever (eds.), *Recent Excavations in Israel: Studies
in Iron Age Archaeology* (AASOR, 49), Philadelphia 1989, 107-24.

been found elsewhere. Of course there are two exceptions, namely the temple in Jerusalem and the huge complex of the Samaritan temple uncovered on the top of their sacred mountain: the mountain of Gerizim, being excavated in recent years by Y. Magen. The beginning of this complex has been established now by hundreds of coins from the Persian period. The plan of this temple highly resembles that of the temple in Jerusalem as it is described by Ezekiel.[17]

How can we explain the complete absence of sanctuaries and, even more significantly, the complete absence of these common cultic figurines in areas of Judaeans (and Samaritans who in this period, considered themselves as Jewish too). Apparently, pagan cults ceased to exist among the Judaeans who purified their worship and Jewish monotheism was at last consolidated. And from this newly established monotheism also sprang the Samaritans. In any case, it seems that this development occurred among the Babylonian exiles and was transferred to the land of Israel by the returning exiles such as Zerubbabel son of Shealtiel and Joshua son of Jehozadak who rebuilt the second temple in Jerusalem, or Ezra and Nehemiah. Certainly not by the Jews from Egypt, for in Egypt the situation was different. From biblical sources we know that there was an Egyptian Diaspora even before the Babylonian destruction of 586 BCE. In Egypt, unlike in Babylon, the Jews continued their pagan customs and, as we know from papyri found on the island of Elephantine in the Nile, even built their own temple and adopted Egyptian and Canaanite pagan names.

---

[17] Y. Magen, "Mount Gerizim and the Samaritans", in: F. Manns, E. Alliata (eds.), *Early Christianity in Context: Monuments and Documents* (SBF.CMa, 38), Jerusalem 1993, 91-148.

Bob Becking   *Utrecht – The Netherlands*

Continuity and Community:

The Belief System of the Book of Ezra[*]

1 Introduction

Traditionally a paper like this would ask for the Theology of the Book of Ezra, or less traditionally, for the Kerygma of the Book of Ezra. The idea 'theology', however, implies a coherent set of propositions on God, on divine attributes, on human sin and divine sanction, just to indicate the most important features. The Book of Ezra, however, does not hint at these features in their entirety, as has been recognized by a variety of scholars.[1] Detecting a 'theology' from this biblical book would be an act of overcharging the evidence.[2] Of course there are elements in the Book of Ezra that hint at a religious understanding of the universe such as the idea of divine guidance in history (Ezra 1:1) and the idea of 'sin' or 'transgression' (Ezra 9–10) to mention a few. Within the Book of Ezra these devices are not presented in a systematic way, nor are they theorized.

2 The Idea of a Belief System

How, then, do we have to deal with the religious understanding of reality in the Book of Ezra? Recently, biblical scholars have been operating with the idea 'belief system' to (re-)conceptualize the religious ideas in a given text. This idea is construed as a set of ideas and religious values underlying a given text. The narrative or hymnic form of a text is seen as the expression of this belief system. A belief system is not necessarily a coherent or consistent set of values and ideas, since it is seen neither as a theory nor as a theology. Used by biblical scholars, the idea is almost equivalent with the idea of a religious code, or a religious symbol system present in a society or in a group within a society and more or less shared by most of that group. Such a belief system finds its expression in rituals, in icons and in texts. This

---

[*]I would like to thank all present at the symposium, but especially Sara Japhet and Christoph Uehlinger for their provocative, yet stimulating remarks that improved the quality of my paper.

[1]See e.g. H.G.M. Williamson, *Ezra and Nehemiah* (OTGu), Sheffield 1987, 77-8.

[2]As has been done by D. Bonhoeffer, "Die Wiederaufbau Jerusalems nach Ezra und Nehemia", *Junge Kirche* 4 (1936), 653-61 = Idem, *Auslegungen und Predigten 1933-1944* (Gesammelte Schriften, 4), E. Bethge (ed.), München 1961, 321-35; F.D. Kidner, *Ezra and Nehemiah* (TOTC), Leicester 1979, 19-27.

is the way in which e.g. Fred Cryer[3] uses the term. Until recently, I thought that this, in a way restricted, sense of the idea was the proper application of the term.[4]

It should be noted, however, that the idea of a 'belief system' has been borrowed from the field of cultural anthropology or non-western sociology.[5] In that field the idea has a much broader, i.e. not a restricted meaning. Basically, the construction of the idea has to do with the following question: How to overcome the differences in 'language games'[6] and 'world making' between cultures?[7] I will try to explain this by hinting at the following example. Some would say: 'The sun moves as you can experience'. Others, however, say: 'The earth turns around its axis, the sun stands still'. A minority-group, having followed a class in astronomy, would say: 'There is no fixed point in the universe; πάντα ῥεῖ'. And, finally, there are cultures whose members belief that it is the solar deity making his or her daily trip across the skies.

Each society, or each group in a society, has its own symbol system and its own social code necessary for group-internal communication.[8] Foreigners, unknown with or unaware of the symbol system of and/or the social code in a society, other than their own, often fail to understand the significance of literary, ritual or other utterances from that society. In other words, misunderstandings between cultures are based on misconceptions of the differing language games in various societies. 'World making' is the often implicit process at work in a person's mind when construing the world outside.[9] The representa-

---

[3]F.C. Cryer, *Divination in Ancient Israel and its Near Eastern Environment: A Socio-Historical Investigation* (JSOT.S, 142), Sheffield 1994, esp. 14-20.

[4]B. Becking, "From Apostasy to Destruction: A Josianic View on the Fall of Samaria", in: M. Vervenne, J. Lust (eds.), *Deuteronomy and Deuteronomic Literature: Festschrift C.H.W. Brekelmans* (BEThL, 133), Leuven 1997, 295-97.

[5]Very instructive is the essay by M. Black, "Belief Systems", in: J.J. Honigmann (ed.), *Handbook of Social and Cultural Anthropology*, Chicago 1973, 509-77; see also the remarks by J.W. Rogerson, *Anthropology and the Old Testament*, Oxford 1978, 46-65.

[6]L. Wittgenstein, *Philosophical Investigations*, G.E.M. Anscombe, R. Rhees (eds.), transl. G.E.M. Anscombe, Oxford 1953, esp. I.7 and I.23; see V. Brümmer, "Introduction: A Dialogue of Language-games", in: Idem (ed.), *Interpreting the Universe as Creation: A Dialogue of Science and Religion* (SPhT, 4), Kampen 1991, 1-17.

[7]N. Goodman, *Ways of Worldmaking*, Indianapolis 1978.

[8]On these concepts see C. Geertz, "Religion as a Cultural System", in: M. Banton (ed.), *The Relevance of Models in Social Anthropology*, London, 1965, 1-46 = Idem, *The Interpretation of Cultures*, New York 1973, 87-125; C. Geertz, *Local Knowledge: Further Essays in Interpretive Anthropology*, New York 1983, esp. 56-70.

[9]Goodman, *Ways of Worldmaking*, 1-22.

tion of the 'objective' world differs from person to person and from
society to society. Texts, rituals and iconic representations of the divine are expressions of the belief of a society or of the most powerful
group in a society. The idea 'belief' in the last clause has more to
do with 'world view' and 'ideology' than with 'faith' in a restricted
religious sense.

All these remarks, superficial as they are, yet indicate two features,

1. That the idea 'belief system' should better be taken in a broader
   connotation. Belief systems are conceptualized gatherings of
   world makings. They include more than the religious dimensions. Or to say the same in other words: In some cultures, religion is not as marginal as in the current western societies. By
   implication 'religion' plays a more important role in the belief
   system of that society.

2. That 'belief system' is a hermeneutical concept that can help
   in detecting the world-view in a society. Searching for a belief
   system is searching for the properties and propositions of the
   members of a society or a culture. It is not asking for the view
   of the outsider: How do the world and the belief of that society
   looks to the scholarly investigator? It is asking for the view
   from inside: How does the world look like for people in a culture
   looking outside? How is the world construed by members of a
   given society? Where asking for the Theology of the Book of
   Ezra would basically be an etic approach, asking for the belief
   system is an emic approach.[10]

3 The Book of Ezra[11]

The trouble with studying ancient civilizations lies in the fact that
we do not have a direct entrance to that kind of cultures. We cannot
go out and interview people living in Persian period Yehud. An anthropologist studying a contemporary culture would go out and live
among Indians in Surinam or with the Sami in Northern Finland to
get insights in the dynamics of the cultures mentioned.[12] Since time

---

[10]The ideas 'emic' and 'etic' were coined by K. Pike, "Towards a Theory of the
Structure of Human Behaviour", in: D. Hymes (ed.), *Language in Culture and
Society*, New York 1964, 154-61; see also Geertz, *Interpretation*, esp. 14.

[11]An informative survey of the present state of research with regard to the Book
of Ezra has been given by T.C. Eskenazi, "Current Perspectives on Ezra-Nehemiah
and the Persian Period", *Currents in Research: Biblical Studies* 1 (1993), 59-86.

[12]This way of doing participating research started with B. Malinowski, *Argo-
nauts of the Western Pacific*, London 1922; instructive on a methodical level are

is irreversible we cannot do a comparable thing with the 'Ezra-group' in Jerusalem in the fifth or fourth century BCE. We are restricted to the existing evidence: Written texts and archaeological findings and we are hoping for new evidence to be found. Here, I would like to confine myself to the Book of Ezra for the following reasons,

1. I consider the Books of Ezra and Nehemiah as two separate books.[13]

2. Evidence on an ancient culture can be compared with the pieces of a jigsaw puzzle. Before I can put a piece in its correct position I have to observe carefully the features of that piece such as size, colour and format.

I read the Book of Ezra as a composition on its own. As has been shown by Williamson and Japhet there is no need to construe Ezra as a part of a so-called Chronistic History writing.[14] Neither do I construe Ezra as part of a composition Ezra & Nehemiah. The Book

---

the essays in G.M. Foster *et al.*, *Long-term Field Research in Social Anthropology*, New York 1979.

[13] Against the view of a common redaction for Ezra & Nehemiah, as expressed by for instance H.G.M. Williamson, *Ezra, Nehemiah* (WBC, 16), Waco, TX 1985, xxxiii-xxxv; Idem, *Ezra and Nehemiah*, 37-47; T.C. Eskenazi, *In an Age of Prose: A Literary Approach to Ezra-Nehemiah* (SBL.MS, 36), Atlanta, GA 1988, 11-4; J.R. Shaver, "Ezra and Nehemiah: On the Theological Significance of Making them Contemporaries", in: E. Ulrich *et al.* (eds.), *Priests, Prophets and Scribes: Essays on the Formation of Second Temple Judaism in Honour of Joseph Blenkinsopp* (JSOT.S, 149), Sheffield 1992, esp. 85; L.L. Grabbe, *Ezra–Nehemiah*, London 1998, 38, 93-9; see the arguments in J.C. VanderKam, "Ezra-Nehemiah or Ezra and Nehemiah?", in: Ulrich *et al.* (eds.), *Priests, Prophets and Scribes*, 55-75; D. Kraemer, "On the Relationship of the Books of Ezra and Nehemiah", *JSOT* 59 (1993), 73-92.

[14] See the arguments in S. Japhet, "The Supposed Common Authorship of Chronicles and Ezra-Nehemiah Investigated Anew", *VT* 18 (1968), 330-71; H.G.M. Williamson, *Israel in the Book of Chronicles*, Cambridge 1977, esp. 1-70; Eskenazi, *In an Age of Prose*, 14-36; E. Nodet, *A Search for the Origins of Judaism: From Joshua to the Mishnah* (JSOT.S, 248), Sheffield 1997, 338-47. *Pace* the classical position that can already be found in the Talmud bBaba Bathra 15a; but first scientifically elaborated by L. Zunz, *Die gottesdienstliche Vorträge der Juden, historisch entwickelt: Ein Beitrag zur Altertumskunde und biblischen Kritik, zur Literatur und Religionsgeschichte*, Berlin 1832, 21-32, 303-5; and later in an almost canonical form by M. Noth, *Überlieferungsgeschichtliche Studien: Die sammelnden und bearbeitenden Geschichtswerke in Alten Testament*, Darmstadt [3]1967, 110-216. In spite of the arguments of e.g. Japhet and Williamson, the common authorship of Chronicles-Ezra-Nehemiah has been defended by A.H.J. Gunneweg, *Esra* (KAT, 19/1), Gütersloh 1985, 24-26; J. Blenkinsopp, *Ezra–Nehemiah* (OTL), London 1988, 47-54; K. Koch, "Weltordnung und Reichsidee im alten Iran und ihre Auswirkungen auf die Provinz Jehud", in: P. Frei, K. Koch, *Reichsidee*

of Ezra presents itself, in its present form, as a composition on its own that should be read as a composition on its own.

In my view the book consists in three narratives:[15]

1. Ezra 1–2 relates the movement of a group of people from 'being in Babylonia' to 'living in Jerusalem and vicinity'.

2. Ezra 3–6 is to be seen as a coherent narrative the main narrative programme of which can be labeled as the abolition of the non-celebration of the Passover. The (re)building of the temple, the change from 'altar' to 'temple' is an embedded narrative programme, apparently necessarily for the celebration of the Passover.

3. The story of Ezra's coming to Jerusalem and the measures taken by him (Ezra 7–10).

The third story is to be seen as a more or less historically reliable report on a string of events from the reign of a Persian king Artaxerxes. In the present form of the Book of Ezra, these three narratives are related in a consecutive order suggesting that the 'events' narrated took place in the narrated order: Return in the time of Cyrus; Rebuilding of the temple under Darius; Reorganization of the community under Artaxerxes.

As for the date of the composition of the Book of Ezra, I would opt for the late Persian period. Ezra's mission is the final event related in the Book. The Persian king אַרְתַּחְשַׁסְתְּא, Ezra 7:1, is to be identified either with Artaxerxes I or with Artaxerxes II. The seventh year would then be either 458 or 398 BCE. 'Die Meinung der Exegeten ist gespalten'.[16] The solution of this chronological problem is related to a variety of other problems, such as (1) The identification of the Persian king Darius in Ezra 5; and (2) The relationship between the mission of Ezra and the exploits of Nehemiah. Were they contemporaries, or did one precede the other and in what order? I will not enter a chronological discussion here. I would, tentatively, prefer a date for Ezra's

---

und Reichsorganisation im Perserreich; Zweite bearbeitete und stark erweiterte Auflage (OBO, 55), Freiburg & Göttingen [2]1996, 220-39. A. Gelston, "The End of Chronicles", *SJOT* 10 (1996), 53-60 has defended the thesis that Ezra 1-6 originally formed the end of the Book of Chronicles. The material was later reused in writing the complex Ezra-Nehemiah.

[15]Applying a different theory of literature, Eskenazi, *In an Age of Prose*, arrives at a different view on the composition and coherence of the narratives in the Book of Ezra.

[16]Koch, "Weltordnung und Reichsidee", 243; very informative are the sections in D.J.A. Clines, *Ezra, Nehemiah, Esther* (NCBC), Basingstoke 1984, 16-24; Nodet, *Search for the Origins*, 25-33.

mission in the reign of Artaxerxes II.[17] The Book of Ezra would be, by implication, a fourth century BCE document, if not later.[18]

Whether the author of the Book of Ezra made use of existing 'sources' is disputed. Williamson[19] and Halpern,[20] for instance, accept the view that the narratives present in the Book of Ezra contain reworked older material that might go back to a Jerusalem copy of Ezra's report for the Persian king, and have taken over authentic Aramaic letters in Ezra 4–6. The decree of Cyrus (1:2-4) and the inventory of temple vessels (1:9-11) reflect, in their view, authentic sources. Grabbe, on the other hand, has seriously reevaluated the authenticity of the sources underlying the Book of Ezra.[21] He questions the authenticity of the Aramaic Documents, the letters in Ezra 5–6, and of the Ezra Memoir (Ezra 7–10), since

1. the comparative material by which to judge the authenticity of the 'Archive material', is too small in number and of uncertain authenticity and since

---

[17] As has first been proposed by A. van Hoonacker, "Néhémie et Esdras, une nouvelle hypothèse sur la chronologie et la restauration juive", *Le Muséon* 9 (1890), 151-80, 315-7, 389-401.

[18] See e.g. T.M. Brolin, "When the End is the Beginning: The Persian Period and the Origins of the Biblical Tradition", *SJOT* 10 (1996), 3-15. A discussion of the text-critical evidence is outside the scope of this paper. On the relation between Ezra and 1 Esdras see e.g. K.F. Pohlmann, *Studien zum dritten Esra: Ein Beitrag zur Frage nach dem ursprünglichen Schluß des chronistischen Geschichtswerks* (FRLANT, 104), Göttingen 1970; D. Böhler, *Die heilige Stadt in Esdras α und Esra-Nehemia: Zwei Konzeptionen der Wiederherstellung Israels* (OBO, 158), Freiburg & Göttingen 1997; Grabbe, *Ezra–Nehemiah*, 109-15. Böhler, *Heilige Stadt*, 382-97, pleads, based on the assumption that Ezra-Nehemia is a reworking of 1 Esdras, for a late Hasmonaean date of the final composition of Ezra-Nehemia. He interprets Ezra-Nehemia as a recension serving the Maccabean rebellion. In view of my remarks on 'Power' (see below § 4.2.) Böhler's view does not make much sense, at least as for the Ezra-material. He might be right in his interpretation of Nehemiah 9–12 as a 'resistance-text', but that would – again – plead for the treatment of Ezra and Nehemiah as two separate books presenting different belief systems.

[19] Williamson, *Ezra, Nehemiah*, xxiii-xxxiii; Idem, *Ezra and Nehemiah*, 20-6, 29-34.

[20] B. Halpern, "A Historiographic Commentary on Ezra 1–6: Achronological Narrative and Dual Chronology in Israelite Historiography", in: W.H. Propp, *et al.* (eds.), *The Hebrew Bible and its Interpreters* (BibJS, 1), Winona Lake 1990, 81-142.

[21] L.L. Grabbe, "Reconstructing History from the Book of Ezra", in: Ph.R. Davies (ed.), *Second Temple Studies*, vol. 1: Persian Period (JSOT.S, 117), Sheffield 1991, 98-106; L.L. Grabbe, *Judaism from Cyrus to Hadrian*, London 1994, 30-41; see also Idem, *Ezra–Nehemiah*, 125-53.

2. in the Persian and Hellenistic period "doctoring of documents to make them more pro-Jewish seems to have been a minor cottage industry", by which is meant that editorial intervention and embedding in a narrative can change the scope and the ideology of a document to such a degree that it is impossible to reconstruct the original text.[22]

In this discussion I intend to take side with Grabbe, but even scholars like Halpern and Williamson will probably agree with the view that the organization of the past in the present Book of Ezra has to be regarded as the author's interpretation of the past and, by implication, is a feature of its belief system.

The Book of Ezra was written in a formative period of Judaism when a variety of Judaisms was nearby as can be assumed. The social setting of the Book and its author is not easy to determine. I tend to agree with Philip Davies who, writing in the mode of a structural-functional sociology,[23] outlines a picture of Persian period Yehud in which a variety of competing forms of Judaisms were present. This variety is also reflected in later Hellenistic texts. The Book of Ezra has been written as a legitimation of one form of Judaism.[24]

4   The Belief System of the Book of Ezra

The last clause of the preceding section can be rephrased as follows: The Book of Ezra has been a written tool to convince groups and persons in Persian period Yehud of a certain world-view. Four elements are important and they will now be discussed.

4.1   Time and the Past: History

The stories in the Book of Ezra contain a reenactment of strings of events. For the author they have truly happened. Moreover, he wants his readers to belief that his representation of the past is the only correct one. The picture of the past he is presenting can be summarized as follows:

1. A mass return in the early years of Cyrus, king of Persia;
2. A rebuilding of the temple despite ongoing obstructions and
3. Ezra's implementation of the תּוֹרָה of YHWH in the community in Jerusalem and Judah.

---

[22]Grabbe, "Reconstructing History", 101-2.

[23]On this term see A.D.H. Mayes, *The Old Testament in a Sociological Perspective*, London 1989, 27-35, 87-117.

[24]Ph.R. Davies, "Scenes from the Early History of Judaism", in D.V. Edelman (ed.), *The Triumph of Elohim: From Yahwisms to Judaisms* (CBET, 13), Kampen 1995, 145-182; Nodet, *Search for the Origins*, 337-66, comes to a comparable conclusion using, however, a more traditional historical method.

As for the 'mass return' some observations have to be made,

1. The return is presented as a fulfillment of prophecies by Jeremiah. Most scholars relate this feature to the prophecies in Jer. 25:12 and 29:10.[25] In my view the author of the Book of Ezra might also have thought at the elements of hope in the so-called Book of Consolation (Jer. 30–31).

2. The Persian king is pictured as standing very friendly toward the Israelites in exile. No mention is made of a comparable liberal policy toward other exiled nations.

3. The returners are supported financially by the Persian king and, on his demand (Ezra 1:4, 6), by their temporary neighbours. The king even returns to them the temple vessels exiled from Jerusalem by Nebuchadnezzar. This is not only a fine gesture by a ruling king, but also an important feature in the belief system of the Book of Ezra, since it presents the, then in the narrative still forthcoming, worship in the second temple as a continuation of the worship in the first temple.[26]

4. Ezra 2:1-70 presents a list of 42,360 returners. An almost identical list is attested in Neh. 7. Critical scholarship has questioned the authenticity of this list. Very intriguing is the interpretation by Weinberg of this list. In his view Neh. 7:7-69 gives the original form of the list the purpose of which is not to describe all those returning from Mesopotamia, but should be interpreted as an indication of the collectives belonging to the 'citizen-temple community' until the year 458/57 BCE. This community consists of descendants of those returning from Mesopotamia from the edict of Cyrus onward.[27] His observations might be correct on the level of the reconstruction of the past. The author of the Book of Ezra wants his readers to believe that this list contains the names of the returners. He especially stresses the continuity

---

[25] See the commentaries on Ezra and W.L. Holladay, *Jeremiah 2: A Commentary on the Book of the Prophet Jeremiah Chapters 26-52* (Hermeneia), Minneapolis 1989, 90.

[26] See P.R. Ackroyd, "The Temple-vessels – A Continuity Theme", in: J.A. Emerton (ed.), *Studies in the Religion of Ancient Israel* (VT.S, 23), Leiden 1972, 166-81.

[27] J.P. Weinberg, "Demographische Notizen zur Geschichte der nachexilischen Gemeinde in Juda", *Klio* 54 (1972), 45-99, quoted after the translation: "Demographic Notes on the History of the Postexilic Community in Judah", in: Idem, *The Citizen-Temple Community* (JSOT.S, 151), Sheffield 1992, 41-3.

with the pre-exilic community by noting that the returners are
identical with those exiled by Nebuchadnezzar (Ezra 2:1). He
even avoids the use of the word 'descendants'.

Regarding the episodes on the building of the temple (Ezra 3–6), it
must be remarked that these units are enigmatic. I will present here
only one problem: The mention of Jeshua and Zerubbabel. They are
mentioned in Ezra 3:2 as laying the foundation of the altar for the God
of Israel. According to the internal chronology of Ezra this event took
place in the reign of Cyrus. According to the same internal chronology
Jeshua and Zerubbabel are still in charge in Ezra 5:2 where they are
initiating the rebuilding of the temple of Jerusalem. This initiative
took place during the reign of a Persian king named Darius who gov-
erned after Cyrus, Ahasuerus and Artaxerxes. Moreover, it took place
after the exchange of letters mentioned in Ezra 4 during the reign of
Ahasuerus and Artaxerxes. Within the text-internal chronology there
is no problem with these textual features except the fact that they
suppose either a quick change in rulership at the Persian court or a
long life for the two officials mentioned. Problems arise when this text-
internal chronology is related to a text-external chronology. So either
Darius mentioned in Ezra 5 is identical with Darius I Hystaspes (522-
486 BCE) or he is identical with Darius II Ochus (424-405 BCE). Both
possibilities provoke problems. The historical reconstruction yielded
by the first identification makes problematical the chronological order
of the letters, since in this reconstruction the correspondence in Ezra
5 took place earlier than the exchange of letters referred to in Ezra 4.
This is rather meaningless in view of the contents of the letters. Ezra
4 stops the building of the temple while Ezra 5 gives permission to
complete the building activities. I do not see the point in a reversed
historical order. The second identification mentioned supposes that
Jeshua and Zerubbabel had lived superhumanly long. Cyrus died in
529 BCE and Darius II Ochus captured the Persian throne in 424 BCE.
This paper, however, is not on reconstructing history. The question
thus must be: What picture of the past is the author of the Book of
Ezra presenting here? Elsewhere, I have discussed this section in more
detail.[28] The author of the Book of Ezra presents in these chapters
the view that

---

[28] B. Becking, "Ezra on the Move . . . : Trends and Perspectives on the Character
and his Book", in: F. García Martínez, E. Noort (eds.), *Perspectives on the Study
of the Old Testament and Early Judaism*, (VT.S, 73), Leiden 1998, 154-79, esp.
168-75.

1. The building of the temple was necessary for the celebration of the Passover-festival,

2. This building has been frustrated by various groups of adversaries and enemies and

3. The building had divine (Ezra 5:1-2) and imperial (Ezra 6:1-5) support.

In the third story, the coming to Jerusalem of the Ezra-group, two events from the past are presented as important,

1. The imperial support for Ezra's mission (Ezra 7:6; 7:11-26),[29]

2. The role of Levites in temple and community.

Note that at the transit camp near the river Ahava, Levites were absent in the group of those going up to Jerusalem until Ezra collected some decent men from the Machli family who belonged to the Levites (Ezra 8:18).

Finally, it is remarkable that there are only a few references to events from the history of the Israelites in the pre-exilic period in the Book of Ezra. The Book refers to kings of Israel and Mesopotamia. Moses and David are mentioned in their respective capacities as lawgiver and initiator of the Jerusalem liturgy. I will discuss the relevant passages.

At two instances the monarchic period in Israel and Judah is referred to. In a text, presented as a letter to Artaxerxes, Rehum, the chancellor, and Shimshai, the secretary, assume that the Persian king will find in the archives of his ancestors a note about Jerusalem, i.e., "that this city is a rebellious city, damaging to kings and provinces, and that sedition has been fomented within it in times past. That is why this city is laid waste" (Ezra 4:15). The Persian king finds this note in the royal records (Ezra 4:19). The author of the Book of Ezra does not say that he himself shares this negative view on the kings of Judah. It is, however, interesting that a feature in the prayer of Ezra is related to a comparable proposition. When Ezra confesses the trespasses of his people, he broadens the historical scope of that confession by saying that "Because of our iniquities, our kings and our

---

[29] Very interesting – from a historiographic point of view – is the essay by P. Frei, "Zentralgewalt und Lokalautonomie im Achämenidenreich", in: Frei, Koch, *Reichsidee und Reichsorganisation*, 5-131, who compares Ezra 7:12-26 with other instances of imperial authorization known from Persian period written sources. For a discussion on this topic see the articles by P. Frei, J. Wiesehöfer and U. Rüterswörden in *ZAR* 1 (1995).

priests have been delivered into the hands of the kings of the lands, of sword, captivity, pillage and open shame" (Ezra 9:7).[30] In phrasing his belief of identification with the Israelites through the ages, Ezra evaluates the sack of Jerusalem as the result of sin.

Two Mesopotamian kings are mentioned in the Book of Ezra. Nebuchadnezzar is portrayed as the king who sacked Jerusalem and exiled the temple vessels to Babylon (Ezra 1:7; 4:12-14). In Ezra 4:2 a group that wants to be cooperative with Zerubbabel in rebuilding the temple, defines itself as sacrificing to the God of Zerubbabel "ever since the time of Esarhaddon, king of Assyria, who brought us here". Esarhaddon is here portrayed in contrast to Cyrus and Darius. He, too, brought people to Israel. This group, however, is not accepted as belonging to the same religious branch by Zerubbabel.

Ezra 4:10 mentions another group of persons presenting themselves as descendants of exiles. Here, a group of people brought to the Samarian area from Erech, Babylon, Susa, Elam and elsewhere by "the great and esteemed Osnappar" are among those who stand against the rebuilding of the temple. The identity of Osnappar is not clear. Often, the name is seen as a confusion of Ashurbanipal, king of Assyria.[31] This identification, however, is not without problems, both philological and historical.[32] Osnappar is *not* presented as a king in Ezra 4:10. He might as well has been an Assyrian, Babylonian or Persian high officer responsible for deportations.

The mention of a "King of Assyria" whose attitude toward the Israelites had been changed by YHWH (Ezra 6:22) should not be taken as a reference to a pre-exilic king, but either as a scribal error or as a stereotyped description of a foreign ruler.[33]

Moses is mentioned only three times in the Book of Ezra. Although the תּוֹרָה is an important theme, especially in the third narrative in the Book of Ezra, it is only at three instances that the תּוֹרָה is related to Moses. Ezra 3:2 narrates that Jeshua and Zerubbabel rebuild "the altar of the God of Israel so that they can probably sacrifice burnt-offerings upon it as prescribed in the law of Moses, the man of God". Ezra 6:18 relates that preparations for the Passover festival were made

---

[30] On the prayer of Ezra see recently H.-P. Mathys, *Dichter und Beter: Theologen aus spätalttestamentlicher Zeit* (OBO, 132), Freiburg & Göttingen 1994, 21-36; J. van Oorschot, "Nachkultische Psalmen und spätbiblische Rollendichtung", *ZAW* 106 (1994), 69-86; H.W.M. van Grol, "Schuld und Scham: Die Verwurzelung von Ezra 9,6-7 in der Tradition", *EstB* 55 (1997), 29-52; Idem, "Exegesis of the Exile – Exegesis of Scripture? Ezra 9:6-9", in: J.C. de Moor (ed.), *Intertextuality in Ugarit and Israel* (OTS, 40), Leiden 1998, 31-61.

[31] See e.g. Blenkinsopp, *Ezra–Nehemiah*, 113; A.K. Grayson, "Osnappar", *AncBD*, vol. 5 (1992), 50.

[32] See A.R. Millard, "Assyrian Royal Names in Biblical Hebrew", *JSSt* 21 (1976), 11-12; Williamson, *Ezra, Nehemiah*, 55.

[33] See e.g. Williamson, *Ezra, Nehemiah*, 85-6; Blenkinsopp, *Ezra–Nehemiah*, 133.

according to the "Book of Moses".[34] Ezra 7:6 informs about Ezra the scribe that he was skilled in the law of Moses. The mention of Moses functions as a device of continuity in the world constructed in the Book of Ezra.

The same holds for the mention of David in Ezra 3:10 and 8:20, where he is portrayed in his capacity as initiator of the liturgy in the pre-exilic temple. It is a remarkable fact that in Ezra 5:11 the building and completion of the first temple are referred to without the mention of Solomon as the "great king of Israel" that constructed the first temple.

4.2 Power

For the author of the Book of Ezra two powers are at work: divine and imperial. Both YHWH and the Persian king are seen as powerful agents steering history.

As for imperial power, it should be noted that the author of the Book of Ezra casts the Persian kings mainly in the role of supporters of Israelite claims about land, worship and ethical conduct. Cyrus is presented as the king promoting the return to Jerusalem and the building of the temple (Ezra 1:1-4; 6:3-5). Darius, too, stands positive toward efforts of rebuilding the temple (Ezra 6:1-13). The unidentified "King of Assyria" whose heart had been changed by YHWH might be interpreted as indicating a Persian king, or as a reference to Persian imperial power as such. Blenkinsopp, taking the final redaction of Ezra 1–6 as a coherent story, construes the "stirring up of the spirit of Cyrus" at the beginning and the "changing of the heart" at the end of this story as an *inclusion*.[35] Artaxerxes, in Ezra 7, is presented as the king supporting Ezra's mission. The only exception is the Artaxerxes mentioned in Ezra 4, who frustrates the process of rebuilding the temple. It is, however, clear that he is manipulated by one, or maybe two groups of adversaries:

    a. Bishlam, Mithredat, Tabeel and their colleagues and
    b. Rehum, the chancellor, and Shimshai, the secretary.

---

[34] Like Williamson, *Ezra, Nehemiah*, xxxvii-xxxix, I do not accept the view of C. Houtman, "Ezra and the Law", in: A.S. van der Woude (ed.), *Remembering all the Way ...: A Collection of Old Testament Studies; Published on the Occasion of the Fortieth Anniversary of the Oudtestamentisch Werkgezelschap in Nederland* (OTS, 21), Leiden 1981, 91-115, that this book would refer to "a law-book with a character of its own which is not transmitted to us" but is different from the Pentateuch.

[35] Blenkinsopp, *Ezra–Nehemiah*, 133.

It belongs to the enigmas of Ezra 3–6 that it is not clear whether
these two groups acted independently or in a cooperative manner.

That the author of the Book of Ezra believed in the power of
YHWH, is detectable from all three narratives in his composition. I
will list a few examples that show the character of this divine rule.
YHWH is presented as "stirring the spirit of Cyrus" (Ezra 1:1), an act
that initiated the process of return. In Ezra 5:1 YHWH is presented
as sending the prophets Haggai and Zechariah. In Ezra 5:5 mention
is made of the fact that "the eye of God was on the elders of the
Judahites". The two clauses are not descriptions of mere facts, but
should be seen as interpretative remarks indicating the belief that
YHWH was encouraging the Judahites even in the period when the
process of rebuilding the temple had entered a dead-end-street and
seemed doomed to fail. In the beginning of the third narrative an
important insight in the belief in divine rule is given. In the textual
unit where Ezra the scribe is introduced (Ezra 7:6) it is said that
YHWH had given the Law of Moses. Although it is not explicitly stated
to whom and when the תּוֹרָה was given it can be assumed that the
author of the Book of Ezra believed that the תּוֹרָה was given in Mosaic
times. In the same verse it is narrated that "The king (of Persia) gave
him (Ezra) ... all he had asked for" and that this happened while
"the hand of YHWH, his God, was upon him". This notion of divine
guidance in the life of Ezra is repeated at Ezra 7:9, 28; 8:18, 22, 31.
In other words, the author of the Book of Ezra interpreted Ezra's
life as steered and conducted by YHWH. Phrased otherwise, he thus
presents his mission and his measures as willed by God and not as
mere human ideas.

These two powers are not construed as mutual exclusive or competing.[36] The Book of Ezra opts for a view in which both powers co-
operate. This synergism of power becomes clear at various instances
in the Book of Ezra. Two of them will be mentioned here: (1) The
"stirring of the spirit of Cyrus" (Ezra 1:1) implies cooperation; (2)
In Ezra 6:14 it is said that the rebuilding of the temple took place
according to the "command of the God of Israel and to the decree of
Cyrus, Darius and Artaxerxes, the king of Persia". This implies (1)
the acceptance of YHWH as supreme power but also (2) the acceptance of Persian imperial power.

Acceptance of YHWH as supreme power implies the veneration
of this deity. In the Book of Ezra this, monotheistic, veneration is
three-dimensional, since it is related to the worship in the temple,

---

[36]See also Williamson, *Ezra and Nehemiah*, 86-90.

the acceptance of the תּוֹרָה of Moses and the clear construction of the boundaries of the community.

The acceptance of Persian imperial power, too, is an implication of the belief in YHWH. In Ezra 1:2 Cyrus, the king of Persia, is presented as uttering the belief that YHWH gave him the rule over all the kingdoms of the earth. Ezra does not preach a revolt against the ruling power as has been done by the former kings of Judah and, but this is not in the text, has been done in the Maccabean era. Two observations must be made,

(1) The existence of this feature in the belief system of the Book of Ezra implies that the pictorial propaganda of the Persian power was effective.[37] (2) As for the general theme of the symposium, it should be noted that an element of discontinuity was provoked by the changed situation. The strive for independence, with or without messianic expectations – a characteristicum of the pre-exilic prophets –, did change into the acceptance of the existence in the periphery of a world power. Later, in Hellenistic times, this position of acceptance was abandoned for rebellion and revolt against the ruling, non-Jewish power.

4.3   Sacred Space: the Temple

The temple is very important in the Book of Ezra. One of the themes of the first narrative is the raising of funds for the rebuilding of the temple. Cyrus, the king of Persia, supplies the temple vessels exiled by Nebuchadnessar. The temporary neighbours in the exilic situation are said to have given silver and gold, goods and livestock (Ezra 1:6). The heads of the families gave freewill offerings toward the rebuilding of the temple on its original site (Ezra 2:68). The central events in the third narrative take place "in front of the house of God" (Ezra 10:1). The middle narrative relates the complex process of the rebuilding of the temple. Many readers of the Book of Ezra will agree with the interpretative remark that the temple was very important for the religious identity of post-exilic Judaism. The temple gave them a home to gather and to worship YHWH in a world where other religions and other forms of Yahwism were present. The Book of Ezra does not inform its readers firmly on the symbolic meaning of the temple.[38] A few glimpses are present, however. As Williamson has stressed already, there are lines of institutional continuity. These lines

---

[37] See Koch, "Weltordnung und Reichsidee", 137-205; Uehlinger in this volume.

[38] I am not convinced by the argument of Eskenazi, *In an Age of Prose*, 54-6, that the expression "the house of God" in Ezra 3–6 would not only refer to the היכל or 'temple-building', but to the city as a whole.

include the temple vessels, the cultic practices and the role of the Levites.[39] These lines of institutional continuity should, however, not be seen as historical descriptions but as part of the belief system of the Book of Ezra. The author wants its readers to believe in the factuality of these lines of continuity. He wants to present the second temple and the worship within it as the only possible continuation of the pre-exilic worship in the temple of Solomon.

As indicated above, I believe the main narrative programme in Ezra 3–6 can be labeled as 'the abolition of the non-celebration of the Passover festival'. This implies that the temple was not seen as a building 'as such' but was necessary for rites of reconciliation.

4.4 Confined Community

Until here, I have been speaking rather naively about 'Israelites' and 'Judahites'. From the Book of Ezra apparently one group of 'Israelites' construe themselves as the true Israel at the exclusion of other groups and persons. The most significant indication for this group can be found in Ezra 9:2. In a message to Ezra, some leaders report the intermarriage of Israelites, priests and Levites with women from other nations with the outcome that "the holy seed has become mixed with the peoples of the land". The idea of divine election is thus reformulated in biological categories.[40] This reformulation should be interpreted as a device of discontinuity. In a way it is an answer to a changed situation. On the political level, Judah had lost its independence. Apart from the difficult question how to classify sociologically the 'Ezra-group',[41] it should be noted that this group is looking for a religious and ethnic identity in Ezra 9–10.

The term 'holy seed' should be seen as a combination of two traditional depictions of Israel: In Deuteronomy[42] Israel is often called a 'holy nation'; elsewhere the depiction of this people as the 'seed

---

[39]Williamson, *Ezra and Nehemiah*, 82-4.

[40]*Pace* Williamson, *Ezra, Nehemiah*, 132, who construes 'holy seed' to be a racial term.

[41]Different classifications have been proposed; see e.g. A. Causse, *Du groupe ethnique à la communauté religieuse: la problème sociologique de la religion d'Israël*, Paris 1937; M. Smith, *Palestinian Parties and Politics that Shaped the Old Testament*, New York 1971; Weinberg, *Citizen-Temple Community*; F. Crüsemann, "Israel in der Perserzeit. Eine Skizze in auseinandersetzung mit Max Weber", in: W. Schluchter (ed.), *Max Webers Sicht des Antiken Christentums*, Frankfurt a.M. 1985, 205-32; R. Albertz, *Religionsgeschichte Israels in alttestamentlicher Zeit*, Bd. 2, (GAT, 8/2), Göttingen 1992, 468-78.

[42]E.g. at Deut. 26:18.

of Abraham' is used.[43] Both depictions are related to the selfunderstanding as elected by God. The term 'holy seed' shows a radical
self-interpretation of the Ezra-group.[44] To them being elected by God
implies that the group may not be defiled by foreign elements. At the
background of the indignation of the leaders in Ezra 9:1-2 and also of
the measures taken by Ezra stand the warnings in the תּוֹרָה of Moses
not to marry with the indigenous population of Canaan because intermarriage would almost certainly lead to syncretism and apostasy.[45]
This proposition is reinterpreted in the Book of Ezra,

1. The negative assessment of intermarriage is still based on fear
   for apostasy and syncretism. The anguish is, however, phrased
   in terms of taboo and fright for the pollution of the group as
   can be detected from the use of the words מעל and תעבה in this
   connection.

2. Texts like Exod. 34 and Deut. 7 only warn and forbid the intermarriage. They do not offer stipulations in case an Israelite
   eventually married a person from another group or nation that
   actually happened in the pre-exilic period as the not negatively
   assessed examples of Ruth and Solomon show. In the Book of
   Ezra measures are taken to dissolve these marriages and to send
   away women and children. These measures, although rigid implications of the תּוֹרָה, are difficult to understand against all said
   in the תּוֹרָה of Moses about the protection of the poor and the
   needy. In other words: The belief in the idea of a 'holy seed'
   is that central to Ezra that he is prepared to overlook other
   features of the moral code.[46]

   It is surprising to note that analogous tendencies are detectable in the
   cultural context. In Zoroastranism, every mingling with people of another
   background is seen as an abomination. In Athens Pericles ordered around
   450 BCE that only persons with a full Attic descent both from maternal and
   from paternal side will be accepted as members of the civil community.[47]

---

[43] See e.g. Isa. 41:8; Jer. 33:26; Ps. 105:6; 2 Chron. 20:7.

[44] The expression might contain an allusion to Isa. 6:13; see J.G. McConville,
"Ezra-Nehemiah and the Fulfilment of Prophecy", *VT* 36 (1986), 218-22.

[45] See Exod. 34:11-16; Deut. 7:1-4; 20:10-18.

[46] One should note that it is an ongoing problem in the ethical discourse when
two propositions from the moral code of a given society turn out to be contradictory in an unforseen situation. On this problem of transvaluation in ethics see
e.g. E.L. Long, *A Survey of Christian Ethics*, New York 1967, esp. 59-72; T.W.
van Willigenburg, *Inside the Ethical Expert: Problem Solving in Applied Ethics*,
Kampen 1991; P.K. Covey, "The Crucible of Experience", in: R. Heeger, T. van
Willigenburg (eds.), *The Turn to Applied Ethics*, Kampen 1993, 53-72.

[47] See R.G. Kent, *Old Persian: Grammar, Texts, Lexicon* (AOS, 33), New Haven

3. As has been observed by Blenkinsopp[48] the Deuteronomic prohibition with regard to intermarriage (Deut. 7:3) includes *both
sexes*, while the prohibition in Ezra (and Nehemiah) is confined
to marrying foreign *women*. By implication, marrying foreign
males does not seem to fall under the post-exilic prohibition.
One can only speculate on the religious, social and demographic
presuppositions and implications of this partial discontinuity of
the traditional code.

This self-complacent interpretation is attested elsewhere in the Book
of Ezra and has implications as for the interpretation of "the other".
I will give an example of both. Ezra 4:1-3 relates the rebuff by Zerubbabel and Jeshua of an offer to help rebuilding the temple by a
group depicted as "the adversaries of Judah and Benjamin". The offer
is declined with an argument of exclusiveness: "You have nothing in
common with us". Zerubbabel and Jeshua appeal to the decree of
Cyrus that only the returners might build a house for YHWH in Jerusalem. In the next section (Ezra 4:4-5) it is narrated that the 'people
of the land' started to frustrate the building process by discouraging
the people of Judah. In an approach that looks for a reconstruction of
the historical chain of events in the Persian period it could be observed
that the acts referred to in 4:4-5 took place in a period quite different
from the acts referred to in 4:1-3[49] or that 4:4-5 contains a 'summary
notation' not giving information on events that took place after 4:1-3,
but summarizing the contents of the preceding textual unit.[50] This
might be true on a historical level, the present presentation in the
narrative order of Ezra 3–6 suggests that the author of the Book of
Ezra believed that this beginning frustration is the reaction of the
"others" to the rebuff by Zerubbbabel and Jeshua.

One final remark concerning the idea of community. Scholars have
long recognized the enigmatic identity of a variety of adversaries and
enemies in the Book of Ezra. Who were the others and how many
groups were there? I do not have an answer to the puzzling question
whether these groups were proto-Samaritans, descendants of Assyrian
settlers, offspring of Judahites that remained in Judah after the cata-

---

[2] 1953, 137-141.157; J. Blenkinsopp, "Temple and Society in Achaemenid Judah",
in: Davies (ed.), *Second Temple Studies*, vol. 1, 59; Koch, "Weltordnung und
Reichsidee", 265-67.

[48] Blenkinsopp, *Ezra–Nehemiah*, 176-7.

[49] Halpern, "Historiographic Commentary", 103-16.

[50] S. Talmon,"Ezra and Nehemiah", in: G.A. Buttrick (ed.), *Interpreter's Dictionary of the Bible*, Suppl. vol., Nashville 1976, 322; Williamson, *Ezra, Nehemiah*,
43-4.

strophe of 587 BCE or whatever there has been proposed.[51] I have an observation, however. What is at hand in the narratives of the Book of Ezra is a mystification of the "others" by being unspecific about them.

In the narratives the two kinds of inimical groups are mentioned. In Ezra 3–6 a variety of groups frustrating the rebuilding of the temple is depicted. In Ezra 7–10 the group of Israelites/Judahites that has no part in the 'holy seed' is outlined unspecifically. First, attention will be paid to the 'others' mentioned in Ezra 3–6:

1. "The peoples of the land". This is an unclear depiction of a group of persons generally construed as Judahites that had remained in the land.[52] They provoked fear amid the 'returners' (Ezra 3:3);

2. Adversaries of Judah and Benjamin, claiming to be descendants of persons deported by Esarhaddon to the Israelite area (Ezra 4:1-3);

3. "The people of the land" a group discouraging the moral of Judahites rebuilding the temple (Ezra 4:4-5). They are not necessarily the same group as 1, although an overlap might be assumed. This group might have included 2. The proposal of e.g. Würthwein[53] to identify this group with the ruling classes in Samaria is premature and cannot be detected from the existing evidence;[54]

4. A group indicated as "they" who wrote a complaint in the reign of Ahasuerus/Xerxes (Ezra 4:6);

5. A group living in the city of Samaria including high officials such as Rehum, the chancellor, and Shimshai, the secretary, writing a letter in a political mode in the reign of Artaxerxes warning the king for the economic effects of the building of a temple in Jerusalem. This group construes itself as settlers from Persia, Erech, Babylon and Susan (Ezra 4:7-16). In doing so this group dissociated itself from both from the indigenous population and from settlers coming later;

---

[51] See the discussion in J. Zsengellér, *Gerizim as Israel: Northern Traditions of the Old Testament and the Early History of the Samaritans* (UTR, 38), Utrecht 1998, 119-37.

[52] E.g. Williamson, *Ezra, Nehemiah*, 46.

[53] E. Würthwein, *Der 'amm ha'arez im Alten Testament*, Stuttgart 1936, 57-64.

[54] See e.g. Smith, *Palestinian Parties*, 193-201; Williamson, *Ezra, Nehemiah*, 50.

6. "Tattenai, the governor of 'Beyond the River', Shethar-bozenai
   and their associates" asking the group who after the prophecies
   of Haggai and Zechariah restarted the rebuilding of the temple
   for their legitimation (Ezra 5:3).

It is not the interest of the author of this narrative to present evidence for a reconstruction of the various factions in post-exilic Yehud.
The aim of the narrative can be seen as follows: Despite a variety of
opponents the temple has been build to function as a house of God
for Israel.

As regards the narrative on Ezra's measures concerning the mixed
marriages, the identity of the "others" is not clear, at least not to me.
There are three possibilities,

1. Members of the group just arrived with Ezra entered mixed marriages.[55] This is an attractive view that explains the fierceness
   of Ezra's reaction since it is then based on Ezra's belief that he
   should keep his group clean from all pollution.

2. Williamson, on the other hand, has argued that families who had
   come to Jerusalem during earlier waves of return are referred to
   and not members of the Ezra-group as such.[56] This view can
   be underscored by the observation that in Ezra 10:6 mention is
   made of Ezra's mourning over the "unfaithfulness of the exiles"
   and that in Ezra 10:7 the בְּנֵי הַגּוֹלָה are summoned to gather in
   Jerusalem. Elsewhere, I have defended the view that in Ezra 7–8
   the move of the Ezra-group from Ahava to Jerusalem is narrated
   in language of movement and not in language of return. Verbs
   like עלה, 'to go up',[57] and בוא, 'to come',[58] are predominant
   while the verb שוב, 'to return', is absent.[59] In this view Ezra's
   measures are a device for differentiation between various groups
   of Judahites and an indication that Ezra's view on Jahwism was
   quickly accepted by others.

3. Finally it is possible to construe those who had entered mixed
   marriages as members of various groups present in Jerusalem

---

[55] E.g. Nodet, *Search for the Origins*, 343.

[56] Williamson, *Ezra, Nehemiah*, 130.

[57] Ezra 7:6, 7; 8:1.

[58] See Ezra 7:8; 8:30, 32.

[59] B. Becking, "Ezra's Reenactment of the Exile", in: L.L. Grabbe (ed.), *Leading Captivity Captive: 'The Exile' as History and Ideology* (ESHM, 2; JSOT.S, 278), Sheffield 1998, 40-61.

and surroundings.[60] The text of the narrative is not very decisive on this point.

Next to this it should be observed that the ethnic entities with which they intermingled are described in a *chiffre*. Ezra 9:6 numbers a list of eight peoples from whom they did not keep themselves apart. This list resembles the lists of the five,[61] six,[62] seven[63] or ten[64] nations in the Pentateuch and the Former Prophets that stand symbolically for the indigenous population of the land in its entirety. Apparently, persons living in Persian period Palestine or Yehud will not have construed themselves as belonging to one of the nations listed. The first four groups mentioned – Canaanites, Hittites, Perizzites and Jebusites – had long been died out by the time of Ezra.[65] In using this traditional language the author of the Book of Ezra is, in a way, demonizing the "other".

In sum, the obscurity about the identity of various groups of "others" functions as a glorification of the community around the character of Ezra.

5   Conclusion

The description of the multi faceted belief system of the Book of Ezra, preliminary and superficial as it is, has made clear the great importance of an intimate and fenced community that construes itself as the only correct continuation of the pre-exilic Judaean/Israelite community. Later readers rather easily criticized this communal idea as 'legalistic', 'particularistic' or 'fundamentalistic'.[66] This, however, is the expression of the look of an outsider. Before criticizing Ezra's belief system one should note that for some proto-Jewish groups such a world-view was needed to survive and to endure in the immense Persian empire.

---

[60]This is about the position of e.g. Eskenazi, *In an Age of Prose*, 68-70; D.L. Smith-Christopher, "The Mixed Marriage Crisis in Ezra 9–10 and Nehemiah 13: A Study of the Sociology of the Post-Exilic Judaean Community", in: T.C. Eskenazi, K.H. Richards (eds.), *Second Temple Studies* (JSOT.S, 175), vol. 2: Temple Community in the Persian Period, Sheffield 1994, 243-65.

[61]Exod. 13:5; ⅏ and ꟺ, however, list seven peoples.

[62]Exod. 3:8, 17; 23:23; 32:2; 34:11; Deut. 20:17; Judg. 3:5.

[63]Deut. 7:1; Josh. 3:10; 24:11.

[64]Gen. 15:19-21.

[65]As is noted by Koch, "Weltordnung und Reichsidee", 265.

[66]See e.g. E. Sellin, *Theologie des Alten Testaments*, Leipzig 1933, 53, 76, 87, 128; L. Köhler, *Theologie des Alten Testaments*, Tübingen 1936, 66-68; G. von Rad, *Theologie des Alten Testaments*, Bd.1, München ⁶1969, 102-5.

Hugh G.M. Williamson *Oxford – United Kingdom*

The Belief System of the Book of Nehemiah

Two reservations need to be expressed about the title prescribed for this article. In the first place, it is superficially curious to focus attention on the book of Nehemiah in isolation from Ezra. In the view of the overwhelming majority of scholars, the separation of this single work into two books is to be ascribed to the activity of later translators only, and it overlooks the deliberate editorial intent to fuse together the roles of the two eponymous reformers, not least in the climactic chapters 8–10.[1] It is true that in recent years one or two voices have been raised in support of the view that these two books were written in separation from one another from the start,[2] but it may be doubted whether this opinion will attract widespread support. While it is, of course, possible to proceed from a literary point of view by selecting any given stretch of writing for analysis, we shall need to be careful, therefore, before we extrapolate from an artificially determined selection towards wider historical conclusions of a sort which this volume is interested to investigate.[3]

In the second place, even greater difficulties attend the use of the language of belief systems in relation to a text, and especially a text as complex as that of Nehemiah. Only people can have a belief system, and there are well-known pitfalls in seeking to move direct from text to history.[4] Even assuming that this hurdle can be overcome, we shall

---

[1]For a summary introduction to the arguments in support of this position, see my *Ezra, Nehemiah* (WBC, 16), Waco, TX 1985, xxi-xxiii.

[2]See J.C. VanderKam, "Ezra-Nehemiah or Ezra and Nehemiah?", in: E. Ulrich *et al.* (eds.), *Priests, Prophets and Scribes: Essays on the Formation and Heritage of Second Temple Judaism in Honour of Joseph Blenkinsopp* (JSOT.S, 149), Sheffield 1992, 55-75; D. Kraemer, "On the Relationship of the Books of Ezra and Nehemiah", *JSOT* 59 (1993), 73-92, reprinted in J.C. Exum (ed.), *The Historical Books: A Sheffield Reader*, Sheffield 1997, 303-21. To these must now be added B. Becking's contribution to the present volume.

[3]One mitigating factor in the present instance may be that the language of belief systems is adopted from the field of cultural anthropology (see Becking's article in this volume), a field which has also provided the model of cultural revitalization. It has been suggested elsewhere that this model may help explain the superficially curious ordering of material in the book of Nehemiah; see K.D. Tollefson, H.G.M. Williamson, "Nehemiah as Cultural Revitalization: An Anthropological Perspective", *JSOT* 56 (1992), 41-68, reprinted in Exum (ed.), *The Historical Books*, 322-48.

[4]While the depth of these 'pits' varies from one text to another, they are not absent even from a text which stands as close to history as the Nehemiah Memoir. Though in exaggerated form, the point is well made by D.J.A. Clines, "The Ne-

need to be clear whose belief systems we are investigating, whether those of Nehemiah himself, or those of the authors of the other sources which have gone into the make-up of the book, or those of the final editor of the work which we now have. In terms of literary study, the work of the final editor is usually the most straightforward to approach, but in terms of our present concern it seems to me to be the most elusive. Since, moreover, it is strongly tied to the question of the relationship between the books of Ezra and Nehemiah already mentioned, I shall have least to say about it. Finally, it remains almost completely unknown to what extent the belief systems reflected in the work of these various authors were shared by others or were regarded as normative by the community at the time.

With these caveats in mind, it seems clear that we must start by separating carefully between the first-person account of Nehemiah himself and the remainder of the material in the book. As I have sought to emphasize elsewhere, for every major achievement for which Nehemiah himself claims credit, there is within the book an alternative account of the same event in which the people as a whole are shown acting in concert under priestly leadership.[5] If this is true, it should be of considerable help to us. Comparison and contrast should add historical depth to the analysis and enable at least one step to be taken towards the disentanglement of core beliefs from individual agendas. It would be too crude simply to distinguish between lay and priestly outlooks. On the one hand Nehemiah was hardly a typical layman of the province; his agenda, at least at the start of his ministry, was strongly influenced by his role as a servant of imperial policy.[6] On the other hand, the remaining material is not simply 'in

---

hemiah Memoir: The Perils of Autobiography", in: *What Does Eve Do to Help? and Other Readerly Questions to the Old Testament* (JSOT.S, 94), Sheffield 1990, 124-64. By "taking account of the genre and associated conventions of this kind of writing", J. Blenkinsopp arrives at rather more conservative conclusions; see "The Nehemiah Autobiographical Memoir", in: S.E. Balentine, J. Barton (eds.), *Language, Theology, and the Bible: Essays in Honour of James Barr*, Oxford 1994, 199-212.

[5]See *Ezra, Nehemiah, passim*, and especially "Post-Exilic Historiography", in: R.E. Friedman, H.G.M. Williamson (eds.), *The Future of Biblical Studies: The Hebrew Scriptures* (Semeia Studies), Atlanta, GA 1987, 189-207. This account of the material still seems preferable to me to the alternative suggestion of D.R. Daniels to uncover "a third source in which Ezra and Nehemiah both appear and which spans Neh 8:1–11:24; perhaps also 12:27-30; and less certainly 11:25–12:26; 12:44–13:3"; see D.R. Daniels, "The Composition of the Ezra-Nehemiah Narrative", in: Idem *et al.* (eds.), *Ernten, was man sät: Festschrift für Klaus Koch zu seinem 65. Geburtstag*, Neukirchen-Vluyn 1991, 311-28.

[6]This point has been rightly emphasized by K.G. Hoglund, *Achaemenid Im-*

278   Hugh G.M. Williamson

house' priestly, but rather reflective of the community under priestly leadership; it is thus likely to present what we might call the public face of the priesthood.[7]

1 The Nehemiah Memoir

In order to clarify these areas of overlap, we need to attend first to some features of Nehemiah's own account which are suggestive of a strongly lay type of belief system. Assuming we may afford his account any credence at all, the fact that he had previously been in service at the heart of the imperial court, and so was not much influenced by the Palestinian priesthood, tends to accentuate these features, though they may nevertheless have been shared to some degree also by others in the land whose normal contacts were outside the restrictive circle of the temple personnel themselves.

A number of points deserve mention under this heading. In the first place, Nehemiah seems to have drawn in an unsophisticated manner on the previous national history.[8] Throughout Neh. 4:1-14 (English versions, 7-20), for instance, there are numerous points of contact with the laws for, and descriptions of, the so-called 'holy war' as represented particularly in Deuteronomic texts.[9] Kellermann[10] lists the following series of connections: the enemy band together against Jerusalem; the people pray before arming themselves; the human resources for defence are slender; the forces are a conscript militia rather than a standing army; the leader proclaims God's involvement in the

perial Administration in Syria-Palestine and the Missions of Ezra and Nehemiah (SBL.DS, 125), Atlanta, GA 1992, whose work on Nehemiah in this regard seems more convincing than that on Ezra.

[7]This aspect of the book of Nehemiah is perhaps overlooked by Kraemer (above, n. 2) in his attempt to drive a priestly versus lay wedge between the books of Ezra and Nehemiah.

[8]I have deliberately omitted reference to 13:1-3 under this heading because there are serious doubts as to whether it was part of Nehemiah's own first-person account; see, for instance, A.H.J. Gunneweg, *Nehemia* (KAT, 19/2), Gütersloh 1987, 163-4.

[9]See the standard collection and analysis of motifs in G. von Rad, *Der Heilige Krieg im alten Israel* (AThANT, 20), Zürich 1951 (English translation: *Holy War in Ancient Israel*, Grand Rapids, MI 1991). The subject has been frequently discussed since; we need note here only the continuing literary use of this material well after our period, as analysed, for instance, by A. Ruffing, *Jahwekrieg als Weltmetapher: Studien zu Jahwekriegstexten des chronistischen Sondergutes* (SBB, 24), Stuttgart 1992.

[10]U. Kellermann, *Nehemia: Quellen, Überlieferung und Geschichte* (BZAW, 102), Berlin 1967, 18; see too Blenkinsopp, "Nehemiah Autobiographical Memoir", 205.

battle[11] and calls for faith and fearlessness; the enemy is discouraged; and the trumpet blast is the signal for battle. It is true that some of these elements do not serve quite the same function as in the earlier, classical texts, but that is only to be expected. This is the language of the laity drawing a general analogy between the present situation and some well-known stories from his people's national history. His aim is simply to encourage them by a straightforward appeal to past victories, not to engage in scribal exegesis.

The same point can be made even more forcefully in the case of Nehemiah's appeal to the example of Solomon in connection with mixed marriages:

> "Was it not on account of such women that Solomon, king
> of Israel, sinned? Among the many nations there was no
> king like him; he was loved by God, and God made him
> king over all Israel; yet even he was led into sin by foreign
> wives."   (Neh. 13:26)

This appeal can be contrasted with the exegetically far more elaborate approach of Ezra in Ezra 9:1-2,[12] where a number of legal texts are combined in order to seek legitimation for the drastic policy of divorce. It is true that Nehemiah appeals to one of the same scriptural passages as does Ezra (Neh. 13:25; Ezra 9:2, 12; cf. Deut. 7:3), but the sophistication of Ezra's legal argumentation is lacking, whereas conversely Nehemiah's simplistic appeal to the negative example of Solomon, which seems to be his trump rhetorical card, is absent from Ezra. For a lay person, a simple reference to a well-known story is more effective, for being more readily intelligible, than legalistic niceties.

Secondly, this same uncomplicated approach to religion is reflected in one of Nehemiah's few references to the temple itself. In an obscure incident, Nehemiah rebuffs the devious Shemaiah's attempt to lure him into the sanctuary with the simple words "Should a man in my position run away? Or who in my state would enter the temple[13]

---

[11] Note especially the stereotypical words of encouragement, "our God will fight for us", in 4:14 [20]; cf. Exod. 14:14; Deut. 1:30; 3:22; 20:4; Josh. 10:14, 42; 23:10.

[12] For varying analyses, see J. Milgrom, *Cult and Conscience: The* ASHAM *and the Priestly Doctrine of Repentance* (SJLA, 18), Leiden 1976, 71-3; M. Fishbane, *Biblical Interpretation in Ancient Israel*, Oxford 1985, 114-23; J. Blenkinsopp, *Ezra-Nehemiah: A Commentary* (OTL), London 1988, 174-7; and my *Ezra, Nehemiah*, 130-32.

[13] The reference to "doors" and the climactic parallelism in Shemaiah's 'poetic' oracle in verse 10 clearly indicate that הֵיכָל here refers to the sanctuary proper, not just to the temple precincts in general, *contra* A.L. Ivry, "Nehemiah 6, 10: Politics and the Temple", *JSJ* 3 (1972), 35-45.

and live?" (Neh. 6:11). While it is true that we should be cautious before drawing far-reaching conclusions from this brief episode in which no more than the minimum response by Nehemiah is expected or required, the attitude which he adopts seems nevertheless to be just what one might expect from a layman, and it finds many parallels even today in the attitudes adopted towards sacred space. He knows that the temple is off limits for him, and that is the end of the matter. Priestly distinctions between the sacred and the profane or the varying degrees of holiness are not his concern.

Thirdly, a typically lay approach is also taken by Nehemiah with regard to some of the fundamental institutions of religion in the reforms which he undertook during his second term as governor. His attitude towards the sabbath in Neh. 13:15-21 is a good example. It is probable that by this time sabbath observance was a distinguishing feature of Jewish culture, and thus important in terms of the community's sense of self-identity. Nehemiah's concern in putting an end to the abuse of trading on the sabbath was thus likely motivated by political as much as religious concerns in so far as these can be separated. Certainly, his methods, including ensuring forcefully that foreign traders should not benefit by Jewish cessation of work, demonstrate his appreciation that more than just Jewish observance was at stake, and indeed, the fact that he set some of his own men, and later the Levites, to work on the sabbath to discourage trade testifies that outward observance overrode other considerations in his calculations. It is, furthermore, noteworthy that no theological reasoning is supplied by way of motivation, but rather another appeal to the nation's past history (verse 18; cf. Jer. 17:27; Ezek. 20:12-24). In Nehemiah's understanding, therefore, the sabbath was more a symbol than a dogma, and he responds to defend it accordingly.

Moving back through chapter 13, we may suggest that the same can be said of what at first sight look like more technically cultic concerns. First, he ejects Tobiah and his belongings from one of the temple chambers and restores its use as a repository for the temple vessels, grain offering and incense (13:4-9). Secondly, on discovery that the Levites had had to go back to agricultural labour because they were inadequately supported, he recalls them, arranges for payment of the tithes to be reinstated, and sets up a committee to look after the accounts (13:10-13). In these cases too, it may be suggested, the concern is predominantly with the externals of the cult as symbol. There is nothing in the text to suggest that in the case of the expulsion of Tobiah Nehemiah was motivated by anything other than a sense of outrage that a former opponent had used his family connections to establish himself in the temple, while his concern for the Levites is very much that of the supportive outsider, seeking to ensure that the cult was adequately financed and administered. I am reminded of a story, for whose truth I cannot vouch, concerning the late Sir Winston Churchill. Asked whether he supported the Church of England, he is said to have replied, "Yes, I support the Church like a flying buttress - holding it up from the outside!" While Nehemiah is certainly portrayed as a man of faith, it would be entirely consistent for him to have viewed the temple and its service as worthy of support in the national interest, but not something about whose inner workings he need bother. That could be safely left to the professionals.

Finally, where did God fit into Nehemiah's belief system? In brief, Nehemiah's God is the one who above all protects his people's interests, both collectively and individually. Collectively, he will give his people success in their enterprise of reasserting Jewish independence and self-respect (2:20; 6:16) and not allow shame to overcome them again (3:36-37 [4:4-5]); he will protect them (4:3 [9]), frustrate the plans of the enemy (4:9 [15]) and fight for them (4:14 [20]) in times of peril; he is expected to uphold the social cohesion of the community (5:13; 13:25); and his help of his people is recognized by the surrounding nations (6:16). In short, he is portrayed as a God who can be relied upon to act positively in the present as he has in the past. It is not that the lessons of past judgment are completely overlooked, but rather they can be simply learnt in terms of avoiding one or two basic errors into which the previous generations had fallen (cf. 13:18, 26). This seems to reflect the uncomplicated faith of an optimistic nationalist who is confident that God is 'on our side'.

The same outlook characterizes his relationship with the individual, principally Nehemiah himself, of course. God's good hand rests on him to prosper his undertakings (2:8, 18), and he prompts Nehemiah to act in certain ways which are always successful (2:12; 7:5). Conversely, the correct attitude to adopt towards God is to fear him (5:9, 15; 7:2; cf. 4:8 [14], הַנּוֹרָא).

Nehemiah's prayers, including the series of "remember" formulae, are indicative of this same pragmatic approach to religion: they reflect a belief that God is available to prosper the undertakings of his servants (2:4; 4:3 [9]; 6:9), to reward the good (5:19; 13:14, 22, 31), to punish the wicked (13:29), and to frustrate the plans of those who would oppose them (3:36-37 [4:4-5]; 6:14).

The one apparent exception to this consistent picture is Nehemiah's more extended prayer in Neh. 1:5-11. Many commentators, of course, have argued on a variety of grounds that this prayer was not an original part of the Nehemiah Memoir, but was added by a later editor.[14] If that is correct, it should not be further considered here. But even on the assumption that it is to be ascribed to Nehemiah himself, it in fact serves to strengthen the picture which has emerged above. Although it certainly fits in general terms within the corpus of post-exilic prose prayers, it has several distinctive features, not least form-critically. It has frequently been compared, for instance, with the communal laments, but it lacks the most characteristic feature of that genre – the complaint in its various forms – and it also switches uncharacteristically between first-person singular and plural address. Equally, while many of the elements of which the prayer is comprised have parallels elsewhere, the manner in which they are here combined is unprecedented. In short, the prayer looks like the work of someone imitating a familiar pattern and using stereotypical phraseology, but without a full understanding of the genre's inner dynamic. That does not make it any the less powerful from a religious point of view, but its idiosyncrasies are nevertheless suggestive of lay authorship.

To sum up, Nehemiah's belief system may be characterized as pragmatic and uncomplicated. His overriding concern is for a strong sense of Jewish identity within an accepted imperial framework. The religious history of his people is what has forged that identity, and the paraphernalia of temple, cultic personnel and practices serve the wider goal by offering points of cohesion and focus; their inner workings and theological underpinning are of little interest. He assumes that God's concerns and values coincide with his own, and he acts accordingly. He appears untroubled by the theological problems which the experience of exile raises for others but adopts a simple and straightforward view of religious continuity. While there is no doubting his firm personal faith, it is the faith of a politician for whom the institutions of religion serve and undergird the wider national interests.

---

[14]Earlier discussions are usefully summarized by Kellermann, *Nehemia*, 9-11, with bibliography. More recent commentators continue to adopt differing positions for much the same reasons as their predecessors. My own approach is based on my understanding that the Nehemiah Memoir developed in two stages. At its base lies a report by Nehemiah to the king on his first year in office. Much later, this was reworked by Nehemiah himself, partly in order to claim the credit for a number of reforms which had been undertaken in subsequent years. On this showing, there is no reason why the prayer should not have been part of the Memoir in this revised form; for brief justification, see my *Ezra and Nehemiah*, Sheffield 1987, 15-19; *Ezra, Nehemiah*, xxiv-xxviii *et passim*.

2   Other Material in the Book of Nehemiah

When we turn by way of comparison and contrast to the remaining material in the book, we find ourselves in a somewhat different world. As has already been mentioned, each of the achievements for which Nehemiah claims personal credit finds a parallel in which the people act collectively under priestly and/or levitical leadership, and so we shall look at these passages next. In some cases, the parallel makes little difference for our purposes, so that there is no need to delay over the details. The account of the wall-building in 3:1-32 is a case in point.[15] Since it lacks the rubrics with which it was presumably once accompanied, we cannot speculate as to whether it reflected similar or different motivations for the undertaking of the task by comparison with those urged by Nehemiah. Much the same could be said of the alternative account of the dedication of the wall into which, I have argued elsewhere,[16] has been spliced Nehemiah's own version of the same event (12:27-43).

Somewhat more informative is the alternative account of the re-population of Jerusalem in 11:1-20.[17] For Nehemiah himself, the whole issue is set within a firmly defensive context (7:1-4), and this may be associated with the imperial policy of militarization which Hoglund suggests Nehemiah was sent to implement.[18] Interestingly, there are some military overtones in the list in 11:3-20 itself, to which Keller-mann has drawn attention,[19] and it is not impossible that these are

---

[15]That this list was not originally compiled by Nehemiah himself seems clear from the facts that its standpoint is that of the task completed, with the "doors, bolts and bars" of the gates all in place, whereas in Nehemiah's own account this point had explicitly still not been reached by 6:1 (but cf. 7:1), that it is in the third person, unlike Nehemiah's consistently first-person narrative, and that it refers to the local leaders as אַדִּירִים (3:5), a word never encountered in Nehemiah's own lists of leaders (e.g. 2:16). This conclusion does not, of course, rule out the probability that Nehemiah made use of the list for purposes of his own when compiling his memoir.

[16]See *Ezra, Nehemiah*, 369-71.

[17]That none of this material, including the first two verses, derives from even a rewritten form of the Nehemiah Memoir seems now to be agreed. It is not in his first-person style, and indeed makes no reference to him; several matters of Hebrew style contrast sharply with his, and the basis for deciding who will move to the city differs from his (cf. 7:4-5). For the details, see Kellermann, *Nehemia*, 41-4, with earlier literature; more recently, Gunneweg, *Nehemia*, 140-1; Blenkinsopp, *Ezra-Nehemiah*, 322-3; Daniels, "Composition", 327.

[18]Hoglund, *Achaemenid Imperial Administration*, esp. 208-26.

[19]U. Kellermann, "Die Listen in Nehemia 11 eine Dokumentation aus den letz-ten Jahren des Reiches Juda?", *ZDPV* 82 (1966), 209-27. While accepting fully the importance of this feature of the list, I have argued that the dating conclusions which Kellermann draws are unjustified; cf. *Ezra, Nehemiah*, 347-8.

to be related to Nehemiah's concern in some way. However, the introduction to the list in 11:1-2 sets the whole issue in a different light.
Lots are cast to choose a tenth of the province's population to settle in
"the holy city", and those who thus "volunteered" are blessed by the
people. There are links here with the closing section of the previous
chapter, notably the emphasis on tithing and the casting of lots,[20] so
that the process is transformed into a sacral act, a tithe for the holy
city paralleling the earlier tithe of produce for the holy place. In this
small instance, then, we seem to have a mirror image of Nehemiah's
belief system. If for him religion was the servant of politics, here a
political undertaking has to be justified in the first place as an act of
the priestly cult and presented on its terms. It is a priestly outlook
which dominates the whole of life.

Finally in this section we need to attend to the pledge in Neh.
10:29-40 [28-39], to some of whose clauses reference has just been
made, though it will be found to contain few surprises. The following relevant points are well known and so require little discussion.
First, the specific clauses of the pledge have close parallels in the substance of the reforms of Nehemiah in chapters 5 and 13. While the historical consequences to be drawn from this observation remain open
for debate, the fact of the overlap is clear, so justifying comparison.
Secondly, the general clauses of the pledge specify in their introduction
that the people will live in obedience to the law of God as mediated
through Moses (10:29-30 [28-29]) and at their close that they will not
neglect the house of God (10:40[39]b). These, then, are the overriding
principles which should govern life, and it is clear that once again
this outlook makes primary what Nehemiah regarded as secondary.
Thirdly, however, in order to implement these general pledges in terms
of specific practice in the present, some sophisticated exegesis of the
law of Moses is needed, and this is precisely what we find, as Clines
in particular has well explained.[21] As we saw, Nehemiah's appeals to
earlier scripture were for the most part unsophisticated and never extended beyond the haggadic. Here, by contrast, the law is supreme as
regulator, not just illustrator, so that the whole text breathes more
the atmosphere of halakah. Concomitantly, it is only to be expected
that the procedures concerning cultic regulation are much more detailed than anything which we find in Nehemiah's writing; it is an
insider's view, unlike his as an outsider.

---

[20]See T.C. Eskenazi, *In An Age of Prose: A Literary Approach to Ezra-Nehemiah* (SBL.MS, 36), Atlanta, GA 1988, 111-5.

[21]D.J.A. Clines, "Nehemiah 10 as an Example of Early Jewish Biblical Exegesis", *JSOT* 21 (1981), 111-7.

To conclude on these alternative accounts of Nehemiah's achievements, we find not so much a contradictory as a complementary belief system. Many of the fundamentals, and all the specifics, are the same, from which we may deduce that we are here close to what was deemed to be central to the community's belief system, but there are distinctions of no small moment in the relative weight to be put upon each. It could well be that Nehemiah's priorities were personal, both in the sense that he was clearly very much of an individual in character and more importantly that he alone was charged with a particular mission by the Persian king which obliged him to adopt several of the local population's standards and values as a tactic to motivate them to co-operate with him. Where differences are to be perceived between these two blocks of material in the book, therefore, it is likely, as was to be expected, that it is what I have called the alternative account which was more typical and widespread. With that provisional conclusion in mind, I turn finally to inquire briefly whether there is any support for it to be found in the work of the book's final redactor.

3   The Final Redactor

Although, as I indicated at the start of this paper, the question of the redactor's viewpoint cannot be fully discussed apart from a consideration also of the book of Ezra, there are perhaps three observations which may be drawn from what I take to be his activity in the book of Nehemiah itself.

First, it is quite obvious that he is responsible for much of the arrangement of the material in the second half of the book. At the start of this section we have in chapter 8 the delayed account of Ezra's reading from the book of the law of Moses, while at its close, from 12:44 to the end, the concern focusses, whether by way of his own composition (probably) at the start of this passage or by way of his use of the final part of the Nehemiah Memoir, on the regular support for the temple cult.[22] These two matters, it will be recalled, were similarly the subject of the opening and closing general statements of intent in the pledge at the end of chapter 10. The values of that pledge are thus given narrative support by the broader framework which has been supplied for it. While it remains the case that the dramatic climax of the book is to be found in the account of the dedication of the wall, where appropriately material from the two major sources has

---

[22] Of course, there are some matters in chapter 13 which go beyond this narrow definition, something which was inevitable given the redactor's method of generally following the material found in his sources in extensive blocks. Despite this, concern for the temple is the major motif even in these verses.

uniquely been woven together, theologically the editor has left a clear
marker that the centre of his concern is to be found in the terms of
the pledge. Law and temple are thus at the heart of his belief system,
and the intricate processes of Ezra's exegesis whereby the latter may
be related to the former are accepted. In this sense, Nehemiah's belief
system may be said to be corrected, or at least recontextualized, by
the redactor.

Secondly, a major concern of the redactor seems to surface in what
is most probably a paragraph of his own composition following the
account of the dedication of the walls (Neh. 12:44-47).[23] Rather than
lingering over the triumphalism of that particular occasion, he hurries
straight on to emphasize that regular support for the temple cult was
immediately arranged ("On that day"). At least two factors point to
the idealized, if not utopian, nature of this paragraph. In the first
place, chapter 13 shows how quickly the portrayal of uninterrupted
financial contributions and faithful service has to be qualified, and in
the second place the implication of verse 47 that this situation had
obtained since the first days of the return from exile is contradicted
both by the preceding narrative and by the implication of the present
paragraph that it was only now that these new arrangements were put
in place. But such pedantry misses the point. The redactor's concern is
to draw attention to the fact that no reform movement can be said to
have succeeded unless it is followed by 'routinization' – the translation
of the values of the reform into a new 'steady state' in the regular life
of the community. By this device, therefore, he demonstrates clearly
what he thinks should be the lasting effects of the events he has
recorded. That they focus on the daily service of the temple cult
reinforces what we have already seen to be the cornerstone of his
belief system.

Finally, it will not have escaped attention that nothing has been
said so far of Nehemiah 9, the great prayer of national confession and
lament. The origins of this prayer are uncertain, but it clearly derives
from circles which are somewhat at variance with the prevailing outlook of most of the remainder of Ezra and Nehemiah, not least in
its closing paragraph.[24] While much discussion could be devoted to

---

[23] For this literary-critical judgement, together with the devices whereby he has
joined this material with the extracts from the Nehemiah Memoir in chapter 13,
so inviting a reading of them as part of the process of routinization, see *Ezra,
Nehemiah*, 380-4.

[24] For arguments against pressing this point too far, see J.G. McConville, "Ezra-
Nehemiah and the Fulfilment of Prophecy", *VT* 36 (1986), 205-24. Even he, however, recognizes that Nehemiah 9 goes rather further than other passages in these
books.

this, the important question for us in the present context concerns its role in the final form of the book and hence the light it sheds on the redactor's belief system.

That it stands appropriately as a confession following the reading of the law in chapter 8 and before the covenant renewal in chapter 10 is widely agreed.[25] Of greater interest, however, is the fact that the redactor has chosen for this confession a lengthy historical recital. From one point of view, this connects with Nehemiah's own use of his people's past history as a primary medium for establishing present identity. From another point of view, however, the understanding of that history and hence the outlook of this prayer differ sharply from his simple and optimistic presentation. The structure and intercessory focus of the prayer betray an understanding of the present as a continuation of the social, political and religious conditions which had obtained in the land since the time of the Babylonian conquest.[26] It is a mistake to assimilate it to the prevailing biblical pattern of exile and restoration; the stance is rather one in which the nation has lost its sovereignty as a result of persistent rebellion against God and now looks to regain its freedom by confession and intercession. It is remarkable that in a work which is so predominantly shaped by the pattern of return from Babylon[27] there is retained this powerful voice of the community which had never been exiled from the land. It suggests that for the redactor who chose to include the prayer, the community's identity was forged not just by past history but also by the continuity of habitation in the land.

In conclusion, it has been possible to detect more than one belief system in the book of Nehemiah, and we have noted elements of similarity and difference between them. Without wishing to press the differences to the point of suggesting that they are incompatible, it is nevertheless apparent that the initially dominant, not to say strident, voice of Nehemiah himself has been significantly modified by the book's final editor in the direction of what I take to be the more widely adopted outlook of the community both at the time and subsequently.

---

[25] See, for instance, Kellermann, *Nehemia*, 90-92; D.J. McCarthy, "Covenant and Law in Chronicles-Nehemiah", *CBQ* 44 (1982), 25-44.

[26] For the details of this, see my "Structure and Historiography in Nehemiah 9", in: D. Assaf (ed.), *Proceedings of the Ninth World Congress of Jewish Studies, Panel Sessions: Bible Studies and Ancient Near East*, Jerusalem 1988, 117-31.

[27] By this I refer principally, of course, to the first return in Ezra 1–2, to Ezra's return in Ezra 7–8, and to Nehemiah's in Neh. 1–2. This motif thus opens each of the major blocks of narrative in the book.

Abbreviations

All abbreviations of series, handbooks and journals in this volume are according to: S.M. Schwertner, *Internationales Abkürzungsverzeichnis für Theologie und Grenzgebiete*, Berlin ²1992. In addition the following abbreviations were used.

AcIr   Acta Iranica (Leiden).

AncBD   D.N Freedman (ed.), *Anchor Bible Dictionary*, New York 1992.

BibJS   Biblical and Judaic Studies (Winona Lake).

CBET   Contributions to Biblical Exegesis and Theology (Kampen; from 1997 onwards: Leuven).

DBHE   L. Alonso Schökel (ed.), *Diccionario Bíblico Hebreo–Español*, Madrid 1994.

DCH   D.J.A. Clines (ed.), *The Dictionary of Classical Hebrew*, Sheffield 1993– .

DDD   K. van der Toorn *et al.* (eds.), *Dictionary of Deities and Demons in the Bible*, Leiden 1995; Leiden & Grand Rapids ²1999.

ESHM   European Seminar in Historical Methodology (Sheffield).

ET   English translation.

EtAs   Etudes Assyriologiques (Paris).

Fs.   *Festschrift.*

GGG   O. Keel, C. Uehlinger, *Gods, Goddesses, and Images of God in Ancient Israel*, Minneapolis & Edinburgh 1998.

HAHAT   H. Donner *et al.* (eds.), *Wilhem Gesenius Hebräisches und Aramäisches Handwörterbuch über das Alte Testament*, Lief. 1–2, Heidelberg ¹⁸1987–1995.

HCOT   The Historical Commentary on the Old Testament (Kampen; from 1997 onwards: Leuven).

IAPN.SP   International Association of Professional Numismatists, Special Publications (Berlin).

HdA   Handbuch der Archäologie (München).

KTU   M. DIETRICH, O. LORETZ, J. SANMARTÍN, *The Cuneiform Alphabetic Texts from Ugarit, Ras Ibn Hani and Other Places* (KTU: second, enlarged edition), Neukirchen 1995.

Trans   *Transeuphratène.*

NABU   Nouvelles Assyriologiques Brèves et Utilitaires (Paris).

NICOT	The New International Commentary on the Old Testament (Grand Rapids).
NRSV	*The New Revised Standard Version.*
OTR	Old Testament Readings (London).
OTW	Oudtestamentisch Werkgezelschap in Nederland en België.
PHAA	Publications d'Histoire de l'Art et d'Archéologie de l'Université Catholique de Louvain (Louvain-la-Neuve).
PredOT	De Prediking van het Oude Testament (Nijkerk).
REB	*The Revisied English Bible.*
SEL	*Studi Epigrafici e Linguistici* (Verona).
SHANE	Studies in the History of the Ancient Near East (Leiden).
SHCANE	Studies in the History and Culture of the Ancient Near East (Leiden).
SOTS	Society for Old Testament Study (UK).
SPhT	Studies in Philosophical Theology (Kampen).
Truma	*Truma. Zeitschrift der Hochschule für Jüdische Studien Heidelberg* (Heidelberg).
TAD	B. Porten, A. Yardeni, *Textbook of Aramaic Documents from Ancient Egypt*, vol. 1: Letters, Jerusalem 1986.
TSSI	J.C.L. Gibson, *Textbook of Syrian Semitic Inscriptions* (Oxford).
UTR	Utrechtse Theologische Reeks (Utrecht).
v., vv.	verse(s).
VveB	Verklaring van een Bijbelgedeelte (Kampen).
WBC	Word Biblical Commentary (Waco, TX).
ZAR	*Zeitschrift für Altorientalische und Biblische Rechtsgeschichte* (Wiesbaden).

Index of Authors

Index of Biblical Texts

Index of Elephantine Texts

Index of Subjects

OUDTESTAMENTISCHE STUDIËN

Edited by Johannes C. de Moor

15. *The Priestly Code and Seven Other Studies.* 1969. ISBN 90 04 03099 9
17. *The Witness of Tradition.* Papers Read at the Joint British-Dutch Old Testament Conference Held at Woudschoten (Holland), September 1970. 1972. ISBN 90 04 03343 2
18. Labuschagne, C.J., C. van Leeuwen, M.J. Mulder, H.A. Brongers, B. Jongeling, L. Dequeker, P.A.H. de Boer. *Syntax and meaning.* Studies in Hebrew Syntax and Biblical Exegesis. 1973. ISBN 90 04 03785 3
19. *Language and Meaning.* Studies in Hebrew Language and Biblical Exegesis. Papers Read at the Joint British-Dutch Old Testament Conference Held at London, 1973. 1974. ISBN 90 04 03943 0
20. *Instruction and Interpretation.* Studies in Hebrew Language, Palestinian Archaeology and Biblical Exegesis. Papers Read at the Joint British-Dutch Old Testament Conference Held at Louvain, 1976. 1977. ISBN 90 04 05433 2
21. Albrektson, B. et al. *Remembering All the Way...* A Collection of Old Testament Studies Published on the Occasion of the Fortieth Anniversary of the Oudtestamentisch Werkgezelschap in Nederland. 1981. ISBN 90 04 06305 6
22. Wilde, A. de (ed.). *Das Buch Hiob.* Eingeleitet, übersetzt und erläutert. 1981. ISBN 90 04 06372 2
23. *Prophets, worship and theodicy.* Studies in Prophetism, Biblical Theology and Structural and Rhetorical Analysis, and the Place of Music in Worship. Papers Read at the Joint British-Dutch Old Testament Conference Held at Woudschoten, 1982. 1984. ISBN 90 04 07035 4
24. *Crises and Perspectives.* Studies in Ancient Near Eastern Polytheism, Biblical Theology, Palestinian Archaeology and Intertestamental Literature. Papers Read at the Joint British-Dutch Old Testament Conference Held at Cambridge, U.K., 1985. 1986. ISBN 90 04 07873 8
25. Woude, A.S. van der (ed.). *New Avenues in the Study of the Old Testament.* A Collection of Old Testament Studies Published on the Occasion of the Fiftieth Anniversary of the Oudtestamentisch Werkgezelschap and the Retirement of Prof. Dr. M.J. Mulder. 1989. ISBN 90 04 09125 4
26. Woude, A.S. van der (ed.). *In Quest of the Past.* Studies in Israelite Religion, Literature and Prophetism. Papers Read at the Joint British-Dutch Old Testament Conference, Held at Elspeet, 1988. 1990. ISBN 90 04 09192 0
27. Boer, P.A.H. de and C. van Duin. *Selected Studies in Old Testament Exegesis.* 1991. ISBN 90 04 09342 7
28. Smelik, K.A.D. *Converting the Past.* Studies in Ancient Israelite and Moabite Historiography. 1992. ISBN 90 04 09480 6
29. Dirksen, P.B. and A. van der Kooij (eds.). *Abraham Kuenen (1828-1891). His Major Contributions to the Study of the Old Testament.* A Collection of Old Testament Studies Published on the Occasion of the Centenary of Abraham Kuenen's Death (10 December 1991). 1993. ISBN 90 04 09732 5
30. Houtman, C. *Der Himmel im Alten Testament.* Israels Weltbild und Weltanschauung. 1993. ISBN 90 04 09690 6
31. Peels, H.G.L. *The Vengeance of God.* The Meaning of the Root NQM and the Function of the NQM-Texts in the Context of Divine Revelation in the Old Testament. 1995. ISBN 90 04 10164 0

32. Lugt, P. van der. *Rhetorical Criticism and the Poetry of the Book of Job.* 1995. ISBN 90 04 10326

33. Eynikel, E. *The Reform of King Josiah and the Composition of the Deuteronomistic History.* 1996. ISBN 90 04 10266 3

34. Moor, J.C. de (ed.). *Synchronic or Diachronic?* A Debate on Method in Old Testament Exegesis 1995. ISBN 90 04 10342 2

35. Tigchelaar, E.J.C. *Prophets of Old and The Day of the End.* Zechariah, the Book of Watchers and Apocalyptic. 1995. ISBN 90 04 10356 2

36. Smelik, W.F. *The Targum of Judges.* 1995. ISBN 90 04 10365 1

37. Sanders, P. *The Provenance of Deuteronomy 32.* 1996. ISBN 90 04 10648 0

38. Keulen, P.S.F. van. *Manasseh through the Eyes of the Deuteronomists.* The Manasseh Account (2 Kings 21:1-18) and the Final Chapters of the Deuteronomistic History. 1996. ISBN 90 04 10666 9

39. Hoop, R. de. *Genesis 49 in its Literary and Historical Context.* 1998. ISBN 90 04 10913 7

40. Moor, J.C. de (ed.). *Intertextuality in Ugarit and Israel.* Papers Read at The Tenth Joint Meeting of The Society for Old Testament Study and Het Oudtestamentisch Werkgezelschap in Nederland en België Held at Oxford, 1997. 1998. ISBN 90 04 11154 9

41. Korpel, M.C.A. and J.C. de Moor. *The Structure of Classical Hebrew Poetry: Isaiah 40-55.* 1998. ISBN 90 04 11261 8

42. Becking, B. and M.C.A. Korpel (eds.). *The Crisis of Israelite Religion.* Transformation of Religious Tradition in Exilic and Post-Exilic Times. 1999. ISBN 90 04 11496 3